The Valentino Mystique

The Valentino Mystique

*The Death and Afterlife
of the Silent Film Idol*

ALLAN R. ELLENBERGER

Foreword by Edoardo Ballerini

McFarland & Company, Inc., Publishers
Jefferson, North Carolina, and London

ALSO BY ALLAN R. ELLENBERGER
AND FROM McFARLAND

Celebrities in Los Angeles Cemeteries: A Directory (2001)

Margaret O'Brien: A Career Chronicle and Biography (2000; paperback 2004)

Ramon Novarro: A Biography of the Silent Film Idol, 1899–1968; with a Filmography (1999)

LIBRARY OF CONGRESS CATALOGUING-IN-PUBLICATION DATA

Ellenberger, Allan R., 1956–
The Valentino mystique : the death and afterlife of the silent film idol / Allan R. Ellenberger ; foreword by Edoardo Ballerini.
    p.   cm.
"The complete filmography of Rudolph Valentino": p.
Includes bibliographical references and index.

ISBN-13: 978-0-7864-1950-0
softcover : 50# alkaline paper ∞

1. Valentino, Rudolph, 1895–1926—Death and burial. 2. Motion picture actors and actresses—United States—Biography. I. Title.
       PN2287.V3E64   2005
       791.4302'8'092—dc22   2004028965

British Library cataloguing data are available

©2005 Allan R. Ellenberger. All rights reserved

No part of this book may be reproduced or transmitted in any form or by any means, electronic or mechanical, including photocopying or recording, or by any information storage and retrieval system, without permission in writing from the publisher.

On the cover: portrait of Valentino by Maurice Goldberg (courtesy the Academy of Motion Picture Arts and Sciences)

Manufactured in the United States of America

*McFarland & Company, Inc., Publishers
Box 611, Jefferson, North Carolina 28640
www.mcfarlandpub.com*

To the memory of

Robbie Coté (1972–2001)
Mabel Ellenberger (1918–2001)
Larry Arthur (1948–2002)
Kenneth Jones (1960–2003)
Jimmy Bangley (1956–2004)

Acknowledgments

No accomplishment, whether trifling or impressive, is ever realized without the help of others. So it is when writing a book. The works of unknown persons can make the research easier, and it is only right to acknowledge these creative souls. It is also necessary and proper to recognize those who have directly shaped our lives and our works by contributing in one way or another, whether sharing specific information or by giving needed encouragement. Both are equally important. I would like to thank the following:

Edoardo Ballerini, for graciously writing the Foreword to this book and taking the time to share his experiences on the making of the short film *Good Night, Valentino* (2003).

Jimmy Bangley, a friend who offered encouragement and advice, and worked hard to obtain interviews and quotes from his many friends and associates. His help was indispensable.

Claire Brandt, of Eddie Brandt's Saturday Matinee, for her help in finding just the right Valentino stills.

The ever generous Kevin Brownlow, who unselfishly shared his knowledge and provided references on Valentino.

Tyler Cassity, owner of Hollywood Forever Cemetery, for continuing the annual memorial services for Rudolph Valentino, and for making available Valentino and June Mathis' cemetery records.

The late Estrellita del Regil, one of the countless "Ladies in Black," who many years ago stood on the corner of Hollywood and Vine and shared with me her stories, love and admiration for Rudolph Valentino.

Emily W. Leider, for her wonderful biography on Rudolph Valentino, and for taking the time to answer questions.

Diane Madsen, for sharing information on her aunt, June Mathis.

Mike McKelvey, a true Valentino fan, for sharing information on the annual memorial services, and for sharing rare photographs.

John Rothman, for sharing his memories of *Good Night, Valentino* (2003).

Tracy Terhune, a Valentino collector for taking the time to share his knowledge and extensive Rudolph Valentino and Ditra Flamé collection.

The following celebrities for sharing their memories: Marsha Hunt, Patricia Medina (costar of 1951's *Valentino*), and director and screenwriter Melville Shavelson.

My fellow authors who offered support, advice and encouragement: Cari Beauchamp (*Without Lying Down: Frances Marion and the Powerful Women of Early Hollywood*), Margaret Burk (*Are the Stars Out Tonight? The Story of the Famous Ambassador and Cocoanut Grove, "Hollywood's Hotel"*), Eve Golden (*Platinum Girl: The Life and Legends of Jean Harlow*), James Robert Parish (*The Hollywood Celebrity Death Book*), André Soares (*Beyond Paradise: The Life of Ramon Novarro*) and Jane Ellen Wayne (*Gable's Women*). A special thanks to writer Robert Young (*Roscoe "Fatty" Arbuckle: A Bio-Bibliography*), who generously supplied me with Valentino stills, a copy of the Valentino estate catalogue, and other eclectic and interesting memorabilia.

Thanks also to the following for their contributions: Bruce Dold of the *Chicago Tribune*; Donna Hill; Gary Hill; Bob King, editor of *Classic Images* magazine; Harry Martin; Linda Peck, daughter-in-law of Ben Ali Haggin; Betty Anne Reiter, Supervisor of Adult Services at Groton (CT) Public Library; Kathee Rhode of the Boyertown (PA) Community Library; Celia Strother (founder) and members of the Rudolph Valentino eGroup on Yahoo!, and Steven Vasilevskiy of Hollywood Forever Cemetery.

To the staff at the Margaret Herrick Library, Academy of Motion Picture Arts and Sciences, Beverly Hills. Specifically I would like to thank two dear friends: Sue Guldin, whom I've known since our days as docents at the former Hollywood Studio Museum, and Allison Berntsen, a sweet and delicate soul that went that extra mile in helping with my research.

To the staffs of the following institutions: Beverly Hills Public Library, Chicago Historical Society, Chicago Public Library, Doheny Library, Francis Howard Goldwyn Library—Hollywood, Glendale Public Library, Los Angeles Central Library, Los Angeles City Archives, New York Museum of Modern Art, New York Public Library, Powell Library at USC, UCLA Research Library.

And in addition to those I've already mention, the dear people that I am proud to call my friends and who have offered encouragement throughout this process: Rock Armstrong, George Barr, Matias Bombal, Pola Brown, George Cress Bujold, Mike Francis, Donna Callahan, Art and Willetta Carrington, Scott Carter, Christine Chapman, Gloria Chapman, Mario Comas, Laura Cramer, Patricia Reese Cummings, Ryan De Korte, James De Menna, Michael "Little Mikey" Dougher, Donna Edwards, Pieter Gertis, Erick Hayak, Max Hoffmann, Deborah Kayser, Adam Kersh, Scott

Khouri, Stacey McAdam, Kevin McCauley, Brenda McElroy, Renée McFadden, Randal Malone, Cynthia Mather, Michelle Mitchell, Margaret O'Brien, Anita Page, Jean Peckson, Max Pierce, Henry Puente, Ann Randolph, Michael Roman, Donna Ross, Michael Schwibbs, Jim Shippee, Martin Terrones, Steve Troha, James Tuttle, Mark Umbach, Justin Wilson, and Carl Youngblood.

Table of Contents

Acknowledgments	vii
Foreword by Edoardo Ballerini	1
Preface	3

Part One. The Last Days of Rudolph Valentino

INTRODUCTION		7
ONE	"Pink Powder Puffs"	9
TWO	The Boxer, the Sage and the Accidental Fiancée	19
THREE	Mending Fences	29
FOUR	"Doctor, Am I a Pink Puff?"	36
FIVE	Final Days	43
SIX	Monday, August 23, 1926	51
SEVEN	Ballyhoo	61
EIGHT	The Fight for Rudy's Body	70
NINE	Requiem in New York	81
TEN	The Journey West	90

Part Two. Homes, Hangouts and Other Places of Interest: Tours of Valentino-Related Sites

TOUR INTRODUCTION		105
TOUR 1	New York City	106
TOUR 2	Hollywood	121
TOUR 3	West Hollywood	135
TOUR 4	Beverly Hills	138

Tour 5	Downtown Los Angeles	142
Tour 6	Suburban Los Angeles and Environs	145

Part Three. Appendices

I	The "Pink Powder Puffs" Editorial and Valentino's Responses	153
II	The Medical Diagnosis, Operation and Treatment	156
III	Tributes and Eulogies	158
IV	Mourners Attending the Funerals in New York and Beverly Hills	173
V	The Last Will and Testament	177
VI	The Estate	180
VII	*Los Angeles Times* and *New York Times* References	187
VIII	Periodical Articles	205
IX	Books	216
X	Film Biographies and Stage Productions	219
XI	Quotations about Valentino	230

The Complete Filmography of Rudolph Valentino	235
Notes	263
Bibliography	275
Index	279

Foreword
by Edoardo Ballerini

The advent of motion pictures was a great step toward fulfilling a long held premise of science fiction: it allowed, for the first time, a person to be in more than one place at one time. Thus it was that a figure like Rudolph Valentino could dance in Paris, ride through the desert in London, and fight bulls in Aurora, Illinois, all at once. But with advances come complications, and mass media was no exception. A new era of mass hysteria arose, and at no time was this more apparent than Valentino's untimely death in 1926. The "Great Lover" was a mere 31 years old.

Valentino.

Even for those who have never seen as much as a photograph of the man, the name somehow still conjures up an image. The romantic hero. The lover. The sophisticate. But unbeknownst to many, the name probably retains its air of mystery as much because of the true events of his life as because of the characters he portrayed. His death, an event that incited riotous mobs and elicited opinions from everyone from Charlie Chaplin to the Pope, may well be the first time in history that the power of a modern media star was tacitly, and frighteningly, understood. And with no uncertain irony, it was this same mass media that helped bring the event about. As is well known to film buffs and historians, Rudolph Valentino spent the better part of his career fighting all manner of accusations from the press— effeminacy and homosexuality chief among them — and the irrational vigor of his defense in the final months of his life ultimately killed him.

Several authors over the decades have tried to examine the psychology of the situation, to "name the disease" (as the great H.L. Mencken put it). Why did Valentino react so poorly to this press? What was he hiding? Further, what was the true cause of his death? Why did crowds fight to catch a glimpse of his body?

Some ascribe the events to a natural result, given Valentino's youth and quasi-superhuman hold over female audiences. Others point to the manipulations of Valentino's manager and studio bosses in trying to excite the crowds in order to line their own pockets. And still others suggest that, well, there is no explanation. It was a phenomenon, and as such cannot truly be described in rational terms. The truth probably lies somewhere within the triangle of these opinions.

But perhaps more relevant to those of us living in the twenty-first century is that Valentino's death seems both prescient and timely, and can teach us something of ourselves. Somehow, it seems this superstar was an everyman, and old attitudes and ways don't seem quite so old after all. It is always sobering to realize how little we've changed as a culture despite our supposed advances.

The book that follows is unique. It is not easy to add to a subject that has sparked interest and debate for over seventy-five years, but as the first author to focus solely on the days leading up to and following Valentino's demise, Allan Ellenberger's poetic and scholarly telling should have both the ardent fan and the unacquainted newcomer furiously turning pages. Some questions will be answered, and still more will be asked, as they should be.

Edoardo Ballerini
Los Angeles, fall 2004

Preface

For whatever reasons, the circumstances surrounding the death of actor Rudolph Valentino have always fascinated me, not to mention thousands of his fans. What is it about the death of a celebrity that causes people to behave in unusual ways? In the instance of Rudolph Valentino's death, there were many contributing factors, including (but not limited to) the emotional state of the crowd, the weather, and the somewhat overzealous police.

To document Valentino's death, I spent countless hours perusing microfilm at several libraries across the country, examining more than twenty newspapers from New York, Chicago, Los Angeles, and other smaller cities. Everything from the prestigious *New York Times* to the scandalous *New York Evening Graphic* helped to fill in the proverbial holes in Valentino's last days.

The "Tours" section developed as I visited sites where the events of Valentino's last days took place. There's something about being at the spot where an historical event occurred that inspires and fascinates. In New York, I was surprised to find that the neighborhood where the funeral riots occurred has completely changed. Buildings within several blocks of the area, including Campbell's, are all gone. The only recognizable landmarks are the median that bisects Broadway, and the subway entrance at 66th Street. A bookstore is now at the Campbell's locale. Across the street is the distinguished Juilliard School. One block south off of Broadway is the Lincoln Center for the Performing Arts. None of these landmarks existed in Valentino's time.

This fact both saddened and intrigued me. What other Valentino haunts and hangouts no longer existed—and if they did, what shape were they in now? Many, of course, have been lost to the march of progress, but some still remain. Fewer still are used for their original purpose. For example, the building where Valentino died is still standing, but is no longer a hospital — it is now residential. In Hollywood, the Sunset Boulevard bungalow of Valentino's love, Natacha Rambova, remarkably survives, but now houses several businesses.

The historian in me was the impetus for the "Appendices" section. Gathering information and making it available in one place has always been a task close to my heart. (Countless times I have desired to have important information at my fingertips when researching a subject). Included is a detailed medical description of Valentino's operation; personal quotes about his death; lists of people attending both funerals; references from the *New York Times* and *Los Angeles Times*; and a complete filmography. All of this and other interesting tidbits make up what I hope is a treasure-trove for Valentino scholars and enthusiasts.

Allan R. Ellenberger
Los Angeles, fall 2004

A special note to the reader: This book is not a biography. It is only biographical in the sense that it covers the last few weeks of Valentino's life. You will not find intimate details on Valentino's childhood, career, or personal relationships (with the exception of the unusual liaison he had with Pola Negri). These subjects have been covered very well, and often, by several biographers over the last eight decades. For anyone interested in the life and career of Rudolph Valentino, I suggest the following books: *Valentino as I Knew Him*, by S. George Ullman, 1926; *Valentino*, by Irving Schulman, 1967; *Rudolph Valentino*, by Alexander Walker, 1976; and *Dark Lover: The Life and Death of Rudolph Valentino*, by Emily W. Leider, 2003.

PART ONE

The Last Days of Rudolph Valentino

Introduction

Some have called the death of actor Rudolph Valentino one of the most severe cases of mass hysteria of the twentieth century. Certainly, few deaths in history, whether the deceased was a sovereign ruler, a war hero, or even a lowly actor, have commanded a more widespread sense of loss than that of the "Sheik." Valentino's quick rise from obscurity to blinding fame, enormous wealth, and romantic appeal makes his story comparable in human interest to any that the screen itself has presented.

When he died in 1926, there were 20,233 motion picture theaters in the United States, with an average of 130,300,000 admissions each week.[1] Thanks to the widespread popularity of film, people everywhere knew his face, and this alone guaranteed him immortality—especially because his death occurred at the height of his fame.

It has been a widely held belief that Valentino was the first actor to die while still popular with the public. That is not so. In 1920, actress Olive Thomas passed away under mysterious circumstances in a Paris hospital, and her death was front-page news for weeks. Dashing Wallace Reid broke the hearts of many of his fans when he succumbed to the effects of drug addiction just three years later. But it was the funeral of the "too beautiful" Barbara La Marr that most resembled the shenanigans at Valentino's bier.

Just seven months prior to Valentino's death, La Marr succumbed from what the newspapers said was nephritis, or inflammation of the kidneys. However, complications from tuberculosis and chronic drug and alcohol abuse were contributing factors. While La Marr's body lay in state for three days, 40,000 people passed by to pay their respects. At her funeral, several thousand of the curious gathered outside the mortuary and on the sidewalk across the street. Men peered from the rooftops, while small boys hung from signboards.

Carmen Cerverra, Miss Spain in the 1962 International Beauty Contest, presents flowers on behalf of Valentino fans in her country.

When the doors to the mortuary opened to the public, a stampede of bodies shoved their way into the chapel, forcing police to throw themselves against the crowd. One woman was arrested as thousands fought to catch a glimpse of LaMarr's casket and of the celebrities who gathered to mourn. As her remains were placed in the hearse, the crowd broke through police lines and rushed the funeral procession. Five women fainted and had to be rescued by police from being trampled by the mob. It took fifteen minutes to push people back so the procession could continue to Hollywood Cemetery. Afterward, hundreds rushed into the mortuary, snatching any souvenir they could find, removing everything, even to the last wreath.

Could scenes such as this and what took place at Valentino's funeral happen again? Could mass hysteria reign at the demise of one of today's superstars? Crowds came to the funerals of such popular idols as Will Rogers, Marilyn Monroe, Elvis Presley and Princess Diana, but there has never since been hysteria to match that found at Valentino's funeral. As one writer put it, "Women still have idols they get irrational about, of course, a fact that everybody from Ricky Nelson to N'Sync has taken to the bank. But, honestly, it's just not the same."

CHAPTER ONE

"Pink Powder Puffs"

"What's wrong?"[1] Valentino asked.

Startled from his concentration, S. George Ullman, Valentino's manager and close friend, realized that Rudy must have discerned the indignation on his face. The two were traveling to New York that Monday morning to publicize Valentino's new film, *The Son of the Sheik*, and were in Chicago waiting for a connecting train. A deadly heat wave was gripping the Midwest, so to find relief they took refuge at the Blackstone Hotel[2] until it was time to leave. In the lobby on the way to breakfast, someone handed Ullman the editorial page of Sunday's *Chicago Tribune*. It was while Ullman read a certain piece entitled "Pink Powder Puffs" that Valentino noticed the change in his manager's countenance.

Ullman hesitated to show him the now infamous editorial, but he knew it was unavoidable. For four years Ullman had been Valentino's business manager, advisor and, more importantly, friend. The former attorney and bank accountant first met Valentino and his fiancée, Natacha Rambova, in 1922 when the actor was involved in a breach of contract suit against Famous Players–Lasky. Disagreeing on how they were handling his career, Valentino walked out on his contract, forcing the studio to serve an injunction to prevent him from appearing on screen while litigation was in progress. This left the actor desperately in need of funds.

At the time, Ullman was associated with the Mineralava Beauty Clay Company. The cosmetic firm was searching for some imaginative promotion, so, after some sleuthing, Ullman found that Famous Players–Lasky's injunction did not prevent the actor from participating in ventures unrelated to acting in motion pictures. When Mineralava offered the Valentinos $7,000 a week to appear in a nationwide promotional dance tour, the couple immediately accepted the offer.

Ullman was, of course, familiar with Valentino through his films, but was caught

An early publicity still of struggling actor Rudolph Valentino.

off guard by their first meeting. "To say that I was enveloped by his personality with the first clasp of his sinewy hand and my first glance into his inscrutable eyes, is to state it mildly," Ullman later wrote. "I was literally engulfed, swept off my feet, which is unusual between two men."[3]

Unknown to Ullman, Rudy and Natacha dabbled in the supernatural and practiced the art of automatic writing. Rudy was, at different times, "advised" by three spirit guides: a Native American by the name of Black Feather; "Jenny," a motherly female spirit (who actually was thought to be the mother of screenwriter June Mathis); and Meselope, an Egyptian of the Hermetic Brotherhood. During one of these sessions, 'Black Feather' prophesied that Ullman was to be his new business manager. At first, when Rudy offered him the job, Ullman refused. After all, he had a family to provide for and Valentino was $50,000 in debt, so he was naturally concerned how his salary would be paid. Ten weeks later, when Ullman relented and accepted the position, neither Rudy nor Natacha were surprised. "I knew you would,"[4] Valentino told a startled Ullman. "These things at first rather gave me the creeps," Ullman later recalled, "but later, because of the sublime confidence of the Valentinos in their psychic control, I became less skeptical and more confident."[5]

The two men had been through many ups and downs during the past four years—mostly over Valentino's tempestuous love affair, marriage, and recent break up with Rambova, a personal drama that affected the actor deeply. The *Chicago Tribune*'s editorial, however, was an attack on Valentino's dignity and masculinity. Ullman reluctantly handed the newspaper to Valentino, who carefully scrutinized the piece. "Instantly I realized how deeply he was moved," Ullman wrote. "His face paled, his eyes blazed and his muscles stiffened."[6]

It seemed that the Chicago writer had taken offense to a powder machine that was installed in the men's room of the Aragon,[7] a new North Side ballroom. He described an apparatus of glass tubes and levers that dispensed a fluffy pink solid; but what most disturbed the anonymous scribe was that the machine was actually being used! He had observed two "'men'—as young lady contributors to the Voice of the People are wont to describe the breed—step up, insert coin, hold kerchief beneath the spout, pull the lever, then take the pretty pink stuff and put it on their cheeks in front of the mirror."

The writer posed to his readers what masculine America was coming to and who was to blame. "Are pink powder and parlor pinks in any way related?" he asked. "How does one reconcile masculine cosmetics, sheiks, floppy pants, and slave bracelets...?" After a detailed discussion of circumstances in cities across the world, he concluded, "Rudy, the beautiful gardener's boy, is the prototype of the American male. Hell's bells. Oh, sugar."[8]

Ullman had no idea why a powder machine had prompted this attack on Valentino's manhood. How was this any fault of his? The well-respected newsweekly *Time*

Roles in films like *The Young Rajah* helped fuel rumors about Valentino's sexuality.

sided with the *Tribune*, calling the editorial an "unequaled opportunity to demonstrate his verbal virility.... Everywhere in the mid-west people read it and groaned for the passing of manhood, seduced by the perfumed ways of a cinema fop."[9]

Regrettably, this indictment was not the first time the "Great Lover's" masculinity had been impugned. In 1922 *Photoplay* published an article by Dick Dorgan entitled "A Song of Hate." Not much is known about Dorgan except that in addition to his journalistic efforts, he also doubled as a newspaper cartoonist. Over the years he worked on such comic strips as "Kid Dugan" and "Mr. Gilfeather." Dorgan's brother, Thomas "Tad" Dorgan, was a well-known and respected cartoonist and sportswriter whom he worked with on the popular comic strip "You Know Me Al" in the mid–1920s.

In the following "A Song of Hate" article from the July 1922 issue of *Photoplay*, Dick Dorgan takes issue with Valentino's popularity with the opposite sex:

> I hate Valentino! All men hate Valentino. I hate his oriental optics; I hate his classic nose; I hate his Roman face; I hate his smile; I hate his glistening teeth; I hate his patent leather hair; I hate his Svengali glare; I hate him because he dances too well; I hate him because he's a slicker; I hate him because he's the great lover of

the screen; I hate him because he's an embezzler of hearts; I hate him because he's too apt in the art of osculation; I hate him because he's leading man for Gloria Swanson; I hate him because he's too good looking.

Ever since he came galloping in with the "Four Horsemen" he has been the cause of more home cooked battle royals than they can print in the papers. The women are all dizzy over him. The men have formed a secret order (of which I am running for president and chief executioner as you may notice) to loathe, hate and despise him for obvious reasons.

What! Me jealous?—Oh, no—I just Hate Him.[10]

Dorgan's resentment of Valentino is overshadowed by the backhanded kudos hidden within his remarks. To further the humiliation, two caricatures—most likely drawn by Dorgan himself—accompanied the article. One was "as the men see him," with glistening teeth, slicked back hair, long eyelashes and adorned with ornamental earrings. The other, "as the women see him," portrayed an attractive, more flattering sketch of the famous Valentino profile.[11]

In Dick Dorgan's view, "A Song of Hate" was merely expressing the thoughts of every red-blooded American male. Valentino was not, however, a fan of, or a stranger to, Dorgan's writings or opinions. Only three months earlier, also in *Photoplay*, Dorgan penned a scurrilous satire of *The Sheik* in which he wrote that, "the Sheik is a bum Arab, that he is really an Englishman whose mother was a *wop* or something like that...."[12]

Valentino was livid. He believed this was not only an attack against him, but also an attack against his mother—something he would not tolerate. With his Italian blood boiling, Valentino stormed the executive offices of Famous Players–Lasky demanding that Dick Dorgan be barred permanently from the studio lot.

Studio heads Jesse Lasky and Adolph Zukor both agreed that this was a thoughtless insult and called James Quirk, editor of *Photoplay*, to express their outrage at Dorgan's comments. Lasky told Quirk that the studio would stand behind Valentino if the actor chose to sue *Photoplay*. Quirk quickly agreed to admonish his wayward writer and, to make up for the affront, would have flattering portraits of Valentino grace the pages of future issues of the magazine.

When "A Song of Hate" came out only three months later, it seemed as though the magazine had ignored the studio's demands altogether. Valentino once more barged into Lasky's Sunset and Vine office and threw a copy of the offending *Photoplay* on his boss' desk. To make matters worse, Lasky had not lived up to his original promise of banning Dorgan from the lot. Pacing the length of the office, Valentino swore to kill Dorgan on sight and insisted that Lasky again call James Quirk. If Lasky failed to agree to these demands, Valentino would neither set foot in Paramount's New York office nor attend the upcoming premiere of *Blood and Sand*. After placating Valentino's anger somewhat with a gift of a silver handled cane, Lasky yielded and made the telephone call.[13]

Was Dorgan correct in his observations of the Valentino persona? If so, why did most of the American male population hold such dislike for the "Great Lover"? Part

Valentino wearing a wristwatch companion to the infamous slave bracelet.

of the problem was Valentino's image. No matter how alluring he was to his swooning, star-struck feminine admirers, their husbands and boyfriends, for the most part, saw him as a sleek-haired foreigner bent on ravaging their women. If not that, then he was viewed as a pretty boy — someone to hold up to derision.

Some referred to him as Rudolph "Vaselino," while others gossiped about his complexion or whether his slave bracelet was a sign of effeminacy. During the last weeks of his life, the press, on several occasions, made numerous references to the bracelet, which they reported as being a gift from his first wife, Jean Acker. In his book, *Valentino as I Knew Him*, Ullman noted that many believed the trinket was an offering from any number of beautiful women, when in reality it was a "Christmas present from his own wife, Natacha Rambova, and was made to order from a design which she herself drew...."[14] From that morning on, and well after their publicized divorce, Rudy never removed the circlet of love. Even though he suffered ridicule and insults from the press because of it, he never once was tempted to take it off. To this day it rests with him in his crypt.

Regarding the offending editorial, Natacha's gift was only part of its inspiration — at least in Rudy's mind. "That harmless little thing," he said, "was the indirect cause of shooting my mercury to the boiling point."[15] There are still other facets of his image that can be attributed to Natacha's influence, such as the film projects she was instrumental in procuring for him. Of these, the most important ones were *The Young Rajah* and *Monsieur Beaucaire*. It can be argued that in both films Valentino's character appears effeminate, if not epicene, especially in the outrageous and scantily clad costumes Rambova designed for him.

Unfortunately, Valentino was not only held responsible for tainting his adoring public, but he was also blamed for affecting his fellow actors. A year after Dorgan's assault, journalist Herbert Howe wrote an article for *Photoplay* in which he opined on the effeminacy of actors.

"From the moment Valentino hoofed that tango in 'The Four Horsemen of the Apocalypse' and set the flappers cuckooing, the movie boys haven't been the same," Howe wrote. "They're all racing around wearing spit curls, bobbed hair and silk panties.... This can't keep up. The public can stand just so many ruffles and no more. Some of the boys better walk up one flight and get some blue serge nifties. It's a cinch if they don't change their panties some of the producers are going to lose theirs."[16]

Even though *Photoplay* was considered a reputable magazine, it was not exempt from titillating and provoking their readers. Oddly enough, James Quirk, *Photoplay's* editor, considered Valentino to be a friend but still allowed these uncomplimentary articles to be published. Apparently selling magazines took precedence over friendship.

Something these articles share in common is that none came close to actually saying what they implied. While the 1920s can be considered the beginning of the era of yellow journalism and lurid little tabloids, yet the word homosexual very seldom saw the light of publication except in sleazy scandal sheets or titillating pulp magazines. This was especially true when the subject was someone of note. Tabloids would only hint at their "deviation," using such terms as effeminate or foppish to describe their purported behavior. Journalists became adept at writing about the sexuality of anyone known to be, or even suspected of being, gay especially in the imagination of the wontedly ultra sophisticate.

The "Pink Powder Puffs" editorial is a perfect example, for without calling "a spade a spade," the author described, in very creative jargon, exactly what he was intimating. "A pink powder machine! In a men's washroom! Homo Americanus!" the writer proclaimed. "Why didn't someone quietly drown Rudolph Guglielmo [*sic*], alias Valentino, years ago?" This insinuation, innuendo or whatever you want to call it, all boiled down to one question in many readers' minds:— was Rudolph Valentino, the great lover of the screen who made female hearts flutter, in fact a deviant—a homosexual?

Today this topic induces heated discussion among so-called Valentino enthusiasts. No subject arouses more hostility, taunting or unwarranted avoidance than expressing one's opinion on Valentino's sexuality—regardless of which side you are camped on. In any event, fans of the Sheik seem to have definite beliefs about their idol's love life. One side will argue that Valentino had to be gay, giving such examples as his marriage to two lesbians as proof. It is a well-accepted fact that actress

Jean Acker, wife number one, was a lesbian, and most will not argue the point. Some Natacha Rambova admirers will concede that Madame Valentino may have been bisexual.

Most movie buffs are not familiar with Dorgan's articles, but the *Tribune* editorial has become a part of film lore, thanks to macabre little tomes such as *Hollywood Babylon*. Oddly enough, very few questioned Valentino's sexuality after his death until the mid–1960s. Since then, many arguments have surfaced that contribute to the Valentino-is-gay theory. The most recent is a book from England which goes so far as to name assumed lovers and describe intimate and detailed liaisons between Valentino and other men. Yet the author gives us very little, if any, documentation, making it difficult to take his allegations seriously.

Only once has any man publicly claimed to have been the lover of Valentino. Ray Bourbon, a flamboyant female impersonator of the 1930s and '40s, while said to be generous, often exaggerated his generosity, telling friends that he discovered Valentino at the Vernon Country Club, where the actor worked as a tango dancer. Author James Gavin, in his book *Intimate Nights*, says that Bourbon claimed to be Valentino's lover and helped arrange for his first screen test. "But as soon as he was signed," Gavin wrote, "Valentino 'deserted him,' later 'throwing him a bone' by getting him tiny parts in films."[17]

Another argument has taken on a life of its own, that regarding the "relationship" between Valentino and actor Ramon Novarro. Long before either had become stars, Novarro worked as a bus boy at the Alexandria Hotel in downtown Los Angeles. During that time he allegedly met and became romantically involved with the struggling Valentino. Years later, when Novarro attained great critical success with the film *Scaramouche*, Valentino, in congratulations, allegedly gave his lover a black lead Art Deco dildo embellished with his own signature. Some reports go so far as to claim that the gift was an actual replica of the Sheik's own phallus. If this were as far as the story went, perhaps — again, perhaps — one may believe there was some truth to it. It was not, however, the end of the story.

Forty-five years later, when Novarro was savagely murdered by two male hustlers, legend has it that the killers committed the deed by shoving Rudy's love gift down Novarro's throat, choking him to death. In reality, the murder weapon was a cane used by the actor in one of his films. During the trial it was proven that the murderers broke Novarro's nose with the cane and knocked him unconscious. After tying him up, they laid him on his back, and blood from his broken nose drained into his throat, drowning him. Not surprisingly, the Art Deco dildo was nowhere to be seen, nor did it ever appear on the inventory list of the actor's estate. Novarro's murder was savage enough without this total work of fiction fashioned from a writer's wild imagination. With that part of the myth proven false, the facts involving a presumed love affair or friendship between Valentino and Novarro remain suspect.

Still, other factions believe Valentino may have been bisexual. Did he enjoy sexual gratification with both genders? Is it possible that, even though he appreciated the company of women, he may have experimented on occasion with members of the same sex? The answer, of course, is yes, it is possible. And because of his popularity, Valentino had ample opportunities to be lusted after and propositioned by both sexes. Some even believe that his Italian heritage and culture allowed him an openness to these little indiscretions.

Then there are those that believe Valentino was 100 percent heterosexual. Some consider it a personal affront to even suggest that Valentino may have had a homosexual thought, let alone an actual encounter. Paul Ivano, a close friend of Valentino and Natacha, would agree, insisting that rumors of the Sheik's homosexuality was "a lot of baloney. He was a nice, normal human being."[18]

Many of the denials, however, come from defenders who honestly believe the facts do not support Valentino's alleged gayness. In many cases this is justified because there is no solid proof to back the claims, thus giving the "straight" argument an edge. But then again, would the desires of others who fantasize of sexual liaisons with the "Great Lover" be crushed if they allowed themselves to believe the rumors?

To sum it up, it is unlikely that Valentino was gay, at least not by today's definition (exclusive sexual relations with members of the same sex). While Valentino seemingly had bad luck with women, especially in his marriages, he consistently proved his love for the fairer sex, especially for Natacha, even if those feelings were not returned in a way he may have hoped. Though in private he may not have lived up to his screen image of the "Great Lover," women were always a part of his life.

Some believed he was more interested in Italian food than he was in women or sex. "He'd turn those slumberous eyes on some woman and she'd just about swoon with delight," actor Stuart Holmes once said, "but he couldn't have cared less. He was usually thinking about the spaghetti and meatballs he was going to have for dinner that evening."[19]

However, another possibility should be considered, and that is Valentino may have had same-sex relationships out of necessity. By his own admission there were times during his early days in New York that he was destitute, living in Central Park or on the streets, pawning his possessions to find shelter. It's possible that he would do things required of him in order to survive. Valentino gives an example of this possibility when relating a story of his early days in New York.

"One rainy evening a man hailed me on the street and dragged me under an awning," he said. "He had a room nearby and we slept that night with our feet in each other's face."[20] The next morning this patron advised him about a job at Maxim's, something that leads us to believe that he either saw the young Valentino dance before or perhaps was given a private show. In any event, the man gives him money. Since Valentino does not name him, it can be assumed that he was a stranger — or was he?

Even so, this does not mean that anything happened between them — it all could have been very innocent. Yet one has to question the possibility, especially when considering other times when men gave him unsolicited help. For example, actor Norman Kerry aided the struggling Valentino several times early in his career. It was Kerry who suggested that Valentino try acting and, when he arrived in Los Angeles, put him up at the Alexandria Hotel. There have been rumors of Kerry's homosexuality;

but even if true, there is no evidence that their relationship was anything more than platonic. These and other stories—such as Valentino being a gigolo—followed his career, serving as the basis for the press' later allegations regarding his sexuality.

The facts of these perplexing quagmires are impossible to verify. Since the sexual activities of actors are not officially documented for posterity; it becomes difficult for those on both sides of the Valentino-sexuality argument. After more than seventy-eight years, anyone who knew Valentino personally is long gone, so it's doubtful if the truth of his sexuality will ever be known. Too much time has passed to arrive at a definite conclusion. It all becomes very confusing very fast. So whether he was straight, gay or bisexual (or tried it out of curiosity or necessity), the point is—so what? As long as fans enjoy Valentino for the pleasure that he gives them on the screen, the subject of his sexuality should be of little importance. Still, it most likely will continue to generate heated debate for years to come.

With all of that said, one can understand the frustration Valentino felt at having a stranger question his sexuality. The same righteous anger he experienced in the past over Dick Dorgan's comments plagued him again. According to Oscar Doob, the press agent in charge of publicizing *The Son of the Sheik*, Doob was the one who suggested that Valentino challenge the "Pink Powder Puffs" editorial writer to a duel.

"He [Valentino] was generally burned up about it," recalled Doob, "and I needed a publicity stunt because we were getting ready to open one of his latest pictures. I wrote the letter of challenge and got Rudy to sign it. He said in his broken English that he didn't mind what they said about him, but he wouldn't have his nation and his father insulted. He was a fine figure of a man and I had a feeling that he would fight like a wildcat if the occasion warranted."[21]

Valentino later alluded to the fact that someone else may have suggested or at least helped with the challenge when, in Chicago ten days later, he said: "I'm not boasting about my physical strength. I never should have allowed my *press agent* to make such a point of the fact."[22] Regardless of who actually wrote the challenge to the nameless editorial writer, Valentino delayed his trip to New York by a few hours. It was decided that the best way to do this was through the *Chicago Herald-Examiner*, the *Tribune*'s biggest competitor and a Hearst newspaper.

"To the man (?) who wrote the editorial headed 'Pink Powder Puffs' in Sunday's 'Tribune,'" Valentino's dare began. "I call you, in return, a contemptible coward and to prove which of us is a better man, I challenge you to a personal test." Valentino expressed that while it was illegal to challenge him to a duel in the historic sense, a boxing or a wrestling match would serve as suitable retribution.

"It's so unfair," Valentino told the *Herald-Examiner* reporter in his suite at the Blackstone Hotel. "They can say I'm a terrible actor if they like, but it's cowardly and low to hold me up as a laughing stock and make fun of my personal tastes and my private life. This man calls me 'a spaghetti gargling gardener's helper' and thanks God for five-yard McCarthy.

"He says 'Blood will tell: heredity and early environment do mould the individual.' What he doesn't know and didn't take the trouble to find out is, that when

I was in college in Italy, I was as well known in athletics as Five-yard McCarthy is here and that there is no more highly respected family in Italy than my father's. As for being a gardener's helper, I specialized in college in landscape gardening because in Italy, that is as fine an art as architecture or painting."[23]

If the offending editorial writer refused to answer his challenge, Valentino would insist on a retraction. Apart from this, there was no response from the editorial writer or the *Tribune* itself. In fact, executives in the "Tribune Tower" secretly suggested that Valentino's ire was a publicity stunt for his new film, *The Son of the Sheik*, which was opening in Chicago the next week. Apart from that, Valentino was about to spend the next several days trying to prove to the world and perhaps to himself that the editorial writer's implications were without merit.

CHAPTER TWO

The Boxer, the Sage and the Accidental Fiancée

New York was enveloped in a suffocating heat wave when Rudy arrived the next morning. An outwardly friendly and urbane Valentino disembarked at Grand Central Terminal toting a book by Freud under one arm while masking the true feelings that churned within him. A few hours later he held court at a press conference from the offices of United Artists Corporation. Valentino restated his original offer of a boxing ring or wrestling mat to prove "in typically American fashion, for I am an American citizen, which is the better man."[1] He wanted it to be clear that the challenge was not for publicity, despite what the executives at the *Tribune* believed. Valentino said that he held no grievance against the newspaper, since he assumed that it got by unnoticed by the directing heads.

Upon returning to his suite at the Ambassador Hotel, Rudy called his old friend and boxing champ, Jack Dempsey, who was in New York training for his scheduled fight with Gene Tunney in the fall. Dempsey, no stranger to acting himself, first became acquainted with Valentino while both were working on the United Studios lot. "He was then making *Cobra*, for which he needed boxing lessons. I obliged," Dempsey recalled. "Valentino was an intelligent, oversensitive individual who allowed himself to be packaged by Hollywood and didn't like the result."[2]

Dempsey was convinced to help in whatever way he could and contacted Frank "Buck" O'Neil, a sports writer and boxing authority for the *New York Evening Journal*. O'Neil was, of course, familiar with Valentino's predicament and what the actor was trying to prove. Curious, he asked several leading questions, with Dempsey defending Rudy as best he could. "Listen O'Neil," Dempsey said, "Valentino's no sissy, believe me. In case you're interested, let me tell you he packs a pretty mean punch."

Boxer Jack Dempsey (left) and Valentino.

"Do me a favor Jack, and cut the crap," O'Neil shot back. "I don't buy it and neither does anyone else. Tell you what I'm gonna do. Since the guy is in a spot, allow me to put him in his place once and for all. Tell him I'll take him on if he's willing."[3]

Dempsey agreed and, after conferring with Rudy, arranged for the bout to take place the following afternoon on the roof of the Ambassador Hotel. Dempsey once again coached Rudy, giving him every pointer to help contend with the heftier and taller O'Neil.[4]

Unfortunately the "Sheik" did not help his case much when, the following morning just before the scheduled bout with O'Neil, he received reporters in his suite, clad only in an orchid bathing suit and lavender lounging robe — something the press was quick to point out.

"I'm going back to Chicago and I'll have satisfaction," Valentino promised.

"But what," he was asked, "would you do if the 'scoundrel' turned out to be a woman?"

"Ah, that goes without saying," he responded. "I should have to laugh it off."[5] If only Rudy could have found humor in the situation, perhaps his future would have turned out differently.

The appointed time came and the two pugilists met on the Ambassador roof before an assemblage of still photographers and motion picture cameras. O'Neil had assured Ullman earlier that he would not hurt Rudy, but was quickly advised that he should look out for himself, as the Italian packed a wicked punch. At first the boxing was light, playing to the cameras until Rudy received a left to his chin and instantly shot back with a short jab to O'Neil's jaw. The writer ducked, however, catching the blow on the side of his head, knocking him to the floor. Rudy apologized for letting that one slip and helped his opponent to his feet.

When it was over, O'Neil admitted that Valentino was no slouch. Rubbing his jaw, the writer remarked, "Next time Jack Dempsey tells me something, I'll believe him."[6] Later, as O'Neil was cleaning up, he told Ullman, "That boy has a punch like a mule's kick. I'd sure hate to have him sore at me."[7]

During the next few weeks, which proved to be the last weeks of his life, Rudy repeated the words "Pink Powder Puffs" more times than any other phrase in all the years Ullman knew him. After his much-publicized boxing match — which seemed to prove nothing — Rudy decided to seek advice on the matter, but not from any so-called Hollywood pundit. The guidance would have to come from someone detached and far removed from the gossipmongers and busybodies of Tinsel Town.

When he learned that a friend, actress and former costar Aileen Pringle, was acquainted with H. L. Mencken, he asked for her help in setting up a meeting with the respected writer. Mencken was a prominent journalist, essayist, and political commentator known for his rapier-like wit. Sometimes referred to as the "Sage of Baltimore," he is probably best known today for his coverage of the Scopes "Monkey" Trial and the publication of the *History of the American Language*.

Mencken first became acquainted with Aileen Pringle at a mutual friend's home in West Chester, Pennsylvania. Pringle was a stage and film star that Mencken found not only attractive but also intelligent and quick-witted. "A very amusing movie gal,"[8] he called her.

Valentino was determined to do everything he could to prove his manliness, as he hoped (in vain) the boxing match with O'Neil would have done. Once again though, the press and the public, as they had when the original editorial came out, just snickered. Many ascribed it to another actor seeking publicity, or, as Mencken put it, to "a vulgar movie ham seeking space." The actor's outrage only added to his scorn.

Many have tried to guess why Valentino reacted as he did. It seemed the more he griped the more people laughed and wondered what, if anything, he was hiding. Edoardo Ballerini, who produced, directed and starred in the 2003 short film *Good Night Valentino*, which was based on the meeting between the actor and Mencken, believes that Valentino's retort is actually a question of his heritage. "He felt like he'd given everything to America," Ballerini said. "He'd become an idol; he'd even become an American citizen and they were still attacking him as this kind of immigrant. I think that's what riled him more than anything."[9]

To Mencken, it appeared that Valentino's masculine honor had once again been slighted. The writer added, however, that honor in America, except where the integrity of a woman was concerned, has only an amusing connotation. "When one hears of the honor of politicians, of bankers, of lawyers, of the United States itself, everyone naturally laughs," Mencken wrote. "So New York laughed at Valentino."[10]

A reporter once questioned Valentino if he, in fact, took the entire "Pink Powder Puffs" editorial seriously. "Not as a detached thing, no," he replied. "I grow recalcitrant because of the misrepresentation it implies—and because it is a printed utterance—and automatically becomes a part of my biography, which some day I will not be here to defend."[11]

Mencken was unclear as to why he was chosen to play the part of the sage. It must have been something he had written that impressed upon Valentino that he was a "judicious fellow," Mencken reasoned. "I had never met him before nor seen him on the screen," he wrote. "The meeting was at his insistence and, when it was proposed, vaguely puzzled me. But soon its purpose became clear enough."

In any event, he agreed to meet with Valentino at Aileen Pringle's suite at the Algonquin Hotel. The night being so warm, the men immediately stripped to their shirtsleeves and, as Mencken wrote, "came to terms at once." Mencken recalled that Valentino wore unusually wide suspenders that appeared absurd, especially on a slim young man and on such a hot summer night. For an hour they communed, while at intervals they wiped perspiration from their brow with handkerchiefs, napkins and even corners of the tablecloth. Thankfully a thunderstorm arose, allowing them a brief respite from the heat. At this time, Pringle excused herself, leaving the two men to converse in private.

Unfortunately, Mencken had little advice to comfort the frustrated actor. He could "name the disease" but could offer no cure. Instead he told Valentino he should have ignored the Chicago writer's taunt or, better yet, countered with a jeer of his own. He also should have stayed away from the New York reporters. Nevertheless the deed was done and nothing could change it. "Let the dreadful farce roll along to exhaustion," Mencken advised.

"That is infamous," Valentino protested.

"Infamous?" the writer argued. "Nothing is infamous that is not true. A man still has his inner integrity."

Back and forth they went, debating the matter and getting nowhere it seemed. Suddenly the agnostic Mencken had an epiphany of sorts. The writer realized that it wasn't the whole "Pink Powder Puffs" incident that was tormenting Valentino, but, as he put it, "the whole grotesque futility of his life." If, for all the years he toiled in motion pictures, he was a success, then that success was useless, "a colossal and preposterous nothing." The sycophantic parasites that had invaded his life did little or nothing but look after their own interests. And the wild adulation that followed his every move, and that at first had bemused him, now caused him alarm.

Although Mencken recognized that an air of commonness surrounded Valentino, he also acknowledged a "touch of fineness." Valentino was a gentleman. Sadly, the results of Mencken's counsel would never be known. Within a month of their fateful meeting, Rudolph Valentino would be dead, and Mencken would write of their meeting in an essay for the *Baltimore Evening Sun*.

Mencken ended that essay with an appraisal of Valentino's life and career: "Here was a young man who was living daily the dream of millions of other young men. Here was one who was catnip to women. Here was one who had wealth and fame. And here was one who was very unhappy."[12]

Was Mencken correct in his assessment of Valentino? Was he truly unhappy? Actor John Rothman, who has conducted intensive research on H. L. Mencken, and portrayed the writer on the stage and in Edoardo Ballerini's short film *Good Night Valentino*, disagrees with much of Mencken's assessment of the actor.

"I think what Valentino was able to communicate on the screen is not nothing," Rothman says. "Mencken's time was before the movies, before the age when movie stars had such an incredible transformative effect on people. I don't think Mencken ever really understood how that would work, how movies would become the great popular art form. I agree that Valentino was very unhappy; clearly, the level of fame and hysteria that he caused probably frightened him. But I don't agree that it was a colossal preposterous nothing. I think it was an extremely powerful something, whatever it was."[13]

A well-dressed Valentino poses for photographers.

One also has to look at whether success breeds happiness. Rudy once admitted that he did not yet consider himself successful, deeming there to be a vast difference between popularity and success. To Rudy, success was a sequence of artistic achievements, which, to his mind, he had not yet realized. "Artistic achievement can come only through economic independence," he told a shocked interviewer. "Don't look so surprised—I don't have it yet."[14]

A confused and emotionally distraught Rudy once told Adela Rogers St. Johns that life was a terrible thing and he was afraid of it. "I have everything—and I have nothing," he said. "It's all too—too terribly fast for me. Where am I? What am I? What is all this about? Where am I going?"[15]

And since Natacha had divorced him, he had no home life to speak of. Hoping to rebuild a family atmosphere, like the one he knew as a child, he brought his brother Alberto, Alberto's wife Ada and their son Jean with him from Europe. At Falcon Lair, he took care of their every need, but that still did not satisfy his longing for companionship. Unknown to Rudy, time was quickly running out, and whatever it was that he was looking for would forever slip from his grasp.

On Saturday, July 24, 1926, Rudy saw Alberto and his family off to Paris on the *S. S. France*. Before Alberto's boat departed, Rudy and Ullman raced by taxi to a nearby pier where General Umberto Nobile[16] was sailing on the liner *Conte Blancamane*. The Italian-born Nobile was designer and constructor of the polar airship *Norge*, and Captain of the aircraft on its recent flight over the North Pole. Rudy, who recently became acquainted with the famed aviator, posed for pictures with him on the boat deck.

The following day, Rudy made a personal appearance at the Mark Strand Theater for the New York premiere of *The Son of the Sheik*. A double line began forming early that Sunday morning and stretched nearly to Eighth Avenue, blocking traffic on Broadway. Included in Valentino's party was Aileen Pringle, James Quirk, and someone referred to by Ullman as Major McCutcheon.[17]

It was incredibly hot that day, somewhere around ninety-eight degrees, yet the crowd waited patiently to be admitted into the air-cooled theater. Ullman was impressed by this crowd's earnestness and respect, "as if a desire to see a great artist rather than a popular movie star motivated them."[18] Inside, an enormous ovation from a standing room–only audience greeted the film. Valentino spoke and gave, as Ullman described, "one of his gracious charming speeches, extemporaneous as usual, and captivated his hearers."[19]

As they were leaving, between three and four thousand fans jammed the entrance to the theater, blocking their escape. It took twenty policemen to clear a pathway from the stage door to their waiting automobile parked at the curb. Because it was Valentino the crowd was waiting for, Pringle, Quirk, and McCutcheon went unnoticed, reaching the car safely. Valentino then placed his hands on Ullman's shoulders and the two plowed their way through the crowd, as if, Ullman wrote, "we were carrying a football to the goal."[20]

Ignoring Ullman, the adoring crowds began grabbing at Valentino, tearing off his tie, snatching his handkerchief, ripping buttons from his coat and even tearing the cuff links from his shirt. Minus several articles of clothing, including his hat, but physically unscathed, Valentino reached the safety of the car. As they pulled away, the excited crowd knocked a frantic female off the running board as she attempted to jump into the car. Concerned for her safety, Rudy wanted the chauffeur to stop, but by now the woman had disappeared into the mob.

Once they made their way through the snarled traffic, everyone went to their respective homes or hotels to change and agreed to meet later for dinner. Back at the Ambassador, Rudy had Ullman call the neighboring police stations for reports of an injured woman, of which there were none.

In spite of his sense of relief, and even though it had been an exciting day, Rudy remained in a solemn mood. He spoke sincerely of his desire to play the piano, and decided that, upon his return to Hollywood, he would secretly take private lessons and surprise his friends with his newfound talent. The conversation soon turned to marriage, and he asked Ullman if it would be wise for him to one day marry a girl who was not an actress. Ullman was noncommittal with his answer, but believed that Rudy had not yet made a decision on the subject — regardless of what a certain Polish actress was telling Hollywood.

The relationship between Rudy and Pola Negri was a puzzler from the beginning. The two had officially met less than a year before at a masquerade party hosted by Marion Davies. Raised in poverty, the Polish born Negri, neé Appolonia Chalupec, had witnessed as a child the arrest and banishment of her father to a Siberian work camp. A bout of tuberculosis forced her to give up her beloved ballet at age thirteen. Trying her hand at acting, she was accepted by the Warsaw Imperial Academy of Dramatic Arts. It was not long before noted stage producer and director Max Reinhardt took notice and brought her to Germany, where she became the toast of Berlin. At the time, Germany's film industry was booming, and before long she was appearing in a string of films, including the Ernst Lubistch classic, *Passion* (1919). This and other films caught the attention of Hollywood, where in 1923 she signed a $3,000-a-week contract with Paramount.

Reportedly, Rudy was first introduced to Pola by director Raoul Walsh in 1924.[21] However, gossip columnist Louella Parsons claims it was she who presented the pair; yet Negri herself gives the credit to Marion Davies. In Parsons' account, Louella and Rudy were lounging around Davies' pool one Sunday afternoon when he requested a favor. "Introduce me to Pola Negri," he said. "I saw her last picture and I think she is fascinating. Can't you arrange for her to come to one of Marion's parties?"[22]

Negri, in her autobiography, referred to Marion Davies as one of Hollywood's great matchmakers. According to Pola, when Rudy casually mentioned to Marion that he would like to meet her, it was enough to "galvanize her into action."[23] At any rate, what Parsons and Negri both agree on is that Pola played hard to get. Louella called it an ancient feminine maneuver that seldom failed to get results. Pola, on the other hand, said that she was frightened and had a feeling of foreboding. "Nobody could understand why I would not want to meet one of the world's most attractive men," Pola said. "I barely understood it myself."[24]

Pola eventually relented and attended one of Marion's famous masquerade parties dressed as Catherine the Great from her recent film, *Forbidden Paradise*. Parsons said that she took her time about presenting Rudy to Pola, even though she could feel the "undercurrent of excitement in both of them from the moment she swept royally into the room."[25] According to Pola, though, Marion introduced her to Rudy as she entered the house. "Here you are, at last," Marion said. "I was about to send out the Texas Rangers." Marion then gestured to a handsome man standing at her side, dressed in full Russian regalia. "May I introduce Rudolph Valentino?"[26]

Surprisingly, Pola has the support of journalist Adela Rogers St. Johns, who was present at Marion's party and witnessed their introduction. "Miss Davies presented him," St. Johns said. "Pola gave him a white, ringed hand and he kissed it. They danced together and somehow the floor cleared so that they were dancing almost alone."[27]

Whomever made the first introduction, the result was certainly a violent affair of the heart from day one. Pola had a reputation for being intense — a child of emotion — and when she suffered, she let everyone know and feel her misery. Whatever it was that attracted Rudy to his "Polita," no one could say. Theirs was a true love-hate relationship. Shortly before Rudy's fatal illness, journalist Harry Carr met Pola on the lot and commented on how lovely she was and how everything must be going well with her. "Business very good; love very bad,"[28] she replied. She had quarreled with Rudolph. These intense quarrels, however, were always followed by passionate lovemaking. "They lived at the top of their emotional natures," said St. Johns. "A passion that swept Rudy along on its turbulent course."[29]

Perhaps Pola brought some sort of mental stimulation and excitement to Rudy's life and made him forget the unhappiness he felt over his recent divorce. Rudy missed Natacha's companionship, which Pola provided in part. The difference being, not once did Rudy stray from his commitment to Natacha; never was there a rumor of dalliance on his part. But with Pola it was different. During their separations it was as if Pola did not exist. Rudy openly dated other women and unashamedly took them out on the town, even though his romantic obligations were reportedly to Pola.

A perfect example is Rudy's last trip to Europe. Actress Peggy Hopkins Joyce joined him for excursions along the Parisian boulevards, as did Jean Nash and the Dolly Sisters, who often took pleasure in his company. In England he became acquainted with Lady Mary Curzon, the barony of Ravensdale. Lady Curzon, or Baroness Ravensdale as she was more commonly known, had long possessed a reputation for wit, beauty and charm. Befriending Rudy almost immediately, she intended to present him to the Royal family; but the death of the beloved Queen Mother, Alexandra, canceled all social events. Still, the Baroness saw to it that Rudy made the party circuit, introducing him to as many of her friends as possible.

"A marvelous dancer Valentino was too," Ravensdale later said, "but a quieter, simpler fellow I have seldom met: his patience with autograph hunters in the night clubs was unending. He discussed with me, with considerable melancholy, his misfortune that his wives would never bear him children, so instead he had a vast house and collected Mexican silver saddles and firearms."[30]

Another titled English beauty that monopolized much of Rudy's time was Lady Sheila Loughborough, who would later incur "Polita's" wrath. The English gossip columns had reportedly carried stories linking Rudy romantically with Loughborough. Pola caught wind of it and decided she would never speak to him again, sending Rudy a cable informing him of just that. Rudy cabled back that there was nothing to the rumors, which seemed to satisfy her jealousies.

Whether it was a coincidence or not, shortly after Rudy's return to Hollywood, both Loughborough and Ravensdale arrived in town. During her visit, Ravensdale stayed with author Elinor Glyn, who was an acknowledged mistress of Baroness Ravensdale's father, Lord Curzon. Glyn saw to it that her distinguished house guest was feted by nearly every star in Hollywood — Charlie Chaplin, Bebe Daniels and, of course, Marion Davies all played court to the Baroness. It's uncertain if a physical liaison existed between Rudy and Ravensdale, or if they were just good friends. In her memoirs, the Baroness only admits to a fleeting encounter with the actor one memorable night, and, incredibly, not being affected by his charm.

"As I came home at four A.M.," she wrote, "I shook myself fiercely, and wondered what was wrong with me that I had been in the company of the Great Lover for hours, but never in a state of swoon from start to finish."[31]

The fact is, they knew each other well and were at least good friends. It could be that as an Englishwoman of title, it would be improper to reveal more of a relationship, especially with a Hollywood actor.

Valentino sets sail for a trip to Europe.

Loughborough's visit, however, proved a bit more tumultuous. Because of her hospitality to Rudy in London, he repaid Lady Sheila's generosity by entertaining her at Falcon Lair. Evidently, Loughborough's presence in town was unknown to Pola, for when she arrived at the festivities, she found Rudy greeting his guests — Joe Schenck and his wife, Norma Talmadge — with the tall, resplendent blonde standing behind him in the position of hostess. Rudy casually introduced Pola to Lady Loughborough.

"I was completely taken aback," Pola said. "Since his cable denying the rumors of their affair, I had forgotten all about her. And here she was in his house, her cool insolent expression seeming to mock me."

Pola tried to be civil about the whole affair, but the rage she felt showed clearly on her face. Norma saw what was happening and told Pola that she must learn to hide her emotions. "You are too transparent,"[32] Norma told her. Rudy also sensed Pola's slow boiling fury and again tried to assuage her concerns. Then Pola noticed that Rudy had two photographs on the dressing table in his bedroom, and only one of them was of her — the other was of Lady Loughborough. According to Adela Rogers St. Johns, there were, to put it mildly, "fireworks." The Schencks maintained that Pola slapped Rudy's face. "At any rate, the quarrel was sufficiently noticeable and Rudy was annoyed," St. Johns said. "The confusion of it all, the swift pace, the continual upset, were beginning to get him."[33]

Rudy and Pola's alleged engagement is still open to conjecture. It should be noted that whether in public or in private, Rudy never admitted to an engagement to the Polish prima donna. In fact, he once told an inquiring reporter that they had not even discussed marriage. "Both of us have lots of work ahead of us," Valentino said. "We are not engaged. I do not like the word 'engagement.' It sounds too much like a contract one has to perform by a certain date."[34]

Even so, rumors ran rampant about their upcoming nuptials, most of which began with the actress herself or those close to her. Only a few weeks before Rudy's death, Pola's mother, Mrs. Elinor Chalupec, when asked if it were true that her daughter was going to marry Rudolph Valentino, replied that it was "more than probable."

"My daughter is very fond of Rudolph and he is very fond of her," Mrs. Chalupec said. "He would make Pola a splendid husband. But she doesn't believe in divorces, and her first marriage ended that way. If she and Rudolph are still fond of each other next March, they will probably be married in France."[35]

Rudy had definite opinions about marriage himself. Shortly after his divorce from Natacha, rumors circulated about a possible romance and marriage to actress Mae Murray. "Marry again?" he exclaimed. "Absurd. While I am what you might call domesticated, I have observed that a man in my profession is happier when he is single. I have no present intention of marrying Miss Mae Murray or any other woman."[36]

George Ullman later commented that even though he was entirely in Rudy's confidence, the actor never once mentioned an engagement to Pola Negri. In fact, many times when reporters would ask Rudy directly if it were so, he would invariably reply, "Ask the lady!" Shortly before his death, Adela Rogers St. Johns asked Rudy point blank if he were going to marry Pola.

"If I ever marry," he said slowly, "it will be a girl of my own people. I should like to have — a home, and children. But somehow I don't think I shall ever have them. Maybe — when I am much older. Then I shall go back to Italy, and live in the country somewhere, and have a wife like my mother and maybe some babies. Not now. Not here. Not while I am in this business."[37]

Rudy once confessed to Ullman that his goal was not to marry until his career was completed. Since he was looking forward to at least another five years of performing romantic leads before becoming a character actor or director, marriage likely was not on his agenda. He also felt there were only two reasons to marry: one was for love, which he already had with Natacha; the other was for a home and children, which he hoped to fulfill one day. One can understand Rudy's hesitancy at getting married again, in particular since his two tries at matrimony had ended in divorce.

But at the moment there were more important things to think about than marriage. Dinner and a night on the town were in order, and the invited guests included Jean Acker, Rudy's first wife. Rudy had recently made amends with Jean, and the two had been seen around town, prompting rumors of reconciliation; but Rudy, as usual, remained mum on the subject.

CHAPTER THREE

Mending Fences

Before going anywhere, Rudy had to change from the suit his fans had ravaged that afternoon at the Strand, into evening attire. On the way to the restaurant they picked up Jean before meeting the rest, which included the gang from that afternoon's premiere and the addition of Rudy's friend, Ben Ali Haggin. A popular Broadway choreographer, set designer and painter, Haggin designed the living tableaux featured in the *Ziegfeld Follies*. It was Haggin's marriage to Rudy's first dance partner, Bonnie Glass, which necessitated his enlisting with Joan Sawyer on her dance tour.

After dinner, the group went to the Playground, a cabaret managed by Tommy Guinan, the brother of Texas Guinan, the so-called "Queen of the Night Clubs." Texas had invited Rudy and his party to the Playground in hopes of propping up the weekend business for her sibling. The headliner of the evening was Rahman Bey, an Egyptian Fakir, or magician, who was appearing in a successful vaudeville act at the Loew's State on Broadway.

For his first trick, Bey, attired in his traditional sheik makeup, jabbed a long hatpin into the arm of Texas Guinan, who took it without wincing. Then some character in the audience blatantly yelled out, "How about the he-man, Valentino, following suit?"[1] Bey approached Valentino at his table and asked if he could drive a needle through his cheek, promising there would be no pain or blood. Put on the spot, Rudy was about to submit to Bey's request when Ullman, concerned about the famous Valentino mug, intervened.

With all he had recently been through, Rudy wasn't about to back out at this point, so he offered to have the trick performed on his arm. Bey agreed, but as Rudy removed his coat, the audience began to giggle — the "Sheik" was wearing red suspenders! That was bad enough, but when Bey pierced Rudy's arm with a pin, the actor shouted "Ouch!" resulting in the second laugh of the evening at Rudy's expense.

"Rudy couldn't stand being laughed at," *Variety* wrote, "so he finally let the pin go all the way, satisfying that bloodthirsty audience."[2] Bey withdrew the needle without any blood, much to Rudy's amazement. Seeing the humor in the situation, Rudy laughed, pulled down his shirtsleeve and returned to his table. Ullman, on the other hand, fearing an infection, sent for alcohol to cleanse the actor's arm.

A few days later, Rudy and some friends were at a performance of the Ziegfeld revue "*No Foolin'*" at the Globe Theatre[3], where a pretty young Titian-haired dancer caught his eye. Afterward, Rudy found Ben Ali Haggin, who choreographed the show, and asked for an introduction. The attractive chorus girl was 21-year-old Marion Benda, who worked in various Broadway shows for the past three years. At first their relationship was purely of a business nature. "Mr. Valentino was looking for someone to play with him in his new picture *Cellini*," Benda remarked. "He thought he might be able to use me. Then we began to see one another almost every night. We were drawn together by a spiritual bond."[4]

They would take cab rides in Central Park, and, after the show, would go for long walks that lasted until dawn. Discovering a mystical commonality between them, Rudy shared his belief that a protective spirit hovered near him, and that everyone had such a spirit. Many times their conversations turned to marriage and to Pola Negri. "He was not engaged to marry Miss Negri," Marion said. "You'll notice that all the statements have come from her. He never denied any of them because he was too fine. He did think a great deal of her but he had absolutely no intention of marrying her, I know."[5]

On Thursday, July 29th, Rudy returned to Chicago for the local premiere of *The Son of the Sheik*. When he appeared before the packed auditorium of the Roosevelt Theater, he was greeted with a thunderous reception lasting several minutes. When the applause died down, Rudy gave what Ullman called "the best speech of his life, receiving upon its conclusion a similarly vociferous acclaim, together with shouts of his name."[6]

Earlier in the day he faced a barrage of questions from reporters, confirming that Estelle Taylor, wife of Jack Dempsey, would be his leading lady in his next film, *The Life of Cellini*. He claimed there was no significance in having dined with Jean Acker a few nights earlier, and that they were just friends. Most of the questions, however, were aimed at his reported feud with the *Tribune* editorial writer. He told them he was making good on his promise to return to Chicago to see what effect slave bracelets have on virility. To prove his point, Rudy went to Mullen's gymnasium and spent several hours punching the bag, shadow boxing, and sparring with attendants. Afterwards, he stayed close to his hotel, waiting for an answer to his challenge.

"I must return to New York tomorrow," he said. "My business there is not completed. But I challenged this man to fight, and that's my business in Chicago now. I'm not boasting about my physical strength. I never should have allowed my press agent to make such a point of the fact. But this critic has called me effeminate and unmanly and I am anxious to correct that impression. Evidently this critic has changed his mind about me for thus far I have heard nothing from him."[7]

Before leaving Chicago, Rudy released a statement to the press once again calling the anonymous writer a "coward." Feeling vindicated by the writer's silence, and reluctantly accepting his silence as a retraction, Rudy praised the vast majority of newspaper men and women, whom he called "absolutely fair and so loyal to their profession and their publications, that I need hardly say how conspicuous is this exception to the newspaper profession."[8]

It would be an understatement to say that the "Pink Powder Puffs" editorial affected Rudy deeply. According to Ullman, that deplorable appellation "stuck in Rudy's craw." In denouncing the writer, Ullman said that it was not so much what the article contained, but the deep hurt that Rudy received from it; and Ullman blamed the editorial for hastening the actor's death.

"Who knows but that, in those last days when he was conscious, able to think, and undisturbed by visitors," Ullman wrote, "his mind might have dwelt on his inability to avenge the insult and that, had his last hours been more free from anxiety, his power to cope with the inroads of the septic poisoning might have been increased, and possibly his life spared."[9]

We will never know whether the writer of that infamous editorial felt remorse or in any way responsible for contributing to Valentino's death. For decades the author of the "Pink Powder Puffs" editorial remained a secret. Ullman stated that he recognized the anonymous attack "as coming from the same poison pen which earlier in the year had, without cause and without reason, attacked my friend."[10] He did not, however, identify the writer.

Some historians have claimed that the writer was none other than Dick Dorgan, the same man who penned the offending "A Song of Hate" article for *Photoplay*. Even with his connections, it is doubtful that Dorgan's meager writing credentials would have allowed him to editorialize for a newspaper as prestigious as the *Chicago Tribune*.

Still another writer to whom the editorial has been attributed was John Origen Herrick,[11] husband of popular *Tribune* writer Genevieve Forbes. At the time, Herrick was questioned about the editorial but had "nothing, nothing whatever, to say."[12] In 1977, film critic Gene Siskel also gave the credit to Herrick,[13] but while the *Tribune* employed the writer at that time, he did not pen the piece.

The true author of the "Pink Powder Puffs" editorial was Clifford Samuel Raymond.[14] Born in Franklin, Pennsylvania, and educated at Wittenburg College and Harvard, Raymond was a scholar and author of several mystery novels.[15] Raymond joined the *Tribune* as a correspondent in 1898 and, in the years that followed, became chief editorial writer until his retirement in 1942. According to his colleagues, Raymond rarely attended motion pictures, and some say it's possible he never saw a Valentino film.[16]

If Raymond had come forward, it is unlikely Valentino would have made good on his threat. Valentino admitted there were only two things that would have prevented him from taking action against the writer — if he were feeble or old, or too young. "If he is too old, he should have known better," Valentino said. "If he is too young, I'll spank him." Even though Raymond was far from feeble, at 51 years of age it is doubtful that he would have made a good sparring opponent for the younger, more virile Rudolph Valentino. Regardless of his years, Valentino added, "All journalists should be ashamed of him, whoever he is."[17] In any event, Raymond never made his identity known, nor has it been recorded how he reacted to Valentino's challenge.

Rudy's personal appearances to publicize *The Son of the Sheik* helped the film's box-office wherever it played. In Los Angeles, the picture was shown at Grauman's Million Dollar Theater, where it came within a close margin of equaling the house record. At every theater, similar scenes were replayed — the same crowds waiting in long lines, experiencing the same high temperatures. The incredible heat wave that gripped most of the country for the previous few weeks had already been blamed for the deaths of more than forty people. Yet the fans stood in line for hours under the blistering sun for the opportunity to catch a glimpse of Rudolph Valentino.

It was the same in Atlantic City, where, at the Ritz-Carlton Hotel, Ullman and Rudy were met by an enormous crowd. Men and women alike jumped on the running board and shoved their hands into the open windows, hoping to greet the star. At the Virginia Theater he was welcomed by a three-minute ovation before he spoke to the crowd.

Afterward, Rudy's friend, vaudevillian Gus Edwards, persuaded him to make an appearance at his revue. Edwards publicly awarded him a pair of boxing gloves, suggesting that he use them on the Chicago editorialist. Before the evening ended, Edwards once more imposed on Rudy, asking him to tango with one of the dancers in his revue. After some gentle persuasion, Rudy, for the last time, did the dance that had made him famous.

A few days later, *The Son of the Sheik* once again played to a standing-room-only crowd at Brooklyn's Strand Theater. Rudy gave an impromptu speech before the packed audience, paying tribute to his two-time costar, Agnes Ayres. Rudy commended the actress for taking such a small part in the film, reprising her role of Diana from *The Sheik*, and thus adding to its success. He spoke with tenderness of how Ayres was also a wife and mother, describing her daughter Maria with such candor that it nearly brought the audience to tears. Ullman said that his eyes shone with an indescribable expression that only came when he spoke of children.

Rudy spent the next two weeks, as they say, burning the candle at both ends. His only commitment was a personal appearance in Philadelphia for *The Son of the Sheik* on August 16th, so until then, his time was his own. Many weekends that summer were spent at "Pleasure Island," the Long Island getaway of Schuyler Parsons, a wealthy bon vivant of a prominent New York family who first met Rudy shortly after his arrival in this country. With a letter of introduction from a mutual Italian architect friend, Rudy made quite an impression, not only on Parsons, but also on several of his lady friends.

One weekend during that last summer, Parsons recalled that his butler witnessed Rudy taking an enormous amount of bicarbonate of soda. "But since I knew that he never drank [was he trying to protect Rudy's reputation?], I thought nothing of it,"[18] Parsons said.

Rudy had been complaining of "nervous indigestion" for weeks but refused to seek medical attention. One evening, just days before his fatal illness, he was having dinner with Joseph Schenck and Norma Talmadge. "Chief, I've a terrible pain in my right side," Rudy admitted. "Do you know I believe I've got appendicitis."

"Don't be silly, Rudy," Schenck laughed. "If you've a pain in your side, go to a doctor, or forget about it."[19]

Rudy kept his body in good physical shape with regular exercise. "There is nothing as brutally truthful as the movie camera," he once said. "The actor's stock and trade is his physical appearance. Constant vigilance plus systematic exercise will keep the chest up, the muscles supple, the eye bright, and the mind clear. I ride, box, run, row, wrestle, fence."[20]

Four days before he went into the hospital, Rudy had breakfast with Jack Dempsey and his wife Estelle Taylor. They discussed details of their next picture, *The Life of Cellini*, in which Estelle was to costar. During the course of their conversation, Rudy boasted of his splendid physical condition. "I never felt better in my life,"[21] he told the couple.

But while he religiously maintained his outward appearance with physical exercise, Rudy also neglected it in many ways. A member of the physical department of the New York Board of Education interviewed him at the Ambassador Hotel about the care of his body. When asked if he smoked, Rudy replied, "Yes, from 40 to 50 cigarettes a day."

"Do you drink?"

"Yes—frequently."

"What about your eating?"

"I eat everything I please."

"What is the secret to your health?"

"I do what I want to do when I want to do it."[22]

That could have been Rudy's mantra in those last days. He thoroughly enjoyed himself, as Ullman recalled, saying that he turned "day into night and having, as he expressed it, the time of his life." One morning very early, Rudy came into Ullman's room as he slept and awakened him. There he stood, still in his evening clothes, holding a glass of Vichy water. "Would you like some water?" Rudy asked.

Ullman rubbed his eyes and questioned the reason for the room service, to which Rudy replied that he thought his friend might be thirsty. "You mean," Ullman said, "that you are bringing me this peace offering, hoping that I will not scold you for getting home at five o'clock in the morning!"

"Well," said Rudy sheepishly, "I did intend to ask you to see that I was not disturbed until noon. I'm going to lunch with Jean at one."[23]

It was George Ullman's belief that Rudy never had a premonition of his imminent death. There were, however, some that disagreed. John Considine, Jr., the producer of *The Eagle* and *The Son of the Sheik*, said that several times Rudy told him that he would die young. "I know it," Rudy told Considine. "And I shall not be sorry. I would hate to live to be an old man."[24] Norma Talmadge also remembered one evening during dinner when Rudy remarked to a guest that he would not live a lengthy life. "In fact, I don't want to be an old man," Rudy told the guest. "I can't bear to think about it. If I meet death at 40, I'll be quite satisfied."[25]

Oddly, Rudy passed many of his last days mending fences and making wronged relationships right, almost as if he knew this were his final chance. Most notable among these was his recent reconciliation with Jean Acker and his old friend, June Mathis.

When Mathis' version of the script for the ill-fated *The Hooded Falcon* failed to impress either Valentino or Natacha, Mathis ended their relationship. "June refused to have anything further to do with us,"[26] Natacha said. So it was a tearful reunion when Valentino saw Mathis with friends at the Los Angeles premiere of *The Son of the Sheik*. "He stopped them, and then and there showed by his cordiality that the old Rudy was again in evidence and at heart had never changed,"[27] Ullman recalled.

Another peace offering was made to his old boss, Adolph Zukor. In 1922 Rudy had disagreed with the way Famous Players–Lasky was handling him and walked out on his contract. When Rudy made it clear that he had no intention of returning, the studio secured an injunction preventing him from working at another studio. An agreement was finally reached, and Rudy returned, making two more films — *Monsieur Beaucaire* (1924) and *The Sainted Devil* (1924) — before being released from his contract.

On Monday, August 9, Zukor received a telephone call from Rudy inviting him to lunch. "It is only that I would like to see you," Rudy said. "No business." Zukor said that he would have agreed in any circumstance, but was sure Rudy was telling the truth since he was already well set with United Artists.

"Certainly," Zukor answered. "Where?"

"The Colony," Valentino responded. Zukor had already guessed his choice. "The Colony was probably New York's most expensive restaurant," Zukor said. "He liked the best. We set the time."

At the restaurant, the two barely had time to sit down when a parade of women who were only slightly acquainted with Zukor made their way to his table. "Though overwhelmed," Zukor said, "I remained in sufficient command of my senses to observe the amenities by introducing each to Valentino." Once the introductions had ceased, Rudy made his point.

"I only wanted to tell you," Rudy said, "that I'm sorry about the trouble I made — my strike against the studio and all that. I was wrong and now I want to get it off my conscience by saying so."

"It's water over the dam," Zukor shrugged. "In this business if we can't disagree, sometimes violently, and then forget about it we'll never get anywhere. You're young. Many good years are ahead of you."

So the subject was dropped. They continued talking of artistic things and of his ambitions, especially his desire to direct when his days as a leading man were over.

Zukor came to the conclusion that perhaps fame had come too rapidly to him and he hadn't known how to deal with it properly. "Telephone me any time," Zukor said as they parted, "and we'll do this again. I enjoyed myself."[28] Sadly, another opportunity would never arise, since two weeks later Valentino was dead.

By all outward appearances, Rudy was feeling better, at least emotionally. The fact that he had been making good on his bad relationships seemed to set well with him. And most importantly, perhaps, he had finally put the whole "Pink Powder Puffs" fiasco behind him. But that is possibly what all the over-indulgences of the past two weeks were about — numbing those feelings to the point that it didn't matter.

In any case, Friday the Thirteenth was a good day for Rudy. He had only one more personal appearance commitment in Philadelphia to fulfill before beginning work on *The Life of Cellini*. Joseph Schenck and Norma Talmadge were leaving town for a few days to visit United Artists president Hiram Abrams at his summer house in Maine. Rudy was with them at Grand Central Terminal when he took Norma aside.

"Norma," he said, "I've been so happy lately that I've simply got to celebrate. Will you and the Chief come to a party I've decided to give in your honor at the Ambassador Hotel next Friday night?"

"We certainly will,"[29] Norma answered.

The Schenck's genuinely liked Rudy and would have returned for Friday's gala regardless. Tragically, they had no way of knowing their return to New York would be sooner than scheduled. Two days later, an unexpected telegram would forever change their lives — and the life of Rudolph Valentino.

CHAPTER FOUR

"Doctor, Am I a Pink Puff?"

Saturday, August 14, 1926

The facts about Valentino's last night on the town vary, depending on who is telling the story and when they are telling it. In Ullman's book, he mentions that Rudy's coloring was bad and urged him to return to his hotel room for a rest. "Why, I feel wonderful!" Rudy replied. "I don't need rest."[1]

Rudy spent the majority of the day at the apartment of Barclay Warburton, Jr., or "Buzzy" as his friends called him. Warburton, the grandson of department store founder John Wannamaker, was a scion of Philadelphia high society. Young, blonde, and handsome, Warburton, who was recently divorced from his first wife, occupied a bachelor apartment full of "soft lights, low couches and luxury."[2]

That evening Rudy was feeling ill but insisted on going to his favorite restaurant, the Colony, for dinner with Warburton and Ullman. Adela Rogers St. Johns was visiting New York and also had rooms at the Ambassador. Rudy stopped on his way to suggest that Adela, James Quirk, and Quirk's fiancée, actress May Allison, join their party. "But we had theater tickets and it wasn't until the next day that we knew the serious results of that gay evening," St. Johns later wrote.[3]

Dagmar Godowsky, Rudy's old friend and former costar, was also having dinner at the Colony that evening. "I saw him the night before he was taken to the hospital," Godowsky later said, "we were at the Colony restaurant. He wasn't a happy man."[4]

After dinner, Rudy complained of indigestion, admitting to Warburton that he had been troubled with it for some time. Regardless of his discomfort, the trio attended the *George White's Scandals*[5] at the Apollo Theater on Forty-second Street. This was the eighth performance of the hit revue that Rudy had attended in the last two weeks. After the show, they met backstage with *Scandals* stars Frances White and

Harry Richman. At some point, the group was invited to a party at the apartment of actress Lenore Ulric, but Rudy declined, saying he was not feeling well. Instead they went to Warburton's apartment, where, later reports said, between fourteen to sixteen people gathered, including Marion Benda, who was just getting out of a performance of the Ziegfeld revue "*No Foolin.*'"

According to Harry Richman, there were "some drinks, music and dancing," but Valentino declined any "refreshments" because he had indigestion.[6] Guests slowly began leaving as the night progressed until only a small group remained. "Rudy was sitting on the couch," Ullman later explained. "Suddenly he collapsed."[7] Richman said that Valentino became violently ill around one-thirty in the morning and was rushed back to the Ambassador.

Sunday, August 15, 1926

The first reports from that morning claimed Rudy arose from bed about eleven-thirty. Still feeling poorly, he refused breakfast, and instead read the Sunday papers. Suddenly, he turned pale, clutched his abdomen and collapsed on the floor. Frank Chaplin, Rudy's valet, called for assistance and notified Barclay Warburton. Ullman and his wife Beatrice, who were in adjoining suites, were with Valentino by the time Warburton arrived. Later in the day, Ullman gave a slightly different version of what happened:

> Mr. Valentino had gotten out of bed, but had not ordered his breakfast. This fact, it may turn out, may save his life. We were sitting around reading the Sunday papers when suddenly he groaned and pressed his hand to his side, complaining of a severe pain in the region of his abdomen. The pain passed off, but a little later he turned pale again and another pain seized him. Then I called a doctor whom I know personally. He came into the hotel and as Mr. Valentino continued to get worse we had him removed to the hospital.[8]

Dr. Paul Durham of the Polyclinic Hospital was a friend of both Ullman and Warburton. Within minutes of his arrival, Durham examined Rudy but waited four hours before calling an ambulance, even though his symptoms appeared to be serious. Several reasons have been given for this delay, one being that it was a hot Sunday afternoon and many physicians were out of town. Valentino's brother, Alberto, believed that no one wanted to take responsibility for operating on Rudolph Valentino, so they waited for a "well-known surgeon, [an] experienced surgeon, to come along."[9]

Still others claim that Valentino had a fear of hospitals. Dr. Arthur Bogart, who worked at Polyclinic Hospital in the late 1940s, was well acquainted with one of Valentino's former physicians (who was still on staff at the hospital). "The doctor told me," Bogart said, "his patient refused surgical intervention which might have saved his life, because he was terrified of surgery."[10]

Whatever the reason, sometime around four-thirty, Rudy was taken by ambulance to the Polyclinic Hospital on West Fiftieth Street. According to Ullman, in his time of need, Rudy sought assistance from his spirit guides. "I remember, too," Ullman recalled, "as he lay in that ambulance, doubled up with pain, unconscious and en route to the hospital where he was to die, he kept repeating the word, 'Jenny, Jenny, Jenny.'"[11]

Shortly after five o'clock that afternoon, Dr. Harold D. Meeker,[12] a consulting surgeon at Polyclinic, examined Valentino. The fifty-year-old Meeker, a graduate of Columbia University, was also professor of Surgery at Polyclinic's Medical School. When Meeker first examined Valentino, the actor was in great pain with a moderate fever, a rapid pulse and a board-like rigidity of the abdomen. Meeker's first diagnosis was a perforated gastric ulcer, but he couldn't rule out other possibilities at that advanced stage of the illness. In his expert opinion, the only way to save Valentino's life was to operate.

At six-thirty the patient was rolled into the operating room. Meeker was assisted by Durham; Dr. Golden R. Battey, senior house physician of Polyclinic; and Dr. G. Randolph Manning, a specialist in diseases of the stomach. During surgery, fluid was found leaking through a round hole one centimeter in diameter in the anterior wall of Valentino's stomach. Meeker's report stated that the "tissue of the stomach for one and one-half centimeters immediately surrounding the perforation was necrotic. The appendix was acutely inflamed from a secondary infection...."[13] Meeker repaired the opening in Valentino's stomach and removed his appendix.

Valentino was taken from the operating room at nine-thirty and transferred to a suite on the eighth floor. Suite Q, the most expensive suite in the hospital, had two luxurious rooms and a bath, a large mahogany bed and dresser, two large easy chairs, handsome rugs and several smaller chairs. It was aptly dubbed the "lucky suite" when Mary Pickford successfully convalesced there in 1912. When Rudy came out of the anesthetic at about ten o'clock, he asked, "Doctor, am I a pink puff?"

"No indeed," Durham replied. "You have been very brave."[14]

Later, when Ullman arrived, Rudy smiled and asked, "How did I take it?"

"You took it fine," he replied.

"Oh well," Rudy whispered. "Once a sheik, always a sheik." He then fell asleep.[15]

Shortly after midnight, Ullman announced that Valentino reacted very well from the operation, but warned that his condition was critical. "Indeed, we fear that it is doubtful if he can survive because the disease had progressed so far without him knowing or suspecting it," Ullman said. "It will be several days at the very least before we can know the outcome."[16]

Monday, August 16, 1926

The next morning, Valentino's illness was front-page news in every paper in the country. The Polyclinic set up a "Valentino Information Desk" on the first floor where bulletins on the actor's progress were given out every few hours. Extra telephone operators were placed on duty to handle the thousands of incoming calls, mostly from women asking for news about their idol.

As the morning progressed, the number of fans arriving at the hospital inquiring about Valentino's condition increased. They finally had to be turned away and the hospital doors closed. Jean Acker, who was planning a trip to Europe at the end of the week, called about Rudy's status, saying she would visit later in the day.

As Rudy requested, Ullman sent cables to Alberto and his sister Maria in Italy, and to Natacha in France. Ullman at first wanted to have Alberto return to New York, but Rudy declined. "By no means," he insisted. "Just cable him that I am a little indisposed and will soon be all right."[17] When Natacha received news of Rudy's illness, all the anger and hurt that she experienced the past year suddenly faded, and the differences that had separated them now seemed unimportant.[18] For support, she turned to her

Valentino and costar Kathleen Kirkham in a scene from *A Married Virgin* (1918). (Courtesy of Robert Young)

mother and aunt, Teresa Werner, who was a favorite of Rudy's. Both women had maintained hope that the couple would be reunited, and felt that this illness might bring them back together.

Rudy asked that a wire also be sent to Pola. "Tell her that I'm all right," he told Ullman. "Tell her not to worry. I'll pull through."[19] When Pola received her telegram, it provided hope for her though his condition remained serious. "Mr. Valentino has been operated on for appendicitis and gastric ulcers," the telegram read. "He is making good progress."[20]

Negri was on the set of her latest film, *The Hotel Imperial*, when she spoke to reporters. "I am so unhappy," she said. "I can't just walk off the set, for I am in the middle of a big picture. But I will go to Rudy just as soon as I can leave my business and as fast as a train will take me to New York. Poor Rudy—I had no idea he was going to get sick—he was so strong and happy when he left and he didn't say a thing about illness in his last telegram."[21]

Rudy's boss, Joseph Schenck, who newspapers reported had a $1,000,000 insurance policy on Valentino's life, was still at Hiram Abrams' summer camp in Maine when he received word of Valentino's condition. Schenck cabled that he and Norma would leave for New York immediately.

After a slight relapse that afternoon, rumors spread that Valentino had died. The actor rallied, however, and briefly regained consciousness. Recognizing his nurse, Pearl Frank, a diminutive and exceedingly attractive brunette, he patted her on the cheek and said, "You're a fine girl. You've been so good to me!"[22]

While Valentino fought for his life, stories circulated up and down Broadway that the star had attended a "wild party" with liquor and showgirls the evening before he took ill. Barclay Warburton emphatically denied that a party of any kind had taken place. Early that afternoon reporters gathered at his Park Avenue apartment as Warburton confirmed that he, Rudy, and Ullman had dined at the Colony before attending *George White's Scandals*. Afterwards, he said, Valentino felt "rotten" and complained of pain. Instead of continuing on, Warburton went to his apartment, and Valentino and Ullman, as far as he knew, returned to the Ambassador. He first learned of Rudy's condition when the actor's valet telephoned him on Sunday afternoon.

The reporters left Warburton's apartment convinced that he was telling the truth. One newspaper, however, revealed that as they were leaving, an attractive young woman arrived, a "member of one of the popular Broadway revues."[23] Some have speculated that it was Ziegfeld Follies girl, and frequent Valentino date, Marion Benda.

Two days after Warburton's denial, Benda related her version of that evening to the *New York American*. She corroborated Warburton's story, saying that she met with Valentino and Warburton (she did not mention Ullman) after the theater. "Mr. Warburton was going home, he said, and Rudy and I decided to go dance some place," she told the tabloid.

Benda claimed they ended up at Club Lido on East Forty-fourth Street, where Valentino again complained of feeling unwell. Later, at Texas Guinan's nightclub, Valentino became upset for reasons unknown to Benda, so she suggested that they leave. "He said he wasn't in the mood for such a place," Benda said, "although we had had such a good time there only a few nights before."[24]

From there, Valentino escorted Benda to her apartment building on West Fifty-fifth Street. "I saw Rudy last at the door of my apartment house," she said. "It was about 3 o'clock in the morning. He said he was going home to bed."[25] However, cab driver Mike Di Calzi told the *New York Evening Graphic* that he picked up Valentino and Benda at her apartment at four-thirty that morning and took them to Warburton's apartment. Frank Gross, the elevator operator in Benda's building, reportedly confirmed that Valentino and Benda did leave her apartment around that time.

The question arises, how could Valentino be with Marion Benda at two nightclubs and her apartment, and be at a party at Barclay Warburton's at the same time? Were the cab driver and elevator operator lying, or did the *Evening Graphic* fabricate the story, which would not be hard to believe considering their reputation. It should also be noted that no one ever came forward from Club Lido or Texas Guinan's to confirm Valentino's presence there that evening.

Regardless, a few days after Valentino's death, Benda changed her original story. This time she stated to a *New York Daily News* reporter (to whom she originally told a few days earlier that she "knew nothing about it"[26]) that they had indeed gone to Club Lido and Texas Guinan's, but they were not alone — Warburton, dancer Frances Williams and "a girl named Hayes" accompanied them. She couldn't remember who else was in the party.

Benda said that when Valentino took ill, the festivities moved to Warburton's apartment, where Dr. Paul Durham was called. At first it was thought that Valentino was suffering from indigestion. "Perhaps he's eaten something that disagreed with him," Durham suggested.

"All he had was a ham-and-egg sandwich," Benda replied.[27]

All evidence points to a party at Warburton's apartment that evening, but whether it was a "wild party" or not is hard to say. In 1920s vernacular, a "wild party" conjures up visions of scantily clad girls dancing on tables drinking champagne. Regardless of Prohibition, it was, in all probability, a simple gathering of a few people having drinks, listening to music and dancing, as Harry Richman stated.

If this were true, why would Warburton lie? He is not convincing when he insists that a party never occurred. Not only are there those who contradict him, there were none that defended him, including Ullman. And the fact that he later avoided the press on the subject generates skepticism. At this point in time, one can only speculate as to why Warburton would choose not to tell the truth. Being that it was the middle of Prohibition, perhaps he was nervous because hard liquor was served. With a well-earned reputation as a playboy, he was known for hosting riotous parties that lasted until all hours of the morning. A former neighbor, who claimed that his dusk-to-dawn soirees kept him from sleeping and forced him to move, had already sued him.[28]

This brings up another consideration — the possibility of a scandal. At the time, it was uncertain whether Valentino would live or die. If the actor died after attending a party where alcohol was present, who knows what the repercussions would be. After all, memories of the Fatty Arbuckle scandal, less than five years earlier, were still fresh in the public's mind. The best defense, it would seem, would be to deny that a party had even occurred.

And what of Marion Benda? There is no question that she was acquainted with Valentino and attended Warburton's party, but why give two different accounts to two different newspapers? If Benda were the mysterious chorine at Warburton's apartment that day, perhaps she and Warburton reached an "agreement" that should back up the playboy's statement. Though only speculation, perhaps the fact that she suddenly includes Warburton in the second version of her story indicates that perhaps any agreement may have gone sour, and this was her way of setting things right.

Tuesday, August 17, 1926

According to hospital statements, Rudy passed a moderately comfortable day. Laying, for the most part, with eyes closed, he opened them only when treatment was administered. At one point Rudy smiled weakly at Ullman and declared, "I've gotten out of worse fixes than this. I'll soon be on my feet again and making pictures."[29] As Ullman left the room, the actor summoned up enough energy to wink "good-bye."

Rudy insisted that the mass of flowers that continued to pour into Polyclinic for him be distributed to the various wards of the hospital. Hundreds of telegrams remained unopened, waiting until he was well enough to read them himself. As he lay there, Rudy surprised Ullman by asking for a mirror. Ullman was at first hesitant because the illness had clearly left its mark on Rudy's face. "Oh, let me have it," Rudy insisted. "I just want to see how I look when I am sick, so that if I ever have to play the part in pictures I will know how to put on my make-up!"[30]

Early that morning, Joseph Schenck and Norma Talmadge arrived from Maine but were not permitted to see the actor. Schenck told reporters that millions of dollars would be lost "in the event of the star's death."[31]

The "no visitors" order, however, did not deter creative fans from attempting to see their idol. Many would-be visitors succeeded in reaching the eighth floor but were stopped before they could enter his room. Marie Markiewz, a determined young woman, demanded that she be allowed to see her "beloved." When told that Valentino was too ill for visitors, she became hysterical and recited poetry that she scribbled down on paper. As they were forcibly ejecting her from the hospital, she sobbed loudly, "Oh, my beloved, I hope you get well."[32] Another admirer was a young man whose only request was to kneel at Valentino's bedside and silently pray for his recovery.

Meanwhile, outside the hospital, crowds watched as reporters photographed the arrival of Betty Hughes, a dancer in a Brooklyn cabaret that Valentino reportedly frequented. Accompanied by her pet monkey 'Pepy,' Hughes told reporters that the simian had often amused Valentino on his visits to the cafe. Neither she nor the monkey got any further than the first floor.

Unfortunately, all this attention generated by Valentino's illness seriously disrupted the hospital's daily routine. After a consultation with Polyclinic's administrator, Ullman hired a private detective to stand guard outside Valentino's suite, hoping to deter further undesirables. In addition to barring the curious and overzealous flappers that tried to force their way in, all reporters, who had been maintaining a "death watch" on the first floor, were ordered out of the hospital shortly before noon.

At seven o'clock that evening the last official bulletin of the day was issued: "There is no change in Mr. Valentino's condition. His temperature is 103.6, respiration 26, pulse 103."[33] Physicians were certain that whatever transpired the next day would determine Rudy's fate.

CHAPTER FIVE

Final Days

Wednesday, August 18, 1926

Valentino once again had a reasonably comfortable night. Letters, flowers, and telegrams continued to flow into Polyclinic Hospital, and more operators were added to handle the influx of calls inquiring about Valentino's status. Meeker's report stated that the actor's condition remained favorable. "Unless unforeseen conditions develop," he said, "recovery is possible. Temperature 100.8. Pulse 85. Respiration 20."[1]

That morning, Rudy, who was experiencing less pain, was given chicken broth and Vichy water, the first bit of nourishment since his operation. It appeared that he was feeling significantly better, but somewhat restless. "How much longer is this damn thing going to last?"[2] he asked Ullman, who was the only person allowed to see him besides the hospital staff.

Rudy tried to concentrate as some of the thousands of telegrams received were read to him. "That's very nice," was his response to Joseph Schenck's message of sympathy. John Gilbert wrote, "Fight, Rudy, fight. Millions need you."[3] Other greetings arrived from John Barrymore, Bebe Daniels, Charles Chaplin and Mary Pickford. Letters and packages from unknown fans arrived daily, including more than a dozen Bibles and a copy of "Bedtime Stories for Grown-up Guys" from a young girl in Chicago.

Natacha Rambova and her Aunt Teresa cabled their good wishes from Paris: "We pray for your recovery. Love."[4] That evening, Natacha arranged a séance with medium George Wehner, who claimed to have contacted Valentino's spirit even though the actor was still very much alive. There appeared to be some confusion in the metaphysical world, since Rudy's spirit believed that Natacha and company were in New York comforting him. Suddenly, Jenny, one of his spirit guides and the one he called for in the ambulance, took control, describing his illness and how his thoughts were directed to Natacha and his beloved Aunt Tessie.

Pola Negri, Valentino's self-proclaimed fiancée, called long-distance and spoke briefly to an operator. "This is Pola Negri. How is Mr. Valentino?"[5] she asked. When assured that he was doing well, she thanked the operator and hung up. Though Pola proclaimed she would take an airplane in order to be at Rudy's side, her employers, Famous Players–Lasky, vetoed that notion, not wanting to risk the safety of their star.

Earlier that afternoon, reports again circulated that Valentino had died. The *New York Evening Graphic* issued an extra with two words in a large black headline— "Rudy Dead." Below, in smaller and lighter type, the headline continued, "Cry Startles Film World as Sheik Rallies." In its story, the *Graphic* recounted a rumor that Valentino had died, but gladly reported that it wasn't true.[6] The headline, however, had done its job. As one newspaper put it, "Theatrical stars, never out of bed before noon, rushed to the hospital, while others telephoned or sent messages."[7]

Calls flooded the hospital switchboard at a rate of thirty-two per minute. Two additional operators were added, performing their duties "standing up." When word reached the Astoria studios of Famous Players–Lasky, they closed for the remainder of the day before the truth was learned. The hospital staff did their best to deny the rumors and denounce its originators, but the damage had been done. In retaliation, Dr. A. A. Joller, superintendent of Polyclinic Hospital, had Jack Miley, the *Graphic*'s reporter and author of the piece, barred from the hospital's press room. When ordered out, Miley said, "Who's going to pay for this press room — Mr. Ullman, Mr. Valentino, or the United Artists?"

Dr. Joller defended his actions and the hospital, saying "For an institution of the high character and standing that Polyclinic enjoys, to tolerate such a fake as charged by the *New York Evening Graphic* would be suicide and would not be permitted for one moment, actor or no actor."[8]

At seven o'clock that evening the final bulletin of the day was issued: "Mr. Valentino's condition remains favorable. Unless unforeseen complications develop, recovery is considered probable. His temperature is 100.8; respiration 20, and pulse 86."[9]

For dinner, Rudy was given broth, French Vichy water, and peptonized milk. Just before midnight he was awakened by an attack of heartburn. "The doctor gave him some medicine and he went back to sleep again," Ullman said. "The attack was not severe but it did interrupt the rest we hoped he would get."[10]

Thursday, August 19, 1926

While still not out of danger, Rudy's condition seemed much improved. The heartburn he suffered the night before appeared to have no ill effect during the day. In fact, oatmeal was now added to his daily regimen, but he grimaced and complained that it didn't "ride so well."[11] His doctors were so confident about his condition that they released the following bulletin: "Mr. Valentino is making satisfactory progress and having passed his most critical period, no further bulletins will be issued unless some unexpected development occurs."[12]

The actor was never told how serious his operation and illness was. In fact, four priests stopped by the hospital but were not permitted to visit, lest the sight of them convince him he was near death. Still, Rudy gave an indication of knowing the seriousness of his illness when he told Ullman, "I was pretty close that time, wasn't I? Closer than I hope to be in the next ninety years."[13]

Ullman promised to bring him a copy of *The Prisoner of Chance*, a novel he was reading before he took ill, but balked when the two-pack-a-day smoker asked for a cigarette. "Oof! Not yet!"[14] Ullman replied. Rudy sent a dozen American Beauty roses he received from Pola Negri to a crippled girl in one of the free wards and appeared uninterested when told that Pola had telephoned daily. He seemed more concerned about where he would convalesce after his stay in the hospital. The summer home of Hiram Abrams in Maine was mentioned in the press, but Rudy favored a retreat in Vermont where he had vacationed a few years earlier.

As Rudy was feeling better, Ullman accepted a list of questions for the actor from the press. Over a period of several hours, so as not to tax his strength, Rudy conveyed his responses:

Q.—*What feelings have been inspired by the hundreds of telegrams, letters and phone calls that have reached you, not only from friends, but from girls and women you have never met?*

A.—I feel grateful, so grateful, and feel my inability to repay all the kindness extended to me. They have helped me mentally to overcome my sickness.

Q.—*What was your mental reaction to a serious illness? Were you afraid of death?*

A.—All I wanted was relief—anything to get rid of the terrible pain. Death would have been better than to have stood it longer.

Q.—*What was your favorite screen character among the parts you played? Did you visualize any of them in your illness?*

A.—The part I like best was my role in *Blood and Sand*. If I had died, I would have liked to be remembered as an actor by that role—I think it my greatest.

Q.—*When you are able to eat full meals again, what do you want most?*

A.—Food? Ugh! The thought of food is nauseating, obnoxious to me. Don't mention it.

Q.—*How are you going to pass the time when you go away to Maine to recuperate?*

A.—I am going to do like the prize fighter—get in condition as soon as possible.

Q.—*For whom was your first thought when you realized you were seriously ill?*

A.—For my brother Alberto and my sister Maria—for them were my first thoughts.

Q.—*Did the fact that your illness was prophesied by an unknown woman who called at your rooms here increase your interest in psychic phenomena?*

A.—Perhaps. My interest in such matters has always been that of the average well-read person. I hope now to learn more about the subject one day.[15]

At the end of the day, Ullman released the following statement from Rudolph Valentino:

> I have been deeply touched by the many telegrams, cables and letters that have come to my bedside. It is wonderful to know that I have so many friends and well-wishers both among those it has been my privilege to meet and among the loyal unknown thousands who have seen me on the screen and whom I have never seen at all. Some of the tributes that have affected me the most have come from my "fans"—friends—men, women, and little children. God bless them. Indeed I feel that my recovery has been greatly advanced by the encouragement given me by everyone.[16]

Friday, August 20, 1926

Press coverage of Valentino's illness was at a minimum because of his reported recovery. The big news centered on Valentino's friend, Barclay Warburton, Jr., who also took ill with an undisclosed illness and admitted himself into Harbor Hospital, a private sanitarium on Madison Avenue. Paul Durham, the doctor who originally treated Valentino, performed an operation described only as "minor."[17] By four o'clock that afternoon, Warburton was reportedly smoking a cigar and talking to his mother on the telephone. To this day, no information has been released pertaining to the nature of Warburton's illness.

Afterward, Durham returned to the Polyclinic to check on Rudy, whose temperature had returned to normal. The actor had another restful night, but fussed after being given orders to be still. He asked to be returned to his suite at the Ambassador but was told he would not be able to sit up for several days. Though he could take light soups and other liquid nourishment without discomfort, he complained when Nurse Frank tried to feed him broth. "I don't want that darned stuff,"[18] he grumbled. Usually all it would take to get Rudy's cooperation was a smile from the attractive Frank.

Because of his apparent recovery, some of the press charged that Valentino's illness was a publicity stunt rather than anything life-threatening. Even Natacha, who received a cable earlier that day from Ullman stating that Rudy was out of danger, laughed and said, "What Rudy won't do for publicity!"[19]

Meeker and Joller were quick with their denials. "The man's life was saved by an immediate operation for two perforated gastric ulcers and the removal of his appendix, which was badly inflamed,"[20] Meeker insisted, adding that the mortality rate for this type of illness was extremely high. Critics quickly pointed out that, according to most medical experts, gastric ulcers did not develop like mushrooms, and some sort of irritant would have been necessary to induce Valentino's sudden attack. Meeker, however, could offer no explanation. It would soon be a moot point since the worst was yet to come.

Saturday, August 21, 1926

Ullman arrived at Polyclinic Hospital around five o'clock that morning. Rudy was sleeping as Ullman read his chart, which noted that his pulse and respiration had increased. Concerned, he called Meeker, who arrived shortly with his associates.

When he awoke, Rudy acknowledged that he felt better. "The pain is all gone and I can feel the place where they made the incision," he told Ullman.[21] After reviewing his symptoms, Meeker explained that Rudy's lack of pain was not a good sign. That afternoon, however, Valentino began experiencing some major distress. At 1:15 P.M., after another consultation, Meeker released the following bulletin: "There is a slight spread of the infection in the abdominal wall causing considerable discomfort. There is nothing about the condition to cause undue anxiety at the present time. His temperature is 101, pulse 90, respiration 22, [Signed] Harold D. Meeker, Paul E. Durham."[22]

Unofficially it was thought that the pain may have been caused by a muscular reaction after the withdrawal of post-mortem drains from the wound, and might not mean a dangerous relapse. However, the doctors soon discovered that pleurisy had developed in Rudy's chest. As a precaution, the hospital staff took blood specimens from Rudy and Ullman in the event a transfusion became necessary. A list of local blood donors was also made available by the hospital.

Nurse Frank told reporters that the actor was making a desperate fight for his life. "He is in great pain and is frequently given opiates," she reported.[23] Shortly before four o'clock, Rudy's condition grew worse, and the chief resident, Dr. William Bryant Rawles, was called in for consultation. Even though no one would comment on his status, it was evident by their facial expressions that Valentino's relapse was more serious than previously thought.

At seven o'clock the last bulletin of the day was issued: "Mr. Valentino has developed pleurisy in the left chest; has had a very restless day. Temperature, 103.2; pulse, 120; respiration 36."[24] The bulletin was signed by Dr. Paul E. Durham, Dr. Harold D. Meeker and Dr. G. Randolph Manning.

An employee of Jean Acker's dropped off a package at the Polyclinic's front desk late that evening. Inside was a white bedspread with lace ruffles and the word "Rudy" embroidered in the four corners. A matching pillow cover over a silk, scented cushion was included in the ensemble. It was hoped that the screen star would live to enjoy it.

Despite Rudy being near death, a report came out of Hollywood that Pola was not as grief-stricken as her press agents led everyone to believe. After Rudy's relapse was reported, a visitor to the set of *Hotel Imperial* purportedly found the actress in "fine fettle, entertaining a roomful of friends with all the spirit of an enthusiastic raconteur."[25]

Pola Negri has received much criticism for what many called a "performance" during her relationship with Valentino and after his death — particularly at the funerals. Pola later claimed that she was deceived and never knew how serious Valentino's illness was. "Oh if I had only known what was being done to me!" she said. "They called it common sense when it was really lying, in the name of business. I was deliberately deluded. Weeks later, I discovered the whole cruel deception."

According to Pola, the studio craftily arranged for false reports to be given to her during Valentino's illness, knowing that she would stop all work on *Hotel Imperial* and rush to New York the instant she learned the truth. Newsboys with extras were kept away from the studio; on her way from her house to the studio, and back again, she was under what she called an "invisible guard of detectives," who watched to see that nothing disturbing should reach her ears. "My servants were instructed to keep all the newspapers from me," she said, "to see that no reporters got to me, and to allow no one to speak to me on the telephone."

Negri went so far as to accuse George Ullman of "staying the machinery of deception" from the New York end. Pola claimed that Ullman arranged for someone to be at the hospital, night and day, to intercept telephone messages and supply her with favorable bulletins instead of the truth. She did concede, however, that no doubt Ullman thought Rudy was going to recover.

"But under all the pretense, it was 'business first,' love and death were secondary," she said. "Such is the heartless law of picture-making."[26]

Sunday, August 22, 1926

To ease the staffs' burden, another specialist, Dr. Eugene Poole, was added, and the nurses were doubled. Meeker remained at Rudy's bedside throughout Saturday night and Sunday morning, watching for any changes in his condition. At 1:45 A.M. a statement was issued stating that Rudy's condition remained unchanged, and that he had been sleeping for several hours.[27]

Rudy received frequent injections of morphine during the night to alleviate his pain. The pleurisy, which began in his left lung, continued to spread, and the septic poisoning in the regions of the incisions increased, causing his temperature to climb to 104 degrees. In order to combat the toxins that were ravaging his body, saline solutions were injected into his chest to moisten the tissues and help fight the infection.

Word quickly spread throughout the hospital and among the press that Rudy was slipping. Telegrams were sent to Rudy's closest friends, and Ullman personally telephoned Rudy's close confidant, John Barrymore, to inform him of his condition. A cable was sent to Alberto requesting his return to New York as soon as possible. The hospital staff once again began intercepting calls from people seeking information.

Actors Ben Lyon and Lowell Sherman arrived in hopes of seeing their friend, but were turned away.

Ullman, who had spent most of the past week at the hospital, said that Valentino had recognized him when he arrived that morning. Ullman appeared fatigued and unsettled when he confronted the press in the afternoon. "Rudy is not suffering much pain," he said. "I was glad of this, but the doctors take it as an ominous sign. They say he should be in greater pain normally. They say he doesn't respond to their treatment. He coughs only a little and then with great effort."[28]

Ullman, until that day, would not allow a priest into Rudy's room for fear the actor would think he was dying. While Rudy's mind was still somewhat lucid, Ullman called Father Edward Leonard[29] of St. Malachy's, known as the "Actor's Church." A meeting with Father Leonard would give Rudy a chance to confess his sins if he so wished, and receive absolution and Holy Communion in accordance with his faith.

On the advice of his physicians, Ullman contacted Joseph Schenck, who was staying at the home of Adolph Zukor. It was suggested that Schenck hurry to the hospital to be at Valentino's side, another indication that he might not survive the night. Schenck and Talmadge had tried to visit several times that week but were turned away.

Weeping and twisting her gloves as she arrived at the hospital, Norma was briefly allowed to visit the stricken star. She noticed that Rudy was very cognizant of his surroundings, even though he had been given large doses of morphine. What disturbed her most was the sound of his breathing, which could be heard above everything else in the room. A nurse explained that his lungs were affected, making the respiration so pronounced.

"I could only stay a minute," Talmadge said. "I couldn't bear the sight of him looking at me and smiling when I had been told he might die. He said he would like to see some of his other friends, but I didn't see anyone else there while I was in the hospital. The poor boy is lonesome, but I guess the doctors know best."[30]

Rudy smiled when he saw Schenck enter the room. "Mighty nice of you to come see me,"[31] Rudy murmured. "I didn't know I was so near death that Sunday. I am beginning to realize only now how serious my condition was."[32] When Dr. Poole entered, Rudy greeted him with a slight wave of the hand and a whispered, "Hello boss."[33] Schenck's visit was also brief. As he left, he told reporters that Rudy had recognized him, but that was all. "He is very low,"[34] said Schenck, who planned to return to the hospital later and pass the night at Rudy's bedside.

A short while later, Frank Menillo, a close friend and former roommate of Rudy's, arrived and was brought up to date on Rudy's condition. Menillo, who was also from Italy, visited briefly and spoke with his friend in Italian. Rudy smiled and answered in English. "Thank you Frank," he said. "I'm going to be well soon."[35]

The only official bulletin issued that day acknowledged that the actor's situation was life-threatening: "Mr. Valentino's condition is considered critical. There has been a slight extension in the pleural process in the left chest. It is impossible to determine the outcome at the present time. Temperature, 104; pulse, 120; respiration, 30."[36]

That evening, Major Edward Bowes, the managing director of the Capitol

Theater and a vice-president of Metro-Goldwyn Pictures, broadcast news of Valentino's relapse on radio station WEAF. Bowes asked the public to hold an encouraging thought for the stricken actor. Before long, and under a light rain, a group of more than one-hundred concerned fans held a vigil outside Polyclinic Hospital in hopes of receiving word on his condition. That number would soon increase.

At eleven o'clock Ullman issued the final report of the evening: "Valentino went to sleep at 10:30 and is resting comfortably. His general condition remains unchanged. His temperature and respiration are about the same. They hold out high hopes for his recovery and there is no doubt that he has a fighting chance."[37]

CHAPTER SIX

Monday, August 23, 1926

Ullman, Schenck, and Frank Menillo, along with the doctors, kept a watch at Rudy's bedside all that night. Shortly after midnight an x-ray revealed that the peritonitis was spreading quickly through Rudy's system. By early morning, he was struggling to breathe against the fluid that was seeping into his lungs, causing him agonizing pain. That, and the difficulty in breathing, were the only things he complained about.

Around three-thirty, Rudy awoke from a restless sleep. Meeker was standing at his bedside as Rudy weakly raised his hand for the physician to draw nearer. "Doctor, do you know what I want to do?" Rudy whispered. "I want to go on that fishing trip we were talking about."

Meeker patted his arm and replied, "You certainly will, old man." Rudy closed his eyes momentarily and then opened them again, frowning. "Look, doctor," Rudy said. "I've left all my rods out in California. Can't get them here in time. Can I borrow some of yours—have you got enough?"

"Plenty, old man; plenty," Meeker replied.[1] Rudy closed his eyes again and tried to sleep. A half-hour later he awakened and gazed up at Meeker, who was seated next to his bed. "Doctor, I am afraid we won't go fishing," Rudy admitted. "Who knows? We may meet again." Then, after a brief silence, he murmured, "Pola—if she does not come in time, tell her I think of her."[2] Meeker nodded and gave him an injection to induce sleep.

During the next few hours, Rudy tossed and turned, murmuring incoherently in Italian, unable to get a fitful sleep. Around six o'clock, Rudy awoke and found Schenck and Ullman sitting at his bedside. Seeing the troubled look on Schenck's face, Rudy said, "Don't worry Chief. I will be all right."[3]

Rudy then turned his gaze to Ullman. "Wasn't it an awful thing that we were lost in the woods last night?" Rudy asked. Ullman, taken aback by his obvious delirium, remained silent and gently stroked his hair.

"On the one hand you don't appreciate the humor of that. Do you?" Valentino asked.

Ullman smiled. "Sure I do, Rudy. Sure I do," he said.

Valentino regarded him quizzically. "On the other hand, you don't seem to appreciate the seriousness of it either."

The sun was slowly rising over the New York skyline and filling the room with light. Ullman was about to pull down the blinds when Rudy waived his hand and smiled slightly. "Don't pull the blinds!" he said. "I feel fine. I want the sunlight to greet me."[4] With those words, Rudy again fell asleep. Doctors considered a blood transfusion but decided that his heart would not be able to stand it. Only a miracle could save him now.

Around eight o'clock, Rudy lapsed into a coma. Ullman regrettably sent word to Rudy's friends that it was now only a matter of time. Within the hour, Ullman's wife Beatrice, James Quirk, and Father Leonard joined Schenck and Ullman. At nine o'clock, a troubled Ullman met with reporters. "Rudy's temperature has gone up half a point," he told them. "It is now 104½. His pulse is 135. We are hoping for the best."[5]

In California, columnist Louella Parsons was celebrating her daughter Harriet's birthday at the Virginia Hotel in Long Beach. Earlier that morning she received a call from her editor requesting that she write Valentino's obituary. "But Rudy's isn't dead," she protested.

"No," the editor replied, "but he is dying, and New York wants the story in the office to send out as soon as the end comes—which the doctor says will be in a few hours."

Reluctantly, Louella sat at her portable typewriter, with tears streaming down her face, and began writing. "This is all very silly," she kept repeating to herself. "Rudy will live and we will laugh over his untimely death tribute."[6]

Over the next few hours, Schenck and Ullman would quietly enter his room for a few moments and then quietly leave. The only sounds that emanated from the actor's lips were incomprehensible words in Italian. Around ten o'clock, Father Leonard summoned Father Joseph Congedo[7] of the Church of the Sacred Heart of Jesus and Mary. Congedo originally hailed from Valentino's home town, but had never met the actor.

"I was interested more in Valentino's soul than in his public career," Father Congedo said. "When I heard that he was facing death without the consolation of his kith or kin, I volunteered to stand at his bedside, not only as a fellow townsman, but as a spiritual counselor."[8]

A container of holy oil, a crucifix, and candles were neatly arranged on a small altar in the actor's room as Father Congedo administered Extrema Unction, the last rites of the church. Schenck told reporters that it was no longer a question of medical science or the doctors. "That all is past," he said. "Medical science has done its all. It's simply a question now of Rudy's resistance. It's his own fight."[9]

Shortly before noon, Jean Acker arrived at Polyclinic by taxi and worked her way unrecognized through the crowds that blocked the Fiftieth Street entrance. Until that day she had not been allowed to visit with her ex-husband. "Every day I called the hospital," Acker said. "But every day it was the same story. They did not need me, they said. I could do no good there." But today was different.

When she was ushered into his room, she noticed that everything—flowers and all unnecessary furniture—had been removed, with the exception of the small altar and the bed that he lay upon. Jean knelt at his bedside and called his name, but he didn't answer. "I bent over and kissed his forehead," she said. "But he did not know I was there. I called him again and again but he made no sign." After several minutes, she was led from the room.

"The last thing I remember was his breathing," she said. "It seemed such a hard thing for him to do. And he looked so, so alone."[10]

A few minutes past noon, Father Leonard once again blessed Rudy, holding to his lips a crucifix that reportedly contained a piece of the true cross; he then stepped back. Meeker, who could no longer do anything physically for his patient, gazed down at Rudy and checked his pulse. "It's only a matter of minutes," he whispered.

Ullman, who had very little sleep during the past few days, was at the point of exhaustion. Stepping into the hallway, he cried, "I can't stand it any longer. I can't."[11] At ten minutes past twelve o'clock, a slight shudder arose from Valentino's body as he drew one last breath; a priest, his physicians and nurses were the only ones at his side. Meeker opened the door and sadly nodded to Ullman. Rudolph Valentino, the great lover and idol to millions, was dead.

With Ullman so distraught, it lay upon Joseph Schenck to inform reporters of Valentino's death. "Just passed away,"[12] was all that Schenck could articulate to the men and women waiting on the first floor. For a brief moment, the only sound heard was the persistent ringing of telephones coming from the nearby "information desk." Someone laid a note before one of the operators, who, upon reading it, broke down and sobbed into the telephone, "He's dead! Rudy's dead!"[13]

Literally within minutes, word of Valentino's death was being transmitted by every available telephone to news offices around the country. The crowd outside the hospital, which before noon had been estimated at about one thousand strong, increased by hundreds more pouring in from businesses along Broadway as news of his death spread throughout the city.

"He's dead! He's dead!"[14] were the cries that sped down Fiftieth Street, as throngs of people seemed to appear out of nowhere. Rosa Rosanova, the actress who played Rudy's mother in *Blood and Sand*, happened to be in a restaurant having lunch with her daughter only blocks from the hospital. Rosanova, who became very close to Rudy during filming, had tried to visit her stricken costar for days, but was denied admittance. "I was not worried," she said at the time. "I knew he had a great constitution." As they were eating, she heard the newsboys crying on the street and sent her daughter to see what had happened. "She returned to tell me that Rudy was dead," Rosanova said. "I screamed and fell in a faint."[15]

At the Polyclinic, men, women, and children, shouting, screaming and staggering over each other, tried to get as close to the front of the hospital as possible. Crowds began herding through the main entrance and into the lobby until police arrived, clearing everyone back out onto the streets. Extra reserves were needed to drive the mob back and across the street from the hospital. Anyone entering Fiftieth Street from Eighth or Ninth Avenues was required to show identification, but many still managed to elude the police.

Meanwhile, Valentino's physicians ordered Ullman to bed. There were, however, several duties that needed his attention before he could afford the luxury of a rest. Frank E. Campbell's Funeral Church was contacted to handle the obsequies. Schenck sent a cable to Valentino's brother Alberto, who at the moment was making his way by train to Paris to await news of his brother's condition. When informed later in the day, a grief-stricken Natacha shut herself into her room for three days, refusing to eat.

Dr. Paul Durham, who was the first doctor to examine Valentino at the Ambassador, worn out by eight days of constant attendance at his bedside, collapsed from the strain. Many assumed that he suffered a heart attack, but hospital attendants refused to give any statements regarding his condition. Durham's associates, however, believed it was from exhaustion and not the result of heart problems as originally reported.

Pola Negri was at her bungalow at the Ambassador Hotel in Los Angeles when her maid informed her of Rudy's death. Even though reports from New York had not been good in recent days, Pola hoped that Rudy would win against his illness. Totally unprepared for the news, the fiery Polish actress became hysterical and the maid called for the hotel's physician.

Within minutes, Pola's secretary, Florence Hein, arrived and called Charles Eyton, the general manager of the west coast studios of Famous Players–Lasky. Eyton and his wife, actress Kathlyn Williams, found Pola prostrated across her bed as her personal physician, Dr. Louis Felger, attended to her. All production was stopped on *Hotel Imperial*, and, after some gentle persuasion, she agreed to return to her Beverly Hills home to rest. "I have lost not only my dearest friend," she sobbed, "but the one real love of my life."[16]

While en route, Pola insisted on going to Falcon Lair, Valentino's hilltop home off Benedict Canyon in Beverly Hills. Eyton was hesitant but relented when Kathlyn mentioned that Falcon Lair would be far from the prying eyes of the press. The opiates that Dr. Felger administered to Pola seemed to have had little or no affect on the actress as she sobbed uncontrollably. "Oh why did he leave me?" she wailed. "Why didn't he come back as he promised?"[17]

At Falcon Lair they tried to comfort her, but to no avail. "There was nothing that anyone could say," Louella Parsons later wrote. "Rudy was gone, a stark, uncompromising truth no words of Pola's and no words of her friends could recall him." Parsons, who had been in Long Beach when Valentino died, left immediately for Los Angeles and, with Marion Davies, found Pola at Falcon Lair. When they arrived, the

The Beltran-Masses portrait of Valentino as the Gaucho, hanging in the library of Falcon Lair. (Courtesy of the Academy of Motion Picture Arts and Sciences)

actress was laying prostrate on a couch in the library where two Beltran-Masses portraits of Valentino hung: one a handsome, young Rudy in his favorite role of an Argentine gaucho, the other a sterner Valentino in the costume of a warrior.

Pola continued to become more and more emotional. When Kathlyn suggested that they return to the Ambassador, Pola insisted on staying in Rudy's home — the home she one day had hoped to share with him. Lying on the couch tossing and sobbing until finally exhausted by her performance and the opiates, she fell asleep. That sleep, however, was short-lived. Before long she awakened with a cry and sobbed Rudy's name over and over again. Suddenly she arose from the couch, pointing to one of the portraits that hung above her. "I want that picture," she cried. "I want that painting of Rudy for my own."[18] The object of her grief was the Beltran-Masses portrait of Valentino as an Argentine gaucho.

Louella Parsons described Pola as a wild, caged jungle beast, pacing from one room to another. "She wept, she wailed, she clutched her long black hair," Parsons wrote, "she fell on her knees crying to high heaven to let her die, too. Never in her most scenery-chewing moments as an actress did Pola stage such a performance as she put on before Marion and me."[19]

When writing her memoirs years later, Pola recounted an entirely different version of that day. As she was dressing in her bungalow at six-thirty that morning (this would make it nine-thirty in New York and more than two and a half hours before Valentino's death) the telephone rang. As her maid was out walking the dog, she answered it herself. It was a reporter from New York asking if he were speaking with Miss Negri's maid. Not wanting to admit who she was to a reporter, she replied that yes, she was Miss Negri's maid.

"Tell me," the reporter asked. "How did she take the news of Valentino's death?" From that point Pola claims to have only vague recollections of the doctor, nurse, and of Marion Davies tearfully embracing her.[20] Gone were the histrionics and the trip to Falcon Lair.

Pola, at last, agreed to return to the Ambassador, since her presence at Falcon Lair was too emotionally draining. Later, Charles Eyton announced that Negri was planning to marry the late actor as soon as their work permitted. "She spent more than an hour there where they both had worked out their ideas for an ideal home which was to be occupied by them after their marriage," Eyton explained.[21] Reports that the couple were secretly married were denied by Kathlyn Williams. "The rumor is too absurd for words," Williams said. "They were an ideal couple and had planned to marry shortly after the first of the year. To imagine the ceremony already had been performed is ridiculous."[22]

Whatever the truth, Famous Players–Lasky released a statement declaring it impossible for Pola to attend Valentino's funeral in New York, as they could not hold up production of *Hotel Imperial*. Those closest to Pola, however, believed that somehow she would have the final say.

Back in New York, the crowds outside the Polyclinic had grown to such an extent that it was impossible for Campbell's hearse to reach the back entrance on West Fifty-first Street. In order to move the crowds, the police spread a rumor that Valentino's body was being removed from the front entrance. Remarkably, the ruse worked, and the majority of the crowd moved slowly back to Fiftieth Street just long enough for the hearse to circle the block and pull up in the space cleared by police.

Inside the hospital a reporter for the *New York World*, exhausted from the week-long coverage, retreated to a back hall of the Polyclinic and slumped down in a small settee. At two-forty that afternoon the stillness was interrupted by the sound of the elevator descending from the floors above. "Something told me — I have no idea what — that Valentino's body was on that elevator," he later said. As the elevator doors opened, the reporter witnessed an undertaker's basket being wheeled out and rolled down the corridor toward the back door.

"I glanced that way," he said. "There waited Campbell's 'wagon.' Almost involuntarily, I got to my feet as that basket passed me. Rudolph Valentino beloved idol of millions going out the back door of Polyclinic Hospital in a wicker basket! That was dramatic enough. But to add to the drama, someone had thrown a piece of gold cloth over the top of the basket!"[23]

By then the crowds outside the hospital finally began dispersing when word filtered through the masses that Valentino's body had been removed via the rear entrance and taken to Campbell's Funeral Church at Broadway and West Sixty-sixth Street.

Rudy's personal effects were later given to Jean Acker by the hospital staff. Why she received them and not George Ullman remains unclear. It may be that she was his ex-wife and technically the only "family" member present. In any event, his belongings included, among other things, a shirt and a small hairpiece about four inches in diameter. While it was obviously a highly guarded secret during his life, as early as 1929, columnist Walter Winchel revealed that, "Valentino actually wore a small toupee on the back of his head."[24]

Surprisingly, many skeptics believe that Valentino's Italian heritage would have blessed him with a thick head of hair, but, in fact, photographs taken just months before his death show that his hairline was receding. The hair loss appears to have started sometime around the making of *Cobra*, possibly aggravated by Rudy's marital problems. By the time filming began on *The Eagle*, director Clarence Brown suggested that his thinning crown and temples be "touched-up." The make-up department perfected a creative hair-weaving appliance for his crown and used a special formula for covering his temples. This was, of course, in addition to any wig, hairpiece, or partial that he may have worn for his screen roles. With the proper lighting, the illusion was complete. And since Valentino's brother, Alberto, and his son Jean also had receding hairlines, chances are that Rudy's would have followed suit.

To sum it up, Ditra Flamé, the flamboyant "Lady in Black," expressed it succinctly in a letter to George Ullman when referring to the many inquiries she received from strangers about the actor: "I am supposed to know such intimate things as how long did Mr. Valentino wear a toupee?"[25]

In any event, Jean Acker kept the toupee and Rudy's belongings in her possession for decades. After her death, these articles found their way into the hands of a private collector in Beverly Hills where, it is believed, they remain as of this writing.[26]

Valentino's death certificate was filed with the Board of Health at three-fifty that afternoon. It stated the cause of death as a ruptured gastric ulcer and general peritonitis, naming also septic pneumonia and septic endocarditis as contributory causes. Valentino's real name, Rodolpho Guglielmi, was inscribed on the certificate. There was some delay in the filing while information was sought as to Valentino's exact age. Dr. William B. Rawles, chief resident of the Polyclinic, signed the certificate.[27]

Later that afternoon, Ullman released the following statement to the press:

> Mr. Valentino was greatly cheered during his last days by the thousands of messages sent him by his friends and motion picture admirers, and while he was too weak to read all of them, it was a great comfort to him to know that so many friends were interested and sympathetic. I know he would want me to express the gratitude he felt. Personally, I want to thank the physicians and nurses and hospital attachés who worked so hard and conscientiously to save his life. Everything humanly possible was done for him.[28]

As funeral arrangements were being made, Alberto anxiously made his way to Paris. He was on a train from Turin when his brother died, so when he arrived at the Lyons station he was not aware that Rudy was already dead. Dressed in a double-breasted suit, polka-dot bow tie and a brightly colored handkerchief protruding from his pocket, one would never guess by looking at him the agony he was experiencing. Guy Smith, who was in charge of the European distribution of Valentino's films, met him at the station. Alberto greeted him and smiled, searching his face for some sign of good news. "Tell me that he is better," Alberto said.

Smith shook his head. "I am most sorry, I cannot." Alberto took a deep breath and collapsed onto his luggage. He began sobbing uncontrollably. To avoid the gathering crowds, Smith helped him to a taxi that took them to a nearby hotel where Alberto released a statement affirming that Valentino would be buried in America.

"This is what he would have desired," Alberto said. "He so loved America that I am sure he wanted to be buried there — rather, even, than beside our father and mother in Italy. He loved Italy, but he loved the country of his adoption and his success more."[29]

Alberto received a telegram of condolence from Pola Negri that evening. He replied, "Dear Pola: Thanks for your sympathetic cable. Sailing tomorrow *Homeric*. Only you and I can appreciate our great loss. Hope to see you on my arrival."[30]

Back in New York, Campbell's employees labored feverishly throughout the night, trying to restore Rudy's emaciated face, working mainly from publicity photos of the dead star. A $15,000 bronze and silver casket was ordered from the Boyertown Casket Company in Boyertown, Pennsylvania. Until its arrival, Valentino would be laid out in Campbell's prestigious Gold Room on a draped catafalque, attired in full evening dress.

"As I understand it," Frank Campbell told reporters, "Mr. Ullman feels that Valentino, like every great artist, belongs to his public. It has been decided, therefore, that unless his brother objects, the body will lie in state, where it may be viewed by any who care to come."[31]

Campbell's Gold Room was indeed a chamber of regal splendor. The windows, with a northern exposure, let in the mid–Manhattan daylight through tawny curtains. On the floor was a rose-covered carpet. The ceiling was low, measuring but seven or

Valentino lying in state in the Gold Room of Frank E. Campbell's Funeral Church.

eight feet from the floor. Located on the third floor, visitors could ascend to the Gold Room in an elevator, though those wishing to view Valentino's body would have to use the stairs. A few shorts steps through a hallway and one would enter the room where Anna Held, Oscar Hammerstein, Olive Thomas and Enrico Caruso once lay in state.

Campbell's publicity stated that European artists of note were commissioned to supply the furnishings, including tapestries in the Gobelin manner that hung on the east and west walls. Scattered about were Louis the 15th chairs, stiff and uncomfortable, and so ornate as to defy any who might wish to sit. To the left, a great concert grand piano in gold by Steinway supplied the musical accompaniment. As nightfall approached, four floor lamps in gold and olive cloth placed about the room shed a subdued light.

It was here, according to Campbell's advertising, that "great men have reposed in state,"[32] and where the body of Rudolph Valentino would lie. It was a decision they would soon regret.

That evening a woman entered the 150th Street Police Station carrying a six-month-old boy. She told police the "foundling" had been left with her the previous

April by its parents, who said they were going to Venezuela for a month and would return for him; but they never did. The woman could no longer care for the child, and something — namely, the death of Rudolph Valentino — prompted her to leave him with the police. As she was leaving the station, an officer asked for the baby's name. The woman stopped, and with tears filling her eyes, replied, "Robert Valentino." The infant was sent to Bellevue Hospital.[33]

CHAPTER SEVEN

Ballyhoo

Now that Valentino was dead, George Ullman could do nothing more for him — at least not physically. Besides supervising the funeral arrangements, Ullman turned his thoughts to the overwhelming task of putting the actor's affairs in order. Having intimate knowledge of his financial status, Ullman knew how badly in arrears Valentino's estate was. While he may have been a great talent on the screen, when it came to his business affairs Rudy was totally inept. In the last year of his life alone he made $200,000 for each picture and received a fifty-percent royalty. Over his career, the actor made millions of dollars, but also spent and gave away millions more.

"Anyone could get money from Valentino," Schenck said. "I think he lent more than he ever spent on himself. Last year he had an income of almost a million dollars and he didn't save a cent of it. That trip to Europe cost a great deal and he brought back many beautiful artistic creations for his California home."[1]

Schenck admitted that Valentino's death was a great loss to the studio, but at the moment that was not on his mind. Though insisting that he was not sentimental, the mogul said, "Next week, perhaps, I will look at the loss from a business point of view, and figure up what Rudy's death cost us. But now, it is too close."[2]

It didn't take long to figure exactly what Valentino's death cost — at least for the actor's estate. Valentino owed Joseph Schenck $187,000, had general debts totaling $236,000, and owed Cinema Film Corporation $106,000. Valentino's major asset was the half-interest he owned in his United Artists films, *The Eagle* and *The Son of the Sheik*. It therefore became imperative for Ullman to keep Valentino's name before the public, since these films were the only property that could bring in needed revenue to both the estate and the studio.

At the time of his death, *The Son of the Sheik* was showing in only a few theaters and wouldn't be in wide release for another two weeks. The problem, however, was that, historically, films of dead movie stars were considered worthless and were usually shelved by producers soon after. Audiences showed an aversion to watching the apparently living actions of a person they knew to be no longer alive. So it was in the case of Olive Thomas, Wallace Reid and Barbara La Marr, all of whom died young and while still popular with the public. Would audiences react the same to Valentino's death, and if so, how would United Artists recoup their sizable investment?

One thing the studio had going for them was the incredible amount of publicity that had already been generated by Valentino's sickness and death — more than to any Hollywood personality before or since. A way had to be found to hold the public's interest. United Artists decided to take a chance and not only continue with the scheduled release of *The Son of the Sheik*, but also re-release *The Eagle*. However, they would need at least a week to rush out prints to theaters across the country and abroad. With that in mind, Ullman and the studio hired forty press agents to handle and publicize the funeral, thus keeping Valentino's name before the public.

The person chosen to oversee this formidable task was Oscar Doob, the man who successfully engineered the New York premiere of *The Son of the Sheik* and reportedly wrote Valentino's response to the "Pink Powder Puffs" editorial. Doob's job was to assist the newspapers (and anyone else, for that matter) that wished to publicize and thus propagate the memory of Rudolph Valentino. Along with his newly formed publicity machine, Doob churned out brief biographies of Valentino and passed out thousands of stills from his films.[3] More than one hundred testimonials were collected from his closest friends and associates. Nearly every star, director, and producer in Hollywood was asked for a statement, including those who had never met Valentino or had only a minor association with him. Once gathered, these tributes were distributed to every newspaper in the country — just in time for the next day's edition.

Among the countless condolences were many sincere and heartfelt tributes. As to be expected, the most poignant came from those closest to the actor. Norman Kerry, who befriended Valentino very early in his career and helped with his start in Hollywood, said simply, "The death of my friend is a great shock and our grief is deep. I had hoped for the best."[4]

Boxer Jack Dempsey, who instructed Rudy in the sport and advised him on several occasions, said, "He was a great lover of boxing and a great admirer of mine. The screen has lost a dandy fellow and a talented actor. I have lost a great friend, and the moving picture industry a popular figure whose place always will be vacant."[5]

But it was June Mathis, Rudy's longtime friend and benefactor, who gave the most moving and honest reaction to his passing. "My long association with Rudolph Valentino endeared him to me, as he has become endeared to everyone who knew him," Mathis said. "My heart is too full of sorrow at this moment to enable me to speak coherently. I only know that his passing has left a void that nothing can ever fill and that the loss to our industry is too great to estimate at this time."[6]

The press willingly cooperated and gave pages of space to Valentino's death and approaching funeral. After all, it helped sell newspapers. Tabloids, such as the *Daily News* and *Daily Mirror* in particular, had a field day trying to outdo each other with so-called "firsts" and "exclusives." Perhaps the most vulgar of the scandal sheets was the *New York Evening Graphic*, (or, as some called it, the "Porno Graphic").[7] The brainchild of media entrepreneur Bernarr McFadden, the *Graphic* was only one in a stable of newspapers and magazines that the publishing magnate owned. The *Graphic* was famous for its use of "composographs," or faked photographs, usually of notable people superimposed on the body of actors posed in concocted scenes. Using this technique, the *Graphic* portrayed a dead Valentino meeting the spirit of the recently deceased singer Enrico Caruso. "Rudy Meets Caruso. Tenor's Spirit Speaks!" the headline blared. This was the same *Graphic* that, the previous week, published the "Rudy's Dead" headline and was responsible for a photo of Valentino lying on the operating table, nude to the waist, surrounded by his physicians.

Other newspapers, not to be outdone, rushed to grab their share of the readership. Sprinkled among the daily goings-on concocted by the studio's publicity team were articles by Valentino associates Joseph Schenck and Norma Talmadge. Talmadge wrote (or perhaps it was ghost written for her) a three-part piece for the *New York American* entitled "Valentino as I Knew Him." The *American*, a Hearst newspaper, also published excerpts from Valentino's book, *Daydreams*, which brought in much needed revenue to the dead Sheik's coffers. Again, the *American*, along with the *Daily News*, reprinted daily installments of Valentino's "My Life Story" that had first appeared in *Photoplay* magazine in 1923.

In addition, global reaction to Valentino's death received wide coverage. He was mourned in his native Italy, despite being criticized for renouncing his Italian citizenship. Flags in his home town of Castellaneta were lowered to half-mast, and placards were posted declaring the city to be "in mourning for our beloved illustrious townsman, Rodolfo Valentino."[8] The British press devoted more space to Valentino's death than was usually accorded to American news. Female Londoners sobbed in theaters as news of his death was announced from the stages. In Paris, women stood in front of Valentino posters and wailed uncontrollably.

The coverage meted out by the press soon incurred the wrath of intellectuals and academics. Pundits were incensed that the recent death of Dr. Charles W. Eliot, president emeritus of Harvard University, was allotted only minimal space compared to the pages given to Valentino. The ninety-two-year-old Eliot, who died the day before the actor, received only short obituaries printed next to (or, in many cases, under) news of the star's condition. In London, the *Daily Herald*, a labor newspaper, gave Valentino nearly a column while Dr. Eliot received only three lines. So many letters of protest were written objecting to the proliferation of space given to the death and glorification of an actor that the *New York Times* responded with an editorial.

"It is not contended that the loss of that great intellectual leader was slighted," the editorialist wrote. "To him, indeed, the press of the whole country paid its admiring tribute. Only by comparison, and owing to the accident of the two deaths coming at the same time, could it appear that the newspaper reports betrayed a distorted sense of values."

The writer pointed out that newspapers are sometimes required to report facts connected to everyday life, regardless of how fantastic or exaggerated they may be, as in the case of Rudolph Valentino's death. It was further noted that much of the blame could be placed on the growing popularity of motion pictures itself. Because of the universal acceptance of film as an art form, millions of people were familiar with Valentino's image and name. Very few in America, let alone Europe, knew who Dr. Charles Eliot was, despite his contributions to the world of education. "Call this a vulgar and deplorable thing, if you will," the *New York Times* wrote, "but there it is—an undeniable fact full of significance."[9]

Was the coverage of Valentino's death a "vulgar and deplorable thing"? Perhaps. Especially if one considers that all of this "free" publicity played right into the hands of the studio's press agents, making their job of keeping Valentino's name on the front pages much easier. Nevertheless, United Artists was not the only ones looking to profit (or, as they saw it, recoup their investment) from the Sheik's untimely death. Some say that Frank E. Campbell's Funeral Church, which provided the funeral arrangements at gratis, also saw this as an opportunity to garner some free advertising.

For more than ten years Campbell's publicity was under the direction of Harry C. Klemfuss, a skilled press agent who had offices in a Manhattan hotel. Klemfuss assisted the press by advancing the distribution of photographs and other material regarding the place where Valentino's body would lie. His first duty was to reveal the embalming methods used to beautify the corpse. Klemfuss noted that it was the same method used to preserve singer Enrico Caruso, who had died just five years earlier. "This process," Klemfuss wrote, "prevents the quick decomposition and makes it possible to preserve the body indefinitely."[10]

Next, Klemfuss hired thirty persons (at a dollar a head) whose chore it was to stand in line outside Campbell's and attract attention. Little did he know how well the "stand-ins" would do, for when the mob came, much to Klemfuss' gratification, Campbell's name was in all the headlines.

Tuesday, August 24, 1926

Regardless of Klemfuss' help, a crowd of about five to six hundred mourners gathered in front of Campbell's before eight o'clock that morning. By noon, their number had increased to an estimated ten thousand, despite a light rain that was falling. Fashionably dressed Park Avenue socialites commingled with tenement wives from Hell's Kitchen, waiting for hours to get what would be a two or three second glimpse of Valentino's corpse. The *New York American* described this motley group as "weeping widows, avid open-mouthed flappers with dresses dripping in the rain, married women desperately clutching their offspring, young men in bell-bottomed trousers and older men, curious of death...."[11]

Assigned to keep the peace over this assorted assemblage were a dozen foot policemen and three mounted patrols from the West Sixty-eighth Street Station. Soon the traffic on Broadway began to jam as the influx of people filled the sidewalk and spread west across the street. By two o'clock, the West Seventy-fifth Street Station was called for back up as the crowd reached 15,000. The light drizzle quickly became a downpour, and the once somber congregation began taking on the characteristics of an unruly mob.

Morning newspapers had announced that the doors to Campbell's would open at two-thirty, but rumors spread that the time was amended to four o'clock. To keep order, the police resorted to charging the lines on horseback, which only made the crowd angrier. Though many had a genuine affection for Valentino, a large percentage was only concerned with satisfying their morbid curiosity. Adela Rogers St. Johns remarked that it was an emotional crowd. "With hysterical emotion as you weren't at all sure what they would do," she said. "Hysterical crowds behave badly at funerals."[12] This crowd was about to prove her right.

The hours of waiting, the constant downpour, and the continuing rushes from the police pushed the throng to its limit. Because of the crowd's mood, the doors to Campbell's were opened as originally announced — at about two-thirty. In their rush to enter the building, the struggling mob stormed the entrance, compelling the mounted patrolmen to drive them back into the streets with repeated charges. Rain-drenched women screamed hysterically as some were thrown under the horses' hoofs and others rushed to get out of their way.

The result of the ensuing melee pushed a line of policemen against a twenty-foot, ceiling-high plate glass window north of the main entrance. The window came crashing down, showering the revelers with pointed shards. Several fragments sliced into the hand of a patrolman. Three women were forced through the window frame and were injured on the jagged glass. A newsreel cameraman documenting the fray was hurled backward along with his camera just as a huge sliver of glass fell, severing the tendons of both his ankles. In all, ten people were injured by the shattered glass alone.

The mounted police raced their horses up the sidewalk, flailing their clubs at anyone who happened to be in their way. Six policemen rushed in and stood in front of the shattered window, hurling back screaming young girls and smacking forceful young men across the back with their clubs as they attempted to leap through the open frame. Four policemen held the door while additional mounted recruits and fifty reinforcements were dispatched to the area.

In the chaos, men and women kicked and clawed at one another while trying to climb on the shoulders of other mourners. After ten minutes, police were able to push the crowds back against the building, revealing a battlefield of scattered hats, purses, shoes, and other personal items. Ambulances were summoned, as four women lay injured and trembling among the wreckage in the rain. An emergency hospital was set up inside, treating, in all, fifteen seriously injured and as many as sixty others less severely hurt.

Acting Captain Hammill of the West Sixty-eighth Street Station telephoned for additional reserves. "This crowd has a real mob spirit," Hammill said. "I never saw anything like it in twenty years on the police force. So many of them are so morbidly curious that they won't go home."[13]

As the police gained a brief reprieve, it was hoped that the continuing downpour would deter the crowd and they would disperse, but instead their numbers increased. Finally, after a brief consultation between the police, Ullman, and the management of Campbell's, it was decided to allow the first group of seventy-five to enter the building and view the body at 3:15 P.M. The moment the doors were reopened, however, the second scuffle began.

Police standing at the doorway were swept back by the initial rush of the multitude forcing their way to get a glimpse of Valentino. Women, knocked to their knees fighting and screaming, engaged in hand to hand combat with police. Six shrieking fans made their way past the first blockade and into the reception room, where several of Campbell's employees, dressed in black cutaways and striped trousers, met the intruders with black-gloved fists.

Outside it was complete mayhem. Men and women fell shrieking; one woman had her foot crushed by the hoofs of an onrushing steed. Suddenly, another rush of the crowd pushed people through yet another window, this one at Brown's "Drive It Yourself" Automobile Company on the corner next door to Campbell's. As the mob was driven out onto Broadway, groups of people were forced back against a parked automobile, overturning it onto a young woman who had been knocked to the ground by a police horse.

The mounted police regrouped and charged the crowd once again. "Go home! Go home!" they shouted while violently swinging their clubs at anything that got in their way. One jostled woman grabbed a man who was assisting police at Campbell's entrance. "Why don't you be a man and let us in?" she shouted.

"Why don't you be a lady and go home?" he responded. The woman, already at the boiling point, lifted her umbrella and forcefully brought it down on the man's head.[14]

Helpless to do anything, George Ullman panicked as he watched the scene from a window on Campbell's second floor. Valentino's body was lying on a catafalque in the Gold Room, making it vulnerable to the riotous mob. Immediately he ordered that the actor's body be placed in his silver-bronze coffin, with a glass covering placed over his face for protection. "This crowd is likely to do almost anything," Ullman screamed. "Some will try to touch the body, others will perhaps try to take a button from his coat — to touch his face."[15]

Meanwhile, downstairs, two doctors with first-aid kits were treating more than a dozen women lying on the floor of the temporary emergency room. One woman was kicked in the abdomen, exposing a fresh appendix scar; two women fainted and awoke in hysterics when they could not find their children. Other injuries were so serious the victims had to be transported to the Knickerbocker Hospital for treatment.

Outside on Broadway a crowd estimated at more than 30,000 stretched from Sixty-seventh Street to Lincoln Square. With more than one hundred officers and a dozen mounted patrols, the police had difficulty controlling the throng. All traffic on Broadway came to a standstill and had to be temporarily diverted to Columbus Avenue.

As the rioting mob fought their way into Campbell's funeral parlor, farther down the Great White Way another type of disturbance was germinating—not one of physical violence, but one involving words. Rumors circulated that there was more to Valentino's death than what was being reported. The *Evening Graphic* was once again the major purveyor of this ballyhoo when they wrote: "Persistent reports along Broadway the past week, hinting darkly that the death yesterday of Rudolph Valentino might be attributed to causes not disclosed in official bulletins by his physicians, may result today in a complete investigation of the film actor's last visit here.

"Soon after Valentino had been rushed from an all-night revel at the cabarets to an operating table in the Polyclinic Hospital these three stories began circulation: 1) Rudolph Valentino had been poisoned by a jealous woman; 2) The sheik had been injured in a fight with a man who had resented Rudy's attention to a woman; 3) Valentino had been shot in a quarrel during a gay party."[16]

The *Graphic* also received confirmation from the "other side" when it conducted a séance that evening under the auspices of the Unbiased Commission for the Investigation of Psychic Phenomena, sponsored by *Ghost Stories Magazine*. The séance was evidently a success, for according to *The Nation* magazine, "the spirits rattled tambourines, moved tables, and said just what the *Graphic* wanted them to say."[17]

The reply was muffled and confused.

"What was the medicine?"

There was a ghastly shriek and a long drawn-out cry. The voice then continued: "But that was not the primary cause. Valentino was poisoned at the party he attended before taken to the hospital for his operation. The doctors there did their best, but they could not work against the poison which he had taken before. Valentino's spirit in the room now."[18]

Whether inspired by the ghostly accusation or their own imaginations, the most-accepted cause of death among Valentino rumormongers was arsenic poisoning. This fed into the theory that irritants were present in Valentino's system, causing the deathly reaction to the perforated ulcers. What better "irritant" than arsenic! Jealousy and revenge were the motive behind the alleged poisoning, but no specifics were given. As these reports spread, Dr. William Rawles, the physician who signed Valentino's death certificate, formally denied that any trace of poison was found in the actor's body. Pearl Frank, Valentino's nurse, concurred. "There is absolutely nothing to the poison story," Frank insisted.[19]

One reason the public and officials seriously considered the poison theory, lending credence to the *Graphic*'s story, was a statement from Dr. M. Del Vecchio, a lung specialist from Brooklyn. Del Vecchio, who closely followed the actor's illness, said that Valentino's symptoms and emaciated features strongly pointed to evidence of poisoning by a foreign substance. "Septic poisoning alone would not do that," the doctor insisted.[20] Del Vecchio went so far as to pressure assistant district attorney

Ferdinand Pecoria to order an autopsy on Valentino. Pecoria cautiously announced that if the poisoning theories and Del Vecchio's claims were presented to him "officially," he would begin an investigation to determine their veracity. Those theories were never embraced, however, and an autopsy was not performed.

Meanwhile, at Campbell's, four o'clock approached and attempts were made to reorganize the lines waiting outside. The reception hall resembled a battle zone, with shards of broken glass, blood, and various articles of clothing strewn across the marble floors. Porters worked feverishly to clear away the debris and remove all pieces of furniture (including many valuable art objects).

Between the hours of four and six o'clock, an estimated 5,000 persons viewed the mortal remains of Valentino. Four large bunches of roses from George Ullman and James Quirk surrounded the casket. Candles burned at the head and foot of the coffin, and behind it was a crucifix and a small statue of the Virgin Mary. Police and Campbell's attendants constantly urged the people in line to "step lively" and to "take that hat off." No one was allowed to linger.

Problems arose as certain members of the crowd tried to pilfer a flower, a candle or any type of souvenir from the Gold Room. To keep the room from being ransacked, the line was stopped at the lower door so that Valentino's body could be carefully moved to the north end of the second floor near a stairway leading directly to Sixty-seventh Street, allowing the crowds to emerge more easily.

The coffin was placed at an angle with only the head and shoulders of Valentino visible beneath the glass top of the casket. "His eyes were closed, his cheeks rouged, his eyebrows penciled," wrote one reporter. "His face was stern and his features rigid in the stillness of death. And so, while the crowd howled, this man lay there. They cried — but he could not hear them. They gazed — but he could not see them."[21]

Around six o'clock, office workers began to swell the crowd's ranks until it was feared the throng would once again overrun the police and storm the building. At seven o'clock the doors were closed for a half-hour until 110 reinforcements arrived. A single line was formed, four abreast, up the east side of Broadway and extending around the corner onto West Sixty-ninth Street. Those admitted during the remainder of the evening were swiftly hustled through. Several touched the glass covering his face, and one young woman was spied kissing it. Every fifteen minutes the line was stopped so that a Campbell's attendant could clean the glass. Lola Pierce, a Broadway chorus girl who told reporters she was a former dancing partner of Valentino's, became hysterical after viewing the body and had to be helped to a taxi by friends.

Outside, thousands more of the curious continued to gather for a last chance to see Rudolph Valentino. Some, either repeat mourners or those who had heard about the police charges that afternoon, scattered powdered soap on the wet pavement, causing the horses to slip and fall on the slick sidewalks.

In spite of the chaos, police made only three arrests that day. One man was sent to jail for disorderly conduct after refusing to get back in line while brandishing an umbrella against a mounted policeman. Two women were jailed for arguing with police, calling them names and refusing to move when ordered.

At ten-thirty the streets were more crowded than at any time that day. Knowing that many women worked during the evening and would have no other time to view the body, Frank Campbell announced that the doors to his mortuary would remain open for several hours past the scheduled midnight closing. The police, however, had other plans. Having been on duty for hours struggling with an unruly mob, their patience and tempers were strained. Captain Hammill told Campbell in no uncertain terms that neither he nor his men would be responsible for the consequences if they were to stay on duty another four hours. After pressuring from Ullman, Campbell agreed and the doors closed promptly at midnight.

As the crowds began to disperse, ten men representing the Fascisti League of North America arrived, attired in their traditional black shirts. Claiming to be there on the instructions of Premier Benito Mussolini, they arranged to have two of their number stand guard over Valentino's body at two-hour intervals throughout the night. They brought a huge wreath bearing in gold letters against a black-silk ribbon the words "Benito Mussolini." Ceremoniously, they placed it at the foot of Valentino's casket for the benefit of the gathered photographers. The rite so impressed both Campbell and Ullman that the Fascisti were permitted to remain.

In the considered opinion of the New York police department, the rioting that transpired that day was without precedent. "For numbers, for unruliness and for complete failure to realize the necessity for some order and the significance of the occasion, was without equal," Captain Hammill said.[22]

Now they were going to do it all over again the next day.

CHAPTER EIGHT

The Fight for Rudy's Body

Many legends concerning Rudolph Valentino have accumulated over the years, but one in particular had its birth at the actor's bier. Several years after Valentino's death, editor James Quirk shocked everyone when he announced that a wax dummy had stood in for Valentino at his funeral. Since the powers-that-be were concerned that grief-stricken fans would rush the casket, a lifelike wax head was fashioned by a sculptor and attached to the body of a store mannequin. Valentino's real body was kept in a hidden room in the funeral home.

There are several problems with this story. First, if it were true, what has become of the paraffin impostor? A curiosity of this importance would surely have shown up in someone's attic or, at the very least, some carnival sideshow. And if the doppelganger were melted down into "Sheik" candle souvenirs, the switch itself would have required that too many people know about it, increasing the chances of the story getting out.

The story may have arisen due to the condition of Valentino's corpse. Campbell's embalmers tried to repair the ravages that pain had etched in Valentino's features, but the effort appeared to be in vain. Describing the appearance of the actor's body, one newspaper said that, "powder and rouge could not take the tautness out of compressed lips or change the distended nostrils and could not remove the traces the disease left. The eyes are closed unnaturally, as if simulating sleep. The hair has lost its sleekness that the movie fans knew."[1]

The wax dummy story was revived as late as 1998 when Quirk's nephew, author Lawrence Quirk, told a reporter, "So while the real Valentino lay in peace in a cool, dark vault, my uncle's wax figure took the brutal punishment from Valentino's hundreds of fans at the funeral parlor."[2] Since the tale originated with the not-always-reliable James Quirk, and was initially disseminated by Quirk's cohort, Adela Rogers

St. John, it is most likely another of Quirk's tall tales. So until the head surfaces in someone's garage, or another more reliable account comes forward to corroborate the story, the legend of the wax head should remain just that — a legend.

Wednesday, August 25, 1926

That morning, radio stations and newspapers announced that funeral services would be held Monday at St. Malachy's Catholic Church. A solemn high mass would be performed at eleven o'clock and would be confined strictly to the traditional Catholic ritual. Father Edward Leonard, the priest who heard Valentino's deathbed confession, would officiate. Afterward, the body would be placed in a receiving vault at Woodlawn Cemetery unless Alberto had arrived from Europe by that time.

Charles Eyton telephoned Adolph Zukor that Pola Negri was overwrought and intended to travel to New York for the funeral. "Put a nurse and a publicity man on the train," Zukor instructed, "and ask Pola to guard her statements to the press."[3] Within hours, Pola, dressed in black satin crepe mourning weeds, departed on the Golden State Limited with her secretary, a nurse, and a studio representative. Charles Eyton, Kathlyn Williams, and Marion Davies escorted her to the station.

As Pola made her farewells, Alberto was boarding the White Star liner *Homeric* to begin his journey. Ullman received a cable from Alberto instructing that the funeral be delayed until his arrival since it would violate family traditions to have the ceremony without relatives present. He also reversed his original decision regarding where his brother's body would rest, stating he needed to discuss it with Maria and Rudy's American friends. Until then, no decision would be made.

Surprised by this turn of events, many wondered where Valentino would be interred. Rudy's sister, Maria, told reporters by telephone from her home in Turin that she wished for her brother to be buried in Castellaneta. "It is my desire that Rudolph be buried in Italy," she said, "and I hope that my brother Alberto, now en route to New York, will agree to this."[4] Citizens of Valentino's home town were in agreement and already making plans to welcome the body of their fellow townsman. A committee was organized to collect funds to erect a stately tomb in the town's cemetery.

Ullman still had hopes of taking his friend's body back to Hollywood. "I think he belongs there and hope to so persuade his brother,"[5] he said. Pola agreed, telling reporters that she too hoped Alberto would bring Rudy's body back to the city where the actor had his greatest success. "Because he spent so many happy hours — his happiest hours — here, and because I am here," she said. "I want him buried in Hollywood. But if his brother should wish him buried in Italy, to lie beside his father and mother — that is different. I can understand that."[6]

Jean Acker sided with the Italian delegation. "I think he would prefer to lie by the side of his mother and father in Italy," she said. "But I have no say in it. Who am I to say anything?"[7] Natacha, from whom little was heard in the past ten days, cabled

Monument dedicated to Rudolph Valentino in his home town of Castellaneta in 1961.

Ullman with an unusual request. "Unless otherwise directed by Rudolph, we prefer cremation, ashes to be placed in temporary security," she wrote. "Later could go to my plot in Woodlawn."[8]

Ullman insisted that this was impossible since the Catholic Church did not allow cremation, and Rudy, who had drifted away from his childhood faith, had returned to it on his deathbed. Ullman recalled that several years earlier they had discussed cremation, and Rudy had said, "Well, when I die I'd like to be cremated and have my ashes scattered to the winds."[9] Ullman insisted that Rudy was joking.

Meanwhile, a contingent of Hollywood producers, directors, and actors cabled Alberto, urging that Valentino be buried in Los Angeles. "We, of the Hollywood motion picture colony, who knew, worked with and loved Rudolph Valentino, urge you to order that his mortal remains be allowed to rest forever here, where his friendships were formed and where he made his home,"[10] they wrote. It was signed by thirty-eight Hollywood personalities, including Charles Chaplin, Marion Davies, Antonio Moreno, Ramon Novarro, Norman Kerry, and Louis B. Mayer.

Alberto was very appreciative of the honor and interest that Rudy's friends bestowed upon his brother, but hoped they would not insist on an immediate decision. "I have communicated with my sister in Turin," he responded by cable. "There are many factors that must be taken into consideration. I cannot reach a decision until I reach New York."[11] The fight for Rudy's body was on, and Alberto was caught in the middle.

In the meantime, several independent efforts were being made to memorialize the actor. Joseph Schenck, Ullman, and James Quirk formed a committee to erect a permanent memorial in Hollywood, financed by public donations. Similar groups were started in Castellaneta and Chicago. Also in the film capital, plans were being drawn up to construct an Italian park on Hollywood Boulevard featuring a large statue of Valentino.

To avoid a repetition of the Tuesday riots, the city posted 112 patrolmen, twenty mounted police, twelve sergeants, and four lieutenants outside Campbell's mortuary. When the doors to the Funeral Church opened, more than 10,000 people were waiting. Police diverted the northern end of the line through Sherman Park, but discovered that it interfered with traffic on Broadway. To ease the congestion, the crowd was redirected back to the east side of Broadway, where it stayed for the remainder of the day.

The enduring rain did not deter the thousands that came to get one last glimpse of their idol, however brief. To help expedite the increasing throng, Valentino's body was moved to Frank Campbell's private office on the first floor. This quickened the movement of the crowd and provided a smoother exit through Campbell's flower shop next door.

Valentino's sister, Maria Strada, and her daughter Gabriella in the 1950s.

Early that morning, Dr. Sterling Wyman of Flower Hospital volunteered his services to supervise the emergency clinic that had been set up at Campbell's. Wyman inspected the room currently being used and decided that a room closer to Campbell's office and the restless mourners would better suit his needs.

Around two o'clock, Jean Acker arrived with her mother and an unidentified woman to view Valentino's body. Dressed in a long brown raincoat, a low-brimmed soft hat, and wearing blue sunglasses, Jean slowly circled the casket as the line was momentarily halted to allow her to briefly gaze upon the face of her ex-husband. For a moment it appeared as though some decorum had been restored — until the crowd recognized her and cameras began flashing. Jean's sobbing could barely be heard over the din of reporters' shouts, asking if she still loved Rudy.

"Yes, yes, I have always retained my love for Rudolph," she sobbed. "I have always been his friend — the divorce didn't change that feeling in my heart and now ... in the last two weeks, I have just learned that he thought the same about me."

In an attempt to clarify her statement, her eyes filled with tears as she explained that even though they had recently reconciled after six years, there were no plans to

Valentino's first wife, Jean Acker (in foreground with head bowed), views the body with her mother and an unidentified woman.

remarry. "I mean that we were going to share that friendship that I always had for him and that I just learned that he had for me," she said.

Nervously turning her sunglasses over and over in her hands, she trembled as her mother reached out to pat her knee. "Please," her mother said, "don't try to talk any more. These gentlemen understand dear. Come home." Not yet convinced that the reporters understood, she continued: "Please, know that this affection I spoke about — that I had for Rudy — for Mr. Valentino, was like a mother, a sister. We never thought of re-marriage."

Jean sank back into the chair and wept uncontrollably as her mother tried to comfort her. "Please, please," her mother begged. "You see she mustn't — can't talk anymore."[12] Once composed, Jean departed through the huge marble-floored reception room, passing the stalwart officers of the Fascisti wearing brightly colored ribbons pinned to their black shirts. This so-called guard of honor was causing quite an uproar among the New York Italians, who claimed that Valentino was not a Fascist and had refused to become one.

Throughout the remainder of the afternoon an organist played softly while mourners passed Valentino's bier. The New York papers, including the respected

Times, listed the names and addresses of each mourner that fainted. One young lady swooned just by gazing upon Valentino's face, while another keeled over after entering the room. One fourteen-year-old girl became hysterical while standing in line and had to be sedated. Still another woman fainted and fell over the casket. When revived, she insisted on another glimpse, but fainted again. After fainting a third time, she was ordered home. To accommodate the weak-kneed and emotionally spent, three doctors and a nurse were stationed near the casket.

Individuals were now passing by Valentino's bier at the rate of forty per minute, but it still wasn't fast enough for some. One overzealous policeman began pushing people through the line by their elbow while chanting, "Little life, here. Hurry up. Little life here."[13]

The situation outside Campbell's was no better. The crowd retained its carnival-like atmosphere while ignoring the respect that was due. Newsreels of the day reveal scores of people laughing and mugging for the cameras. Those who truly came to mourn left hearing the laughter of scoffers echoing in their ears. Still others made it a business of selling their place in line for a dollar or two, while others sold umbrellas, sandwiches, and rubber boots.

Even the Vatican found time to comment on the goings-on in New York, saying that the manifestations over the death of Rudolph Valentino were "collective folly." The Pope's representative remarked that the actor, at the point of death, certainly felt that life was a serious thing, not a romance. Concluding, the Vatican declared, "This thirst for screen romances constitutes a folly which is a clear symptom of a profound moral and civil decadence."[14]

It would appear that Ullman agreed with the Vatican, given that the general disrespect, hysteria, and lack of somberness in the crowd brought about his decision to close Campbell's door to the public. "This has gone far enough," Ullman said. "From midnight on, Valentino's body will be viewed only by friends and associates under my personal supervision. The lack of reverence shown by the crowd, the disorder and rioting since the body was first shown, have forced me to this decision."[15]

Fearing another riot because of the unexpected closing, an additional one hundred patrolmen were added to the area, bringing the total force on duty to three hundred. At 11:40 P.M. the police cut the line off at Broadway and Sixty-eighth Street. When more than 5,000 people beyond that point realized they were not going to get in, they cursed, booed, and screamed at the police. One young man was arrested for disorderly conduct, opting to spend a day in jail rather than pay his three-dollar fine.

The angry crowd was not their only problem. Members of the Anti-Fascist Alliance announced they would not be responsible for what might happen if the Fascisti guard at Valentino's bier was not removed at once. As a safeguard, a detail of ten police was stationed in the funeral chamber. Oddly, representatives of Mussolini in Rome denied that they had authorized a guard of honor for Valentino. The cable also claimed that the American organization was not acting on Mussolini's instructions, nor did the Italian dictator send a wreath to be placed at Valentino's casket. They did concede, however, that the Fascist organizations abroad had the authority to act on their own in such matters, without the permission of Rome.

Pietro Allegra, secretary of the Anti-Fascist organization, sent a telegram to Ullman protesting against the "black shirts." It read: "We hold that their presence is an insult to the memory of this great artist, who in life manifested his opposition to the anti-democratic policies of Mussolini and was for that reason outrageously treated on his last visit to Italy."[16] Allegra said that when Valentino became an American citizen the previous year, his films were boycotted throughout Italy on the order of Mussolini. Many in Italy, whether Fascist or not, felt that Valentino was a traitor to his country, so much so that in some theaters where his films were shown, some in the audience would shoot at the screen. Allegra also claimed that the American Fascists were acting on the orders of Mussolini, on whom they placed their allegiance. "Now the Fascists of New York are sending a black-shirted guard to Valentino's funeral chamber to delude the people of America into believing that he endorsed the actions of Mussolini and was one of them," Allegra concluded. "This is not true."[17]

The dispute provoked Ullman to call a conference between the two Italian coalitions to decide what should be done. "I permitted the Fascists to stand guard," Ullman explained, "only because I thought Rudy would have liked it. He was always afraid that Mussolini didn't approve of him and this seemed like proof that there was no basis for this fear."[18]

In Atlantic City, Acting Mayor Anthony M. Ruffu, Jr. released a statement claiming that Valentino was indeed a Fascist. According to Ruffu, who spoke with Valentino during his recent trip to that city, the actor told him that Mussolini "had done wonders for Italy."[19] Ullman countered that by saying, "Rudolph had a superstitious fear of the Fascisti, but he wanted to be friends with them. I did not ask them to place a guard about the casket, but I did ask them to leave."[20]

As it turned out, the whole Fascisti ordeal was a publicity stunt concocted by Harry Klemfuss, Campbell's head of publicity. Even though the American Fascists were genuine, they were hired and coached by Klemfuss, who instructed them on military formalities and how to stand guard at Valentino's casket. As for the wreath from Mussolini, it was later discovered to have come from Campbell's own flower shop.[21] Regardless of the fraud, officials feared another riot if the Anti-Fascist sympathizers gained entrance to the mortuary. In order to calm raw nerves and save face, the so-called "black shirts" agreed to withdraw their guard, and were escorted by twenty detectives to their headquarters on West Forty-fifth Street.

With that problem solved, Frank Campbell's plans for a stately funeral procession was abandoned, and the public would no longer be permitted to view the body. Only personal friends displaying a card of admission issued by Ullman would be allowed to enter the funeral chamber. Ullman felt, however, that Rudy's true friends would choose not to visit the mortuary, but instead wait until the funeral. "They seem to prefer to remember Rudy as he was in life, a robust, joyous boy," Ullman said. "And the unruly demonstration of the mob undoubtedly kept many away who would have come. They are content to send flowers and to be present at the church services

Monday."[22] Mary Pickford, who arrived that day from a European trip, agreed, saying she would not view the body but would attend the funeral.

Since the actor's death, Ullman was besieged with all sorts of requests. Sculptors offered to make death masks of Valentino, and singers and organists volunteered to perform at the funeral, but Ullman refused them all, making it clear that everything from that point on would be private. "The public has nothing more to do with the funeral rites of this gentleman who was my friend," Ullman insisted. "All decency has been violated in the last two days. From this minute on, it is a simple private affair."[23]

New York was not the only city experiencing extreme reactions to the death of Valentino. Late that evening, word was received about a young English girl who allegedly committed suicide over Valentino's passing. Peggy Scott, a 27-year-old actress, was found dead from poison in the bedroom of a London flat. When police entered, they discovered several pictures of Valentino and a number of letters supposedly written by the actor in her possession. Friends of Scott said the actress had first met Valentino while vacationing in Biarritz, and that there were rumors at the time of a romance. Scott left several letters in which she expressed tremendous grief over the actor's death.[24]

Thursday, August 26, 1926

When the doors to Campbell's funeral chapel were finally closed to the public, city officials estimated that roughly 100,000 people had viewed the earthly remains of Rudolph Valentino. Though it was announced in the newspapers and on radio that his body would no longer lie in state, the curious continued gathering outside the mortuary. Two hundred police remained on duty around the funeral church and on its side streets to keep the crowds moving — no one would be permitted to loiter. Ullman continued to express his disappointment at the lighthearted attitude of the crowds. "They showed the most gross irreverence," Ullman said. "I am sorry they were allowed to see him at all."[25]

"When I came to the funeral church yesterday, it struck me that people were acting disgracefully. Women and girls laughed; and some men, you would have thought, were going to a picnic or a three-ring circus."[26]

Friday, August 27, 1926

New York health laws prevented Alberto's request to delay the funeral until his arrival the following Wednesday. Even so, Ullman called at the home of the Commissioner of Health, Dr. Louis L. Harris, to ask permission to keep Valentino's casket at Campbell's instead of having it placed in a receiving vault at Woodlawn Cemetery. That way, Alberto could, if he so wished, view his brother's body one last

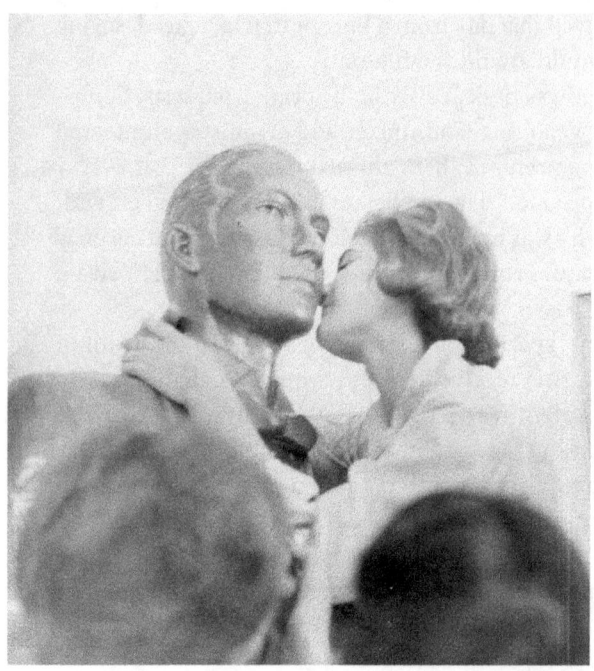

A young fan kisses a statue of Valentino that once stood in his birthplace of Castellaneta.

time. Harris agreed to a forty-eight-hour extension on the condition that the casket be sealed and that no one be allowed a viewing after the funeral except for Alberto.

Ullman was confident that Alberto would consent to interring Valentino in Hollywood. The subject became a hot topic for the nation's newspapers, some of which quoted the opinions of stars such as Douglas Fairbanks, who released a statement on behalf of himself and Mary Pickford.

"Since Hollywood was the scene of Valentino's rise to fame, and since the most important events of his life transpired there, it is fitting that his body be taken there for burial," Fairbanks said. "Both Mrs. Fairbanks and I feel that his funeral should be as simple as possible, without the mob scenes that now take place around his body."[27]

The Mayor of Castellaneta, Valentino's birthplace, cabled Alberto on the *Homeric,* imploring him to have the actor's body returned there for burial with ceremony. Valentino's sister Maria, who at first wanted her brother brought back to Italy, now concurred with the Hollywood delegation, thanks in part to the suggestion of William Randolph Hearst. She wired Alberto that while she was leaving the matter in his hands, it would be only just for her brother to rest forever in his adopted country. At a train stop in Hutchinson, Kansas, Pola wired that she intended to plead with Alberto and Ullman to make them realize that Rudy's friends have the first right to ask for his burial in Hollywood, the place where he became famous as an artist. "I will not ask it, however, for myself," she added piously.[28]

But Pola was curious, so at a stop in Topeka, Kansas, she asked a porter to bring her copies of the local papers in case there was news of the funeral arrangements. As she turned the page of one newspaper, she came upon a photograph of the dead Valentino lying on his bier. The shock was apparently too great, for Pola uttered a low cry and collapsed, sobbing on her berth. The nurse was called to sedate her, but the crying continued for nearly fifteen minutes. After this, Pola refused visitors, choosing to stay in her drawing room in seclusion with the blinds drawn until arriving in New York.

Meanwhile, in Hollywood, a riderless horse with a pair of empty riding boots reversed in the stirrups held center stage at a memorial tribute to Valentino at the Breakfast Club. The ceremonies were attended by scores of celebrities, ranging from Charlie Chaplin to Emmett Flynn, the director who had cast Valentino in *Alimony*, one of his first films. The horse was Rudy's own, which he had ridden in the foothills above Falcon Lair, and the saddle and boots were his as well. His close friend Norman Kerry held the bridle as the eulogies and prayers were said. The bugle played "taps," with a photograph of Valentino from *The Son of the Sheik*, draped in mourning, occupying a prominent place.

Saturday, August 28, 1926

Valentino news was temporarily forced off the front pages when New York held a ticker tape parade for Gertrude "Trudy" Ederele, the first woman to swim the English Channel. "Rudy Forgotten by Crowd for Trudy,"[29] one newspaper headline read. It was, of course, just a temporary setback, as Pola's expected arrival the following day would once again put Rudy back on top.

When Pola's train arrived in Chicago, she was reportedly too weak and would not meet with reporters during the three-hour layover. Her car was cleansed, switched to the New York Central tracks, and attached to the Twentieth Century, which was scheduled to pull out at 1:40 that afternoon, Chicago time. The only visitor she received was actor Thomas Meighan, who was also traveling East for Valentino's funeral. Florence Hein, Pola's secretary, read a statement from the actress in which she begged to be excused from interviews.

"Mme. Negri is truly sorry that she cannot grant interviews," Hein stated. "Her strength has completely given out. She knows the ordeal that awaits her in New York and feels you will understand her sorrow. Until the last moment she hoped that Mr. Valentino would recover. His final relapse was a great shock to her, and it will take considerable time before she is herself again."[30]

Pola's self-imposed exile did not prevent reporters from shouting questions and comments through her compartment door. One asked if it were possible that, on his deathbed, Valentino still felt spiritually bound by his first marriage to Jean Acker. Upon hearing that, Pola found her voice and the strength to reply. Throwing open the door to her compartment, she screamed, "No, no, no. It is not so. Everybody on the coast knows it is not so."[31]

Perhaps to prove her love to the public (or maybe even to herself), Pola ordered a blanket of four thousand Mme. Pierson red roses, eleven feet long and six and one-half feet wide, to cover Valentino's bier upon her arrival. In the middle of this huge pall, white roses spelled out "Pola" in Spenserian script. The actress ordered them at a cost of $2,000, replacing the yellow roses and orchids placed by the Schencks.

Actor Ben Lyon, who was assisting with the funeral arrangements, received a call in his room at the Ambassador Hotel informing him of Pola's new "flower arrangement." To Lyon, Pola's self-promotional florets made it appear like opening night for the Polish actress. "Under no circumstances will those flowers be placed on that casket," Lyon said. "Of course she was furious and put up a terrific fight. It was a premiere for Pola Negri."[32]

Regardless of whether Pola's floral tribute was a self-aggrandizing act or a memorial to her dead love, nothing would compare to the performance that New York and the world was about to witness.

CHAPTER NINE

Requiem in New York

Sunday, August 29, 1926

The Twentieth Century arrived at Grand Central Terminal just before noon. Pola was composed as she stepped from the train clad in a reportedly $3,000 mourning garb. When she met Ullman and his wife on the platform, she wept softly, placing her head on Beatrice's shoulder while sobbing, "Oh why didn't you bring him back to me?"[1] As Ullman escorted Pola to the upper level, hundreds of fans and reporters waited under the huge dome of Grand Central. News cameras flashed as the curious called out her name. Pola's visage at first expressed anger, but then broke into impassioned weeping. "No, no!"[2] she cried to the legion of peering eyes standing before her — then she fainted.

The *New York Daily Mirror*, under their now famous banner, "Pola, Faints, Faints, FAINTS," reported that Negri was the screen's greatest emotional actress both on and off screen. "Anyone who saw her yesterday won't doubt it," the tabloid wrote. "Our regret is that the kliegs and cameras were missing. No acting Pola will do upon the screen will compete with the performance she gave before the mob of curiosity seekers who haunted the portals of Grand Central."[3]

The *Los Angeles Times*, a considerably more respectable newspaper, also got their digs into the actress, even if a little more eloquently. "She wept and collapsed," the *Times* reported, "and gave to the public all of the spectacle of grief that the greatest of the dramatic writers had pictured in song, story and opera from the beginning of things theatrical."[4]

A waiting cab took Negri and the Ullmans to the Ambassador, where she fainted once again in the lobby. "She is on the verge of a mental collapse," Ullman later told the press. "She just sits there in her suite, crying and mourning and murmuring indistinguishable phrases to herself."[5]

At three o'clock, crowds were waiting at Campbell's when Pola arrived, escorted by police through a side entrance on West Sixty-seventh Street. Pola, who began weeping as she entered the bouquet-adorned Gold Room, was given special permission by the Board of Health to view Valentino's body. On the casket was a blanket of red roses, replacing the larger and more conspicuous offering she originally ordered.

Pola trembled as the casket lid was lifted. For five minutes she stood there and stared through the glass covering, gazing upon Valentino's cold, emaciated countenance. Suddenly she reeled and began sobbing bitterly. "It's cruel—cruel. I didn't know,"[6] she cried. Composing herself, she knelt before the casket while reciting the "Litany of the Dead." As she uttered the last words of the prayer, Pola threw up her hands and collapsed into Ullman's waiting arms. Attendants carried her to a couch where she remained unconscious for twenty minutes.

That evening, Pola received reporters in her suite at the Ambassador, dressed in a black silk mourning gown. One paper wrote, "She looked more tragic than in any picture she ever made."[7] Pola still insisted that she and Valentino were to be married, proclaiming her love for the actor as the greatest of her life. "I shall never forget him," she said. "I loved him not as one artist might love another, but as a woman loves a man."[8]

Monday, August 30, 1926

As the funeral mass was said in New York, services were simultaneously being held in cities across the country and around the world. In Rio de Janeiro more than 200 women and young girls attended a special mass at St. Joseph's Church. At Chicago's Trianon Ballroom, where just two years earlier Rudy and Natacha had danced for a standing-room-only audience, more than two thousand fans gathered to hear a eulogy given by Judge Francis Borrelli, president of the new Valentino Memorial Association. "Valentino's appeal was universal," Borrelli declared. "He was ever the personification of romance. He is the ideal of love — at once the Cyrano, the Romeo and the Don Juan."[9]

In order to prevent a repeat of the previous week's disorder, fifty patrolmen, five sergeants and four mounted police were present to watch over the three thousand gathered at Campbell's. Dressed in a simple black suit, Jean Acker arrived first, accompanied by her mother and an unidentified woman. The rosary she had carried during her visit the previous week was encased in a miniature gold casket and placed in Valentino's clasped hands.

The crowd reached six thousand by the time Pola and the Ullmans arrived. Unadorned by jewelry, the actress wore a mourning dress of black satin and a long black veil that floated from the brim of her hat to her waist.

Shortly before eleven o'clock, Valentino's silver-and-bronze casket was placed in a hearse to begin the short trip to St. Malachy's. Twelve motorcycle police led the funeral cortege of fifteen cars, as a well-behaved crowd of 100,000 lined Broadway.

With five hundred policemen standing shoulder-to-shoulder and arms locked, the crowd was compelled to behave.

Only those presenting a black-bordered engraved invitation from Ullman had access to West Forty-ninth Street between Eighth and Ninth Avenues. Father Edward Leonard, who heard Valentino's deathbed confession, waited at the entrance as the honorary pallbearers followed Valentino's rose-covered casket, carried on the shoulders of eight of Campbell's assistants. Actors Ben Lyon, Clifton Webb, and Richard Dix were among those who served as ushers.

Beams of sunlight streamed through the stained glass windows of St. Malachy's as Father Leonard led the procession down the center isle. A requiem resounded on the organ, and the casket was gently placed in front of the altar. Ullman, his wife, and the heavily veiled Pola Negri took their seats in the sixth row next to the casket. Behind them sat Jean Acker and her mother, Norma and Constance Talmadge, and Mary Pickford. Natacha Rambova's sister, Nora Van Horn, represented the Hudnut family.

The scent of incense floated through the church as the sextet softly sang Spoth's "Miserere." The six tall candles flanking the casket

Crowds wait for Valentino's body to be removed from Campbell's Funeral Church.

trembled with each resonating note from the organ. "Eternal rest give them, O Lord, and let perpetual light shine upon them," Father Leonard began. "Brethren we will not have you ignorant concerning them that are asleep." After this followed the sacred "Dies Irae."

"And O what trembling there will be, when the Judge comes in majesty to try the world unsparingly."[10] With each verse, the choir repeated the words.

Solemn High Funeral Mass
for Rudolph Valentino
St. Malachy's Church
West 49th Street
between Broadway and 8th Avenue
Monday August 30th 1926 at 11 A.M.

This card must be presented
for admission to the Church
it is also necessary for passage
of Automobile through Police Traffic Lines

Invitation card needed for admittance to Valentino's funeral at St. Malachy's. (Courtesy of Tracy Terhune)

The emotion-filled congregation remained hushed during the mass. With tears coursing down her cheeks, Pola knelt with her head bowed, several times sinking forward as if she were about to faint. Norma Talmadge steadied a kneeling Jean Acker as Constance passed forward a bottle of smelling salts. Only the echo of women weeping lingered throughout the church as former costars Gloria Swanson and Lois Wilson sat quietly with their husbands. Others present included Madge Bellamy, Marilyn Miller, Harry Houdini, Mary Philbin, Valentino's former dance partner Bonnie Glass, and night club entrepreneur Texas Guinan.

Demetri Onotri of the San Carlo Company sang "Ave Maria" during the offertory. Before presenting communion, Guido Ciccolini of the Chicago Opera Company sang Massenet's "Elegy." Father Leonard blessed the corpse, asking God to "show mercy, we humbly beseech Thee for the soul of Thy servant Rudolph Valentino."[11]

At one point, two tabloid photographers were discovered hiding, one in a confessional and the other, Izzy Kaplan of the *Daily Mirror*, in the choir loft. Gloria Swanson's husband, the Marquis de la Falaise de Coudray, expelled Kaplan, dragging him to the church doorway and brusquely kicking him down the steps, where his camera and exposed plates shattered on the sidewalk.

As the ritual ended, members of Campbell's undertaking staff placed Pola's shroud of pink roses onto the casket before gently lifting it to their shoulders. At the door to the church, as Chopin's "Funeral March" played, a stocky little man fell to his knees in front of the procession, crying, "Goodbye Rudolph! Goodbye, my friend. I will never see you again." The ushers restrained him as he shouted, "He's gone! He's gone." The man was later identified as Nicola Abrazze, a barber from Brooklyn who claimed to be a boyhood friend of Valentino's from Castellaneta.[12]

To avoid a possible charge by the crowd, the cortege returned to Campbell's by way of Ninth Avenue. The honorary pallbearers stood at attention as the casket was placed in the Gold Room to await Alberto's arrival. As Pola was leaving, Mary Pickford gave her a letter from Valentino's physician, Dr. Harold Meeker, who was away on vacation but wanted to communicate a message to Pola before her return to Los Angeles. While reading the letter, Pola once again fainted.

Later that evening, Pola invited reporters to her blossom-filled suite at the Ambassador where George Ullman attended, as did Norma and Constance Talmadge. With her shoulder-length hair in disarray, the actress made quite a vision as she entered

Valentino's funeral procession makes its way to St. Malachy's for the service.

the room on the arm of her nurse. Eyes reddened and radiating great indignation, Pola stood before the assemblage holding the letter from Meeker in her hand.

"The newspapers have been very cruel," she said in hushed tones. "But I suppose some of you understand."[13] Her statement appeared to be in reference to the printed implications by many newspapers, some represented in the room, that her performance at the funeral bier and her announced engagement was more a publicity stunt than genuine grief. Pausing a moment for effect, she sat down to read Meeker's letter.

"About 4 o'clock Monday morning I was sitting by Rudolph alone in the room," Meeker wrote. "He opened his eyes, stretched out his hands and said, 'I'm afraid we won't go fishing together. Perhaps we will meet again. Who knows?'

"His mind was still clear and this was the first time he seemed to realize that he would not get well. He was perfectly clear in his mind. He gave me a message for the chief, Mr. Schenck, and then he said: 'Pola — if she does not come in time, tell her I think of her.'"[14]

As she finished, Pola swooned, grasping the hand of her nurse. "There!" she cried. "If you knew, if you could only look into the bottom of my heart, you could not do

Valentino's casket leaving St. Malachy's Catholic Church, also known as the "Actor's Church."

the cruel things you have done."[15] For Pola, this was her counterattack against the menacing press—her proof that Valentino did indeed love her and wanted to marry her. With trembling hands, she pressed the letter to her face, sobbing uncontrollably. The note with Valentino's last farewell fell from her hands to the floor. The reporters that clustered about her began moving uneasily as Norma and Constance chose that moment to leave the suite. Pola stood as she regained control and faced her accusers. "This was his last message to me," she said. "I must rest. You will please excuse me."[16] As she left the room supported by her nurse, she took Ullman's arm and asked that he be "nice to her guests."

Tuesday, August 31, 1926

Douglas Fairbanks and Mary Pickford left New York immediately after the funeral to return to Hollywood. During their layover in Chicago, reporters bluntly asked whether Valentino was in his right mind when he made his dying statements about Pola. "That is too big an order for me," Mary replied, "but I do believe they were in love and I believe they intended to be married." While Pickford was not personally acquainted with Negri, she admitted that the actress was certainly grief stricken when Mary handed her the note from Dr. Meeker.

"Pola had no makeup on when I saw her and her nose was red at Rudy's funeral," she added. According to Mary, Meeker admitted that had he been called two hours earlier, Valentino's life might have been saved. "But the trouble spread quickly and had gone too far when he arrived," Pickford said.[17]

That afternoon, several New York newspapers reported that Pola left the sanctuary of her hotel suite to go on a shopping spree. Adelaide Valencia, Pola's nurse, vehemently denied the rumor, saying that Pola was a very sick woman on the verge of a nervous breakdown. "She was permitted one visitor today only for five minutes," she added. "That was Adolf Zukor."[18]

Another rumor circulated that Valentino's body would travel in a special funeral car, complete with a miniature chapel and kneeling bench, but Ullman denied this. "The body will be taken West in a private car in the most simple and dignified manner possible," he said. "That is all. There will be none of the ostentation which disgusted me early last week."[19]

Wednesday, September 1, 1926

The question lingering in everyone's mind was whether Alberto would allow the burial to be in Hollywood or if he would take his brother's remains back to Italy. The night before, Alberto cabled the Associated Press from the *Homeric*, repeating that he could not make a decision before conferring with Ullman. Confident that Alberto would comply with public opinion, Ullman announced plans to return Valentino's body to Hollywood. "The funeral party will leave Grand Central depot tomorrow [Thursday], at six-thirty. Two private cars have been engaged — one which will contain the body of Mr. Valentino and the other the members of the party."[20]

The *Homeric* arrived in New York harbor that evening after a brief delay at sea. Pola remained in seclusion all day after suffering another relapse at her hotel, but insisted on meeting Alberto's ship, much against Dr. Wyman's orders. At the dock, Ullman, his wife Beatrice, Pola, Wyman, and Rudy's friend Frank Menillo pushed their way through a sea of reporters and bystanders. While Pola, Beatrice, and Wyman waited in the Customs office, Ullman, Menillo, and several reporters took a tug down the bay to Quarantine where they boarded the *Homeric*. Menillo came along as an interpreter, given that Alberto's English was not very good.

Alberto greeted them as they boarded the ship. "What is the estate worth?" were the first words Alberto allegedly asked Ullman as he stepped aboard.[21] Without replying, Ullman introduced Alberto to reporters whose first questions were about Valentino's burial locale. Alberto repeated that he would not make a decision until he conferred with Ullman. That said, the three men entered Alberto's cabin and remained there for half an hour before inviting reporters to join them. As he stood,

Alberto broke down and sobbed uncontrollably in broken English, saying to the effect, "My brother belonged to America and his resting place shall be Hollywood. What is more, I shall adopt the name of Valentino and shall perpetuate that name through my children."

Alberto was so distraught that Frank Menillo stepped in to translate. He explained that the decision had the support of Valentino's sister Maria in Turin, who, if she had known the seriousness of Rudy's illness, would have joined him in New York. "We decided to give to America our dearest possession — the body of our brother," Alberto explained through Menillo.[22]

At 6:40 the *Homeric* docked at Pier No. 69 at the foot of West Seventeenth Street. An Italian delegation waving their native flag greeted Alberto as Pola fell into his outstretched arms. Placing her head on his shoulder, the two began to weep. "Let us both be brave," he whispered in Italian as Pola kissed him. Several sharp-eyed reporters noticed the tags on Alberto's luggage already denoted his proposed name change. "Chevalier Alberto Guglielmi Valentino,"[23] one reporter read aloud. Through Menillo, Alberto explained that he would, of course, have to obtain the permission of Mussolini's government in order to legally change his name.

After clearing customs, Dr. Wyman chauffeured the party in his limousine, dropping Pola at the Ambassador before proceeding to Campbell's. Ullman escorted Alberto to the Gold Room where, nervous but composed, he viewed his brother's body for fifteen minutes and was then joined by Father Congedo for prayer in an adjacent room. As Ullman looked on, Valentino's casket was sealed one last time, never to be opened again. Once Alberto decided to inter Valentino in Hollywood, a second requiem high mass, to be said at Father Congedo's Church of the Sacred Heart, was abandoned.

Thursday, September 2, 1926

The outer gold-bronze box that Valentino's casket was placed in for protection bore a simple inscription with the actor's real name, Rodolfo Guglielmi, and his stage name. At four o'clock, as his remains left Campbell's for the last time, only a small number of onlookers braved the light rain that fell. Few paid notice to the hearse as it traveled south on Broadway, across Forty-sixth Street and then to its final destination, Grand Central Terminal. The funeral party entered through the Forty-fifth Street baggage entrance, where an elevator transported the casket down to the train platform. Frank Campbell and his attendants stood guard until the casket was loaded onto the Lake Shore Limited.

Pola placed a small bouquet of lilies on the casket next to a huge floral offering of snapdragons, larkspur, and roses from the Ullmans. Two drooping flowers from five-year-old Cynthia Wyman, daughter of Dr. Sterling Wyman, lay nearby. Outside on the concourse, hundreds lined the balconies, crowded the gates and stood patiently on the stairway from Vanderbilt Avenue, hoping to get a glimpse of the casket and funeral party.[24] Among those making the trip west were James Quirk, Chicago newspaper correspondent Catherine Donovan, Frank Campbell, William H. Hull (manager of Campbell's Funeral Church), and Harry Klemfuss.

Pola and Alberto refused all requests for interviews but gave out written statements through Dr. Wyman. Both expressed their deepest thanks to friends and sympathizers in New York. "It is a great consolation to know that the last remains of my beloved will find a resting place in California," Pola said. Alberto's thoughts were of his sister Maria, who could not join him, "so she remained sorrowing in Italy with my family."[25] Ullman denied reports that an autopsy would be performed, adding that a thorough medical report on Valentino's illness would be made public, in part to quiet the rumors that he was a victim of poison or violence.

Hollywood most likely would pay their respects at a mass held Tuesday morning at the Church of the Good Shepherd in Beverly Hills. The choice for the interment site, which had not yet been decided, was between Hollywood Cemetery and Calvary, the official final resting place of the Catholic Diocese. If Hollywood Cemetery were chosen, a special dispensation from the Catholic Church would be required.

The Lake Shore Limited, temporarily dubbed the "Valentino Funeral Train" by the press, carried Rudolph Valentino on his final journey. Ullman announced the formation of the Rudolph Valentino National Memorial Committee, headed by Joseph Schenck, which would erect a memorial in Valentino's honor. Public donations collected through theaters and newspapers would finance the project, which tentatively envisioned a heroic bronze equestrian statue of Valentino in his role as the Sheik standing before a Roman temple.

As the funeral train returned to Hollywood, on the steps of a Sicilian church on the beach of Emerald Bay, California, many of the extras employed by Valentino in his last film, *The Son of the Sheik*, held a special service to his memory. The extras were employed in Sam Rork's production of *The Blonde Saint*. Rork, who gave Valentino one of his first film roles, in *Passion's Playground*, suspended shooting so he and former Valentino costars Lewis Stone and Doris Kenyon, director Sven Gad, and others could attend the services. Rork sent a telegram to Joseph Schenck, extending the company's sincere condolences. "We all feel a personal loss in the death of Mr. Valentino,"[26] the telegram read.

CHAPTER TEN

The Journey West

Friday, September 3, 1926

"We went across country and it was amazing," Alberto said. "You probably can't believe me, but it's true, that to see the people and the way they were trying to show their shock and affection for Rudy. I was awakened early in the morning 'cause it was just dawn. I was informed that a group of people from Erie came with guitars and mandolins. The great majority were Italians living here in this country. They asked my permission if they could sing and play some of the Italian songs for the memory of Rudy. It was very touching."[1]

When the train arrived in Chicago, a steady rain fell as the police, a group of reporters, and members of the Valentino Memorial Association gathered on the runway at La Salle Street Station. Hawkers of Valentino souvenirs were peddling their wares long before the train arrived. Buttons with Valentino's image could be seen on practically every rain-soaked coat and hat in the group.

As the afternoon progressed, the gathering crowds ignored police warnings, forcing their way through barricades and spilling over onto the tracks. With the help of railroad employees, the determined mob was driven from the train shed, but lingered in the falling rain as police lines held them back.

The thousands, who waited hours in the rain hoping to get a glimpse of his casket, rushed the train when it pulled in at five o'clock, but the police lines held. Pola's face grimaced as she peered through the fogged windows at the mass of gaping, rain-soaked women who fought for a quick look at her or at one of the famous mourners. "Well, I suppose that they mean to be kind," Pola observed.[2] Ullman supervised the transfer of the actor's remains to the Golden State Limited of the Rock Island Line as police guarded the entrance to the car. Only reporters and a few of Valentino's Chicago friends were permitted a last glimpse of the casket.

In Los Angeles, Bishop Cantwell of the Catholic Diocese granted a special dispensation so that the actor's body could be laid to rest in Hollywood Cemetery instead of Calvary. Valentino's friend and benefactor, June Mathis, offered her own crypt in the mausoleum temporarily until an appropriate memorial could be built. In order to hold a second service at the Church of the Good Shepherd, Ullman would have to get the Bishop's consent, inasmuch as Catholic Church ritual allows only one high mass.

Many questioned why Valentino was being permitted a Roman Catholic burial in the first place, considering his two divorces. The church was mostly concerned with whether Valentino was ever validly married and concluded that he wasn't, at least not in the eyes of God. According to church edict, a Catholic marriage is valid only when it is contracted before a duly authorized priest and two witnesses. Even though Jean Acker was a Catholic, a minister performed their wedding, and Valentino's two marriages to Rambova were both civil service ceremonies.

Father Leonard, when called to Valentino's bedside, found a public sinner bound neither in the eyes of the Church or State by a previous marriage. Whereas Valentino had received the last sacraments, he had died as a Catholic and was thus entitled to a Catholic burial. "The Church gave him what she gives all her children," the Archdiocese of New York explained, "simply this and nothing more."[3]

Saturday, September 4, 1926

For much of the journey, Pola stayed in her stateroom, but would occasionally glance out her window at mourners assembled along the tracks. Pola told a group of reporters at a stop in Missouri that, while no formal engagement existed between her and Valentino, plans were being made for their wedding the following April. Alberto said that Pola and his brother were together constantly from the time they became acquainted, more than eight months before. "I believe there was no ring and no announcement," Alberto said, "but we all knew the engagement existed and were very glad. We like Pola very much."[4]

Sunday, September 5, 1926

The Hearst newspapers published an article for their Sunday readers written by Valentino two weeks before leaving for his ill-fated trip to New York. Entitled "Why Marriage Was a Failure in My Case," it was widely touted as "the last that he wrote before his death."

"I shall have to disappoint the reader who expects something sensational," he wrote. "I did not beat Natacha. She did not throw flat-irons at me. Sorry — but we did not do those things. Nor did I object to her having a career — her own career. Nor did I demand that she bear children."[5] Valentino was reluctant at first to write about his failed marriage, but did so because of the many false stories printed, thinking it best to tell his version of the truth.

As the "Valentino Funeral Train" inched its way to Los Angeles, the *New York Times* reported that Dr. Sterling Wyman, Pola Negri's attending physician, was in truth an impostor and former convict. Identified as Stephen Jacob Weinberg, the Brooklyn-born hoaxer was known to Federal authorities under eleven different aliases, and had impersonated the U.S. Consul to Morocco, a Romanian envoy, and a Serbian military attaché.

The impostor's most well-known masquerade occurred in 1921, when he befriended Princess Fatima of Afghanistan and arranged a meeting with her and then–President Warren G. Harding. Weinberg was eventually found out and convicted for impersonating an officer. He was sentenced to eighteen months in the Federal Penitentiary in Atlanta. The *Times* also reported that Wyman had served a sentence at the Dannemora State Hospital for the Criminally Insane for forging the name of former United States Senator William M. Calder of Brooklyn, New York.

Wyman or Weinberg explained that he had known George Ullman for several years and had offered his services because of Valentino's death. He denied assertions that he had represented himself as Pola Negri's physician. The assumption came, Wyman claimed, when someone at the Ambassador ran into Ullman's suite saying that Pola had fainted. "I asked whether she had fainted or whether she was simply hysterical," Wyman said. "I was told that she seemed to be hysterical and I only suggested that they give her some aromatic spirits of ammonia."[6]

When reporters informed Ullman of Wyman's apparent deception at a stop in El Paso, he insisted that he had never met Wyman until Valentino's death, when the so-called doctor approached him and offered his services. "Wyman was very courteous and attentive to me during the funeral," Ullman said. "He showed a police badge and drove a police car, which he said was at my disposal. As we were leaving New York, he repeated his wishes to be of service to me. Wyman must be laboring under some derangement if he is asserting that he represents me in any manner."[7]

As the train carrying the body of Rudolph Valentino roared through the heat-oppressed desert, sun-bronzed cowboys stood with plain-looking women, paying tribute with bared heads as the entourage passed. This scene repeated itself at every little stop where farmers and ranchers gathered for a chance to pay their respects. Outside Yuma, Arizona, the train rolled past the huge sand dunes where Valentino filmed portions of *The Sheik*. As Alberto immersed himself in this sight, a white-robed man on horseback appeared through a swirling sand cloud, reared his mount and saluted, palm first.

The funeral train made a brief stop at the Yuma station where two hundred people, many who worked as extras on *The Sheik*, were waiting. For the first time since leaving Chicago, the side door to Valentino's coach was opened, revealing a mountain of flowers, wilted and brown from the desert heat. Kneeling next to the bier, Pola gave another performance worthy of one of her Hollywood scenarios. "Ah dear boy,"

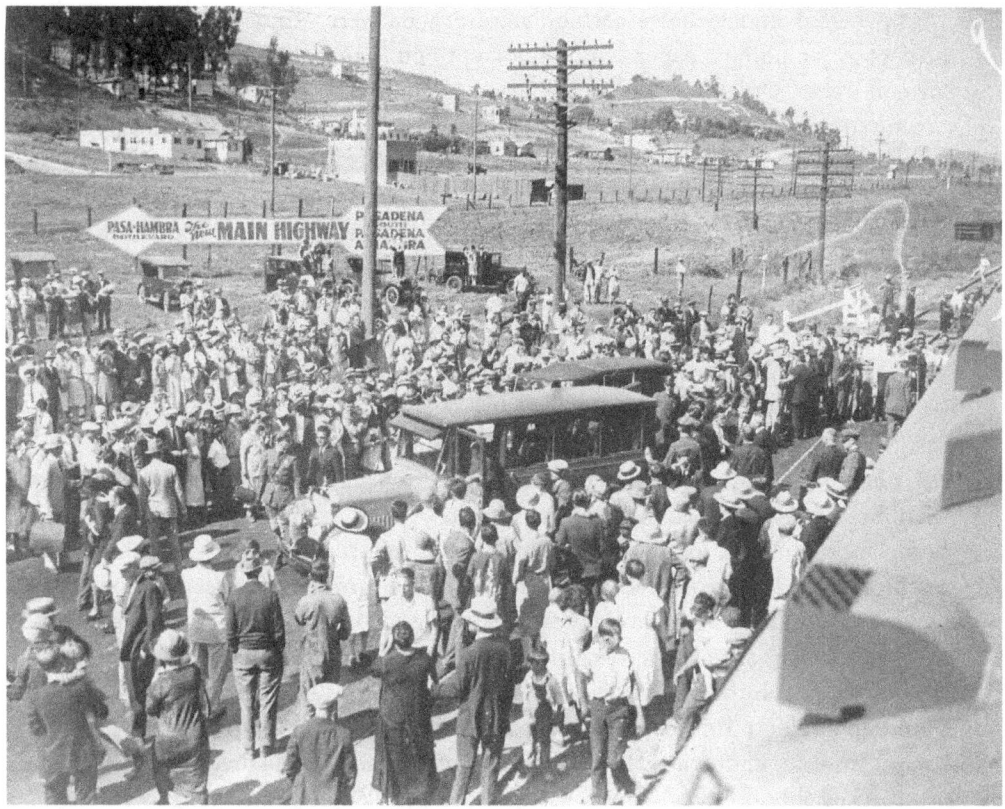

Valentino's body arrives in Los Angeles at the Pasa-Hambra railroad crossing. (Courtesy of the Academy of Motion Picture Arts and Sciences)

she sobbed, "we will soon be home; home, my dear, where you were so happy and life and love were so sweet."[8]

Monday, September 6, 1926

The blistering heat continued into the night as the Southern Pacific Golden State Limited clamored across the Colorado River Bridge and into California. At Narod, several of Valentino's Hollywood friends, including Charles Eyton, Kathlyn Williams, John Considine, Jr., and Marion Davies, boarded the train.

The train was scheduled to arrive at the Los Angeles station at 2:45 P.M., but because of concern that there might be a replay of the events in New York, Ullman decided to remove Valentino's body at the Boulevard Park station. Despite the secrecy surrounding Valentino's return, more than 300 people were waiting at this obscure railroad crossing as engine No. 4319 slowly crept to its destination. Murmurs of, "He's coming,"[9] could be heard from the crowd, many of whom came from a small park less than a mile away where Labor Day festivities were taking place.

Sprinkled among the gathering that afternoon were people hawking Valentino mementos, including a paper-bound book entitled *Rudolph Valentino: His Romantic Life and Death*. Quickly put together, it was written and published by a Hollywood screenwriter, Ben-Allah, and sold for 25 cents. For the moment though, peddlers were ignored as motorcycle officers halted oncoming traffic for an approaching gray hearse. As the doors to the club car opened, Joseph O'Connor of the Cunningham & O'Connor Mortuary supervised several attendants as they lifted Valentino's casket from the train into the waiting hearse.

Pola, dressed in black and carrying a bouquet of yellow roses, clutched tightly to the arm of Dr. Felger as she stepped from the train. Followed closely by Marion Davies, Pola made her way to Valentino's casket as it was placed in the waiting hearse. Before the doors closed, Pola raised the bouquet in a final farewell as an attendant took the flowers and placed them on the casket.

The funeral party quickly entered waiting cars that followed the hearse along Alhambra Avenue and Mission Road to its downtown destination. Other cars took their place in line and followed the procession of mourners, led by several motorcycle officers. The long motorcade slowly made its way through the streets of Los Angeles, past Lincoln Park where holiday crowds paid a silent tribute, and then on to Little Italy where many of Valentino's countrymen bowed their heads in respect. In other parts of the city, hundreds of people stopped their daily activities to watch silently as Rudolph Valentino passed by for the last time.

Meanwhile, in downtown Los Angeles, more than 1,000 people, mostly teenage girls, packed the spacious lobby of Central Station. People waited for more than an hour after the train's arrival, thinking they might catch a fleeting glimpse of their dead idol's coffin. Instead, all that remained was a dusty wreath of evergreen and a white ribbon with purple letters spelling out the star's name.

Sirens blared several blocks from Cunningham & O'Connor's South Grand Avenue mortuary as Valentino's funeral cortege edged closer to its destination. More than three thousand spectators filled the streets, taking advantage of every vantage point, including the windows of every building on the block. At first the cordon of police had their hands full trying to restrain the crowd, but when the hearse stopped and the doors were opened, a hush came over those watching. Pola remained in her cream-colored Pierce Arrow town car, peering out from behind curtained windows. Valentino's eleven-hundred-pound, flower-draped casket was lifted onto the shoulders of a dozen men and carried into the mortuary's Guardian Angel Chapel, where it would remain until morning.

Later that afternoon, Alberto arrived at Hollywood Cemetery to inspect the marble-faced crypt that writer June Mathis was temporarily providing. Located in the southeast corner of the mausoleum, it was above the crypt of Mathis' mother, Virginia (or Jenny, as she was called). Many times Valentino left flowers at this very spot, next to the huge stained-glass window that emitted soft-colored light into the marble corridor.

Interred in the same mausoleum, just two corridors over, is Virginia Richdale

Kerrigan (crypt 1399), the daughter of William W. Kerrigan, one-time manager of Universal Studios and the twin brother of actor J. Warren Kerrigan. Virginia had the distinction of being the first baby born on the Universal Studios lot in 1915. Rudy first met William Kerrigan while working on the set of *Delicious Little Devil* with Mae Murray. At the time, Kerrigan was managing his brother's career and was soon doing the same for Valentino. Rudy became attached to little Virginia, spending many hours at her Ivar Avenue home, often taking her for rides in his car.

On December 26, 1924, nine-year-old Virginia ran to a neighbor's house to model a new dancing frock she received for Christmas. As she twirled across the floor, her dress brushed over an open gas heater and ignited. Virginia was rushed to Hollywood Hospital, where the next day she died from her burns. According to Virginia's brother Patrick, Valentino, who always had a profound love of children, was devastated by little Virginia's death and would often leave flowers at her crypt.[10]

Tuesday, September 7, 1926

That morning, Pola, dressed in deep-mourning garb, emerged from her bungalow at the Ambassador to meet the waiting press. Joe Hergesheimer, an author now under the employ of Famous Players–Lasky, was staying in the bungalow across from Pola and watched as she exited with her veil thrown back. As cameras rolled, someone yelled out, "Pola — the light's not good on your face — will you do it again?"

"And," Joe later told a friend, "darned if she didn't! It's the only time I ever saw a retake on mourning."[11]

While Pola was doing her close-up, an estimated 3,000 spectators gathered under the willow trees lining the sidewalk across from the Church of the Good Shepherd in Beverly Hills. Many were there to catch sight of a celebrity, not to pay their respects to the dead actor. Though more than 200 policemen were on duty, the crowd needed little restraining except for an occasional reprimand to get back in line.

Baroness Ravensdale, who was still visiting Hollywood, received one of the 500 invitations sent out by Ullman, but had no mourning attire. "But in my maid's black dress, held up by elastic," she said, "and in Elinor Glyn's black toque and one of her satin capes, I attended that bewildering ceremony."[12]

Newsreel cameras captured the arrival of mourners, including Mary Pickford, Douglas Fairbanks, Ruth Roland, June Mathis, and San Francisco Mayor James J. Rolph.[13] Wood wardia ferns and dahlias graced the vestibule of the church as the haunting sounds of the organ and choir emanated from within. Ravensdale and Glyn were seated at the rear of the church with William Randolph Hearst. Marion Davies, Hearst's companion and mistress, sat with her sisters in a group huddled nearer the front of the church.

Charlie Chaplin, director George Fitzmaurice, Samuel Goldwyn (a replacement for Norman Kerry, who injured his leg on a film set), and others carried the coffin, which was covered with a ravishing canopy of red rose buds (a gift from Pola) and a cross of white roses and lilies (from Alberto). Behind them walked Pola, arriving ten minutes late and dressed in deepest widow's weeds, a veil hanging over her tear-streaked face, clutching the arm of Alberto.

The casket was placed on a bronze catafalque, draped by a purple velvet cover. Pola wept audibly as Father Michael Mullins, rector of the Church of the Good Shepherd, chanted the solemn requiem mass for the repose of the soul of Rudolph Valentino. "Requiescat in pace," Father Mullins intoned. For more than an hour the officiating priests droned, and the choir retorted as the aromatic scent of incense drifted through the open air. From the choir, Richard Bonelli, a baritone from the Chicago Grand Opera, sang the melodramatic "Ave Maria."

"We beseech Thee for the repose of the soul of Thy servant Rudolph," Father Mullins prayed, as the priests, followed by the altar boys, stepped down and sprinkled holy water on the flower-draped casket. "Requiescat in pace," chanted the priests. "May this, Thy servant escape from pains and penalties and may Thy angels lead him into Paradise. And may he rest in eternal peace."[14]

The melancholy rituals of the Catholic Church had a disheartening effect on Baroness Ravensdale. "I was particularly depressed by the innumerable prayers sending him to the bottomless pit of Hell," Ravensdale said, "since, Mr. Hearst told me, his many marriages were not recognized by the Church, and his poor dead body was being told so in pretty plain language."

Hearst, Ravensdale, and Glyn withdrew from the service early, just moments before Valentino's casket was placed in a waiting hearse. The funeral procession was led down Santa Monica Boulevard to Hollywood Cemetery, where the streets were lined with "thousands of hysterical, weeping people,"[15] recalled Ravensdale.

At the gates of the cemetery, another large crowd pushed against police lines. Future director, actor, and Academy Award–winning editor Robert Parrish, who in 1926 was a ten-year-old student at neighboring Santa Monica Boulevard School, recalled the excitement that accompanied Valentino's funeral that morning. "When I arrived at school, at 7:55 A.M., weeping women were blocking Santa Monica Boulevard in front of the cemetery from Van Ness Avenue to Gower Street," Parrish said. "The big red Pacific Electric streetcars crawled through the crowd, bells clanging, motormen cursing."[16]

In the midst of this, would-be entrepreneurs hawked black-bordered stills of the great lover from his last film, *The Son of the Sheik*. Silver Valentino slave bracelets, gypsy earrings, hair grease, and black arm bands were also being huckstered about the bereaved mass of bystanders.

As the crowds increased, the assistant fire chief arrived at eleven o'clock and advised the principal to close the school. The children were told to go straight home, but, of course, many did not, including Parrish and his buddy, Ely Novic. When the two boys crawled through a secret hole in the high cedar hedge that surrounded the cemetery, they saw thousands of people casually wandering around the grounds, including regal looking women in wicker chairs, dressed as if attending a garden party. "As the ladies trampled across the graves of various prop men, cameramen, extras, and other lesser Hollywood figures," Parrish said, "we followed in their wake, hoping to get a look at whatever was going on."

Their adventure was foiled when Bud, a cemetery worker, began chasing them. The boys sprinted to the back of the cemetery and wormed their way through the fence and onto the Paramount lot, where they climbed onto a square-rigged, four-masted schooner — one of many standing sets that dotted the back lot.

"We climbed to the crow's nest at the top of the tallest mast and had a bird's-eye view of the whole show," Parrish recalled. "Every time Bud looked our way, we thumbed our noses, raised the middle finger of our right hand, and cried in unison, 'Bud, Bud, Peter Pud! How do you like it? Fried, stewed, or barbecued?' To this day, I don't know why we did this, but it seemed like a sensational thing to do at the time."[17]

As the hearse arrived at the steps of the Cathedral Mausoleum, Father Mullins and the altar boys greeted the imposing granite building's newest resident. As Valentino's body made its final trek, two airplanes swooped down over the crowd to a height of 100 feet, dropping thousands of flowers—a salute from Valentino's employee, Luther Mahoney, and several others. "No one will ever know how bad I felt the day he was buried," Mahoney later said. "For years I always looked back and thought what a wonderful idea it was that I had the thought to bed his path to the Great Beyond with roses."[18]

The blossoms drifted through the morning air, carpeting the entrance to the mausoleum as the casket was carried through the open bronze doors. "The mausoleum looked like a hotel lounge," Ravensdale said, "with plaques, cubicles and vases of flowers all over the place."[19]

An elderly woman approached Italian actress Rosa Rudami and handed her a small bundle of blossoms. "They won't let me in but I want him to have them," she said.[20] Rudami smiled graciously and added the woman's tiny offerings to her own. The crowd watched as Douglas Fairbanks, Mary Pickford, Charles Chaplin, Harold Lloyd, June Mathis, Marion Davies, William Randolph Hearst, Baroness Ravensdale and others entered the imposing granite edifice and the bronze doors clanged shut behind them.

The procession reverently made their way through the marble corridors of the mausoleum to the sunny corner where a black hole five feet from the floor waited, in contrast with the sameness of the neighboring closed crypts. As the hoisting apparatus maneuvered Valentino's casket into place, Father Mullins spoke a final word of blessing over the remains and waiting tomb. The silver-bronze casket creaked as it slid along the grooves of the marble crypt, and Pola's rose canopy fell silently to the floor. "May his soul and the soul of the faithfully departed through the mercy of God, rest in peace, Amen," intoned Father Mullins.[21]

Ravensdale noted that as the casket slid into the burial chamber, Pola, in a final fit of emotional agony, "made a dramatic crucifix gesture in front of it, screamed and swooned, and had to be carried out...."[22] In contrast, Alberto prayed quietly before the open crypt, but stopped as his grief overwhelmed him. As a final gesture, he leaned towards the casket, placed his forehead on the end and kissed it. "Addio, Rodolfo—addio,"[23] he sobbed. For the first time, Alberto broke down and had to be helped out.

As friends and family slowly made their way down the short corridor, June Mathis, who so graciously loaned her own crypt for Rudy to rest in, touched the casket and said, "Rudy, you can stay here 'till they place me in it."[24]

Postmortem

As most of the film capital was saying their final good-byes to Rudolph Valentino, Frances Howard Goldwyn was at the Good Samaritan Hospital giving birth to Samuel Goldwyn, Jr. The following day, director King Vidor and actress Eleanor Boardman were married at the Beverly Hills home of Marion Davies. Even Pola Negri, after her exhausting performance of the last two weeks, returned to work on the set of *Hotel Imperial*. "I must work," she said. "My work and my memories are all that is left to me."[25]

Now that the obsequies had been completed, the thought of how Valentino would be remembered was foremost in everyone's mind. The city of Chicago, home of the infamous "Pink Powder Puffs" editorial, formed the Rudolph Valentino Memorial Association in the hopes of erecting a remembrance of some kind. The Arts Association of Hollywood proposed a monument that would be the forerunner of a series of memorials to pioneers of the film industry.[26] A committee of local Italians, which included director Robert Vignola, Silvano Balboni, and his wife June Mathis, suggested the construction of an Italian park on Hollywood Boulevard with a memorial theater and a large statue of Valentino as its central feature.[27] Despite those grandiose projects, no memorials actually materialized — and it slowly became apparent that the same would happen with Valentino's final resting place.

The fight over Valentino's estate received considerable press coverage over the following year, eclipsing the attention paid to his as-yet-unresolved resting place — that is, until June Mathis died unexpectedly in New York on July 27, 1927. Mathis and her grandmother, Emily Hawkes, were attending a performance of *The Squall* at the 48th Street Theatre, when, during the last act, Mathis suddenly rose with her hands pressed against her breast and screamed, "Mother, I'm dying."

Actress Blanche Yurka, the star of the play, recalled that when she heard the commotion in the audience she assumed that someone had been overcome by the heat. When the final curtain was lowered, she sent her maid to check on what happened. "Miss Blanche," her maid said upon returning, "the lady's dead; she's lying on the steps in the alley, stone dead." Horrified, Yurka sent her costar, Mervin Williams, to obtain more information.

"It's June Mathis, the scenario writer," Williams told her, "you know, the one who discovered Valentino. She had a heart attack. They telephoned the coroner's office; they say she mustn't be moved until they arrive."

Yurka went to the alleyway and saw Mathis' body lying on the steps surrounded

Artist's conception of the front and overview of Valentino's planned memorial.

An impression of the memorial, standing in classic silhouette against a dark background of trees

Artist's conception of the planned resting place of Rudolph Valentino at Hollywood Cemetery.

by a physician and Mathis' grandmother. Refusing to believe her granddaughter was dead, Hawkes rubbed Mathis' wrist and cried, "If you will only let me take baby home, I know I can make her get well. Why don't you let me take baby home?"[28] Mathis' body lay on the steps of the theatre for several hours before the coroner finally arrived around two o'clock in the morning. Ironically, Mathis body was taken to Campbell's Funeral Church where Valentino was on display less than a year earlier.

Now that Mathis was in need of her own crypt, a decision had to be made about what to do with Valentino. As a good-will gesture, Silvano Balboni offered to have Valentino's casket moved to his crypt next to Mathis' until the Valentino estate ironed out its problems. On August 8, cemetery workers entered the Cathedral Mausoleum and, one last time, moved Valentino's remains to the adjoining crypt, number 1205.

While public memorials were being considered, Valentino's body continued to lay in a borrowed tomb. At the time of his death, architects were asked to submit designs for a mausoleum, with an estimated cost placed at $10,000. *Photoplay* magazine published plans for a proposed tomb by architect Matlock Price in the November issue. The design incorporated an exedra, a half-circle of columns standing serene and dignified against a dark background and curving towards the observer. Within that half-circle, a "heroic" bronze figure of Valentino as the Sheik, seated on an Arabian horse, towered above the onlooker. Following the curve of the exedra, a broad bench sat under two pergolas running across the ends of the terrace, which was paved with red Spanish tile.

These plans also went nowhere, and a permanent mausoleum for Valentino has never materialized. In May 1930 a memorial to Valentino was finally erected in De Longpre Park in central Hollywood, the only one of its kind dedicated to an actor in the film capital. In April 1934, after Valentino's body lay in a borrowed tomb for almost eight years, Silvano Balboni sold the crypt to Alberto.

Every year on August 23rd at 12:10 P.M. (the time that Valentino died in New York), scores of fans gather near his crypt at Hollywood Forever Cemetery to remember the man. Regardless of the circus atmosphere that has sometimes prevailed at these events during the past seventy-eight years, whether it be reports of the actor's ghost or the appearance of mysterious, dark-veiled women, it is hoped that somehow the spirit of Rudolph Valentino, the "Great Lover," now rests in peace.

PART TWO

Homes, Hangouts and Other Places of Interest: Tours of Valentino-Related Sites

Tour Introduction

Rudolph Valentino worked and played in New York and Los Angeles for thirteen years. But if the film idol were to visit any of his old stomping grounds today, he would discover that much has changed since 1926. Many of today's landmarks and tourist attractions in New York and Los Angeles did not exist during Valentino's lifetime. Valentino never saw a movie at Grauman's Chinese or the Pantages Theater. He never spent a night at the Roosevelt Hotel or had dinner at the Brown Derby. In New York, the Empire State Building was just a dream, as were Radio City Music Hall and Rockefeller Center. All of these venues were built after his death. Additionally, many of the buildings that were familiar to him no longer exist. Gone are the Hollywood Hotel, Metro Studios, and even his own home, "Villa Valentino." Many of the actor's haunts and hangouts no longer exist, and many that do have been altered remarkably. The indication "site" appearing with a location means that the building or location has been razed and no longer exists.

TOUR 1

New York City

City Hall / Chinatown

The Tombs [site], 100 Centre Street, between Franklin and Leonard streets.

"The Tombs" was mainly a prison for detention where persons accused of crimes were confined until trial and sentencing. After Valentino's arrest at Georgia Thym's apartment, he spent three days confined here under $10,000 bail as a witness against a police officer charged with extortion and accepting bribes. Two days later, the bail was reduced and Valentino was set free. In 1972, the seventy-year-old building (actually the second prison on that site) was replaced by the present Manhattan Detention Complex, but "the Tombs" name still persists.

East Midtown

Ambassador Hotel [site], 345 Park Avenue, northeast corner of Park Avenue and East 51st Street.

The opulent Ambassador Hotel stood on this site for more than forty-five years. Valentino was staying here when he collapsed in his suite prior to being rushed to the hospital. It was on the roof of the Ambassador that Valentino staged a boxing match with sports writer Frank "Buck" O'Neil. Located just a few blocks from Grand Central Terminal, the Ambassador was one of New York's most luxurious hostelries. The hotel opened in April 1921, immediately attracting the attention of the rich and

Opposite: The Ambassador Hotel in New York. Valentino boxed with Frank "Buck" O'Neil on the roof of the hotel, and it was here that Valentino took ill before being rushed to the Polyclinic.

famous. In 1958 the 537-room hotel was sold and renamed the Sheraton-East. Then, on July 9, 1966, almost forty years after Valentino's death, the hotel closed its doors to the public, and its contents were sold at auction. Sadly, a behemoth 44-story office building replaced the stylish hotel. At the time, the *New York Times* editorialized that the destruction of the former Ambassador Hotel "will be an inestimable loss in the city's sophistication and character and in the practice of the dwindling art of living."[1]

Club Lido, 47 East 44th Street, between Vanderbilt and Park Avenue.

Club Lido was one of the many night spots Valentino frequented on his trips to New York. According to Marion Benda, they danced here the Saturday evening before he took ill however, no one ever came forward to confirm her story.

Grand Central Terminal, 42nd Street at Park Avenue.

The Beaux-arts Grand Central Terminal, built in 1913, is the world's largest and busiest transportation building, occupying 49 acres. Whenever Valentino arrived in New York, he would invariably pass through Grand Central. In particular, he saw Joseph Schenck and Norma Talmadge off to Maine from here the day before he took ill. When Pola Negri arrived to attend Valentino's funeral, mobs gathered inside the main concourse of Grand Central in order to get a glimpse of her. And, of course, the "Valentino Funeral Train" left from here for the actor's last trip back to Hollywood. Grand Central almost suffered the same fate as Pennsylvania Station, but preservationists like Jacqueline Kennedy had it declared a landmark in the mid–1960s. Although the Terminal had suffered neglect in the 1970s and '80s, a massive four-year restoration project has been recently completed.

Park Avenue Apartment [site], 270 Park Avenue, between East 47th and East 48th streets.

Natacha and her Aunt Teresa moved into an apartment on this site in August 1925. Valentino listed this address as his place of residence on his application for citizenship the following November. In 1926 an advertisement for the building described the apartments as having large rooms, high ceilings, and a great garden quadrangle that gave it a "stateliness and individuality, which appeal so strongly to the family desiring a particularly fine city residence."[2] Demolished in the late 1950s, the apartment complex gave way to the J. P. Morgan Chase & Co. building.

Flatiron / Lower Midtown

Brunswick Records, 16–18 West 36th Street, between Fifth and Sixth avenues.

"The original records are being highly valued as memorials of the famous star and particular value has been laid upon the fact that one, the 'Kashmiri Love Song,' was taken from his great role of *The Sheik*."[3] — Brunswick executive, 1930.

In 1920, Brunswick Records moved into the top two floors of what was then a newly constructed thirteen-story building. The main offices, furnished in mahogany and white, were located on the twelfth floor. Two state-of-the art recording rooms, fully equipped with modern devices, occupied the top floor. This is where Valentino recorded two songs in May 1923—"El Relicario" and the "Kashmiri Song." The recordings were placed in Brunswick's libraries until, all but forgotten, their existence was eventually traced through a letter written by Valentino to Natacha Rambova. Ralph Mazziotta, vocal coach for the Metropolitan Opera House, was present when the songs were recorded and verified the authenticity of the records in 1930. These are the only recordings of Valentino's voice known to exist.

Madison Square Garden [site], 51 Madison Avenue, at 26th Street.

Valentino judged a beauty contest for Mineralava at the old Madison Square Garden in November 1923. Budding filmmaker David O. Selznick produced a short film about the contest entitled *Rudolph Valentino and His 88 American Beauties*. In 1925, Madison Square Garden was demolished and the venue moved to Eighth Avenue and Forty-ninth Street. In 1928 the New York Life Insurance Company building was erected on the site of the original. The current Madison Square Garden is located above Pennsylvania Station, between 31st and 33rd Streets, and Seventh and Eighth avenues.

Maxim's Restaurant-Cabaret, 108–110 West 38th Street, between Broadway and Sixth Avenue.

"That morning I went to a fellow who was playing the piano in the orchestra at Maxim's."[4]—Rudolph Valentino.

At Maxim's, a popular nightspot offering European cuisine, live music and dancing, Valentino worked as a "taxi-dancer," or dancer-for-hire, entertaining female guests without escorts. As part of the arrangement with Maxim's, he was given a room with a Victrola on one of the upper floors where he could give dancing lessons. A popular physical fitness club now utilizes the bottom floor where Valentino once danced with paying female guests.

Hell's Kitchen

Jean Acker's Apartment [site], 320 West 57th Street, Apt. 422, between Eighth and Ninth avenues.

At the time of Valentino's death, Jean Acker lived with her mother Margaret in a building that once stood on this site but has since been razed.

Chez-Fysher, West 55th Street (exact address unknown).

"Then Bonnie Glass opened the Chez-Fisher [*sic*] on 55th street, a very popular and exclusive place. I danced with her there until she married Ben Ali Haggin and retired."[5] — Rudolph Valentino.

Prior to this, Valentino danced with Bonnie Glass at the following establishments: *Delmonico's*, 56 Beaver Street; *Rector's*, Broadway at West 48th Street; *Winter Garden Theatre*, 1634 Broadway at 51st Street (1911–present); *Colonial Theatre* [site], 1887 Broadway at 62nd Street (built 1905, demolished in 1977 and replaced by condominiums); *Orpheum Theatre*, Rockwell and Fulton, Brooklyn; *Palace Theater*, 1564 Broadway at 47th Street (1913–present) and the *Boulevard Café*.

Photoplay Magazine, 25 West 45th Street, between Fifth and Sixth avenues.

Photoplay's New York headquarters were located in this building.

Polyclinic Hospital, 345 West 50th Street, between Eighth and Ninth Avenues.

New York's Polyclinic Hospital and Medical College, where Valentino died, played host to the ills of many prominent people over the years. Actress Mary Pickford, gangster Arnold Rothstein, singer Peggy Lee, and Marilyn Monroe are only a few of the famous folk who passed through these doors. After Valentino's death, the 334-bed hospital remained politically and financially strong, and continued to function for decades as a totally independent hospital. A merger with the French Hospital in 1972, however, paved the way for bankruptcy and its eventual closing in 1976, fifty years after Valentino's death. The former hospital building, while still standing, is now residential. The eighth-floor suite where Valentino died is most likely reconfigured. Still, the windows on the east side, though some are bricked up, remain visible.

St. Malachy's Catholic Church, 239 West 49th Street, between Eighth Avenue and Broadway.

Founded in 1903, St. Malachy's, today known as "the Actor's Chapel," still ministers to Broadway's Catholic actors. Valentino's New York funeral was held here, as was the 1929 marriage of Douglas Fairbanks, Jr., to Joan Crawford. For information on services, call (212) 489-1340.

Lower East Side

Angeline Celestina's Attempted Suicide, 34 Cherry Street, between Catherine and Market streets.

A documented suicide attempt took place here two months after Valentino's death. On Halloween morning, 1926, gunshots were heard coming from an apartment here on New York's lower east side. When neighbors rushed in they found twenty-year-old Angeline Celestina, mother of two small children, lying on the floor of her

The former Polyclinic Hospital as it looks today, now a residential building. Valentino died here in his suite on the eighth floor.

apartment surrounded by photographs of, and articles about, Valentino. With her husband and children away, Celestina told police that she wanted to be with the actor in death, so she drank iodine and took two shots at herself. She was arrested and charged with violating the Sullivan law (she had a .22-calibre pistol in her possession without a permit), and was taken to the prison ward of Beekman Street Hospital (117 Beekman Street). The physicians treating her were not certain if she would recover; however, word of her death was never reported, so it is assumed that she survived.[6]

Times Square / Midtown

Apollo Theatre, 219 West 42nd Street, between Seventh and Eighth avenues.

It was at the Apollo Theatre, on the evening before he took ill, that Valentino, along with George Ullman and Barclay Warburton, attended a performance of *George White's Scandals*. The Apollo Theatre, originally called the Bryant, was built in 1920 and was known exclusively for its run of *George White's Scandals*, which played annually from 1924 to 1931. Over the years, the Apollo has also shown motion pictures and in the late 1930s it served as a burlesque house run by Minsky's. In 1978 it once again hosted live theater, including runs of *On Golden Pond*, *Bent* and *The Fifth of July*. While the exterior of the Apollo remains, in 1996 it was gutted (along with the Lyric Theatre next door) in order to build the Ford Center for the Performing Arts, the Broadway home for the Livent Producing Organization. Significant architectural elements were saved from both the Apollo and the Lyric for future display in the new theater.

Astor Hotel [site], 1515 Broadway between 44th and 45th streets.

"And so I used to go into the Astor Hotel—up on the mezzanine floor—and write letters to her [his mother] on their beautiful stationery telling her how happy and successful I was."[7]—Rudolph Valentino.

So his mother wouldn't worry, Valentino would write her letters on stationery from the opulent Astor Hotel, which opened in 1904. At other times his correspondence would come from the Waldorf Astoria, which was then located on the present site of the Empire State Building. Virginia Mathis, mother of screenwriter June Mathis, died at the Astor on September 7, 1922. In 1967 the Astor Hotel was demolished and a 54-story office building built in its place. It is now the home of the Minskoff Theatre and MTV Studios.

Marion Benda's Apartment, 145 West 55th Street, between Sixth and Seventh avenues.

"I saw Rudy last at the door of my apartment house. It was about 3 o'clock in the morning. He said he was going home to bed."[8]—Marion Benda.

Ziegfeld Follies girl Marion Benda lived here during the time she dated Valentino. According to Benda, Valentino dropped her off at the front door early on the morning he took ill. Other witnesses claim that Valentino was actually a visitor to the apartment that night.

Central Park

"I was engaged as an apprentice landscape gardener in Central park until such time as I was able to pass the examination and take a regular position on the park staff."[9] — Rudolph Valentino.

Cornelius Bliss gave Valentino a letter of introduction to the Central Park commissioner; Rudy was given a job picking bugs off rose leaves. At one low point, without money for shelter, Valentino had to sleep in the park.

John de Saulles Residence, 2 West 57th Street, at the corner of Fifth Avenue.

Valentino first met John de Saulles here in 1916. At the time, de Saulles was involved in an affair with Valentino's dancing partner, Joan Sawyer, and used this address for their rendezvous.[10]

Famous Players–Lasky, 485 Fifth Avenue, between East 41st and East 42nd streets.

Famous Players–Lasky's corporate headquarters were located in this building when Valentino was under contract to the studio. It is directly across the street from the New York Public Library.

Forty-third Street and Broadway Apartment [site] (exact address unknown).

"It was a cubby-hole in which brooms and mops were kept. There was an iron sink. I wiped my hands on newspapers. It was too luxurious for me, I couldn't afford to keep it."[11] — Rudolph Valentino.

Valentino paid two dollars a week for a skylight room in a boarding house near this intersection in the middle of Times Square.

Giolito's [site], 108–110 West 49th Street, between Sixth and Seventh avenues.

"My friend had told me of an Italian place, Giolitto's, in West 49th street, where I could probably obtain rooms."[12] — Rudolph Valentino.

Valentino's first residence in New York when he arrived in December 1913 was originally on this site. McGraw-Hill Companies publishers now have their headquarters here.

H & H Automat, 545 Fifth Avenue at 45th Street.

"On the great days when I was blessed with a job I would go to the place of 'The Hungry and Homeless'— the H & H Automat."[13] — Rudolph Valentino.

The H's in H & H Automat were actually the initials of the restaurant's founders, Joseph Horn and Frank Hardart. Other locations included those at 106 West 50th Street (now Rockefeller Center), 104 West 57th Street, and the last to survive, 200 East 42nd Street (closed in 1991).

Anabel Henderson's Residence [site], 24 West 59th Street (Central Park South), between Fifth and Sixth avenues.

"At that time mother had an apartment next to the Plaza Hotel."[14] — Anabel Henderson.

In 1941 a woman named Anabel Henderson came forward with a five-part article about her relationship with Rudolph Valentino. Entitled "I Was Valentino's Mystery Woman," it told of her remarkable twelve-year, on-and-off relationship with the "Great Lover." When they first met in 1914, Anabel Henderson lived here with her mother and stepfather, and reportedly entertained Valentino in their apartment. Ironically, the building where they lived is the only one on this upscale block of hotels and townhouses that has been razed.

King Cole Room, Knickerbocker Hotel, 42nd Street and Broadway.

"When I saw Jean Acker in disguise, I didn't know whether to commit suicide or sing 'Baby Shoes.'"[15] — Texas Guinan.

The King Cole room, located in the Knickerbocker Hotel, was one of Texas Guinan's early speakeasies. It was here that Valentino and Natacha had an unusual run-in with the ex–Mrs. Valentino, Jean Acker. This particular evening, Valentino was the guest of honor at one of Guinan's "movie nights." Guests included the Barrymores, Ivor Novello, and Peggy Hopkins Joyce, who paid one hundred dollars for a table near the Valentinos. At Peggy's table was a mysterious woman introduced as the Countess of Itch, with spiked hair and a multitude of pearls. As the Valentinos danced, the Countess loudly began to rattle her plates, making all sorts of noise and taking the attention away from the guest of honor. When it suddenly dawned on Texas Guinan that the alleged Countess was actually Jean Acker, she roared with laughter — as did Valentino. The painting of "Old King Cole," which decorated the room for years, now hangs in one of the smaller bars of the St. Regis Hotel.

Knickerbocker Hotel, 152 West 42nd Street at Broadway.

Valentino met singer Enrico Caruso in 1916 while the singer was living here, and later tangoed on the hotel's dance floor with actress Mae Murray. The martini was allegedly perfected in the Knickerbocker's bar in 1912. In 1921 the hotel was closed and converted into office space, at one time serving as the headquarters for *Newsweek* magazine. In 1980 it was again converted, this time into residential lofts. Previously, an entrance from the subway station led directly up to the hotel. The entrance is no longer open to the public, but the brass sign above it still reads "Knickerbocker." Today the building is known as 6 Times Square.

Mark Strand Theater [site], 1585 Broadway at West 47th Street.

This 3,500-seat movie palace designed by Thomas W. Lamb opened in 1914. Valentino made personal appearances at this theater for the premieres of *The Eagle* (1925) and *The Son of the Sheik* (1926), and on both occasions adoring fans mobbed the actor. In the 1970s, even though the Strand's noble three-story facade of Corinthian pilasters remained intact, the theater's interior was divided and renamed the RKO Warner Twin. The former Mark Strand Theater was demolished in 1981, and the site is now headquarters for Morgan Stanley.

June Mathis' Death [site], Forty-eighth Street Theatre, 157 West 48th Street, between Sixth and Seventh avenues.

"Oh Mother, I'm dying."[16] — the last words of June Mathis to her grandmother, Emily Hawkes.

Screenwriter June Mathis died in the arms of her grandmother in the alley behind the Forty-eighth Street Theatre that once stood on this spot. On August 23, 1955, a water tower collapsed and fell through the roof of the theatre, completely destroying it. Attempts to reconstruct the building proved unsuccessful, and a parking structure now occupies the site, which is next to Rudy's Music Shop.

Persian Garden, Winter Garden Theatre Building, 1634 Broadway at West 50th Street.

Valentino danced with Joan Sawyer at the Persian Garden after Bonnie Glass' retirement. He also appeared with Sawyer at the *Woodmansten Inn* (Pelham Parkway) and Williamsbridge Road (in the Bronx).

The Playground, 201 West 52nd Street, between Broadway and Seventh Avenue.

Popular nightclub hostess Texas Guinan set up her brother Tommy in this establishment located on the second and third floors. It was here in July 1926 that Valentino met the Egyptian fakir Rahmen Bey, who convinced the actor to allow him to push a hat pin through his arm without pain or drawing blood. The space is now above Rosie O'Grady's Bar.

Rector's [site], Broadway and 48th Street.

"Accordingly, after getting my apartment, I went to Rector's for lunch, and after partaking of the entire menu I started back to the boat to get my trunks."[17] — Rudolph Valentino.

Valentino had his first meal in New York at Rector's, a place to buy lobster and rub shoulders with other pleasure seekers. Later, he reportedly waited tables here and at one time danced with Bonnie Glass.

The 300 Club [site], 151 West 54th Street, between Sixth and Seventh avenues.

Texas Guinan's new speakeasy opened here in January 1926. The following July, Valentino was seen escorting his ex-wife, Jean Acker, to the 300 Club, prompting rumors of a reconciliation. A favorite nightspot of Valentino's, he partied here several times with Ziegfeld Follies girl Marion Benda, who claimed that she came here with the actor the evening before he became ill. However, no one came forward to verify her story. The original building has been razed, and the site is now the Rihga Royal Hotel.

Georgia Thym's Residence, 909 Seventh Avenue, between 57th and 58th streets.

On September 5, 1916, Valentino was arrested for false witness and "instigation to prostitution" in a raid of a woman suspected of operating a brothel on the premises. It is unclear why Valentino was here that evening, but the police assumed that he worked for Mrs. Thym (the true reason for Rudy's presence, whether as an employee or to secure the services of a prostitute, will probably never be known). The building is directly across the street from Carnegie Hall.

United Artists Corporation, 729 Seventh Avenue, southeast corner of West 49th Street.

The corporate headquarters for United Artists was located in this building. Valentino held a news conference here on July 20, 1926, to publicly challenge the *Chicago Tribune* editorial writer who called him a "Pink Powder Puff."

West 57th Street Residence, 264 West 57th Street, between Eighth Avenue and Broadway.

Valentino lived here in 1916 during the John and Bianca de Saulle divorce trial.[18]

Upper East Side

The Colony [site], 667 Madison Avenue at East 61st Street.

The Colony, at one time one of New York's most popular and expensive restaurants, was also Valentino's favorite. The actor made amends with Paramount mogul Adolf Zukor over lunch at the Colony two weeks before his death. It was also here that Valentino had his last meal before becoming ill.

Harbor Sanatorium, 677 Madison Avenue, between 61st and 62nd streets.

Valentino's friend and party host, Barclay Warburton, Jr., had a mystery operation here just days after Valentino took ill. Dr. Paul Durham, who was the first doctor to examine Valentino, performed the procedure. The nature of Warburton's operation was never revealed, and many speculated that it was connected to Valentino's illness.

Barclay Warburton's Residence, 925 Park Avenue, at East 80th Street.

"He now occupies a bachelor apartment full of soft lights, low couches and luxury."[19]—*New York Daily News*.

It was here that the infamous all-night party was held when Valentino first took ill. A few days later, Warburton told reporters that there was no party, but his claims were refuted by almost everyone who attended the 'phantom' soirée.

Upper West Side

Frank E. Campbell's Funeral Church [site], 1970 Broadway at West 66th Street.

When Frank E. Campbell took over this building on Broadway in 1915, he dedicated it to creating "a service so sublimely beautiful, in an atmosphere of such complete harmony, as to alleviate the sorrow of parting."[20] Unfortunately, this so-called atmosphere of harmony did not manifest itself at Valentino's viewing held here eleven years later. The mortuary remained at this site until 1938, when it moved to its present location at 1076 Madison Avenue at 81st Street. Many of the entertainers and people of note who have made Campbell's their last curtain call include: Florence LaBadie (1917), Anna Held (1918), Vernon Castle (1918), F. W. Woolworth (1919), Oscar Hammerstein (1919), Olive Thomas (1920), Enrico Caruso (1921), June Mathis (1927), Jeanne Eagels (1929), Texas Guinan (1933), Fatty Arbuckle (1933), Frank Campbell (1934), Montgomery Clift (1966), Dorothy Parker (1967), Judy Garland (1969), Igor Stravinsky (1971), Joan Crawford (1977), John Lennon (1980), Mae West (1980), Ayn Rand (1982), Jack Dempsey (1983), Ethel Merman (1984), James Cagney (1986), Rita Hayworth (1987), Billy Martin (1989), Vladimir Horowitz (1989), Aileen Pringle (1989), Jim Henson (1990), Jackie Kennedy Onassis (1994), Notorius B.I.G. (1997), Douglas Fairbanks, Jr. (2000), Aaliyah (2001), Celia Cruz (2003), and Dorothy Louden (2003). The original building on Broadway where Valentino's body lay in state was demolished, and a commercial building now occupies the site.

Hotel des Artistes, 1 West 67th Street, between Central Park West and Columbus Avenue.

Built in 1913, this stately mass of luxury co-ops was originally designed to house bohemians who had moved beyond their romantic garret stage. While Valentino waited for his divorce to become final from Jean Acker, he and his roommate, Frank Menillo,[21] stayed here. Natacha shared a hotel apartment further down the block with her Aunt Teresa.

Barclay Warburton's apartment building at 925 Park Avenue. It was at a party here that Valentino first became ill.

Frank E. Campbell's Funeral Church, where crowds wait to view Valentino's body.

New York's Century Theatre [site], Central Park West at 62nd Street.

In 1923, just prior to their Mineralava tour, Valentino and Natacha danced the Tango at a benefit for the Actors Fund at New York's Century Theatre (built 1909, demolished 1930).

Natacha Rambova's Apartment, 9 West 81st Street, between Columbus Avenue and Central Park West.

Natacha and her Aunt Teresa took an apartment here shortly before traveling to France and officially separating from Valentino. Today the numbers range from 7 to 11, and there is no number 9. It's possible the building was renumbered at some point. It is across the street from the American Museum of Natural History.

Washington Square / SoHo

Mills Hotel, 160 Bleecker Street, between Sullivan and Thompson streets.

"I went to the Mills hotel and got a room for twelve cents. For one night only. The next night I didn't have twelve cents."[22]—Rudolph Valentino.

At one of his lowest points, Valentino pawned whatever he could and got a room at the Mills Hotel (erected in 1896), a hostel for men with little money. The Mills offered 1,500 tiny rooms at affordable rates. The establishment operates today just as it did in Valentino's time.

Beyond Manhattan

Astoria Studios, 34–12 36th Street, between 34th and 35th avenues, Astoria.

More than 150 films were produced by Famous Players–Lasky at the Astoria Studios between its 1920 opening and 1932, when the studio moved all operations back to the west coast. Valentino filmed *Monsieur Beaucaire* and *A Sainted Devil* entirely at the Astoria Studios. During World War II the army made training films there. Today it is known as Kaufman Astoria Studios, and Stage E, where *The Cosby Show* was taped in the 1980s, is the largest soundstage in the United States east of Hollywood.

The Bronx Zoo, Fordham Road and Bronx River Parkway, the Bronx.

"One Sunday morning as we were walking through the zoo in Bronx park, I halted squarely in front of the monkey cage and declared I'd never move another step until Alex taught me to tango."[23] — Rudolph Valentino.

Valentino received his first tango lesson from his friend, Count Alex Salm of Austria, here at the historic Bronx Zoo, which first opened its gates in 1899.

An eighteen-year-old Valentino arrived at Ellis Island on the *S. S. Cleveland* on December 23, 1913.

Ellis Island, New York Harbor.

Ellis Island opened in 1892 — and for the next fifty years more than twelve million people came through it on their way into the United States. Valentino first set foot on American soil here, when he arrived on December 23, 1913, on the *S. S. Cleveland*.

Strand Theater, 647 Fulton Street, between Rockwell and Ashland Place, Brooklyn.

Valentino made his last public appearance at this downtown Brooklyn theater for the premiere of *The Son of the Sheik* in August 1926. During his speech to the audience, he spoke lovingly of costar Agnes Ayres and her willingness to take a small part in the film, in addition to her being a devoted mother. Built in 1919, the former Strand Theater is now the headquarters of the Brooklyn Information and Culture Center (BRIC), an organization dedicated to the visual and performing arts.

TOUR 2

Hollywood

Jean Acker Residence, 1954 Pinehurst Road, north of Bonita Terrace.

The 1920 Los Angeles City Directory lists Jean Acker as living here. Acker most likely moved here from the Hollywood Hotel after her marriage to Valentino.

Jean Acker and Grace Darmond's Residence, 1337 Orange Drive, west side between De Longpre and Fountain avenues.

Jean Acker and her lover, actress Grace Darmond, lived together here during the time that Acker was married to Valentino—including the divorce trial period. Remarkably, the small bungalow has escaped the wrecking ball and still stands, surrounded by nondescript apartment buildings, hidden behind a multitude of lush shrubbery.

Acker–Valentino Marriage [site], 5051 Hollywood Boulevard, northwest corner at Mariposa Avenue.

"The Karger's were giving a farewell party that evening to Richard Rowland, president of Metro, who was returning to New York. Mr. Karger suggested that we procure our license and turn the party into a wedding."[1]—Rudolph Valentino.

Valentino and Jean Acker were married on November 5, 1919, in the house that once stood on this location. When Metro executive Maxwell Karger heard of the couple's plans to get married, he suggested that the nuptials take place at a party being held in honor of Metro president Richard A. Rowland at the home of Joseph Engel, the studio's treasurer. After saying their "I do's," the newlyweds had supper with the guests before jumping in Jean's car and making the ten-minute trip down the boulevard to the Hollywood Hotel where Acker had a room. The Engel house was razed in the late 1920s, and a small neighborhood market now occupies the site.

Marion Benda's Suicide, 1825 North Wilcox Avenue, west side between Franklin Avenue and Yucca Street.

Marion Benda, a former Ziegfeld Follies girl and self-proclaimed Lady in Black, who dated Valentino two weeks before his death, made several attempts at suicide over the years. The first recorded attempt occurred in November 1945 when Benda's cousin, Perry Combs, found the ex-chorine unconscious in her Santa Monica home (1425 Ocean Front). Benda's neighbor at the time told the press that the former show girl had secretly married Valentino and had two children by him. "One is a girl, now about 20," the neighbor revealed, "living with Valentino's sister in London now and the younger is an 18 year old boy who served with the Italian army." Benda's cousin, Perry Combs, confirmed the marriage, saying that it remained a secret because of concern it would hurt Valentino's appeal at the time. Combs revealed another "secret" when he admitted that Benda was indeed the original Lady in Black, the mysterious veiled woman that visited Valentino's crypt each year.

Valentino's first wife, Jean Acker, during her career as an extra in films, circa 1930s.

Alberto Valentino told reporters it would be very farfetched to assume that his brother, who was well know to everyone, could have secretly married in 1925, particularly since he still wasn't divorced from his second wife, Natacha Rambova. When asked, George Ullman admitted that Rudy dated Marion from time to time, but he was sure there was no marriage. "As for her having a child by Rudy," Ullman said, "there were 35 women who advanced that claim after he died."[2]

Less than six months later, Benda once again attempted suicide, taking forty sleeping pills at the Regent Hotel (6162 Hollywood Boulevard) in Hollywood. Then in November 1951, Benda was arrested and taken to the Lincoln Heights Jail on a narcotics charge, once again for taking an overdose of sleeping pills. Just a week later, the former Ziegfeld Follies girl made one more attempt to take her life — this one, however, proved successful. On November 30, 1951, Marion Benda committed suicide in her apartment in this building by ingesting barbiturates. Benda was laid to rest in an unmarked grave at Santa Monica's Woodlawn Cemetery.

Viola Dana's Residence [site], 7280 Hillside Avenue, on southeast corner of Fuller Avenue.

> "What are you doing for Christmas?" Dana asked.
> "Well, nothing," Rudy replied.
> "Have you any place to go?"
> "Well, no I don't."
> "You sure do. You're going to come home with me. This is our big night."[3]

For Christmas 1919, Valentino had nowhere to celebrate, so actress Viola Dana invited him to her house. To make him feel welcome, she dressed him as Santa Claus in a red cape and cotton beard and had him give out the presents. The house where this happened was razed long ago to make way for an apartment building.

Grace Darmond's Apartment [site], 7316 Franklin Avenue, south side between Vista and Camino Palmero streets.

> "He [Valentino] called at the house and asked for his wife [Acker] and when I told him she was upstairs, he pushed me aside and was very angry."[4] — Alice Johnson, mother of Grace Darmond.

During Valentino's divorce trial, it was revealed that Jean Acker was staying at Grace Darmond's apartment in a building owned by Darmond's mother. Frustrated at not being able to communicate with his wife, Valentino forced his way into Darmond's apartment and confronted Jean. A shouting match followed, ending with Valentino striking her on the face and knocking her to the floor. Valentino begged for her forgiveness and escorted her to the lobby, where she told him she would seek a Reno divorce. A newer apartment building is now on this site.

De Longpre Park, south side of De Longpre Avenue between Cherokee Avenue and June Street.

Developed in 1924 for $66,000, De Longpre Park is named after painter Paul De Longpre, whose celebrated home at Hollywood Boulevard and Cahuenga Avenue was the first tourist attraction in Hollywood. On May 5, 1930 (Valentino's 35th birthday), at twelve o'clock in De Longpre Park, actress Dolores del Rio drew back a velvet curtain to reveal the bronze figure of a man with face uplifted. The statue, entitled "Aspiration," was designed by sculptor Roger Noble Burham and was paid for with contributions from fans and admirers. The inscription reads: "Erected in the Memory of Rudolph Valentino 1895–1926. Presented by his friends and admirers from every walk of life — in all parts of the world, in appreciation of the happiness brought to them by his cinema portrayals."

A week later, neighbors, who insisted that they were not consulted on the matter (and that the only statue in the park should be of De Longpre himself), made an official protest. Regardless, nothing came of the matter and the statue remained. No more was heard of the statue until a few years later when a woman named Zunilda Mancini came forward, claiming to have donated $6,900 towards the statue, which

The statue "Aspiration," dedicated to Valentino's memory, still stands in De Longpre Park.

actually cost only $1,500. She sued George Ullman in court and was awarded the difference of $5,400.

The year after the unveiling, a fourteen-year-old girl was found on a bench near the statue. Police said she had been chloroformed and most likely sexually assaulted. She died at Hollywood Hospital without regaining consciousness. Three years later, on November 1, 1934, the caretaker of the park found the lifeless body of thirty-year-old Ann Johnston in a rest room just a few feet away from "Aspiration." Next to her was an empty poison bottle. Since she left no note, it remained unclear whether her suicide was related to Valentino or, as the police surmised, was due to a nervous breakdown she recently suffered.

The statue has been the object of vandalism several times over the years. On February 2, 1952, it was found broken from its base and lying on the park lawn. Taken to the city service yard for repairs, it was not returned for nearly twenty years. In July 1979 a bronze bust of Valentino, sculpted by Richard Ellis and paid for from the estate of one of his fans, was mounted on a tall, white pedestal several feet from "Aspiration." Shortly afterward a group of concerned neighbors initiated a campaign to revamp the neglected park. To this day, "Aspiration" is the only monument ever erected to honor an actor in Hollywood. (*Warning*: De Longpre Park is located in a rather shabby part of town, surrounded by a metal fence and locked up at night. Please take reasonable precautions when visiting.)

Famous Players–Lasky Studios [site], 1500 North Vine Street, northeast corner at Sunset Boulevard.

The studio where Valentino made many of his films, including *The Sheik* (1921), *Beyond the Rocks* (1922), and *Blood and Sand* (1922), was located on the northeast

Valentino imitator Rudolph Florentino in his apartment-shrine to the Sheik above the old Apollo Theater.

corner of Sunset Boulevard and Vine Street, stretching east to El Centro Avenue and north to Selma. In June 1926, shortly before Valentino's death, the studio moved to its present location on Melrose Avenue and became Paramount. The studio buildings were demolished (with the exception of the original barn, which was moved to the new lot) sometime in the 1930s and replaced with NBC Studios (built 1938, razed 1964) and the Hollywood Palladium. A bank now stands on the corner where Mary Pickford's dressing room once stood. Colorful mosaic images on the bank's marble facade portray such stars as Pickford, Fairbanks and, of course, Rudolph Valentino.

Rudolph Florentino Apartment [site], Apollo Theater, 5546½ Hollywood Boulevard.

Rudolph Florentino, nee Dominick Giordano, was considered, after the Lady in Black, one of Valentino's most ardent admirers. Here in his apartment above the Apollo Theater Florentino transformed the interior into a scene from Valentino's film *The Sheik*. Complete with a full-size Arab tent, sand on the floor, silken divans, and photographs of his idol on the walls, Florentino held court for a bevy of Valentino admirers. Employed as a brass welder, Florentino claimed to be, at different times, a dancer and film extra, Valentino's stuntman in *The Son of the Sheik*, and a former caretaker of Falcon Lair. Valentino's gaucho hat from *The Four Horsemen* and a number of other sacred relics were scattered around the tent apartment.

In May 1953, Florentino made the front pages of several newspapers when he threatened to kill himself here. When police arrived at the apartment, a .32 revolver and a sword cane were at his side; both were confiscated. He then told police that he really didn't intend to kill himself, but was in love with a married woman. "I taught her how to tango, like Valentino," he said. "We had a quarrel, and I wanted to scare her."[5]

A few years later, Florentino opened his apartment to the public as the Valentino Memorial Shrine. Silent film star James Kirkwood spoke to the press as a bevy of middle-aged slave girls lounged in pantaloons beneath a life-size portrait of Valentino. Florentino modeled several authentic costumes, in addition to displaying Valentino's engraved cigarette case, an engraved ring and various costumes worn by the Great Lover. The exhibit was well received, though it attracted mostly elderly women. The Apollo Theater and the apartment where Florentino had his shrine have since been demolished — the only building on that block to suffer such a fate. Rudolph Florentino died on December 8, 1978, at the age of seventy-five.

Formosa Apartments [site], 7139 Hollywood Boulevard, north side between Formosa and La Brea Avenues.

Valentino put down a deposit on an apartment at the Formosa when he married Jean Acker in 1919; but that, of course, fell through. The following year he shared an apartment here with his friend Paul Ivano. The Formosa was demolished decades ago, and a modern apartment building now occupies the site.

Hall of Arts Studio [site], 1753 Highland Avenue, west side at Yucca Street.

It was here (where Yucca Street meets Highland) that Valentino's personal effects were auctioned off in December 1926. The Hollywood Renaissance Hotel, part of the new Hollywood and Highland complex, now occupies the site.

Hollywood Athletic Club, 6525 Sunset Boulevard, north side between Schrader Boulevard and Wilcox Avenue.

Built in 1923, the Hollywood Athletic Club's penthouse was reportedly used by Valentino for romantic trysts.

Hollywood Forever Cemetery, 6000 Santa Monica Boulevard, south side between Gower Street and Van Ness Avenue.

Founded in 1899, the former Hollywood Memorial Park Cemetery is the final resting place of Rudolph Valentino. It is also the site of the annual Rudolph Valentino

Two teenagers pay their respects at the 25th anniversary of Valentino's death at his crypt at Hollywood Cemetery.

Memorial service held each year on August 23 at 12:10 P.M., the time of his death in New York.

Many of Valentino's costars, family and friends interred at the cemetery include: Kathleen Kirkham and Vera Sisson from *The Married Virgin* (1918); Duncan Mansfield (editor) from *The Homebreaker* (1919); Sidney Franklin and Harry Dunkinson from *A Rogue's Romance* (1919); Eunice Woodruff from *Virtuous Sinners* (1919); Tony Gaudio (cinematographer) from *An Adventuress* (1920); Maxwell Kargar (producer and best man at his wedding to Jean Acker) from *The Cheater* (1920); Virginia Rappé from *An Adventuress* (1920); Allen Holubar (director) and Dorothy Phillips from *Once to Every Woman* (1920); Edward J. Connelly, Mark Fenton, June Mathis, Josef Swickard and John St. Polis from *The Four Horsemen of the Apocalypse* (1921); William Orlamond from *Camille* (1921); Carl Gerard and Rhea Haines from *Uncharted Seas* (1921); Ralph Lewis and Rolfe Sedan from *The Conquering Power* (1921); Agnes Ayres, Jesse L. Lasky and Adolphe Menjou from *The Sheik* (1921); Gertrude Astor from *Beyond the Rocks* (1922); Walter Long from *Blood and Sand* (1922); Wanda Hawley from *The Young Rajah* (1922); Bebe Daniels and Flora Finch from *Monsieur Beaucaire* (1924); Spottiswood Aitken and Carrie Clark Ward from *The Eagle* (1925); Adrian (costume designer), George Barnes (cinematographer), Erwin Connelly and Karl Dane from *The Son of the Sheik* (1926); and Alberto (brother) and Ada Valentino.

Hollywood High School Mural, southeast corner of Orange Street and Hawthorn Avenue.

Located on the west side of Hollywood High School (1521 North Highland Avenue) is a large mural of Valentino in profile as *The Sheik* in full headdress blowing in the wind. Until the 1930s, the Hollywood High School athletic teams were known as *The Crimson* (in emulation of Harvard). It was around this time that a newspaper journalist wrote an article about one of the school's teams and nicknamed them *The Sheiks* after "the brave warrior-lover hero in the Rodolf [*sic*] Valentino film classic of the 1920s." After the article was printed, the school adopted the name, and they have remained "the Sheiks of Hollywood High" ever since. To view the mural, travel south on Orange Street from Hollywood Boulevard. The mural is just past Hawthorn Avenue and overlooks the school's football field.

Hollywood Hotel [site], northwest corner of Hollywood Boulevard and Highland Avenue.

Built in 1905, the Hollywood Hotel is where Jean Acker locked Valentino out of his honeymoon suite on their wedding night in 1919. After the marriage ceremony, Valentino and Acker returned to the hotel and danced in the ballroom until the early morning hours. When it came time to retire, the bride, for whatever reason, had a sudden change of heart. As they were about to enter her room (Room 264), Jean suddenly bolted past Rudy and slammed the door in his face. Thinking his bride was being playful, Rudy laughed and knocked on the door. Inside, he could hear Jean crying and pleading for him to go away. Puzzled at first, Rudy became angry and began pounding on the door, but to no avail. Frustrated, he soon gave up and returned to his rented room at a downtown boarding house.

Another version of the story has the night clerk of the Hollywood Hotel questioning whether they were really married and refusing to let Rudy into his honeymoon chamber. According to reports, Jean Acker returned to the Hollywood Hotel in the early fifties and asked to see her old room, looked at it momentarily, and left without a word.[6]

On the ceiling of the Hollywood Hotel's old-fashioned dining room were actor's names on gold stars, among them Valentino, Fairbanks, and Nazimova, all of whom supped there regularly. Through the years tales have abounded that Valentino's bed was still in use at the hotel. Whenever a lady guest complained that she did not sleep comfortably, the manager would invariably tell her, "You probably slept in Valentino's bed."[7] The hotel was demolished in 1956, and for more than forty years a characterless high-rise and parking lot were located on this corner. In 2001 the new Hollywood and Highland complex was completed on the site, including the Kodak Theater, the new home of the Academy Awards ceremonies.

Hollywood Knickerbocker Hotel, 1714 North Ivar Avenue, east side between Yucca Street and Hollywood Boulevard.

Built in 1923, the Knickerbocker Hotel was originally two separate apartment buildings until 1929, when the middle section was added, connecting the two structures. Later it would become a hotel. While it is possible that Valentino visited this building during his lifetime, the association to the actor is purely a supernatural one. Valentino's ghost reportedly has been seen here on various occasions walking through the walls of what was at one time the hotel's bar, but most recently housed the "All Star Cafe."[8] In 2002 the Cafe lost its lease, and the hotel once again took over management. It's not known if Valentino's ghost continues to make personal appearances for the hotel's residents.

Paul Ivano's Residence [site], 6820 Whitley Terrace, Whitley Heights.

Valentino's friend, Paul Ivano, lived here in 1921 and "officially" shared the house with the actor while Natacha was living at their new residence on Wedgewood Place.[9] Ivano's house suffered the same fate as Villa Valentino, and was razed when the Hollywood Freeway was built in 1951. The only way to reach the site is to take Whitley Terrace (a short dead end street) from Cahuenga Boulevard. In 1926, Ivano was living at 1000 N. Larrabee Street in West Hollywood.

W. W. Kerrigan's Residence, 2050 Ivar Avenue, north of Franklin Avenue.

William Wallace Kerrigan, Valentino's first manager, was the twin brother of actor J. Warren Kerrigan. Valentino would often visit this home, taking Kerrigan's young daughter Virginia for rides in his car. When the nine-year-old died of burns she received at a neighbor's house on the day after Christmas in 1924[10], Valentino was devastated. He continued to lay flowers at her Hollywood Cemetery crypt (number 1399) until his death two years later.

Lasky–De Mille Barn, 2100 Highland Avenue (across from the Hollywood Bowl).

The Lasky–De Mille Barn is presently home to the Hollywood Heritage Museum. At one time this simple wood-frame structure was part of Famous Players–Lasky's studio, and stood on the southeast corner of Vine Street and Selma Avenue. Built in 1895, the barn was where *The Squaw Man* (1914), the first full-length motion picture filmed in Hollywood by Cecil B. De Mille, was shot. Valentino would certainly have used this building at different times during his tenure at the studio. For information on visiting the barn and museum, call (323) 874-2276 or (323) 874-4005.

Lasky Ranch [site], 6300 Forest Lawn Drive.

In 1912 Universal Studios owned what was then called Providencia Ranch before their move to Universal City. D. W. Griffith filmed the battle scenes for *The Birth of a Nation* here in 1914. On August 4, 1918, Famous Players–Lasky leased the 1,000-acre property, renaming it the Lasky Ranch. Valentino filmed the exterior scenes for *Blood and Sand* here, and portions of his other films for the studio. The former Lasky Ranch is now Forest Lawn-Hollywood Hills Cemetery, located across the Los Angeles River from Warner Bros. Studios. Many of the stars that once worked at the Ranch are now buried here.

Metro Studios [site], 6300 Romaine Street, between Cole Avenue and Lillian Way.

At one time Metro Studios covered five city blocks on both sides of Cahuenga Boulevard south of Romaine Street. Standing outdoor sets were located on the east side of Cahuenga, while studio buildings occupied the west side. This is where Valentino made his first major hit, *The Four Horsemen of the Apocalypse* (1921), and it is also where he first met Natacha Rambova. Abandoned after the merger with Goldwyn Pictures and Louis B. Mayer in 1924, the studio stood empty and in ruins until finally being razed in the 1930s. No trace of the old studio remains today. The west side of the street is now a huge parking lot, while industrial buildings (including several film rental studios) occupy the land on the east.

Montmartre Cafe, 6757 Hollywood Boulevard, north side between Highland and Las Palmas avenues.

A one-time popular nightclub and restaurant, the Montmarte Cafe opened on the second floor of this building in 1923. Lunchtime dances were popular with Charleston aficionados, including then-budding actress Joan Crawford. Valentino and Pola Negri reportedly danced the tango here on many occasions, as did Chaplin, Marion Davies, and other film stars. While performing here, Bing Crosby met his first wife, Dixie Lee. The building still stands, but the second floor, where Hollywood elite danced the night away, has been empty for years. The doorway on the right opens to the stairway that once took Valentino and other patrons to the Montmartre Cafe.

Morgan Place Residence [site], 1825 Gramercy Place, west side between Hollywood Boulevard and Franklin Avenue.

"At the time I was living in Morgan Place in Hollywood, directly opposite Wally Reid's home. Wally and I used to have hot battles. He declared that the cut-out of my car woke him up every Sunday morning, and I claimed that his darned saxophone kept me from going to sleep. Our argument developed into a neighborhood joke."[11]— Rudolph Valentino.

Sometime in the 1930s, the name of this street was changed from Morgan Place to Gramercy Place. Valentino lived here during the winter of 1918-19 while recovering from the Spanish influenza. The building where he lived has been demolished and replaced by a nondescript apartment complex, and the same has happened to Reid's home (1822 Morgan Place) across the street. While many of the original buildings on the block are gone, a few from the era still remain, giving an idea of what the old neighborhood was like.

Paramount Studios, 5555 Melrose Avenue, between Gower and Van Ness avenues.

Originally built by producer Robert Brunton, this rental lot became United Studios in the early 1920s. Valentino made his film *Cobra* here in 1925, and the following year Famous Players–Lasky (now Paramount) bought the property. It remains there to this day. Valentino's ghost reportedly haunts the costume department and has been seen walking through the wall shared by Hollywood Forever Cemetery at the Lemon Grove Gate.

Natacha Rambova's Bungalow, 6612 Sunset Boulevard, south side between Cherokee Avenue and Seward Street.

"Rudy would come out and do all sorts of handy jobs about the house for me. He'd do electric wiring and he'd make little perfume tables and smoking stands and hang all of my prints and pictures."[12] — Natacha Rambova.

Natacha rented this one-bedroom bungalow, and shared it with Valentino and Paul Ivano. One night, according to Ivano, Valentino woke him — panic-stricken, completely nude, and sporting an erection. Natacha had passed out during lovemaking, and Valentino was sure that he had killed her. Ivano revived her by sponging her face with water. It was also here that the trio devised a scheme to make extra money by peddling signed autograph pictures of Valentino to his adoring fans. At one point, Natacha bought a lion cub that they named Zela, who lived in the bungalow along with an assortment of other animals. One night Zela bit the leg of an intruder that turned out to be a private detective hired by Jean Acker. Though converted into offices, the original bungalow still survives.

Natacha Rambova and Theodore Kosloff's Residence [site], 1519 Poinsettia Place, west side between Sunset Boulevard and Hawthorn Avenue.

In 1919 Natacha shared a house at this location with her former dance partner, Theodore Kosloff. At the time, Natacha was teaching at Kosloff's Imperial Russian Ballet School (839 S. Grand Street). A Ralph's grocery store is now on this site.

The Ritz, Inc. [site], 1643 North Highland Avenue, west side between Hollywood Boulevard and Hawthorn Avenue.

In 1924 Valentino bought the Ritz, a cleaning and dyeing shop on Highland Avenue. Unfortunately, the business was not successful, and in March 1927 George Ullman sold it on behalf of the estate. At some point the entire block was demolished; it is now a parking lot.

Rudolph Valentino Productions, 6606 Sunset Boulevard, south side between Cherokee Avenue and Seward Street.

In the late 1920s, Valentino's manager, S. George Ullman, had offices on the second floor of this building, and also based the actor's production company here. The structure still stands, and is located next door to Natacha Rambova's bungalow. In the early 1930s the production offices were located at United Artist Studios, 7211 Santa Monica Boulevard.

Sunset Boulevard Apartment [site], 7369 Sunset Boulevard, north side between Vista Street and Martel Avenue.

"Every day when I returned to my little room on Sunset Boulevard I would run the last block, so anxious was I to see if a letter awaited me."[13] — Rudolph Valentino.

Valentino was living here when he received news of his mother's death (she died on January 18, 1918).[14] A restaurant and a strip mall now stand on the site.

Valentino Building, 716 North Valentino Place, between Melrose Avenue and Marathon Street.

Over the years, stories have claimed that Valentino owned this Tudor-style building now used as offices by Paramount. Still others have said that he wooed Jean Acker in an apartment — or had an office — here while he worked at Paramount (the actor never worked for the studio when it was at this location). In 1979 the short block in front of the building was changed from Irving Boulevard to Valentino Place, in honor of the actor.

This is another spot where Valentino's ghost has reportedly been seen. One night an unidentified woman was falling asleep when she sensed something or someone sitting on the edge of her bed. Though terrified, the woman slowly opened her eyes and saw next to her the ghost of Rudolph Valentino, and immediately passed out. In 1990 Paramount bought the building and converted it into offices. The short stretch of Valentino Place and the Valentino Building has been engulfed by the studio's recent expansion and are no longer accessible by the public.

Villa Valentino [site], 6776 Wedgewood Place, Whitley Heights.

Built in 1922, this was the site of the home Valentino shared with Natacha Rambova in upscale Whitley Heights just north of Hollywood. The house remained in the actor's estate for several years after his death, being occasionally rented out. As early as 1934 the house stood empty and was declared unsafe. Bank of America, the administrator of Valentino's estate at the time, disclosed that the patio was weakened by dry rot, and the gently sloping back lawn and once flowering terraced gardens were overgrown with tall grass. Because of pending litigation over an income tax lien on the estate, the bank refused to make extensive improvements on the property.

Weird tales of haunted corridors and nocturnal visits by the departed actor were vigorously reported by former tenants and the estate administrator. Spiritualists held séances under the shadowy outline of the hillside building in an effort to evoke Valentino's spirit.

In 1951 the state of California paid the last owner $90,000 and condemned Villa

Valentino poses with his car in front of Villa Valentino, which once stood in stately Whitley Heights. The house was razed in 1951 to make way for the Hollywood Freeway.

Valentino, intending to demolish it to make way for the Hollywood Freeway. However, by the time the wreckers arrived, much of the building was already gone. Valentino fans helped things along by carting the house away piece by piece. Gold-leaf wallpaper was stripped from the walls of the bedroom; while plumbing fixtures, the medicine chest, and even toothbrush holders were yanked out of the lavish bathroom.

The foundation of the home survives and can still be seen from the freeway. Over the years, many Valentino fans have held amateur archeological digs on the foundation, taking away pieces of tile and bricks. In late 2002 a sound wall was erected between the street and the foundation, preventing any future digs. To view the foundation, travel south on the Hollywood Freeway (101); as you approach the Cahuenga exit, look up at the sign that reads "Cahuenga/Vine Street" (Warning: for safety, do not do this if you are driving). The foundation is visible on the hill next to the sign.

Walk of Fame Star, 6166 Hollywood Boulevard, south side between Argyle and El Centro Avenue.

Rudolph Valentino's star on the "Walk of Fame" was one of the original 1,500 installed in 1959. The spot where his Star is located was at one time the front entrance to the Hastings Hotel (formerly the Regent), built in 1925 by producer Al Christie on land where, many years earlier, he had filmed one of the first movies made in Hollywood. It was also in this hotel that former Ziegfeld Follies girl Marion Benda made one of her many suicide attempts. The hotel was badly damaged in the 1994 Northridge Earthquake and was demolished. The site is now a parking lot used for the Pantages Theatre and the new subway.

"You Are the Star" Mural, southeast corner of Hollywood Boulevard and Wilcox Avenue.

This mural portrays an audience of Hollywood movie stars sitting in a movie theater, as it might be seen if viewed from the screen. Those represented in the mural include Marilyn Monroe, Clark Gable, Humphrey Bogart, Bette Davis, Charlie Chaplin, and Rudolph Valentino. The mural gives the impression that the actors are watching the "viewer" up on the silver screen.

TOUR 3

West Hollywood

Garden of Allah [site], 8150 Sunset Boulevard, southwest corner of Crescent Heights Boulevard.

The home of actress Alla Nazimova was originally called "Havenhurst" before being dubbed the "Garden of Alla." Valentino would have made many visits here, especially at the beginning of his relationship with Rambova. Because of money problems, Nazimova sold the property to developers, who converted it into a popular hotel the year Valentino died. Nazimova lived in an apartment of the original house until her death in 1945. The Garden of Allah was demolished in 1959 to make way for a bank and strip mall.

George Ullman Agency, Inc. [site], 8979 Sunset Boulevard, north side between Wetherly Drive and Hilldale Avenue.

After Valentino's death, Ullman continued as a manager and agent, representing such stars as child actor Baby Peggy and silent film vamp Theda Bara. For years he was associated with the Hallam Cooley Agency before opening his own offices here on the Sunset Strip. The original building that housed Ullman's agency has been replaced with a modern office complex.

June Mathis' Residence [site], 1500 North Laurel Avenue, northeast corner at Sunset Boulevard.

The house that once stood on this site was originally the home of June Mathis' parents, Virginia and William Mathis (her step-father). It wasn't until after William's death in 1923 (Virginia died in 1922) that June moved in. She continued to live here after her marriage to Silvano Balboni. Mathis' mother was interested in the occult

Screen writer June Mathis, Valentino's friend and benefactor.

and occasionally performed séances that Valentino allegedly attended. Mathis told friends that she had a vision of Valentino in her bedroom on the night he died. She had been reading and glanced up briefly to see his phantom form.[1] When Mathis died a year later in New York, columnist Louella Parsons was the first to break the news to Balboni here at this house. A parking lot is now on the site. During the making of *The Four Horsemen of the Apocalypse*, Mathis lived at 5826 Hollywood Boulevard, which has also been razed.

Natacha Rambova and Theodore Kosloff's Residence [site], 1325 Gardner Street, west side between De Longpre and Fountain avenues.

According to the 1920 Census, Rambova and Kosloff lived in a bungalow at this address. It was here that Kosloff reportedly shot Natacha in the leg when he returned unexpectedly from a hunting trip and found her in the process of leaving him.[2] This house was razed and replaced with an apartment building.

United Artists Studio, 1041 North Formosa Avenue, southwest corner at Santa Monica Boulevard.

Films have been made on this lot since 1918, when it was known as the Hampton Studios. Douglas Fairbanks and Mary Pickford took over in 1922, renaming it the Pickford–Fairbanks Studios. The couple, along with D. W. Griffith and Charlie Chaplin, had formed United Artists in 1919 and used the lot to make many of the new company's films. Scenes for *The Son of the Sheik*, partly filmed here, required loads of sand trucked in from the desert. In the 1930s, Rudolph Valentino Productions, Inc. had its offices here. In 1939 it became the Samuel Goldwyn Studios and then Warner-Hollywood in 1980. Today it is simply called "the Lot."

Alberto Valentino's Residence, 1444 North Orange Grove Avenue, east side between Sunset Boulevard and De Longpre Avenue.

Alberto lived here at the time of his death in 1981 (his wife Ada died in 1976). In addition, Alberto lived at the following addresses over the years: 318 North Mariposa Avenue, Los Angeles (1927); 1636 North Stanley Avenue, Hollywood (1929); 608

Poinsettia Place, Hollywood (1930); "Falcon Lair," 1436 Bella Drive (1932); "Villa Valentino," 6776 Wedgewood Place, Whitley Heights (1935).

Jean Valentino's Residence, 1540 Sunset Plaza Drive, north of Sunset Boulevard.

Valentino's nephew, Jean Guglielmi Valentino, lived in this house for several decades.

TOUR 4

Beverly Hills

Church of the Good Shepherd, 505 North Bedford Drive, northwest corner at Santa Monica Boulevard.

Valentino's west coast funeral was held at the Church of the Good Shepherd on September 7, 1926. Built in 1924, the church has hosted the funerals of many Hollywood celebrities, including Carmen Miranda (1955), Gary Cooper (1961), William Frawley (1966), Rosalind Russell (1976), Peter Finch (1977), Jimmy Durante (1980), Alfred Hitchcock (1980), Vincente Minnelli (1986), Rita Hayworth (1987), Danny Thomas (1991), Eva Gabor (1995), Mary Frann (1998), and Frank Sinatra (1998). In addition, the funeral scene for the 1954 version of *A Star Is Born* was filmed here. Celebrity weddings have included those of Mae Murray to Prince Mdivani (Valentino was the best man) in 1926, Valentino's costar Vilma Banky to Rod La Roque in 1927, Elizabeth Taylor's short-lived nuptials to Nicky Hilton in 1950, and singer Rod Stewart's 1990 marriage to model Rachel Hunter.

Falcon Lair, 1436 Bella Drive.

Falcon Lair was built in 1923 by Beverly Hills realtor George Read, who liked it so well that he and his family occupied it until he sold it to Valentino in 1925. Valentino originally bought the mansion to share it with his wife, Natacha Rambova. However, before they could move in, Natacha went to Europe and divorced Rudy. The actor redecorated the home and lived here less than a year before his death. At the estate auction, the house was sold to Jules Howard, a New York diamond broker, for $145,000. For reasons unknown, the sale was never completed. Falcon Lair remained empty but was occasionally rented out (actor Harry Carey, for a time, paid $200 a month to live there).

Falcon Lair remained a part of Valentino's estate until December 1934 when it was sold to Juan Romero for $18,000 (90 percent of its appraised value at that time). Rumors circulated that Pola Negri was interested in purchasing the house, and, in fact, Pola visited the house in October of that year. "It has been one of the big dreams of my life to own and live in the home of Rudolph Valentino," Pola declared. "And now my wish is to come true."[1] Sadly, her dream remained unfulfilled.

For the next three years Romero expended well over $100,000 restoring the estate in the manner in which he believed Valentino was attempting at the time of his death. Many of the actor's original possessions that could not be sold at auction remained with the house, including two portraits by Beltran-Masses—one of Valentino and the other of Senorita Gaditana, a one-time famous dancer.

After Romero, owners of Falcon Lair have included actress Ann Harding and philanthropist Gypsy Buys, who sold it in 1949 to five women identified only as "the group." The women intended to turn the house into a shrine for lovelorn women wishing to worship Valentino's memory. In 1951 the estate was bought by food importer Robert L. Balzar for $100,000. In 1953 Gloria Swanson rented the house during a stay in Los Angeles and invited tobacco heiress Doris Duke for a visit. Duke, impressed by the house, bought it from Balzar that same year and drastically remodeled the estate. For the next forty years Duke owned Falcon Lair, and died there in 1993 at the age of 80. In 1998 Falcon Lair was sold to a Florida architect for almost $3 million. In 2003 a major renovation was once again underway both inside and out, but most of the exterior remains as Valentino knew it.

Falcon Lair's Stables, 10051 Cielo Drive.

"He and Fred [Marion's husband] deliberated at great length as to where Rudy could put his stable. Finally it was decided, as per usual, to blast away part of the hill near the road that led up to the Lair."[2]—Frances Marion.

Valentino's stables, now converted into a private residence, are located across from the entrance/driveway of the former Sharon Tate murder house (10050 Cielo Drive, razed 1994). Surrounded by buildings and walls, the tiled roof is the only feature of the former stables that can be seen from the street.

Pauline Frederick's Residence, 9419 Sunset Boulevard, north side between Mountain Drive and Hillcrest Road.

"It was at a party at Pauline Frederick's that I met Miss Jean Acker."[3]—Rudolph Valentino.

In the fall of 1919, Rudy and a friend, director Douglas Gerrard, attended a party given by actress Pauline Frederick at her Sunset Boulevard mansion, which she had built the previous year. It was here that Jean Acker first became acquainted with Valentino, who asked the russet-haired actress to dance (instead, they sat under the moon and talked late into the night). MGM's "Boy Wonder," Irving Thalberg, bought the mansion and married actress Norma Shearer in the backyard in 1927.

Valentino outside Falcon Lair's stables, which have since been converted into a private residence.

Monument to the Stars, Beverly Drive and Olympic Boulevard.

The "Monument to the Stars," a bronze-green spiral of camera film sitting upon an octagonal base, was erected in 1959 to commemorate the eight film luminaries that led the fight to prevent annexation of Beverly Hills to the city of Los Angeles in 1923. Because of their efforts, Beverly Hills remains a totally independent community today. The eight were: Mary Pickford, Douglas Fairbanks, Will Rogers, Conrad Nagel, Tom Mix, Harold Lloyd, Rudolph Valentino, and director Fred Niblo. The monument is located on a traffic island about a half-mile south of Wilshire Boulevard at a three-way intersection of Beverly Drive, Olympic Boulevard, and Beverwil Drive.

Pola Negri's Residence, 621 Beverly Boulevard.

"When Rudy returned from Europe, he came directly to my house. He bounded out of the car and raced to the door, shouting, 'Polita, I am free! I am free!'"[4] — Pola Negri.

Actress Pola Negri lived here during her relationship with Valentino in 1925–26. She sold the house several months after Valentino's death.

Pickfair, 1143 Summit Drive.

"One day Rudolph Valentino made an unexpected appearance on the Pickfair lawn, which, in the warm months, was our outdoor living room. I never saw Douglas act so fast, and with such painful rudeness, as he did in showing Valentino that he wasn't welcome."[5] — Mary Pickford.

When newlyweds Douglas Fairbanks and Mary Pickford moved into this former hunting lodge, the press dubbed it "Pickfair." When the Fairbanks divorced, Mary wed actor Buddy Rogers and lived at Pickfair until her death in 1979. Singer Pia Zadora moved into Pickfair in 1988, and two years later had the historic house razed to build a larger home. Valentino visited Pickfair, the home of Douglas Fairbanks and Mary Pickford on many occasions (most friendlier than the one noted above).

S. George Ullman's Residence, 701 Foothill Road, northwest corner at Elevado Avenue.

S. George Ullman lived here during the time he worked as Valentino's manager.

TOUR 5

Downtown Los Angeles

Alexandria Hotel, 501 South Spring Street at West Fifth Street.

"At Los Angeles I was met by Norman Kerry, who insisted that I put up at the Alexandria Hotel, the best in the place."[1]—Rudolph Valentino.

When Valentino first arrived in Los Angeles, his friend, actor Norman Kerry, put him up for a time at the opulent Alexandria Hotel. Built in 1906, the Alexandria was *the* place to stay when visiting or doing business in Los Angeles. D. W. Griffith used the Alexandria as his base for many years, and future actor Ramon Novarro was a busboy there in the teens. At any time of the day you could see celebrities walking through the hotel's luxurious lobby. In the late 1920s the film crowd moved to the newer Biltmore and Ambassador Hotels, leaving the Alexandria to slip into a decline that only ended with a $2 million face-lift in the late 1970s. The Alexandria functions today mainly as a residential hotel. One of its rooms is named the Rudolph Valentino Suite.

The Auditorium [site], 427 West Fifth Street, between South Olive Street and South Hill Street.

"Mr. Griffith kept me in mind, and when he presented *The Greatest Thing in Life* at the Auditorium in Los Angeles, I was engaged to dance with Carol Dempster in a prologue."[2]—Rudolph Valentino.

Valentino danced here for three months in 1919 for one hundred dollars a week. Home to the Los Angeles Philharmonic, it was here that Griffith premiered *The Birth of a Nation* in 1915, when it was called Clune's Auditorium. The edifice was razed in 1985 to make way for a new office building and a hotel (Pershing Square Center) that never materialized. A huge parking lot now occupies the site.

Biltmore Hotel, 515 South Olive Street, between West Fifth and West Sixth streets.

The Biltmore was the largest hotel east of Chicago when it opened in October of 1923. The Academy of Motion Picture Arts and Sciences was founded here the year following Valentino's death, on May 11, 1927. Rudy attended many functions here, including a costume party sponsored by the Sixty Club. Rudy wore his toreador costume from *Blood and Sand*, and his date, Pola Negri, dressed as a Spanish dancer—the couple won first prize.

Valentino and Pola Negri won first prize in a costume party held at the Biltmore Hotel.

Cunningham & O'Connor Mortuary [site], 1031 South Grand Avenue, at Olympic Boulevard.

Cunningham & O'Connor, the mortuary that handled Valentino's funeral in Los Angeles, began operations in 1898. The business prospered, and in 1906 a new facility was built on Grand Avenue near Olympic Boulevard. This was the first building in the United States to be designed specifically as a mortuary. Valentino's body remained here until his funeral services the following day in Beverly Hills. The site where the building once stood is now a parking lot.

Grand Avenue and Fifth Street Residence [site], 434 South Grand Avenue at Fifth Street.

"Realizing it was silly to stay any longer at the Alexandria hotel, which was very expensive, I decided to take a small apartment at Grand avenue and Fifth street."[3]
— Rudolph Valentino.

Valentino's first apartment in Los Angeles, which he shared with entertainer Bryan Foy, oldest of the "Seven Little Foys," cost eight dollars a week. The original buildings from Valentino's era at this intersection have been demolished. Although Valentino does not give the exact address, the most likely location is the southeast corner where a boarding house once stood. A tall office building now stands on this site. The Biltmore Hotel addition and the Los Angeles Central Library occupy two other corners.

Grauman's Million Dollar Theater, 307 South Broadway at West Third Street.

Built in 1918 by impresario Sid Grauman, the Million Dollar Theater hosted the Los Angeles premiere of *The Son of the Sheik*. On opening night, as Valentino was ending a brief speech at the close of the first showing, he noticed that a fourteen-foot vase on the edge of the stage was about to fall into the audience. The actor ran across the stage and put his shoulder against the vase to steady it, but it was too heavy. Both the vase and Valentino fell into the orchestra pit. Knocked unconscious by the fall, Valentino later regained consciousness and returned to his seat amid thunderous applause.[4] The Million Dollar Theater continued to offer live entertainment along with a movie for several decades. In the 1950s the theater featured Spanish-language variety shows, including headline acts from Mexico City.

Los Angeles Athletic Club, 431 West Seventh Street, between Olive Street and Mercury Court.

"The Los Angeles Athletic Club was a center where the elite of local society and business gathered at the cocktail hour. A young man, a bit player, used to sit around the lounge — a lonely fellow named Valentino who had come to Hollywood to try his luck but was not doing very well."[5] — Charlie Chaplin.

Valentino would spend hours in the lobby and lounge of the Athletic Club, hoping to run into anyone who could further his career. It was here at a party hosted by his friend Douglas Gerrard that he first met actress Pauline Frederick. The Athletic Club, built in 1912, still offers an array of services to its members at this location.

Rialto Theater, 812 South Broadway, between West Seventh and West Eighth streets.

The star-studded premiere for *Blood and Sand* was held at the Rialto Theater (built 1917) on August 5, 1922. Eager fans waited in line the entire day to catch a glimpse of Valentino, Natacha, and the other stars of the picture. The theater's original marquee, which Valentino would have been familiar with, was taken down in the 1930s and replaced with the current marquee, which is the longest on Broadway. The interior of the theater has been converted into retail shops.

Valencia Street Rooming House, 692 Valencia Street at West Seventh Street.

Valentino lived here for a time, presumably when he married Jean Acker and before moving into the Formosa Apartments in Hollywood. Self-proclaimed "Lady in Black" Ditra Flamé maintained that she first met Valentino in 1919 while he lived here.[6] The building has recently been restored.

TOUR 6

Suburban Los Angeles and Environs

Ambassador Hotel and Coconut Grove, 3400 Wilshire Boulevard at South Alexandria Avenue.

The Ambassador Hotel and Coconut Grove opened in 1921 and instantly became a haven for the rich and famous. The interior of the Grove is lined with palm trees said to have been props from Valentino's film *The Sheik* (1921). Valentino and Natacha hosted a dinner party in the Ambassador's ballroom for such guests as Charlie Chaplin, John Barrymore and journalist Adela Rogers St. Johns, who left the festivities early because of Natacha's tardiness. Valentino was best man at Mae Murray's wedding to Prince David Mdivani at the Ambassador, and a few months later it was here that Pola Negri learned of Valentino's death. In 1989, exactly 68 years after it opened, the Ambassador Hotel closed its doors; its future remains uncertain.

Baron Long's Watts Tavern [site], 108th Street and Central Avenue.

"About that time Baron Long opened the Watts tavern, a road house near Los Angeles. He offered me thirty-five dollars a week to dance there."[1]— Rudolph Valentino.

Valentino danced at this popular and rowdy tavern with partner Marjorie Tain. According to Baron Long, the owner of Watts Tavern, he was the only employer to fire Rudolph Valentino. Continuing for several years, Watts Tavern later became known as Jazzland and the Plantation Club. Valentino also danced at another Baron Long establishment, the Vernon Country Club.

Valentino was best man at Mae Murray's marriage to Prince David Mdivani at the Ambassador Hotel. From left: Pola Negri, Mae Murray, Prince Mdivani, Valentino.

Ditra Flamé Residence, 613 West Vesta Street, between San Antonio Avenue and Bonita Court, Ontario.

Ditra Flamé, the so-called "Lady in Black," lived here the last years of her life. She died of a heart attack on February 23, 1984. Flamé was buried at San Jacinto Valley Cemetery in neighboring Hemet, California.

Holy Cross Cemetery, 5835 Slauson Avenue at Bristol Parkway, Culver City.

Holy Cross Cemetery is the final resting place for several of Valentino's friends and family, including Norman Kerry, Douglas Gerrard, ex-wife Jean Acker Valentino, and his nephew Jean G. Valentino.

Los Angeles Pet Memorial Park, 5068 Old Scandia Lane, Calabasas.

The Los Angeles Pet Memorial Park was founded and dedicated on September 4, 1928. Just four months later, Valentino's favorite dog, a Doberman Pinscher named Kabar, died, allegedly from a broken heart at the death of his master. Kabar was one of the first celebrity pets to be buried at the new cemetery. Prince, another of

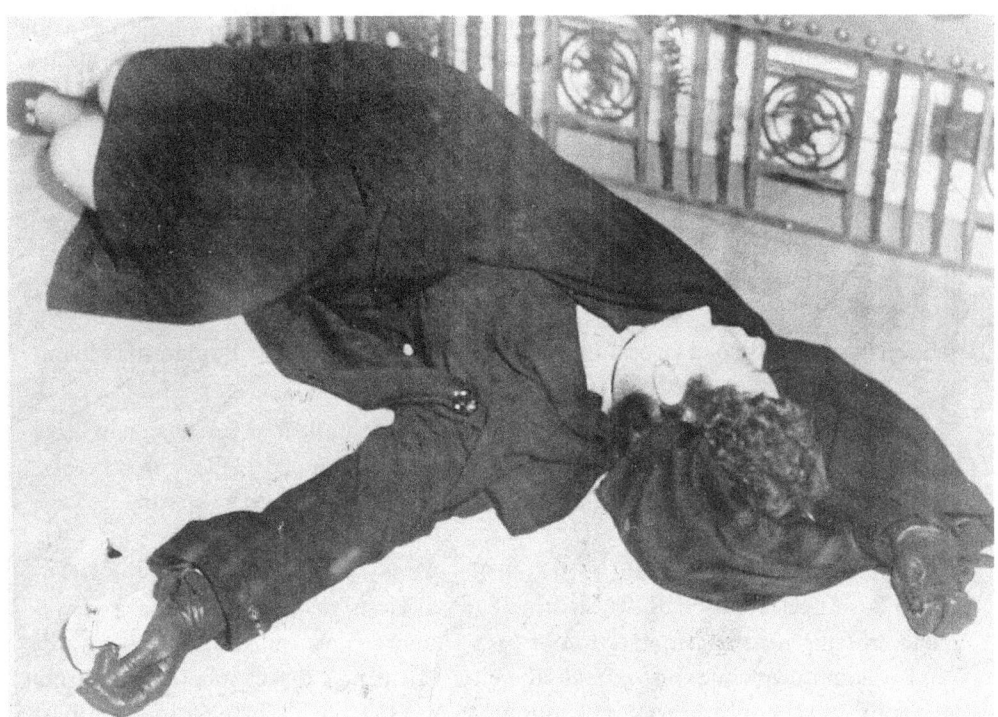

"Lady in Black" Ditra Flamé faints in front of Valentino's crypt in 1951.

Valentino's dogs, a blueblood German Shepherd, died just four months after Kabar, on May 15, 1929. According to reports at the time, Prince disappeared shortly after Valentino's death. Many thought that he had been stolen. Miraculously, several months later Prince walked into an office in San Leandro, California (a community outside San Francisco, an astounding 400 miles away), still wearing the identification collar Valentino had placed on him. Weak and emaciated from hunger, Prince found a home with Mildred Pacheaco, who cared for him until he died, reportedly of grief.

As for Kabar, since his burial at the pet cemetery, visitors describe being licked or hearing panting near his grave. Others report sensing him nipping at their heels. Just as at Valentino's crypt in Hollywood, a Lady in Black has been spied leaving daisies or a single rose for Kabar. Jean Acker's dog, "Bunky Valentino" (1928–1945), is also here. Other star pets interred at the cemetery include Topper, Hopalong Cassidy's horse; Droopy, Humphrey Bogart's dog; Boots, Charlie Chaplin's cat; and Scout, Tonto's horse from *The Lone Ranger*.

Maryland Hotel [site], Colorado Boulevard, Pasadena.

"I met some very fine people from Pasadena who suggested that I try for an engagement dancing at the Hotel Maryland, one of the most exclusive hotels in Pasadena."[2]—Rudolph Valentino.

Valentino's first engagement at the Maryland Hotel was on Thanksgiving Day

1917, dancing with Katherine Phelps. Valentino was offered a permanent engagement here but declined because he could not accept the terms. The hotel was demolished in 1937.

Movieland Wax Museum, 7711 Beach Boulevard, Buena Park.

With more than 300 wax figures, the Movieland Wax Museum is reportedly the largest of its kind in the country. One wax effigy is a likeness of Valentino as the Sheik, his most famous role.

Pasa-Hambra Railroad Crossing, Alhambra Avenue and Valley Boulevard, Alhambra.

"Yesterday ... autos bounced into the open fields as the long procession of black motors slowly moved along Alhambra avenue ... they stopped at the railroad crossing near Pasa-Hambra avenue ... a strange crowd slowly gathered ... waiting ... waiting..."[3] — *Los Angeles Record.*

Because of concerns that the riots in New York would be repeated at the downtown Los Angeles Station, the "Valentino Funeral Train" debarked at a little used railroad crossing near the intersection of Pasa-Hambra (now called Valley Boulevard) and Alhambra Avenue, just outside the city. Valentino's casket was removed from the train and taken by hearse to Cunningham & O'Connor's Mortuary in downtown Los Angeles.

Natacha Rambova's Death, Las Encinas Hospital, 2900 East Del Mar Boulevard, Pasadena.

Natacha had been in poor health for some time when family members brought her to live in California in 1965. She first stayed at the Methodist Hospital in Arcadia before transferring to Las Encinas Hospital on her birthday. Natacha Rambova died here on June 5, 1966. Her death certificate lists 3805 Mayfair Drive, Pasadena, as her place of residence — the home of her cousin, Ann Wollen. It was also at Las Encinas Hospital that comedian W. C. Fields died in 1946, and where Jack Osborne, son of rocker Ozzy Osborne, was treated for drug and alcohol abuse in 2003.

San Fernando Mission, 15151 San Fernando Mission Boulevard, Mission Hills.

The San Fernando Mission, seventeenth of the twenty-one missions founded by the Franciscans in California, was established in 1797 and named for Saint Ferdinand III, King of Spain. Portions of *The Four Horsemen of the Apocalypse* were filmed here, including the well-known scene of Valentino on horseback standing before the long corridor (which still exists).

Ship Cafe [site], Abbot Kinney Pier, Venice.

The Ship Cafe was built to resemble Spanish explorer Juan Cabrillo's galleon that discovered California. One evening, Valentino interrupted the festivities of a now-famous dinner party held in honor of the great Russian actress Alla Nazimova. Actress Dagmar Godowsky, who had first met Rudy in New York, was about to introduce the smiling young Italian when Nazimova slowly lowered her head and froze. The whole table took its cue from her and one by one they too lowered their heads. Godowsky's voice trailed off and so did Valentino. Afterwards, Nazimova, who mistakenly believed rumors that a New York socialite had somehow involved Valentino in the murder scandal of her businessman husband, rebuked Godowsky. A little more than a year later a fire ravaged the entire pier, destroying the Ship Cafe. The cafe was soon rebuilt, but was placed parallel to the beach instead of facing out to sea.

Universal Studios, 3900 Lankershim Boulevard, Universal City.

Founded by Carl Laemmle in 1914 on the site of a 230-acre chicken ranch, Universal has been making movies at this location ever since. Valentino made several films here, including *The Delicious Little Devil* (1919) and *The Big Little Person* (1919), both with Mae Murray. Screening rooms 1, 2 and 3 are still in use from the Valentino era, though they have been remodeled countless times.

Alberto Valentino's Death, Southland Geriatric Center, 11701 Studebaker Road, Norwalk.

Alberto Valentino died here from heart failure on June 4, 1981.

PART THREE

Appendices

APPENDIX I

The "Pink Powder Puffs" Editorial and Valentino's Responses

What follows is the entire text of the infamous "Pink Powder Puffs" editorial from the *Chicago Tribune* and Valentino's two responses, which were published in the *Chicago Herald-Examiner* and other newspapers across the country.

"Pink Powder Puffs"

A new public ballroom was opened on the north side a few days ago, a truly handsome place and apparently well run. The pleasant impression lasts until one steps into the men's washroom and finds there on the wall a contraption of glass tubes and levers and a slot for the insertion of a coin. The glass tubes contain a fluffy pink solid, and beneath them one reads an amazing legend which runs something like this: "Insert coin. Hold personal puff beneath the tube. Then pull the lever."

A powder vending machine! In a men's washroom! Homo Americanus! Why didn't some one quietly drown Rudolph Guglielmo [*sic*], alias Valentino, years ago?

And was the pink powder machine pulled from the wall or ignored? It was not. It was used. We personally saw two "men" — as young lady contributors to the Voice of the People are wont to describe the breed — step up, insert coin, hold kerchief beneath the spout, pull the lever, then take the pretty pink stuff and put it on their cheeks in front of the mirror.

Another member of this department, one of the most benevolent men on earth, burst raging into the office the other day because he had seen a young "man" combing his pomaded hair in the elevator. But we claim our pink powder story beats his all hollow.

It is time for a matriarchy if the male of the species allows such things to persist. Better a rule by masculine women than by effeminate men. Man began to slip, we are beginning to believe, when he discarded the straight razor for the safety pattern. We shall not be surprised when we hear that the safety razor has given way to the depilatory.

Who or what is to blame is what puzzles us. Is this degeneration into effeminacy a cognate reaction with pacifism to the virilities and the realities of the war? Are pink powder and parlor pinks in any way related? How does one reconcile masculine cosmetics, sheiks, floppy pants, and slave bracelets with a disregard for law and an aptitude for crime more in keeping with the frontier of half a century ago than a twentieth-century metropolis?

Do women like the type of "man" who pats pink powder on his face in a public washroom and arranges his coiffure in a public elevator? Do women at heart belong to the Wilsonian era of "I Didn't Raise My Boy to Be a Soldier"? What has become of the old "caveman" line?

It is strange social phenomenon and one that is running its course not only here in America but in Europe as well. Chicago may have its powder puffs; London has its dancing men and Paris its gigolos. Down with Decatur; up with Elinor Glyn. Hollywood is the national school of masculinity. Rudy, the beautiful gardener's boy, is the prototype of the American male.

Hell's bells. Oh, sugar.

—*Chicago Tribune*, July 18, 1926

Valentino's initial response:

To the man (?) who wrote the editorial headed "Pink Powder Puffs" in Sunday's "Tribune":

The above mentioned editorial is at least the second scurrilous personal attack you have made upon me, my race, and my father's name.

You slur my Italian ancestry; you cast ridicule upon my Italian name; you cast doubt upon my manhood.

I call you, in return, a contemptible coward and to prove which of us is a better man, I challenge you to a personal test. This is not a challenge to a duel in the generally accepted sense — that would be illegal. But in Illinois boxing is legal, so is wrestling. I, therefore, defy you to meet me in the boxing or wrestling arena to prove, in typically American fashion (for I am an American citizen), which of us is more a man. I prefer this test of honor to be private, so I may give you the beating you deserve, and because I want to make it absolutely plain that this challenge is not for purposes of publicity. I am handing copies of this to the newspapers simply because I doubt that any one so cowardly as to write about me as you have would respond unless forced by the press to do so. I do not know who you are or how big you are but this challenge stands if you are as big as Jack Dempsey.

I will meet you immediately or give you a reasonable time in which to prepare, for I assume that your muscles must be flabby and weak, judging by your cowardly mentality and that you will have to replace the vitriol in your veins for red blood — if there be a place in such a body as yours for red blood and manly muscle.

I want to make it plain that I hold no grievance against the *Chicago Tribune*, although it seems a mistake to let a cowardly writer use its valuable columns as this "man" does. My fight is personal — with the poison-pen writer of editorials that stoop to racial and personal prejudice. The *Tribune* through Miss Mae Tinee, has treated me and my work kindly and at times very favorably. I welcome criticism of my work as an actor — but I will resent with every muscle of my body attacks upon my manhood and ancestry.

Hoping I will have an opportunity to demonstrate to you that the wrist under a slave bracelet may snap a real fist into your sagging jaw and that I may teach you respect of a man even though he happens to prefer to keep his face clean, I remain with

Utter Contempt
Rudolph Valentino

P. S. I will return to Chicago within ten days. You may send your answer to me in New York, care of United Artists Corp., 729 7th Avenue.

—*Chicago Herald-Examiner*, July 19, 1926

Valentino's final statement:

"It is evident you cannot make a coward fight any more than you can draw blood out of a turnip. The heroic silence of the writer who chose to attack me without any provocation in the *Chicago Tribune* leaves no doubt as to the total absence of manliness in his whole makeup.

I feel I have been vindicated because I consider his silence as a tacit retraction, and an admission which I am forced to accept even though it is not entirely to my liking.

The newspaper men and women whom it has been my privilege to know briefly or for a longer time have been so absolutely fair and so loyal to their profession and their publications, that I need hardly say how conspicuous is this exception to the newspaper profession."

—*Chicago Herald-Examiner*, July 30, 1926

APPENDIX II

The Medical Diagnosis, Operation and Treatment

The following is a letter to S. George Ullman from Dr. Harold E. Meeker, the surgeon who operated on and attended Rudolph Valentino during the illness preceding his death.[1]

August 28, 1926
Mr. S. George Ullman
Hotel Ambassador, New York

Dear Mr. Ullman: I examined Rudolph Valentino for the first time at 5:15 Aug. 22 [sic] at the Polyclinic Hospital. He was suffering great pain, had a moderate rise of temperature, a very rapid pulse, a board-like rigidity of the entire abdominal wall and presented the picture of a rapidly spreading vicious peritonitis. A diagnosis of probable perforated gastric ulcers was made, although other possibilities could not be excluded at this advanced stage. I urged immediate operation as his only chance for life.

OPERATIVE FINDINGS

The abdominal cavity contained a large amount of fluid and food particles. All the viscera was coated with a greenish gray film. A round hole one centimeter in diameter was seen in the anterior wall of the stomach, three centimeters from the pylorus, and two centimeters below the lesser curvature. There was no walling off by natural processes and fluid was still coming through the opening. The tissue of the stomach for one and one-half centimeters immediately surrounding the perforation was necrotic. The appendix was acutely inflamed from a secondary infection, turned on itself, and so fixed by a plastic exudate at its tip and by an old band at its midpoint as to constrict the terminal ileum.

The Operation Step by Step

Median vertical incisions over the right rectus. All possible fluids and foreign particles removed by suction apparatus. Necrotic tissue around mar of ulcer excused, the edges of the opening were approximated by mattress sutures through wall coats, except the mucosa. A portion of the lesser omentum was stitched with fine linen over this suture line; this was in turn reinforced by a portion of greater omentum over it. A rubber drainage tube was stitched in place with fine catgut. The appendix was removed because it was constricting the gut, otherwise it would not have been touched at this time.

A second drainage tube was placed in the right illac fossa and the abdominal wound closed. The patient was placed in bed in position most favorable to gravity drainage. He was in profound shock when put on the operating table, with a pulse of 140, and this condition did not change appreciably during the operation.

Progress

There was a steady improvement up to the fifth day. Abdominal drainage ceased on the third day. Pulse and temperature normal on the fifth day. On the morning of the sixth day the patient had a slight chill, complained of severe pain in the upper left abdomen and left chest. An area of pleurisy was detected; this rapidly extended and scattered areas of pneumonia developed in the left lung. On the seventh day there was a marked improvement of the valves of the heart. The patient died about noon on the eighth day, overwhelmed by the sepsis.

The above is a true account of the last illness of Rudolph Valentino as observed by me.

— Harold D. Meeker

APPENDIX III

Tributes and Eulogies

Here are more than 100 tributes (arranged by the name of the person making the tribute) that resulted from the efforts of the publicity team formed by S. George Ullman and United Artists Studios. Not before or since has such an outpouring of reaction to an actor's death been collected. All were issued within 24 hours of Valentino's death by newspapers around the world, which chose only select ones for publication.[1]

Hiram Abrams (1878–1926), president of United Artists:
"We are greatly grieved and shocked at the great loss. Every one hoped for the best, especially since the boy had waged so great a fight against huge odds. The loss is a great blow to us personally as he was our friend, and surely a blow to the motion picture industry in which he stood so high."

Jean Acker (1892–1978), actress and ex-wife:
"What is there to say? He is gone. What good to talk now?"

Marcus Adams (1875–1959), photographer:
"Valentino was an artist to his finger tips. A wonderful actor."

George Archainbaud (1890–1959), actor:
"It is useless for me to attempt to say how much I feel the loss of Rudolph Valentino. He stood alone in his work and I know of no one who can take his place."

Mary Astor (1906–87), actress:
"He was such a splendid actor, so fine and cultured and immensely popular. I feel that we have lost someone who is very dear to us."

Agnes Ayres (1898–1940), actress and costar:

"His death is doubly affecting to me because not only were our careers so closely linked in the struggle for picture success, but he had ever proved himself a loyal friend."

Silvano Balboni, cinematographer:

"Rudolph Valentino was an artist whose place it will be impossible to fill, just as it will be impossible to fill the empty place in our hearts, caused by his death. I am very deeply grieved."

Vilma Banky (1898–1991), actress and costar:

"Playing opposite Rudolph Valentino taught me the meaning of courtesy and consideration in a fellow actor. If he was one of the screen's greatest lovers, he also was one of Hollywood's most perfect gentlemen. I will mourn him as a friend, but I also will be happy to remember that I had the opportunity of working opposite him."

Reginald Barker (1886–1945), president of the Motion Picture Directors Association:

"The screen will never have another Valentino. He had a distinctiveness all his own, and his loss to the cinema world is an irreparable one. News of his death is a great shock to the industry and members of the Motion Picture Directors Association were stunned by the tidings of his passing. The name of Valentino will linger long in the memory of screen fans and members of the film industry, for he was equally popular in private life, as he was in the estimation of the millions who admired his acting."

John Barrymore (1882–1942), actor:

"Mr. Valentino was a most colorful personality and a fine artist. His loss, artistically, must be considered as very great, stricken as he was at the height of his career. The personal loss to his friends will be incalculable."

Lionel Barrymore (1878–1954), actor:

"Rudolph Valentino has not died; he has simply changed from a present personality to a character in history—for in the screen's history he will always live as one of the greatest artists."

Noah Beery (1882–1946), actor:

"One thing I admired of him above all else, and that was his sincere appreciation of home life. He was unfortunate in marriage, it appears, but he had the reputation of preferring the quiet home life of a country gentleman to the glitter of metropolitan existence. To those who knew his courageous rise to eminence, the memory of a gracious and estimable fellow-artist will live forever."

Wallace Beery (1885–949), actor:

"Without a doubt, he was one of the greatest artists of the screen. His passing will be mourned throughout the world with profound regret."

Fred W. Beetson (1876–1953), secretary and treasurer of the AMPP:

"Rudolph Valentino was one of our greatest men and greatest leaders. He filled a distinctive place in the scheme of things. His passing leaves us a beautiful memory of a man who believed in playing fair. His loss will be felt keenly by the whole industry and by his legion of admirers."

David Belasco (1853–1931), Broadway producer:

"It is indeed pitiful that so talented an actor, so young a man, with prospects so bright, should be called from this world."

Madge Bellamy (1899–1990), actress:

"His was a distinctive personality that cannot be replaced."

Marion Benda (1905–51), Ziegfeld Follies girl:

"I'm just sick. I loved him dearly."

Monte Blue (1890–1963), actor:

"In Valentino the screen has lost one of its dearest friends, a loss beyond repair, for there was only one Valentino."

Betty Blythe (1893–1972), actress:

"He has been as great a personality abroad as he was here."

Frank Borzage (1893–1962), director:

"I regarded Rudolph Valentino as one of the screen's greatest artists. I feel his death keenly."

Major Edward Bowes (1874–1946), vice president of Metro-Goldwyn-Mayer Studios:

"The shock of Valentino's death is overwhelming. He was a great actor, a fine person and a sincere friend. He was a hard, honest and sincere worker in his profession, and, as I happen to know personally, a clean-living man. He gave the best that was in him to his work and appreciated fully the responsibility which went with the high esteem in which he was held by the public. He will long be remembered and respected."

Charles Brabin (1883–1957), director:

"No loss could have been greater and I, for one, can say that I am overcome by sadness at the news of Rudolph Valentino's passing."

Herbert Brennon (1880–1958), director:

"A charming gentleman and brilliant actor who had but scratched the surface of his great talent."

Heywood Broun (1888–1939), journalist:

"Valentino had become that priceless thing — a symbol... It is a long sleep to which he has gone, and very soon the thousands will have another symbol to take his place."

Clarence Brown (1890–1987), director:

"Valentino's death is the biggest loss the screen has ever had. Not only was he a great artist but an influence that worked for good throughout the entire industry; an influence that made all pictures better."

Lon Chaney (1883–1930), actor:

"I don't know when a piece of news has so affected me. Valentino held a place in the art of the screen that made new history in the silent drama."

Charles Chaplin (1889–1977), actor:

"The death of Rudolph Valentino is one of the greatest tragedies that has occurred in the history of the motion picture industry. As an actor he achieved fame and distinction; as a friend he commanded love and admiration. We of the film industry, through his death, lose a very dear friend, a man of great charm and kindliness."

Al Christie (1881–1951), producer:

"Although Valentino is gone he will live always through the many fine roles he created for motion picture audiences throughout the world."

Charles Christie (1880–1955), president of the Motion Picture Producers Association:

"The loss of Rudolph Valentino is one not only to us of the motion picture industry alone, but is a loss that will reach film goers, whose number are incalculable."

George M. Cohan (1878–1942), Broadway producer:

"I did not know Valentino well. But I know he was an accomplished artist with a brilliant future and his death is surely a great loss to the profession in which he so distinguished himself."

John W. Considine, Jr. (1898–1961), producer and supervisor of United Artists:

"Several times Valentino told me 'I will die young, I know it. And I shall not be sorry. I should hate to live to be an old man.'"

Ricardo Cortez (1899–1977), actor:

"In the passing of Valentino the picture industry has lost one of its true geniuses. Always happy and good natured, news of his death is to me one of the most tragic notes in the history of the screen."

Alan Crosland (1894–1936), director:

"Mr. Valentino's death is a keen blow to millions of admirers and a terrible shock to his friends. Few actors in the history of the stage or screen caught the popular imagination as did Rudolph Valentino."

James Cruze (1884–1942), director:

"Anything that might be said sounds weak and futile. I with his millions of admirers throughout the world, share in the sorrow of his passing."

Bebe Daniels (1901–71), actress and costar:

"The loss of a true friend and a great artist leaves one with a helpless feeling of inexpressible remorse. The screen and it's followers will never forget him."

Marion Davies (1897–1961), actress:

"The news of Rudolph Valentino's death came as such a shock that I cannot yet believe it. I feel that with his passing the screen has lost a great actor and his associates have lost a great friend. He was a wonderful artist, a staunch friend, a fine, manly young man and a good loyal American."

Cecil B. De Mille (1881–1959), director:

"In Mr. Valentino's death we have lost a great artist. But fortunately we can look on death as progress and not as the finish."

Jack Dempsey (1895–1983), world heavyweight boxing champion:

"He was a great lover of boxing and a great admirer of mine. The screen has lost a dandy fellow and a talented actor. I have lost a great friend, and the moving picture industry a popular figure whose place always will be vacant."

Reginald Denny (1891–1967), actor:

"We have suffered an irreparable loss. We have lost a real artist and a real man."

Richard Dix (1893–1949), actor:

"The public knew and loves Rudy as an artist — we knew and loved Rudy as a man."

Allan Dwan (1885–1981), director:

"The world will miss Valentino as an actor. I miss him as a friend."

George Fitzmaurice (1887–1940), director:

"He was one of the finest gentlemen as well as one of the most finished character actors whom I have ever directed. Rudy knew everybody in his company, from the property man up, and he could call each by name. His consideration and unfailing courtesy won him the respect and admiration of all of us. In his death I have lost a friend."

Victor Fleming (1889–1949), director:

"I have never directed Rudolph Valentino in a picture, but I have known him. He was possessed of many fine qualities and he had a film following that was amazing, particularly among feminine fans."

William Fox (1879–1952), head of Fox Film Corporation:

"I deeply regret the passing of so great a star. As life is measured by accomplishment, he did well."

Morris Gest (1881–1942), Broadway producer:

"In the death of Rudolph Valentino, I have lost a dear personal friend and the world has lost a great artist."

Hoot Gibson (1892–1962), actor:

"A calamity has struck the screen. Who is there to take his place in the hearts of his fellow workers or on the screen?"

John Gilbert (1899–1936), actor:

"The death of Valentino is a terrific loss to the screen. He brought it happiness, beauty and art as perhaps no other has. His loss can never be replaced. There was and can be only one Valentino: a great artist and one of the finest gentlemen it has ever been my privilege to call a friend."

Elinor Glyn (1864–1943), author:

"With the deepest grief I heard the sad news this morning and I want to pay tribute not only to Valentino's art, which has held the world ever since the *Four Horsemen*, but to this extraordinary and indomitable pluck—having taken his reverses in good part and having steadily regained his old place in public favor. The reports of his illness showed that this great courage endured to the end that he never once made a complaint, but showed that he felt cheerfully. The highest tribute that can be paid to any man is to write the one word 'courage' on his epitaph."

Samuel Goldwyn (1882–1974), producer:

"This is a tragedy. Not only has our film world but the entire universe has lost a man who made the world better for having lived in it. He was a hero not only in the path of make-believe but in everyday experience. Valentino exemplified clean living and the belief and respect for a hereafter. He was an inspiration for all who came in contact with him. The passing of Rudolph Valentino leaves a niche in motion picture circles which will never be filled."

Harold "Red" Grange (1903–91), football player:

"Please accept my sincerest sympathies and condolence for the death of Rudolph Valentino. His passing brings to the industry the loss of a great personality, a sportsman and a gentleman."

Sid Grauman (1879–1950), theater owner:

"The screen has lost a great artist in the death of Rudolph Valentino. Hundreds of his friends in Hollywood are mourning today as are millions of his admirers all over the world. In my career as a showman I found Valentino to be a marvelous box-office attraction because of the distinctive characterizations as the ideal lover that he gave to the silver sheet. He had a wonderful personality and in private life was at all times a perfect gentleman and unaffected by the laurels with which he had been crowned. It will be hard to fill his place on the screen."

Gilda Gray (1901–59), actress:

"In life he was without peer as an actor. In death he becomes a glorious memory."

Raymond Griffith (1890–1957), actor:

"The memory of Valentino will live long in the hearts of screendom. In life he was inimitably an artist, and his passing leaves a hollow void of regret."

Maria Guglielmi, sister of Valentino:

"I, who so deeply feel the need of love and sympathy in this, my time of grief, extend to the people of America and particularly those of Hollywood, who knew and loved my brother, a sister's love and gratitude for their thoughts in this hour and my heartfelt sympathy in our common loss."

Neil Hamilton (1899–1984), actor:

"I mourn the passing of a true friend in whom the screen found an unfaltering artist of unparalleled ability."

Hope Hampton (1897–1982), actress:

"His death marks the passing of a great public idol, who can never be forgotten by the millions who admired him."

Einar Hanson (1899–1927), actor:

"The world will mourn as I do the passing of Rudolph Valentino who has made himself a place in the art of screen pictures the world over."

Will H. Hays (1879–1954), President of the Motion Picture Producers and Distributors Association of America:

"I deeply regret Mr. Valentino's death. He has had a distinguished career and was prepared to do yet greater things. His death is a great loss."

Jean Hersholt (1886–1956), actor and costar:

"A co-worker, a great figure will receive no more screen credits. His friends, Hollywood, and the world mourns his loss."

Jack Holt (1888–1951), actor:
"The news of the death of Valentino struck me like a thunderbolt. Nothing in many years has caused me greater grief."

Lloyd Hughes (1897–1958), actor:
"Rudolph Valentino was one of nature's noblemen as well as a splendid actor, and I am grieved beyond measure at the news of his passing."

Rex Ingram (1893–1950), director:
"Valentino was a type of actor who could never be replaced."

Jim Jeffries (1875–1953), heavyweight boxing champion:
"That's too bad. He made good."

Leatrice Joy (1893–1985), actress:
"Rudolph Valentino's death means, perhaps, the greatest loss the screen ever has had. He was a genuine artist and above all a gentleman."

Buster Keaton (1895–1966), actor:
"Death surely chose a shining mark when it robbed the world of Rudolph Valentino. His sudden end shocks me beyond words. I valued his friendship highly and admired him as one of the world's outstanding actors."

Sidney R. Kent (1885–1942), general manager at Paramount:
"Valentino had a God given personality."

Norman Kerry (1894–1956), actor:
"The death of my friend is a great shock and our grief is deep. I had hoped for the best."

Laura La Plante (1904–96), actress:
"It was a great shock. The passing of Valentino leaves a gap in Hollywood that cannot be filled. He was the leader."

Rod La Rocque (1898–1969), actor:
"Rudy was a true friend, a real sportsman, an athlete and a gentleman, and one of the greatest individual figures our industry ever has developed. The loss we all feel is beyond description."

Jesse Lasky (1880–1958), producer at Famous Players–Lasky:
"Please convey to Miss Negri and to Rudolph Valentino's grieving friends my most sincere condolences. His death is an irreparable loss to screendom. His passing causes me to mourn the loss of a great artist, a true friend and an admirable man."

Marcus Loew (1870–1927), head of Metro-Goldwyn-Mayer:

"I cannot express my grief over the loss of Valentino. He was a friend."

Ben Lyon (1901–79), actor:

"I am deeply shocked at his death. The motion picture industry has lost one of its most wonderful actors."

John McCormack (1884–1945), concert singer:

"The news of Rudolph Valentino's death came to me as a fearful shock and I can scarcely find words with which to express my feeling of sadness. He was not only a great artist, but a fine man and his passing will be mourned by millions."

Jeanie McPherson (1887–1946), screenwriter:

"Personally as well as professionally I always have had the greatest admiration for Mr. Valentino. The entire motion picture industry grieves over the loss of a true gentleman and an exceptional artist."

Percy Marmont (1883–1977), actor:

"One of the most likable and courageous artists the screen has known becomes a poignant memory with the regrettable death of Valentino."

June Mathis (1892–1927), screenwriter:

"My long association with Rudolph Valentino endeared him to me, as he has become endeared to everyone who knew him. My heart is too full of sorrow at this moment to enable me to speak coherently. I only know that his passing has left a void that nothing can ever fill and that the loss to our industry is too great to estimate at this time."

Louis B. Mayer (1885–1957), head of Metro-Goldwyn-Mayer:

"News of the death of Valentino has left me at the mercy of my emotions. In the passing of this beloved actor the motion picture world and millions of motion picture patrons have lost one of the screen's greatest personalities. Rudolph Valentino's service to humanity was as great as that of any rabbi, priest or clergyman. He gave happiness to thousands of suffering souls and brought cheer to sad hearts that had little else in the world."

Thomas Meighan (1879–1936), actor:

"Rudolph Valentino's death was a great shock to me. He was a remarkable actor and the picture industry loses one of its most colorful personalities in his passing. Personally, I have lost a dear friend."

George Melford (1877–1961), director:

"In losing Rudolph Valentino the world has lost a great actor at the peak of his career."

H. L. Mencken (1880–1956), journalist:

"Valentino was a dedicated artist — inimitable and incomparable — whether it came to acting or writing fine sensitive poetry. A great loss to the world."

Colleen Moore (1900–88), actress:

"I do not know how to say how deeply I am affected by the sad news. Mr. Valentino was a fine gentleman, a splendid actor, and his loss is something that must bring sorrow to the entire world."

Antonio Moreno (1887–1967), actor:

"No one will be able to take Rudolph Valentino's place. No one ever will be able to imitate his personality. He was a great actor and a fine man. He still lives in the hearts of his friends. As an actor he was unique. Nobody ever was like him or ever will be like him again."

Charlie Murray (1872–1941), actor:

"At a time like this one feels one's self bereft of words with which to express his feeling and I know that I am merely voicing the words of millions when I say that I am deeply grieved at the death of Rudolph Valentino."

Mae Murray (1889–1965), actress and costar:

"Valentino's greatest quality was a deep sincerity underlying a great strength of character. Like every great genius he had an infinite capacity for hard work and an earnestness which carried him to the highest peak of his art."

Nita Naldi (1897–1961), actress and co-star:

"He was a fine actor and a cultured and educated man."

Pola Negri (1899–1987), actress:

"I have lost not only my dearest friend, but the one real love of my life."

Marshall Neilan (1891–1958), director:

"Probably no man in film history was more beloved than Valentino. His passing is like the extinguishing of a beacon light."

Ramon Novarro (1899–1968), actor:

"Valentino's death has robbed art of a true son. His work and his personality were inspiration to all who knew him."

George O'Brien (1900–85), actor:

"My father and I always were proud of our friendship with him. Rudy was a sportsman, a great actor and an accomplished musician, and above all a gentleman."

Louella Parsons (1881–1972), journalist:

"But while the world grieves for a lost idol, Hollywood mourns for a friend. Only those of us who were privileged to know the real Rudy realize what a generous soul he possessed. What an ability to understand, what a sense of sympathy and what loyalty he had."

Mary Pickford (1893–1979), actress:

"Mr. Valentino was the greatest matinee idol that ever lived. He will never be equaled."

Natacha Rambova (1897–1966), ex-wife:

"There is a void in our hearts which can never be filled."

Harry Rapf (1880–1949), M-G-M producer:

"Valentino filled a unique niche in pictures that worked a great influence for betterment."

F. G. Reiss (dates unknown), German theatrical photographer:

"Rudolph Valentino, the world's most beautiful man, possessed a film face. On the screen Valentino possessed those rare physiognomical and photogenic qualities which transformed him into an Apollo Belvedere. The movies may wait long before another such striking case arises."

Irene Rich (1891–1988), actress:

"It is almost inconceivable that yesterday the idol of all is today but a shattered grief."

Theodore Roberts (1861–1928), actor:

"The passing of Valentino is the loss of one of my closest friends. I knew him as did perhaps no other actor. He consoled me in my illness and cheered me in my sorrow. He will always remain as one of the truly great and loyal friends."

Al Rockett (1889–1960), manager of the production unit of First National Pictures:

"Valentino's death means a loss to the millions who found their dreams of romance embodied in one of the most colorful figures that the photoplay has produced."

Mayor James Rolph, Jr. (1869–1934), mayor of San Francisco:

"Whenever I was in Los Angeles he would call on me and every time he came to San Francisco he would visit at my home. Only a few weeks ago when he was at my home he took a fancy to one of my cocker spaniel dogs and I made a present of the dog — one of the best I had. He sent his car for it and took it to Los Angeles, where he made a pet of it. He was one of those who captivated me and his death will be a shock to everyone."

Richard Rosson (1893–1953), director:

"I have know him since 1918, when we were both struggling actors and lived in a hall bedroom in Hollywood. His tremendous success and popularity never changed him."

Richard Rowland (1880–1947), general manager of First National Pictures:

"Besides a brilliant actor, he was a most lovable man and a credit to the industry."

Alma Rubens (1897–1931), actress:

"Rudolph Valentino was a great idol and his death will be greatly felt throughout the world. Rudy, through greatness, will now mount to the highest peak. His passing was a great blow. It is hard to realize that Rudy will never answer the call of the camera again. We never realize our affection for a friend until too late. But I am sure that Rudy's greatness will now reach its peak."

Malcom St. Clair (1897–1952), director:

"Nothing has ever affected me so deeply. Rudy had a tremendous personality which made him loved by everyone who was able to get within his natural reserve."

Joseph M. Schenck (1878–1961), Chairman of the Board of Directors of United Artists:

"The film world has suffered an irreparable loss in the death of Rudolph Valentino. Perhaps, in time, some undiscovered star may come to the fore to thrill and entrance movie-lovers as he has done, but I doubt it. I feel that we will never see, in this generation at least, a film actor to compare with Valentino. He was in a class by himself."

Nicholas M. Schenck (1882–1969), vice president, Metro-Goldwyn-Mayer:

"The passing of Valentino finds the entire motion picture industry mourning. His death is a loss to all the world."

B. P. Schulberg (1892–1957), associate producer at Famous Players–Lasky:

"No greater tragedy has clouded the film colony than the passing of Rudolph Valentino. As a former member of this organization he was loved by all. I, with my co-workers, express the deepest sorrow and regret."

Norma Shearer (1900–83), actress:

"Valentino's passing means more than the passing of a great artist — he was one of the greatest artists of all times."

Lee Shubert (1871–1953), Broadway producer:

"The death of Rudolph Valentino will be regretted through the whole field of the drama. The screen loses a splendid figure. He came to America unknown and without financial resources. He reached the heights through his own personality and efforts. He was an inspiration to many young men."

Milton Sills (1882–1930), actor:
"Words are inadequate to express my sorrow at the death of Rudolph Valentino."

Lewis Stone (1879–1953), actor:
"The saying, 'In the midst of life we are in death,' was never more deeply emphasized than in the news of Valentino's untimely passing. Not only an artist of great charm and ability, but a gentleman in every sense of the word, his passing was a national and international loss and I am too deeply grieved to be able to express my feelings adequately."

Hunt Stromberg (1894–1968), M-G-M producer:
"Valentino was more than a great artist; he was a world ideal. His passing could almost be called a calamity."

Gloria Swanson (1899–1983), actress and costar:
"He was a real artist, a charming gentleman, a true sportsman and a good friend. Both the motion picture industry and the public have suffered a great loss. May the thoughts and prayers of the millions who loved Rudy help him on his journey to the unknown. As a personal friend and admirer my humble prayers follow him."

Blanche Sweet (1895–1986), actress:
"The memory of Valentino, the fine, lovable and loyal, will live always."

Mrs. Margaret Talmadge (1870–1933), mother of the Talmadge sisters:
"Millions knew him as a great screen artist but they did not know of many other things which endeared him to his family, his friends and his co-workers. Some of these qualities were his kindliness, his loyalty to his family and his eagerness to help others."

Natalie Talmadge (1900–69), actress:
"Millions will mourn Rudolph Valentino but I know no spot in the world will feel his loss so keenly as here in Hollywood, where we knew and loved him."

Norma Talmadge (1897–1957), actress:
"He put up a gallant fight and died, as he lived, a very brave man."

Estelle Taylor (1899–1958), actress:
"I cannot believe yet he is really gone. He was so young and strong looking. It is hard to associate him with death."

Alice Terry (1900–87), actress and costar:

"As one who played with Valentino in his two first successes, *The Four Horsemen* and *The Conquering Power*, his loss to me is a very keen one personally. He was one of the most wonderful personalities on the screen. I know that Rex Ingram, now in Europe, will be terribly broken up when he learns of his passing. My husband and I adored him and admired his exquisite art."

Irving Thalberg (1899–1936), producer at Metro-Goldwyn-Mayer Studios:

"With the passing of Valentino has gone a great artist and one of nature's finest noblemen. His art the world knew and exulted in; his influence on the screen was so great that words cannot describe it. And we, his friends knew him also as a lovable soul and a true friend whose loss is truly a great one. Valentino has passed — but his memory will live with us always."

Lenore Ulric (1892–1970), actress:

"It is a pity one so young should have to die. He was a boy at heart and a charming companion. He was a truly great screen artist and his art was growing. It will live through his pictures for many years to come."

Alberto Valentino (1892–1981), brother:

"What can I say regarding my brother's death. I thought him to be the most affectionate brother in the world and can say no more, as words fail me."

Florence Vidor (1895–1977), actress:

"I, and millions of other admirers, am bowed with sorrow. He will stand out to me as one of the most gallant and truly chivalrous members of the film colony."

Erich Von Stroheim (1885–1957), director:

"I mourn his passing, not only as a true and talented genius but as a staunch and loyal friend as well. Through his work on the screen he will remain forever in the hearts of millions of admirers throughout the world and through his helpfulness to his coworkers in the film colony his memory will linger always."

Jack L. Warner (1892–1978), co-founder of Warner Brothers Pictures, Inc.:

"Words fail to express my feeling. The motion picture industry has had one of its greatest losses since its conception."

Roland West (1885–1952), director:

"The motion picture world mourns one of its greatest figures and countless people mourn a true friend."

George White (1890–1968), producer of *George White's Scandals*:

"All who knew him admired and respected him. I know few men who possessed such qualities of personal magnetism. He will be missed and mourned by many thousands."

Lois Wilson (1894–1988), actress and costar:
"I am deeply shocked. I feel that I have lost a personal friend."

A. H. Woods (1870–1951), Broadway producer:
"I consider him one of the most charming and lovable men that I have ever had the pleasure of knowing."

Florenz Ziegfeld (1869–1932), Broadway producer:
"With the entire world I grieve over the untoward death of Rudolph Valentino. Certainly we all admired him, but he was more than a personality, he was a symbol of manly courage and prowess."

Adolph Zukor (1873–1976), head of Famous Players–Lasky:
"Rudolph Valentino was a great artist. His death comes as a profound shock to all of us who have watched his amazing career on the screen. In his death the motion picture loses a vivid personality who has brought romance and entertainment into the lives of millions throughout the world. It was only two weeks ago today that I had lunch with him. He was the picture of health and full of enthusiasm over his work. Valentino was every inch an artist. He tried to live the characters he played. The screen has lost an artist. I knew him as a gentleman. He was a credit to his profession."

APPENDIX IV

Mourners Attending the Funerals in New York and Beverly Hills

New York City Funeral
St. Malachy's Church
239 West 49th Street, Manhattan

"Solemn High Funeral Mass for Rudolph Valentino. St. Malachy's Church, West 49th Street between Broadway and 8th Avenue. Monday, August 30th 1926 at 11 A.M. This card must be presented for admission to the Church. It is also necessary for passage of automobiles through Police Traffic Lines."—*Invitation to New York Funeral*

CELEBRANTS

Father Edward Leonard (rector of St. Malachy's Church), celebrant; Father Joseph Congedo (Church of the Sacred Heart of Jesus and Mary), deacon; Father William Donohue (Chaplain of the Catholic Actors Guild), subdeacon; Father Joseph McKenna, master of ceremonies; Father James O'Reilly, master of ceremonies.

USHERS

Marquis de la Falais de Coudray, Richard Dix, Richard Gallagher, Johnny Hines, Ben Lyon, Captain Alastaire Macintosh, Kenneth MacKenna, Robert McCullough, Clifton Webb.

HONORARY PALLBEARERS

Hiram Abrams, Douglas Fairbanks, Sidney Kent, Marcus Loew, Frank Menillo,

James R. Quirk, Frank Romano, Michael A. Romano, Richard Rowland, Malcom St. Clair, Joseph M. Schenck, Nicholas Schenck, Adolph Zukor.

MOURNERS (NOT COMPLETE)

Nicolo Abrazze, Edith Acker, Jean Acker, Mrs. Margaret Acker, Calise Barberetti, Madge Bellamy, Ben Bernie, Major Edward Bowes, Louise Brooks, Jules Brulatour, Nathan Burkan, Gene Buck, William J. Burns, Frank Carroll, William Collier, Jr., Ruth Donnelly, Fortuno Gallo, Bonnie Glass, Texas Guinan, Ben Ali Haggin, Hope Hampton, Harry Houdini, George Jessel, Ruby Keeler, Edward Kelley, George Kleine, Wilton Lackaye, Irving Lesser, Mary Lucas, Major Wallace McCutcheon, Dorothy Mackaill, Thomas Meighan, H. L. Mencken, Maude Odell, Marilyn Miller, Pola Negri, Greta Nissen, Warren Nolan, Clara Palmer, Edward Parker, House Peters, Mary Philbin, Jack Pickford, Mary Pickford, Lola Pierce, Harry Richman, Corinne Riley, Nellie Savage, Victor Shapiro, Valeria Senelle, Gloria Swanson, Constance Talmadge, Norma Talmadge, Brandon Tynan, Beatrice Ullman, S. George Ullman, Nora Van Horn, Lois Wilson, Dr. Sterling Wyman.

MEMBERS OF THE PRESS

Jane Dixon (New York *Evening Telegram*), William A. Johnson (*Motion Picture News*), "Red" Kann (*Film Daily*), Martin J. Quigley (*Exhibitor's Herald*), William Reilly (*Moving Picture World*), Fred Shaeder (*Variety*), John Spargo (Chief of Staff, *Exhibitor's Herald*).

Beverly Hills Funeral
Church of the Good Shepherd
505 North Bedford Drive, Beverly Hills

"Solemn Requiem High mass will be celebrated in the Church of the Good Shepherd, Beverly Hills, for the repose of the soul of Rudolph Valentino on Tuesday morning, September seventh at ten o'clock"—*Invitation to Hollywood Funeral*

CELEBRANTS

Father Michael J. Mullins (Church of the Good Shepherd), the celebrant; Father Patrick Concannon (St. Ensullins Church), master of ceremonies; Rev. Father Daniel O'Connell (St. Phillip Church of Pasadena), deacon; Rev. Father Patrick Dunne (Mother of Sorrows Church), sub-deacon; Mgr. Joseph Tonello of Turin, Italy.

USHERS

Lon Chaney, John Gilbert, Montague Love, Malcom McGregor, Antonio Moreno, George O'Brien.

IV. Mourners Attending the Funerals

ACTIVE PALLBEARERS

Tullio Carminati, Mario Carrillo, Charles Chaplin, John W. Considine, Jr., George Fitzmaurice, Emmett Flynn, Count Gradenigo, Douglas Gerrard, Samuel Goldwyn (replaced Norman Kerry).

HONORARY PALLBEARERS

Reginald Barker, John Barrymore, Charles Christie, James Cruze, Cecil B. DeMille, Charles Eyton, Douglas Fairbanks, William S. Hart, Harry Langdon, Jesse L. Lasky, M. C. Levee, Hal E. Lloyd, John McCormick, Henry McRae, Louis B. Mayer, Marshall Neilan, P. A. Powers, Manuel Reachi, Hal Roach, Col. William N. Selig, Mack Sennett, William R. Sheehan, Winfield S. Sheehan, S. George Ullman, Erich Von Stroheim, Sol Wertzel.

HONORARY PALLBEARERS REPRESENTING THE CITY OF LOS ANGELES AND THE CHAMBER OF COMMERCE

Dr. Frank E. Barham, John B. Burke, Harry Chandler, Mayor George E. Cryer, Maurice De Mond, Edward A. Dixon, Motley H. Flint, A. Frank, Frank Galloway, A. P. Giannini, Segundo Guasti, Jr., M. A. Hamburger, William Randolph Hearst, Marco Hellman, A. J. Hill, John W. Kemp, Joseph Marchetti, Thomas May, W. W. Mines, Oro E. Monnette, Enrico Piana, William Simpson, Carmen Smith, James Wood, Boyle Workman, George G. Young.

MOURNERS

May Allison (Mrs. James R. Quirk), Mr. and Mrs. E. M. Asher, Gertrude Astor, Agnes Ayres (Mrs. Manuel Reachi), King Baggot, Silvano Balboni, Monty Banks, Mrs. Frank F. Barham, Fred W. Beetson, Clara Beranger (Mrs. William C. de Mille), Paul Bern, Eleanor Boardman, Olive Borden, Harry Brand, Evelyn Brent (Mrs. Bernard P. Fineman), Mr. and Mrs. H. B. R. Briggs, Mr. and Mrs. (La Runa) Tyler Brooke, Mr. and Mrs. (Ona) Clarence Brown, Melville W. Brown, Mr. and Mrs. (Alice) Tod Browning, Francis X. Bushman, Mrs. Thomas E. Campbell, Jewell Carmen (Mrs. Roland West), Mary Carr, Fred Chaplin, Charles Chase, Ethel Clayton, Ruth Clifford, Eddie Cline, Ray Coffin and mother, Mr. and Mrs. E. R. Collins, John W. Considine, Sr., Mr. and Mrs. (Lillian) Jack Coogan, Jackie Coogan, Mrs. (Isabel) George E. Cryer, Frances Dale, Bebe Daniels, Ethel Davies, Marion Davies, Rose Davies (Mrs. George Van Cleave), Mildred Davis (Mrs. Harold Lloyd), Marguerite de la Motte, Dolores Del Rio, William C. de Mille, Reginald Denny, John S. Dillon, Mrs. Edward A. Dixon, Warren Doane, Mike Donlin, Billie Dove, Winfred Dunn, E. A. DuPont, Mr. and Mrs. Don Eddy, Betty Egan (Mrs. John Harron), Fred W. Eldridge, Robert Fairbanks, Virginia Browne Faire, Dr. and Mrs. Louis Felger, Helen Ferguson (Mrs. William Russell), Dick Ferris, Margaret Fielding, Bernard P. Fineman, Mr. and Mrs. (Mary) John Ford, Trixie Friganza, Tom Gallery, A. P. Gianini, Hoot Gibson, Lillian Gish, Elinor Glyn, Edmund Goulding, Mrs. D. J. Grauman, Alfred E. Green, Lita Grey (Mrs.

Charlie Chaplin), Eddie Gribbon, Frank Griffin, Corinne Griffith, Alberto Guglielmi, Mr. and Mrs. James Haggarty, Irene Haisman (Mrs. Reginald Denny), Alan Hale, John Harron, William S. Hart, Gretchen Hartman (Mrs. Alan Hale), Mr. and Mrs. Irving Hellman, Mr. and Mrs. Ben Hendricks, Jr., Mr. and Mrs. (Connie) Hobart Henley, Mr. and Mrs. (Via) Jean Hersholt, Milton Hoffman, Hylda Hollis (Mrs. Edward Sloman), Herbert Howe, Madeline Hurlock, Julianne Johnston, F. Richard Jones, George Karamano, Buster Keaton, J. Warren Kerrigan, W. Wallace Kerrigan, Norman Kerry, James Kirkwood, Hans Kraly, Peter B. Kyne, Mr. and Mrs. (Peppi) Edward Laemmle, Laura La Plante (Mrs. William A. Seiter), Rod La Rocque, Mr. and Mrs. (Bessie) Jesse L. Lasky, Lila Lee (Mrs. James Kirkwood), Paul Leni, Mr. and Mrs. Louis Leighton, Robert Z. Leonard, George Lewis, Harold Lloyd, Mr. and Mrs. Ernst Lubitsch, A. MacArthur, May McAvoy, Leo McCarey, John McCormick, Mrs. Henry McCrae, Francis McDonald, Katherine Macdonald, Violet McDonald, Cora McGeechie, Roxana McGowan (Mrs. John M. Stahl), Robert Macgowan, Charles McHugh, George McManus, Allen McNeil, Jeannie Macpherson, Charles W. Mahoney, Mr. and Mrs. Luther Mahoney, Guilda Marchetta, Shirley Mason, June Mathis (Mrs. Silvano Balboni), Mrs. Thomas May, Patsy Ruth Miller, Marylyn Mills, Colleen Moore, Daisy Canfield Moreno (Mrs. Antonio Moreno), Walter Morosco, H. Landon Morris, Mr. and Mrs. John L. Murphy, Mae Murray, Pola Negri, Marshall Neilan, Mabel Normand, Mary O'Connor, Agnes O'Malley, Pat O'Malley, Ella O'Neal, Mr. and Mrs. Sidney Olcott, Gertrude Olmstead (Mrs. Robert Z. Leonard), Mr. and Mrs. Robert Parker, Louella O. Parsons, Thomas Patten, Mrs. Charlotte Pickford, Jack Pickford, Mary Pickford (Mrs. Douglas Fairbanks), Mary Philbin, Dorothy Phillips, ZaSu Pitts (Mrs. Tom Gallery), Harry Pollard, Mr. and Mrs. Guy Price, Aileen Pringle, James R. Quirk, Jobyna Ralston, Mr. and Mrs. Harry Rapf, Baroness Mary Curzon Ravensdale, Mr. and Mrs. Joseph Reddy, Ruth Roland, Mayor James Rolph, Jr., Rosa Rudami, Wesley Ruggles, William Russell, James Ryan, Adela Rogers St. Johns, Ivan St. Johns, Mr. and Mrs. Edwin Schallert, B. P. Schulberg, William A. Seiter, E. Lloyd Sheldon, George Siegman, Edward Sloman, Frank Spearman, Mr. and Mrs. Herman Spitzel, John M. Stahl, Mr. and Mrs. (Louise) Hayden Stevenson, Mr. and Mrs. (Katherine) Hunt Stromberg, Blanche Sweet (Mrs. Marshall Neilan), Mrs. Margaret Talmadge, Natalie Talmadge (Mrs. Buster Keaton), Estelle Taylor (Mrs. Jack Dempsey), Sam Taylor, Irving Thalberg, P. K. Thomajan, Mr. and Mrs. Ralph Trueblood, Hector Turnbull, Mr. and Mrs. (Babette) Ben Turpin, Beatrice Ullman (Mrs. S. George Ullman), Virginia Valli, George Van Cleave, King Vidor, R. T. Von Ettisch, John Waldron, H. M. Walker, Johnnie Walker, Millard Webb, Lois Weber, Roland West, Tim Whelan, Kathlyn Williams (Mrs. Charles Eyton), Mr. and Mrs. Cary Wilson, Mrs. Boyle Workman, Hugh Wynne, Mrs. George G. Young.

APPENDIX V

The Last Will and Testament

Judge of the Superior Court,
Attest: L. E. LAMPTON, County Clerk
By G. W. McDonald, Deputy.

Filed: NOV 10 1926,
L. E. LAMPTON, County Clerk,
By G. W. McDonald, Deputy.

ENTERED: DEC 4 1926,
By D. Keene,
Compared A. Lyle [signature] Deputy.

No. 83678
LAST WILL AND TESTAMENT OF RUDOLPH GUGLIELMI

IN THE NAME OF GOD, AMEN: I, RUDOLPH GUGLIELMI, of the city of Los Angeles, County of Los Angeles, State of California, being of sound and disposing mind and memory and not acting under the duress, fraud or undue influence of any person or persons whatsoever, do hereby make and publish this my LAST WILL AND TESTAMENT in the manner following, that is to say:

FIRST: I hereby revoke all former Wills by me made and I hereby nominate and appoint S. George Ullman of the city of Los Angeles, County of Los Angeles, State of California, the executor of this my LAST WILL AND TESTAMENT, without bonds, either upon qualifying or in any stage of the settlement of my said estate.

SECOND: I direct that my Executor pay all of my just debts and funeral expenses, as soon as may be practicable after my death.

THIRD: I give, devise and bequeath unto my wife, Natacha Rambova, also known as Natacha Guglielmi, the sum of One Dollar ($1.00), it being my intention, desire and will that she receive this sum and no more.

FOURTH: All the residue and remainder of my estate, both real and personal, I give, devise and bequeath unto S. George Ullman, of the city of Los Angeles, County of Los Angeles, State of California, to have and to hold the same in trust and for the use of Alberto Guglielmi, Maria Guglielmi and Teresa Werner, the purposes of the aforesaid trust are as follows: to hold, manage, and control the said trust property and estate; to keep the same invested and productive as far as possible; to receive the rents and profits therefrom, and to pay over the net income derived therefrom to the said Alberto Guglielmi, Maria Guglielmi and Teresa Werner, as I have this day instructed him; to finally distribute the said trust estate according to my wish and will, as I have this day instructed him.

FIFTH: Should any other person after my death be able to establish in any Court of competent jurisdiction by proper judgment and decree therein, that he or she is entitled as an heir-in-law, or otherwise, to any share or portion of my estate, I give, devise and bequeath to such person, and each of them, the sum of $1.00 and such person shall take no other or further share in my estate.

SIXTH: In case any person or persons, to whom any legacy, gift, devise or benefit out of, from or by reason of this my Will, shall come, shall commence suit in any Court whatsoever, or by any ways or means sue and disturb or cause to be sued or disturbed by Administrator, my Executor, Administratrix or Executrix, or any other person or persons whatsoever to whom anything is by me given in this my Will, from the recovery, quiet-enjoying and possession of what is by me herein given as aforesaid, and in such manner as is therein mentioned, then my Will and meaning is that all and every, the legacy and legacies, gift and gifts, benefit or benefits herein by me given to any such person or persons, whatsoever, who shall so sue and disturb, as aforesaid, shall cease, determine and be utterly void, and to such person or persons, so suing or disturbing I hereby give, devise and bequeath in the place and stead of such legacy, gift, devise or benefit, the sum of $1.00 each, and no more.

IN WITNESS WHEREOF, I have hereunto set my hand and seal this 1st day of September, 1925.

Rudolph Guglielmi

The foregoing Instrument consisting of three pages, including the page signed by the Testator, was at the date hereof by the said Rudolph Guglielmi, signed, sealed and published and declared to be his last Will and Testament in the presence of us, who at his request and in his presence, and the presence of each other have subscribed our names as witness thereto.

Raymond A. Fager
Residing at 38 St. James Park, Los Angeles, Cal.

Margaret Neff Waters
Residing at 835 McCadden Place, Los Angeles, Calif.

NOTE: On February 4, 1931, during the Valentino court case, a ragged carbon copy of instructions asserted to have been given by Rudolph Valentino for the disposition of his estate was admitted into evidence. Luthor Mahoney, one-time employee to Valentino, said the actor drew the instructions on September 1, 1925, signed them and had Mahoney sign them as witness. The signed original vanished, according to the testimony of Valentino's attorney, Raymond W. Stewart, who noted that the stenographer who typed it was dead.

The instructions, which were addressed to Ullman according to the copy, stated in part:

"It is my desire that you perpetuate my name in the picture industry by continuing the Rudolph Valentino Productions, Inc., until my nephew Jean shall have reached the age of 25 years."

The letter further provided that when there were profits from Rudolph Valentino Productions, Inc., the sum of $400 a month was to be paid to Alberto Guglielmi, brother of Valentino and father of Jean Guglielmi; $200 to Mrs. Maria Guglielmi Strada, his sister; and $300 a month to Mrs. Teresa Werner, whom Valentino described as "my dear friend." The residue would go to Jean when he turned 25.

Raymond Stewart, the attorney who drew up Valentino's will, said he was unable to find the written instructions after the actor's death but came across the carbon copy a year earlier. He said the copy had been misplaced in the divorce file of Natacha Rambova.

Mahoney testified he last saw the written instructions in Valentino's safe the day the actor left for New York early in July 1926. On that day, Valentino, garbed in a dressing gown, met Mahoney in the office of his home, Falcon Lair. There Valentino opened a safe and Mahoney saw a letter of instructions to Ullman regarding postmortem payments to Alberto, Maria and Mrs. Werner. "I found the next day that I could not open the safe," Mahoney testified. "Mr. Guglielmi told me that he had changed the combination." That was the last that anyone claims to have seen the original signed letter.[1]

APPENDIX VI

The Estate

Beginning on December 10, 1926, S. George Ullman held a public sale of Rudolph Valentino's personal effects at the Hall of Art Studios in Hollywood. While Ullman expressed regret at having to dispose of his friend's intimate belongings, he explained the one consolation it gave him in the forward to the estate catalogue:

> Although I dislike the necessity of putting up for public sale things which Mr. Valentino loved with such boyish enthusiasm, still my aversion to such a sale is lessened when I realize that it will give those who loved him the opportunity of possessing a cherished momento of one of the most honored personalities of this age.[1]

What follows are select items from the auction catalogue and their sale price. The number of the item listed corresponds with the number in the estate catalogue. In some instances the buyer of the item is included. If you look carefully, you may see the names of some famous actors.

No. 1— Falcon Lair: No. 2 Bella Drive (now 1436 Bella Drive), Beverly Hills. Located just within the city limits of Los Angeles, overlooking Beverly Hills, at the head of the Benedict Canyon Road, entering from the first street west of the Beverly Hills Hotel, and north approximately one mile beyond and overlooking the "Thomas Ince" and "Harold Lloyd" estates.

No. 2— Beverly Terrace Unimproved Acreage: This acreage consists of approximately six and eight-tenths acres of scenic hill-top property, located in Los Angeles County adjacent to the Francis Marion estate and Fred Niblo estate. It is beautifully located overlooking Beverly Hills, $21,000. Sold to Dr. Frank McCoy, Hollywood.

No. 3— Villa Valentino: 6776 Wedgewood Place, Whitley Heights, Hollywood. Four lots, making approximately one acre. Facing Wedgewood Place and extending through

VI. The Estate of Rudolph Valentino

Advertisement for the auction of Valentino's personal effects.

to lower rear street. Beautifully located on the hillside overlooking Highland Avenue. Not Sold.

No. 4—Santa Monica Swimming Club membership (par value $550.00), $210.

No. 5—Edgewater Beach Club membership, $210. Sold to C. S. Seymour.

No. 6—20 shares Hollywood Music Box (par value $2,000), $500. Sold to T. W. Wurn of New York; **No. 6A**—25 shares Rex Service, Inc. (par value $2,500); **No. 6B**—900 shares Ritz Cleaners, Inc. (par value $9,000).

No. 7—Isotta Fraschini Automobile. Italian, 1925 Model. Five-passenger town car with Landolet Fleetwood aluminum specially built body, $7,900. Sold to Alex Davidson, Amarillo, Texas.

No. 8—Avion Voisin Automobile. French, 1925 model, $2,200. Sold to Alex Davidson.

No. 9—Franklin Coupe Automobile. 1926 Model, $2,100. Sold to Alberto Guglielmi.

No. 10—Chevrolet Roadster Automobile. 1925 Model. Standard build and equipped. In first class condition.

No. 11—Ford Truck Automobile. 1922 Model, $112.50. Sold to T. S. Pettijohn, 417 Beethoven Street.

No. 13—Saddle Horse, "Firefly," Black Gelding. Arabian strain, approximately 15.2 hands, six years old, good walk trot horse (used by Valentino in the film *The Son of the Sheik* and valued at more than $3,000), $1,225. Sold to J. Moran.

No. 14—Saddle Horse, "Yaqui," Black Gelding. Arabian strain, approximately 15.2 hands, seven years old, $425. Sold to Cy Clegg, Culver City, Calif.

No. 15—Saddle Horse, "Ramadan," Gray Gelding. 16 hands, seven years old, $1,000. Sold to Cy Clegg, Culver City, Calif.

No. 16—Saddle Horse, "Haroun," Gray Gelding. 15.1 hands, seven years old (used by Valentino in the film *The Eagle*), $600. Sold to Cy Clegg, Culver City, Calif.

No. 17—Three Great Danes. Pedigreed. From the Francis X. Bushman Kennels.

No. 18—Two Italian Mastiffs. (Shaitain and Sheila) Pedigreed. These dogs were brought from Italy and raised by Mr. Valentino, $58. Sold to L. C. Brackett, 2032 Highland Avenue.

No. 20—One Irish Setter. Pedigreed. From the William Randolph Hearst Kennels, $60. Sold to H. H. Waters, 6120 Romaine Street.

No. 21—Power Boat—32 foot Standardized "Fellows-Craft" Cruiser. "Phoenix," $2,300. Sold to Harvey Priester.

No. 24—2 Western bridles, $64. Sold to Saul Morris, 751 S. Los Angeles Street.

No. 36—1 Lady's Side Saddle, complete with cover, "Martin & Martin's," $35. Sold to J. Volt, 303 Crescent Drive.

No. 71—1 Set Horse Hair Reins, $24. Sold to F. C. Blackman.

No. 79—Tuscan Gothic Oak Cabinet, $390. Sold to Adolphe Menjou.

No. 80—Ligurian Walnut Cabinet, $810. Sold to Olive Wall, Beverly Hills.

No. 88—Oriental Rug, $875. Sold to H. Bertillotti, 721 So. Crenshaw.

No. 89—Player Grand Piano, $2,100.

No. 90—Imported Carved Spanish Screen, $750. Sold to Adolphe Menjou.

No. 94—Antique Walnut Arm Chair, $95. Sold to Mrs. Morton Castor, 4329 Victoria Park.

No. 95—Magnificent Gothic Canopy Arm Chair, $415. Sold to W. F. Schuyler.

No. 96—French Throne Chair, $300. Sold to Maurice De Mond of the "Breakfast Club."

No. 99—Small Moorish Octagonal Tabouret, $83.

No. 101—Overstuffed Davenport, $225.

No. 125—Wrought-Iron Floor Lamp and Parchment Shade, $60.

No. 126—Wrought-Iron Table Lamp and Parchment Shade, $40.

No. 148—Writing Desk, $72. Sold to Adolphe Menjou.

No. 157 to **No. 167**—Mr. Valentino's Bedroom Set (sold as one lot): **No. 157** Bedstead; **No. 158**, **No. 159**—Two Dressers with Detached Cicular Mirrors; **No. 160**—Two Bedside Cabinets; **No. 161**, **No. 162**, **No. 163**—Three Small Round Pedestal Tables; **No. 164**—One Overstuffed Settee; **No. 165**—Upholstered Arm Chair; **No. 166**—Large Cushioned Lounging Seat; **No. 167**—Slipper Side Chair, $875. Sold to Mrs. Frank McCoy.

No. 169—Incense Lamp, $16.

No. 189—East Indian Wine Bottle, with Spout, $50. Sold to Allen H. Ratterree, Beverly Hills.

No. 191—Humidor, East Indian Design, $40. Sold to Allen H. Ratterree, Beverly Hills.

No. 193—Humidor, $25. Sold to Mrs. E. J. Ryan.

No. 196—Miniature Silver Knight, $141.

No. 207—Interesting Antique Key, $20.

No. 208—Curious Medieval Spiked Silver Ring, $25.

No. 209—Carved Ivory Scepter, $51.

No. 211—Small Antique Bronze Armored and Crowned Figure, $8.

No. 212—Very Important Bronze Horse by Gianbologna, $5.

No. 216—Important Antique Crucifi, $93.

No. 221—Lacquer Fan Case, $6.

No. 233—Sculptured Marble Hand of Mr. Valentino. White Carrara marble hand mounted on block of black marble. Made by "Prince Trobetskoy," Europe's famous sculptor, a great personal friend and admirer of Mr. Valentino, $150. Sold to Mrs. A. I. Cowen.

No. 249— Cigar Humidor, $50. Sold to Allen H. Ratterree of Beverly Hills.

No. 250— Large Cigar Humidor, Ebony Color, Porcelain Lining, $35. Sold to Allen H. Ratterree, Beverly Hills.

No. 262— Wide High Back Gothic Monastery Seat with Canopy, $365.

No. 263— Long, Gothic Monastery Seat, $115.

No. 264— High Back Gothic Throne Chair with Beautifully Carved Canopy, $60.

No. 265— Elaborate Carved Gothic Sideboard, $260.

No. 266— Antique Carved Wood Comb, $63.

No. 268— Large Portrait — Rudolph Valentino. By Beltran-Masses. Full length standing figure, in Argentine costume, entitled "Caballero Jerezano," $1,550. Sold to Teresa Werner.

No. 269— Large Portrait — Rudolph Valentino. By Beltran-Masses. Full-length standing figure, in full armor and costume of ancient Persian war lord of the time of the Crusades, with youthful female figure of the same period, seated on crossed feet, looking up at the standing figure.

No. 270— Portrait of Senorita Gaditana by Beltran-Masses. Semi-nude portrait of Europe's famous dancer, Senorita Gaditana, $1,900. Sold to Jules Howard.

No. 273— Portrait of Elizabeth Foscari, $435. Sold to Maurice De Mond.

No. 290, No. 291— Two Small Miniature Portraits on Parchment, $50 each.

No. 316— Valuable Gold Embroidered Cashmere Brocade, $2,965. Sold to Leo Youngworth.

No. 317— Valuable and Unusual East Indian Hanging, $3,475.

No. 318— Antique Herald's Tabard, $90.

No. 337— Old Spanish Silk Shawl (estimated value, $2,000), $350. Sold to F. W. Vincent.

No. 338— Two Large Moorish Tent Entrance Embroidered Hangings, $75.

No. 363— Round Pillow, $26.

No. 369— Ice Pail, with Tongs, $20.

No. 374— Twelve Almond Cups, $40.

No. 378— Eight Ash Trays [Note: only six were sold], $21.

No. 383— Antique Demi-Tasse Cup, Saucer and Spoon, Ivory Handles, $ 30.

No. 388— Small Oak Whiskey Keg and Stand, $27. Sold to C. L. Latty of Lakewood, Ohio.

No. 396— Silver Trophy. Awarded to Mr. Valentino in popularity contest, $30.

No. 397— Oval Tray and Gravy Boat, $20.

VI. The Estate of Rudolph Valentino

No. 406—Large Cocktail Shaker, $20.

No. 412—Sterling Flat Silver, Two Hundred and Twenty-five Pieces, Plate Beautiful Design, Monogrammed (R V G), $515. Sold to Mrs. Thomas Santschi.

No. 422—Set of Crystal Glasses, 59 Pieces, $77.

No. 423—One Set of Black Glassware, 35 Pieces, $60.

No. 424—Lot of Odd Glasses, $9.

No. 432—Curious Wine Bottle, with Four Separate Compartments, $25.

No. 437—Bavarian China Dinner Set, 95 Pieces; Service for Twelve, $125. Sold to Mrs. Alice N. Black.

No. 438—One Complete Luncheon and Breakfast Set, 107 Pieces, "Iona" Porcelain, $60.

No. 536—Fine Double Barrel French Flint-Lock Gun, $235. Sold to Bebe Daniels.

No. 537—Important Old Italian Wheel-Lock Gun, $360. Sold to Mrs. B. L. Lang.

No. 539—Small Hispano-Arab Flint-Lock Gun, $155. Sold to Bebe Daniels.

No. 542—Primitive Arab Flint-Lock Gun, $110. Sold to Bebe Daniels.

No. 543—Two Old Italian Wheel-Lock Pistols, $185. Sold to Bebe Daniels.

No. 544—Two Fine Old Flint-Lock Dueling Pistols, $275. Sold to Bebe Daniels.

No. 546—Indo-Persian Flint-Lock Pistol with Trigger Spring Bayonet, $245.

No. 553—Hispano-Moorish Dagger, $8.

No. 556—Interesting Scotch Highland Stocking Dagger, $300.

No. 564—Fine Spanish Cup-Hilted Rapier, $425.

No. 588—French "Small Sword" or Court Rapier, $180.

No. 594—Indo-Persian Battle Axe, $95.

No. 595—Fine Indo-Persian Round Shiel, $140.

No. 599—Indo-Persian Helmet, $135. Sold to director, Monta Bell.

No. 627—French Gaumont (all metal stereo camera), $180.

No. 630—German Goerz Tenax (vest pocket camera), $72. Sold to Alberto Guglielmi.

No. 631—Eastman Professional Home Portrait Graflex, $195.

No. 633—French Debrie All Metal Motion Picture Camera, $850.

No. 713—1 Set of Star Sapphire and Platinum Cuff Links with Stud, $775.

No. 715—1 Gold Longines Wrist Watch, $150.

No. 721—1 Baquet Shape Diamond Ring in Platinum Mounting, $675.

No. 723—1 Unusually Fine Combination Calendar Watch, $1,150.

No. 726—1 Solid Gold Hand Chased Pocket Cigar Lighter, "Dunhill Design," $85.

No. 732—1 Unusual Onyx Pocket Watch, $1,100.

No. 739—1 Platinum and Sapphire Wrist Watch, $613.

No. 740—1 Cabachon Sapphire Ring, $925.

No. 756A—White Gold Watch; very thin model, $150.

No. 757—Two Large Sterling Hammered Silver Picture Frame, $45 each.

No. 760—One Cut Glass Perfume Bottle, with Silver Mounts, $25.

No. 772—Hunting Knife, $16.50.

No. 785—Desk Clock, Small, Bronze with Cloisonne Inlay, $57.

No. 804—Fine Eight Day Clock, Tortoise Shell with Silver Mounts, $45.

No. 830—1 "Mauser" Automatic Pistol, 32 Calibre (carried by Valentino during making of *Four Horsemen of the Apocalypse*), $20. Sold to F. F. Long.

No. 831—1 "Smith & Wesson" Revolver, 45 Calibre, with Leather Holster, $40.

No. 832—1 "Smith & Wesson" Revolver, 45 Calibre, with Leather Holster and belt, $38.

No. 833—1 "Luger" Automatic Pistol, 32 Calibre, with Holster, $40.

No. 834—1 Spanish Automatic Pistol, 32 Calibre, with Gold Inlaid Design, $37. Sold to Virginia B. Martin.

No. 1095—Large Blue Cushion (made for **The Hooded Falcon**), $95.

No. 1-B—6 Volumes, History Conditions and Prospects of the Indian Tribes of United States, $82.

No. 215-B—China Costumes, $300. Sold to Teresa Werner.

No. 217-B—1, Punishment China, $16.

No. 256-B—1, Black Bound Book of Stills of Mr. Valentino's Picture, "Monsieur Beaucaire," $140.

APPENDIX VII

Los Angeles Times *and* New York Times *References*

Key

EXAMPLE: "05 Aug 1922   I 1:7   Valentino denies he is 'Great Lover.'"

Date: 05 Aug 1922
Reference: I (Section) 1:7 (Page and column)
Summary: Valentino denies he is "Great Lover."

Note: Section, page and column reference is given for "most" listings. The references for the *Los Angeles Times* from 1919 through 1936 were taken from hand written cards used by the newspaper. The handwriting at times was somewhat illegible and the best effort was made to decode it. If the reference you are searching for does not appear in the section or page listed for that date, please try other sections of the newspaper for the same date.

Los Angeles Times, *1919–2003*

06 Nov 1919   II 5:4   J Acker marries R Valentino.
19 Jan 1921   II 5:2   J Acker seeks alimony.
16 May 1921   II 1:2   J Acker files divorce.
16 Nov 1921   II 1:5   Stars in court battle.
23 Nov 1921   II 7:3   J Acker gives testimony in divorce trial.
24 Nov 1921   II 1:6   G Darmond testifies in Valentino divorce trial.
26 Nov 1921   II 9:1   R Valentino testifies in divorce trial.

Date	Ref	Description
30 Nov 1921	II 11:4	Missed evidence.
01 Dec 1921	I 1:8	Rambova picture.
17 Dec 1921	II 7:1	Divorce case submitted.
10 May 1922	II 11:4	Valentino engaged to N Rambova.
13 May 1922	I 9:2	Valentino denies marriage.
16 May 1922	II 1:4	Bigamy hinted at.
17 May 1922	II 1:6	D Gerrard tells of wedding ceremony.
18 May 1922	II 1:3	Separated from bride.
19 May 1922	I 1:8	Marriage investigated.
20 May 1922	II 2:1	District attorney gets evidence.
22 May 1922	II 1:4	Wife in New York.
23 May 1922	II 1:1	Attacks state statute.
24 May 1922	II 7:3	To hear law.
25 May 1922	II 11:6	Documents reach city.
31 May 1922	II 1:6	Attacks bigamy law.
02 Jun 1922	II 7:2	Pajamas figure in trial.
03 Jun 1922	II 1:7	Nazimova in case.
04 Jun 1922	I 13:2	New point in law.
06 Jun 1922	II 5:1	Charge dismissed.
07 Jun 1922	I 7:4	Valentino gets gun permit.
08 Jun 1922	II 1:8	No precedent.
09 Jun 1922	II 9:2	Case may be reopened.
05 Aug 1922	I 1:7	Valentino denies he is "Great Lover."
11 Aug 1922	II 11:3	Valentino goes east.
12 Aug 1922	II 1:4	Strike.
20 Aug 1922	III 13:5	Latin Lover (Wicox).
27 Aug 1922	III 32:3	N Naldi's opinion of R Valentino.
01 Sep 1922	II 1:1	In Adironacks; tries to heal contract with Lasky Co.
03 Sep 1922	I 2:5	J Acker still admirer.
03 Sep 1922	I 11:6	N Rambova to go to Paris.
04 Sep 1922	II 1:5	N Rambova did not go to Paris.
10 Sep 1922	III 35:1	Lasky trouble may go to court.
15 Sep 1922	II 11:6	Injunction (temporary).
19 Sep 1922	I 7:4	Trial starts.
01 Oct 1922	I 3:6	Valentino must keep Lasky contract.
05 Oct 1922	II 11:6	Art pictures.
07 Nov 1922	II 5:3	Rival found?
25 Nov 1922	II 2:4	Sued by agents.
02 Dec 1922	4:6	"An Illiterate."
03 Dec 1922	1:4	Valentino explains non-appearance in St. Louis.
09 Dec 1922	II 1:7	Loses in film suit.
10 Dec 1922	III 33:1	May play Ben-Hur.
11 Dec 1922	7:2	Valentino to work in Europe.

17 Dec 1922	33:1	May make phonograph records.
20 Jan 1923	4:4	Can't act but may work.
21 Jan 1923	V 14:6	To remarry Miss Hudnut in Paris.
25 Jan 1923	II 1:7	In N. Y. vaudeville.
25 Jan 1923	II 11:3	Still popular in N. Y.
08 Feb 1923	II 1:1	In now with Detroit employer.
11 Feb 1923	4:6	May go back to Lasky.
13 Feb 1923	II 10:3	In St. Louis.
23 Feb 1923	II 10:7	Popular with women.
27 Feb 1923	II 10	J Acker in Chicago.
06 Mar 1923	II 10:1	To remarry soon.
13 Mar 1923	II 10:1	Divorce final now.
15 Mar 1923	II 10:5	Married.
30 Mar 1923	3:5	Unknown.
31 Mar 1923	II 6:6	Unknown.
05 May 1923	9:6	To take vacation in L. A.
02 Jun 1923	4:3	Goods siezed to pay bill.
12 Jul 1923	II 9:3	To go to Europe.
18 Jul 1923	2:3	To make films for Ritz-Carlton.
22 Jul 1923	III 25:5	Unknown.
25 Jul 1923	3:6	Valentino leaves for Europe.
10 Nov 1923	II 7:6	To film in London.
13 Dec 1923	II 11:5	Rumors.
16 Dec 1923	IV 12:3	N Rambova sails.
18 Dec 1923	II 9:6	Unknown.
21 Dec 1923	II 11:6	N Rambova to make pictures abroad.
26 Dec 1923	II 11:4	Signs with Lasky.
16 Jan 1924	1:3	Back from overseas; ready to work.
20 Jan 1924	III 11:5	Literary efforts kidded by reviewers.
18 May 1924	III 22:3	Resting in Miami before beginning *Sainted Devil*; to begin with Ritz-Carlton when through with Lasky in June.
15 Aug 1924	II 9:4	Just where does Valentino's charm lie? (Whitaker)
17 Aug 1924	IV 29:1	*Monsieur Beaucaire.*
07 Sep 1924	8:2	To return here for work soon; mgr seeks studio.
11 Sep 1924	II 2:5	N. Y. loses Sheik; will transfer his producing activities to Hollywood at United Studios.
30 Sep 1924	1:3	J Acker applies for citizenship.
02 Oct 1924	II 11:3	Famous Players–Lasky to distribute films.
18 Nov 1924	8:3	Condemned by barbers for wearing whiskers.
19 Nov 1924	18:8	Due here Saturday with whiskers.
23 Nov 1924	10:2	Fans, officials to meet train—comments on whiskers.
25 Nov 1924	II 2:3	Sued by Robertson and Webb film agents.

30 Nov 1924	II 29:1	Aims to make production primary issue.
06 Dec 1924	10:3	To shave off famous beard; will begin filing *Cobra* as first independent film.
21 Dec 1924	II 25:4	Write-up by Whitaker.
26 Dec 1924	II 7:5	To present a gold medal each year to the best actor or actress.
11 Jan 1925	III 23:8	Denies that sister Maria is coming to America to enter films.
24 Feb 1925	II 2:6	Selects A Hale to direct next picture, *The Hooded Falcon*.
01 Mar 1925	II 12:6	Saddle is stolen; worth $600.
05 Mar 1925	II 1:3	May join United Artists; split with Ritz-Carlton hinted.
09 Mar 1925	II 1:2	Robertson and Webb employment agency seeks to recover commission.
10 Mar 1925	II 8:7	Signs with United Artists.
14 Mar 1925	II 5:2	Scores in fee case.
29 Mar 1925	8:1	N Rambova barred from studio lot in new contract; *Hooded Falcon* abandoned; story of old California may be next picture.
25 Apr 1925	16:2	To build home at Palm Springs.
07 May 1925	II 2:3	Celebrates 30th birthday.
21 May 1925	II 10:3	Cast for role of Tarter bandit in *Untamed*.
24 May 1925	III 19:8	To be great Russian lover in next film *The Untamed*.
26 May 1925	II 21:7	Hold magazine ban breaks contract; wrote article on "Our Jazz Age."
21 Jun 1925	III 15:8	Former landlord tells of period when 5 dollars was fortune to Valentino.
28 Jun 1925	15:2	Medal for screen acting presented to J Barrymore; painting of Valentino in Beltran-Masses exhibit.
12 Jul 1925	III 17:1	Valentino now plays comedy; *Black Eagle* light tale of Russian guard; star refuses to capitalize his personality.
20 Aug 1925	II 1:2	N Rambova to sue for divorce; Valentino says only marital vacation.
21 Aug 1925	II 3:1	Valentino admits break; property settlement is made; Rambova says separation is vacation.
29 Aug 1925	II 1:7	Valentino in motor accident.
30 Aug 1925	II 2:5	Returns to studio.
01 Sep 1925	2:6	Income tax.
03 Sep 1925	II 1:2	Fails to appear in court to answer speeding charge.
04 Sep 1925	II 15:4	Fails to appear in court to answer speeding charge.
05 Sep 1925	II 16:5	May hold hearing on studio lot.
09 Sep 1925	II 2:5	Court refuses to go to studio; Valentino ordered to appear Friday for hearing.
10 Sep 1925	II 20:6	Hurt on location; sprain and mustang's kick halt production.

03 Oct 1925	II 1:7	Rambova is shadowed by detectives before sailing for Paris; Valentino denies responsibility.
25 Oct 1925	10:3	N Rambova signs to appear in film.
28 Oct 1925	13:6	N Rambova interviewed in Paris; returning to U. S. but not to Hollywood.
04 Nov 1925	II 2:3	Not to see Rambova; says he has discovered what joys married men miss; leaves for N. Y.
08 Nov 1925	1:6	N Rambova arrived in N. Y.; will never marry again.
11 Nov 1925	1:4	N Rambova interviewed in N. Y.; doesn't want babies.
13 Nov 1925	2:3	Scouts idea wife sued for Paris divorce.
14 Nov 1925	2:2	Confirms report of Paris divorce; will do all he can to hasten it; Santa Monica seer foretold marital difference.
15 Nov 1925	1:4	N Rambova says she will not wed again; Valentino's pride hurt.
22 Nov 1925	13:5	Through with marriage; denies hatred of Rambova's dogs; arrives in England.
23 Nov 1925	8:5	N Rambova atty in Montreal.
29 Nov 1925	10:3	Valentino steps out in Paris.
01 Dec 1925	6:3	N Rambova failed to file suit in Paris.
06 Dec 1925	14	Mother Hudnut sails for Paris; Rambova awaits divorce.
07 Dec 1925	5:1	Italians seek to boycott films.
11 Dec 1925	II 9:3	Recalled from Europe by J Schenck to make another film.
13 Dec 1925	2:7	Italian films boycotted.
14 Dec 1925	3:6	French women mob Valentino; Mrs. Hudnut says Winifred will file divorce; Italian gov't halts mob a picture show.
18 Dec 1925	4:3	N Rambova files divorce action; resents press agent stories.
19 Dec 1925	4:3	Valentino refuses to discuss divorce.
22 Dec 1925	II 9:5	To play sheik role again in *Son of the Sheik*.
29 Dec 1925	16:2	To spend New Year's on Riviera with M Murray.
09 Jan 1926	1:3	*Monsieur Beaucaire* howled off screen by Italian fans.
10 Jan 1926	23:3	Valentino and Rambova meet on friendly terms.
13 Jan 1926	1:3	Divorce up for hearing.
14 Jan 1926		Citizen Rudolph.
20 Jan 1926	1:7	N Rambova awarded decree on charge of desertion from support; Valentino sails for New York wearing stiletto sideburns.
09 Feb 1926	II 1:7	Valentino welcomed here; Pola missing at depot denies going to meet actor; Valentino accompanied by brother Alberto Guglielmi and dog.
22 Jun 1926	II 9:6	Valentino appears in court as defendant.
23 Jun 1926	II 21:8	Valentino will have to pay assignees of C Robertson and C Webb on Lasky contract.

19 Jul 1926	3:1	Italy removes ban on Valentino's films.
20 Jul 1926	15:1	Valentino in Chicago; wedding up to Pola.
16 Aug 1926	1:6	Valentino collapses.
17 Aug 1926	1:1	Valentino improving.
18 Aug 1926	1:1	Valentino "death watch" set with crisis near.
19 Aug 1926	1:1	Valentino on mend.
20 Aug 1926	1:1	Valentino winning.
21 Aug 1926		Valentino continues to improve.
22 Aug 1926	1:5	Valentino's condition reported very serious.
23 Aug 1926	1:5	Valentino lies hovering on borderline of death.
24 Aug 1926		Death comes peacefully to Valentino.
24 Aug 1926		Valentino's films still to be seen.
24 Aug 1926		Film world mourns for Valentino.
24 Aug 1926		P Negri prostrated.
24 Aug 1926		Mayor Rolph pays tribute to Valentino.
24 Aug 1926		Breakfast Club plans services for Valentino.
24 Aug 1926		British artist sounds praise for Valentino.
24 Aug 1926		Hint Valentino poisoned.
24 Aug 1926		Film colony mourns Valentino's passing.
24 Aug 1926		Monument for Valentino sought.
24 Aug 1926		Valentino popularity explained.
24 Aug 1926		Valentino rich in relics.
25 Aug 1926		Scores injured in battle to see Valentino.
25 Aug 1926		Funeral services to be conducted next Monday.
25 Aug 1926		Valentino's first chief harks back.
25 Aug 1926		Estate of Valentino negligible.
25 Aug 1926		Parisian papers pay tribute to Valentino.
25 Aug 1926		Two dispute Valentino's nuptial aim.
25 Aug 1926		Valentino burial in Italy predicted.
26 Aug 1926		Valentino shielded.
26 Aug 1926		Screen colony plans service.
26 Aug 1926		P Negri on sad mission.
26 Aug 1926		Valentino declared lovelorn.
26 Aug 1926		Dr Eliott given less attention than Valentino.
27 Aug 1926		Valentino rests in peace.
27 Aug 1926		Film world to pause as its tribute to Valentino.
28 Aug 1926		Valentino burial delayed.
28 Aug 1926		Breakfast Club pays tribute to Valentino.
28 Aug 1926		B Warburton slips out of hospital.
28 Aug 1926		Valentino burial awaits his brother.
29 Aug 1926		Valentino pall bearers named.
29 Aug 1926		Vatican calls scenes collective madness.
30 Aug 1926		P Negri prays at casket.

VII. Los Angeles Times *and* New York Times *References*

30 Aug 1926		Friends seeking chapel for Valentino rites.
01 Sep 1926		Valentino's body to return to Los Angeles.
02 Sep 1926		Valentino's body leaves N. Y. for Los Angeles.
02 Sep 1926		Valentino's body not to lie in state at Chicago.
03 Sep 1926		Valentino train begins for Los Angeles.
04 Sep 1926		Chicago throngs foiled as star's body arrives.
05 Sep 1926		Players ready for Valentino.
05 Sep 1926		P Negri planned wedding in April.
06 Sep 1926		Valentino's body due in Los Angeles today.
07 Sep 1926		R Valentino to be laid at rest today.
07 Sep 1926		Valentino funeral rites this morning.
07 Sep 1926		Officer leading Valentino cortege injured in crash.
08 Sep 1926		Last services for Valentino.
08 Sep 1926		Few see Valentino rites.
08 Sep 1926		P Negri plans to bury grief and resume work today.
08 Sep 1926		Final tributes paid Valentino.
08 Sep 1926		Floral tributes profuse.
08 Sep 1926		Valentino's favorite dog to go abroad.
09 Sep 1926		Valentino will gives surprise.
10 Sep 1926	II 1:1	Valentino will fight impends.
11 Sep 1926	II 1:2	Valentino will fight may continue.
12 Sep 1926	Edit.	"Valentino and Eliot."
12 Sep 1926	16:8	First will leaves estate to 2nd wife, held void.
14 Sep 1926	II 6:8	Probate hearing set for Oct. 4.
27 Sep 1926	4:3	Beltran-Masses tells of Valentino's attempt at suicide following divorce.
05 Oct 1926	II 8:1	Will fight impends—heirs demand Valentino's brother be name co-executor.
12 Oct 1926	II 1:3	Will to be contested by brother and sister of Valentino; instructions give Ullman by deceased is basis for attack; contest to be delayed.
27 Oct 1926	12:4	"Loves and Life of R Valentino" written by E Ramond of Paris.
29 Oct 1926	II 10:7	Architects invited to submit designs for mausoleum.
02 Nov 1926	6:4	Mrs. Werner thinks contest unlikely—says Guglielmi misinformed.
03 Nov 1926	Edit.	"Old Shoes"—left 1,000 pairs of socks, 300 neckties and 50 pairs of shoes.
07 Nov 1926	6:4	Gov't files income tax lien for $6490 against estate for 1924 income tax.
14 Nov 1926	II 1:7	Matinee idol (Lancer).
26 Nov 1926	1:1	Valentino's ex-wife, W Hudnut gets message through spiritualist medium; aspires to legitimate stage of astral

		plane; visits theaters showing his pictures here; no mention of P Negri; A Guglielmi scoffs at spirit message story.
27 Nov 1926	II 8	P Negri shocked at attempts to publicize the matter as profane.
29 Nov 1926	4:6	J Acker says Valentino did not believe in spirits.
02 Dec 1926	II 20:1	Art works to be auctioned.
11 Dec 1926	11:3	H Hoyt, motion picture director believes Miss Hudnut sincere in spirit message story.
11 Dec 1926	II 2:2	Valentino's mansion sold in auction.
12 Dec 1926	17:3	Whitley Heights house gets no bidders.
15 Dec 1926	II 22:5	Valentino's personal effects sold; several thousand people turned away for lack of space; stars buy treasures.
16 Dec 1926	II 21:6	Bidding spirited at second day of say; B Daniels buys ancient guns.
17 Dec 1926	II 14:7	Further sales plans announced.
19 Dec 1926	Edit.	"The Lair of the Falcon."
19 Dec 1926	23:2	Crowd falls off at sale.
21 Dec 1926	II 2:5	Costumes for *Hooded Falcon* auctioned.
25 Dec 1926	II 16:3	P Negri files claim for $15,000 against estate.
29 Dec 1926	10:8	Bidding wars at auction; 2 more days of sale.
30 Dec 1926	II 6:8	Low mark in attendance at Valentino sale.
14 Jan 1927		Court honors P Negri's claim on Valentino estate.
21 Jan 1927	II 3:1	Ullman's claim on Valentino's estate granted.
01 Feb 1927	II 7:4	Possessions of Valentino to be sold in San Francisco.
02 Feb 1927		Last auction of Valentino items held next week.
07 Feb 1927	II 3:1	Doctor sues for fee in Valentino's case.
09 Feb 1927	1:7	Auction in San Francisco gets eager bidders.
10 Feb 1927	3:4	Payment made by Valentino to J Acker taxable.
19 Feb 1927		Valentino's sister M Guglielmi arrives to pray beside tomb.
24 Feb 1927		Valentino income tax lien dismissed.
02 Apr 1927	II 9:2	Agreement reached between Ullman and Feature Productions re film *The Firebrand* which was underway when actor died; advance salary had been drawn and notes given by Valentino.
21 Jun 1927	II 11:6	Young cafe dancer has resemblance to late Valentino.
17 Jul 1927	V 9:5	Valentino auto sold to J M Close.
27 Jul 1927		J Mathis dies.
03 Aug 1927	II 1:4	Valentino's remains to be removed.
06 Aug 1927		J Mathis laid at rest.
17 Aug 1927	II 2:4	Valentino memorial next week.
18 Aug 1927	II 20:8	New Valentino service plans.

19 Aug 1927	II 2:4	Hundreds to do honor to Valentino.
23 Aug 1927		Valentino will be paid tribute by films today.
24 Aug 1927	II 1:5	Anniversary of Valentino death observed here.
24 Aug 1927	II 4:4	"Vogue of Valentino."
28 Aug 1927	II 2:2	Undeveloped films taken by Valentino found on anniversary.
06 Oct 1927		Woman's kindness to Valentino begets riches.
19 Oct 1927	II 14:2	A G Valentino sports new face.
03 Mar 1928	II 5:2	Valentino's estate now totals $287,462.
18 Mar 1928	II 9:2	Valentino heir turns up by mail.
24 Mar 1928		A Guglielmi opens estate fight.
10 May 1928	II 9:4	A Guglielmi, brother of late R Valentino ready for a film career.
14 May 1928		S Wyman arch-imposter squelched.
31 May 1928	II 11:2	Rites for Valentino.
17 Aug 1928		Valentino case will be argued.
18 Aug 1928	II 1:1	Dispute over estate settled.
21 Aug 1928	II 13:5	Valentino rites set.
24 Aug 1928	II 7:4	Memorial rites for Valentino conducted here; memory honored in England in gardens of Italian Hospital in Queen's Square.
31 Aug 1928		Federal liens filed in court.
06 Sep 1928	II 8:5	A Guglielmi gets part in *Tropic Madness* film.
31 Dec 1928	II 18:8	Income tax lien filed against Valentino estate.
17 Feb 1929	II 5:2	Suit develops over plans for Valentino crypt.
19 Apr 1929	II 10:4	Valentino estate tax liens filed.
16 May 1929	I 21:6	Prince, Valentino dog, dies.
16 May 1929	II 2:4	Income tax lien filed against Valentino Productions.
29 Jun 1929	II 6:1	A Valentino asks $9 damages to car from woman who bumped into him.
09 Jul 1929	I 7:3	J Valentino on way to Hollywood on pilgrimage to tomb of his uncle.
13 Jul 1929	II 10:7	J Valentino, nephew of Valentino arrives in L. A. with T Schipa.
19 Jul 1929	II 1:6	A Guglielmi gets $9 for damages.
23 Aug 1929	II 1:8	Memorial rites for Valentino today.
24 Aug 1929	II 3:4	Tribute to Valentino impressive.
31 Mar 1930	II 1:4	Ghost stories at Falcon Lair.
10 Apr 1930	II 5:4	Large sum paid from Valentino estate.
07 May 1930	II 20:7	Valentino memorialized.
16 May 1930	II 8:5	Valentino monument protest turned down.
17 May 1930	II 13:5	Valentino estate fraud charges outs executor.
20 May 1930	II 1:4	Valentino executor raises veil on "tricks."

30 May 1930	II 3:2	Ullman defends actions as Valentino executor.
06 Jun 1930	II 5:5	Valentino executor again hit.
08 Jul 1930	II 7:5	Valentino's friend out of estate.
09 Jul 1930	II 1:1	Bank to handle Valentino's estate.
11 Jul 1930	II 5:2	Judge continues disposition of Valentino's estate.
31 Aug 1930		"Ghost" of Valentino.
21 Sep 1930		Monuments to film fame rise.
22 Oct 1930	II 2:7	Valentino will dispute finds way to court.
04 Nov 1930		Valentino's phonograph records discovered.
05 Nov 1930		Valentino suit comes up today.
06 Nov 1930	II 1:4	S G Ullman tells court how he balleyhooed Valentino's funeral
07 Nov 1930	II 3:1	Valentino lost money in dry cleaning shop.
08 Nov 1930	II 6:1	Valentino safe raid asserted.
11 Nov 1930	II 8:5	Valentino case gets surprise.
13 Nov 1930	II 3	Two Valentino bank notes offered.
14 Nov 1930	II 3:3	Fame of Valentino cited in court.
28 Nov 1930		Valentino will row heats up.
23 Dec 1930	II 16:6	Valentino estate case trial delayed.
05 Dec 1930	II 2:8	Lawyer backs Valentino will.
06 Feb 1931	II 2:5	Valentino's good-by scene to P Negri disputed.
07 Feb 1931	II 6:3	Valentino case given to Judge.
02 Aug 1931	II 11:6	Can C Gable be another Valentino?
24 Aug 1931	II 3:4	Memory of Valentino kept fresh.
11 Oct 1931	I 9:4	Abatement of $61,432 to Valentino estate for over assessment of taxes.
21 Feb 1932	II 1:2	Estate of Valentino practically insolvent.
06 Jul 1932	II 2:5	Medium rushes through courtroom — says sent by spirit of Valentino.
24 Jul 1932	I 13:2	J Guglielmi, Valentino nephew arrived in L. A. from Turin where he was studying.
18 Aug 1932	II 1:1	Judge rules Ullman made unauthorized expenditures and order to repay.
22 Nov 1932		A Valentino and wife involved in car accident.
07 Jan 1933	II 1:2	Ullman appeals to State Supreme Court.
10 Jun 1933	II 2:2	Valentino photograph basis of $100,000 suit.
18 Dec 1933	II 10:5	Tax lien filed against estate of Valentino.
10 Feb 1934	II 2:6	Woman is awarded difference from cost of Aspiration statue.
06 Jul 1934		A Valentino and wife to return from Mexico and apply for US citizenship.
09 Sep 1934	II 1:2	Does death of star kill film at box office?
13 Oct 1934	II 3:2	R Valentino echo stirs court spectators.

11 Dec 1934	II 1:2	Falcon Lair sale approved by court.
18 Apr 1935	II 2:7	Judgment in Valentino fight upheld for woman.
26 Apr 1935	II 2:7	Burglars steel $100 worth of furnishings from Villa Valentino.
01 Jun 1935	I 5:4	Woman asserts receiving messages from Valentino dictating menus.
21 Jul 1937		J Acker, former wife of Valentino appears in film as extra.
23 Aug 1937		Blonde beauty due at crypt of Valentino.
24 Aug 1937		Valentino lures fans to crypt.
23 Aug 1938		Mystery woman due to keep tryst today at Valentino's tomb.
24 Aug 1938		Scores visit Valentino's tomb.
23 Aug 1939		Valentino service plans abandoned.
19 Aug 1940		Valentino tribute set for Friday.
24 Aug 1940		J Acker visits Valentino tomb on death anniversary.
13 Nov 1940		Mystery of Valentino ring partly solved by publicist.
22 Aug 1941		Valentino anniversary to be marked at crypt.
12 Jul 1944		Valentino still hero to S G Ullman.
28 Jul 1946		Valentino art books offered for sale.
03 Aug 1946		R Valentino tests to start mid-month.
24 Aug 1947		"Lady in Black" joins in tribute to Valentino.
13 Sep 1947		Valentino family sued by lawyer.
15 Sep 1947		Nephew J Valentino, settles fee suit.
22 Dec 1947		Valentino's estate hangs fire 20 years.
07 May 1948		Spirit of Valentino returns, so they say, but turns coy.
24 Aug 1948		"Lady in Black" visits Valentino tomb again.
24 Aug 1949		Valentino crypt visited by dozens.
06 Jun 1950		D Gerrard found dying in street.
16 Jul 1950		Valentino film secrets now out.
20 Jul 1951		A Terry files suit over Valentino film.
01 Dec 1951		M Benda commits suicide.
15 Oct 1952		"Substantial amount" to family in $500,000 Valentino Suit.
06 Jan 1953		A Terry suit over Valentino film settled.
25 Aug 1953		Memory of Valentino honored on anniversary.
24 Aug 1955		"Lady in Black" missing at Valentino ceremony.
24 Aug 1957		"Lady in Black" fails to attend Valentino rites.
24 Aug 1958		100 attend memorial for Valentino.
25 Aug 1959		50 attend memorial services for Valentino.
24 Aug 1963		"Lady in Black" visits at Valentino crypt.
06 Aug 1966		N Rambova obituary.
24 Aug 1967		Valentino legend lives on after 41 years.
08 May 1972	I 2:3	Valentino remembered by fan club.

Date	Ref	Description
24 Aug 1972	I 1:4	Valentino mourned 46 years after death.
14 Nov 1973		Valentino's leading lady silent star L Lee dies.
21 Aug 1974	IV 16:1	Four Horsemen / death.
13 Jul 1975	X 11:2	Valentino still keeps home fire bright.
20 Aug 1975	IV 1:2	"Valentino—Return of a Loving Legend."
22 Aug 1976	Cal 1:1	A 50-year swoon song for R Valentino.
24 Aug 1976	II 1:4	Hundreds attend Valentino memorial rite.
02 Sep 1976	I 3:5	Portrait of Valentino—"Ghost" to go public.
23 Aug 1977	IV 5:1	*Son of the Sheik* review.
24 Aug 1977	II 1:1	51st anniversary of death. Valentino still an idol.
29 Sep 1977	II 4:4	Valentino heir's suit tossed out on appeal.
29 Nov 1977	IV 5:1	"Rudolph Valentino" A Walker review.
02 Dec 1977		Original *The Sheik* due at museum.
12 May 1978		Valentino Place: landlord asks street renaming.
19 Aug 1978	I 28:1	J Acker obituary.
31 Aug 1979	II 1:1	De Longpre Park facelift hits a bureaucratic snag.
15 Jun 1981	I 20:1	A Valentino obituary.
29 Feb 1984	II 1:1	D Flame obituary.
19 Apr 1984		P Ivano obituary.
25 Jul 1985		10 noteworthy statues that enhance the city's sense of history.
25 Aug 1988		Remembering Valentino.
02 Jun 1989		J Romero obituary.
24 Aug 1989		200 mark Valentino's death.
24 Aug 1989		"Woman in Black" to be reunited with Valentino.
24 Aug 1990		Valentino draws crowd 64 years after death.
28 May 1991	E 1:2	J Smith discusses his recent viewing of *The Sheik*.
24 Aug 1991	B 2:1	Fans of R Valentino gather at his grave in Hollywood.
17 Aug 1992	B 1:2	For 60 years women dressed in black have visited crypt of R Valentino.
20 Aug 1996	F 3:1	Silent Movie Theater's 6th annual film festival features *Cobra*.
26 Sep 1996		J G Valentino obituary.
04 May 1997		Hot Property.
20 May 1997		Only in L. A.
03 Jan 1998		Morning Report: Automobiles.
01 Nov 1998		Hot Property.
01 Mar 2000	A 5	Review of *The Married Virgin*.
02 Mar 2000		Theater owner urges Valentino Oscar.
23 Mar 2000	A 49	Review of video release of *The Sheik*.
18 Aug 2000		Eternal adulation.
05 Apr 2001	B 8	A Dexter obituary.
03 May 2001		Birthday boy.

18 May 2002	F 16	HBO documentary tells how a bankrupt Hollywood cemetery is made into a spiffed-up screenland shrine.
26 Jun 2002		Memories of a glamorous age.
11 Jul 2002	F 38	Review of video release of *The Sheik*.
23 Aug 2002	E 1	As in the last 75 years, a motley group congregates today at a cemetery at the exact time Valentino died.
29 Aug 2002	F 48	Falcon is the latest supper club with late-night food in an intimate setting.
11 May 2003	R 2	Review of *Dark Lover: The Life and Death of Rudolph Valentino*, by Emily W. Leider.
28 Aug 2003	E 14	Review of *Monsieur Beaucaire*.

New York Times, *1916–1996*

06 Sep 1916	6:4	Mrs. G Thyme and R Guglielmi arrested.
10 May 1922	19:1	Engaged to W Hudnut.
16 May 1922	10:3	Marriage to Hudnut declared invalid.
18 May 1922	19:4	Dist Atty inquiring into bigotry.
19 May 1922	10:1	Feds may cite Mann White Slave act.
20 May 1922	3:3	Bride's real name is Shaughnessy.
21 May 1922	16:1	Arrested on bigamy charges.
23 May 1922	36:2	Acker denies she will aid him.
04 Jun 1922	12:2	Bridal apparel shown at hearing.
06 Jun 1922	20:2	Freed on bigamy charge.
02 Sep 1922	10:3	Explains quarrel with Famous Players–Lasky.
03 Sep 1922	12:2	N Rambova reported to have sailed for Paris.
04 Sep 1922	3:3	N Rambova did not sail.
15 Sep 1922	12:2	Famous Players–Lasky gets injunction.
16 Sep 1922	18:5	Famous Players–Lasky gets injunction, cont.
19 Sep 1922	14:4	Court reserves decision in injunction suit.
01 Oct 1922	II 1:6	Famous Players–Lasky wins injunction.
11 Nov 1922	14:4	J Acker asks court to use Valentino name.
19 Nov 1922	II 1:5	Objects to Acker using his name.
02 Dec 1922	8:2	Appellate Div reserves decision about injunction.
09 Dec 1922	11:2	Loses appeal.
23 Dec 1922	4:6	Addresses American Radio Exposition.
20 Jan 1923	13:4	Appellate div modifies injunction by Famous Players–Lasky.
30 Jan 1923	12:2	N Rambova fails to appear at Palace Theatre.
31 Jan 1923	8:2	N Rambova fails to appear in court to pay taxicab fine.
28 Feb 1923	17:1	Reported that he will rewed N Rambova.
01 Mar 1923	19:8	Plans to remarry.

06 Mar 1923	7:2	Wedding put off until Mar 9.
13 Mar 1923	2:6	Obtains final divorce decree.
15 Mar 1923	21:5	Remarries.
20 Mar 1923	24:2	N Rambova appears at the Palace.
30 Mar 1923	36:2	Ind Dep Atty Gen hold marriage is illegal.
02 Apr 1923	23:3	Report of shattered nerves denied.
21 Jun 1923	30:4	Property attached in suit by A B Graham.
19 Jul 1923	18:3	Signs with Ritz-Carlton Pictures.
24 Jul 1923	21:4	Attracts crowd outside restaurant; police.
25 Jul 1923	3:3	Sails for Italy with N Rambova.
27 Nov 1923	2:6	Beauty contest judge.
28 Nov 1923	20:4	Beauty contest continued.
29 Nov 1923	30:1	Beauty contest winners announced.
09 Dec 1923	II 5:8	Sails for Europe.
27 Dec 1923	10:2	Re-joins Famous Players–Lasky.
16 Jan 1924	21:5	Surprised Salm-VonHoogstraeten did not marry Miss Coffee.
25 Jan 1924	20:3	Crowned King of the Movies.
26 Feb 1924	14:1	Awards prize for best review.
11 Apr 1924	17:1	Buys Benguiat art collections.
24 Apr 1924	20:1	Buys art objects at American Art Gallery.
10 Jul 1924	24:4	Sued by Robertson & Webb for commission.
03 Aug 1924	VII 2:1	*Monsieur Beaucaire.*
30 Sep 1924	14:3	J Acker files to restore citizenship.
11 Nov 1924	20:3	Return from trip to Spain.
18 Nov 1924	27:6	Banned by barbers in Chicago.
04 Feb 1925	14:2	J Acker regains citizenship.
11 Mar 1925	19:1	Future productions released by UA.
21 Aug 1925	8:1	N Rambova visits parents in France.
10 Sep 1925	28:2	Injured on horse on film set.
25 Sep 1925	2:3	Natacha denies divorce rumors.
04 Nov 1925	24:2	Leaves L. A. for New York; statement on marital troubles.
08 Nov 1925	18:1	Arrives in N. Y.; troubles with wife.
10 Nov 1925	1:5	Testifies in plagiarism suit against Mme. Petrova.
11 Nov 1925	16:2	Takes out citizenship papers; explains being a slacker during World War.
14 Nov 1925	2:6	Will establish domicile in France where wife has filed suit for divorce.
15 Nov 1925	26:1	Sails for London.
15 Nov 1925	VIII 5:1	Acting in film, *The Eagle.*
08 Dec 1925	24:2	Wife sues for Paris divorce.
19 Dec 1925	3:2	Denies knowledge of wife's suit.

22 Dec 1925	9:3	Arrives in Berlin; denies rumor of engagement to M Murray.
31 Dec 1925	10:5	Wife refuses to appear in same program.
09 Feb 1926	22:6	N Rambova appears in vaudeville.
08 Jul 1926	28:5	Mother of P Negri says Miss Negri may marry next March.
21 Jul 1926	17:2	Seeks fight with author of editorial in *Chicago Tribune* on powder puffs for males.
22 Jul 1926	11:6	Challenge ignored by *Chicago Tribune* editor.
25 Jul 1926	2:7	Sees Gen U Noble off on return to Italy.
30 Jul 1926	19:6	Still wants fight with Chicago editor; E Taylor will be next leading lady.
03 Aug 1926	19:4	Welcomed at Atlantic City.
16 Aug 1926	1:5	Operation for gastric ulcer and appendicitis.
17 Aug 1926	1:4	Condition, messages of inquiry.
18 Aug 1926	1:7	Condition, messages of inquiry.
19 Aug 1926	1:5	Condition, messages of inquiry.
20 Aug 1926	2:6	Condition, messages of inquiry.
21 Aug 1926	3:8	Condition, messages of inquiry.
22 Aug 1926	1:3	Develops pleurisy.
23 Aug 1926	1:6	Alarming worse.
24 Aug 1926	1:6	Death.
24 Aug 1926	7	Had premonition of early death.
24 Aug 1926	3	Career; tributes; mourned in Italy; attending physician, Dr. P E Durham, ill after long strain.
24 Aug 1926	20:5	Fame compared with Kipling's.
25 Aug 1926	1:1	Riot at bier; Fascisti place guard at coffin; plans for funeral.
25 Aug 1926	3:5	Praised in Paris papers; 14 co-workers in Hollywood send message of regret to J M Schenck; P Negri, reported fiancée, will attend funeral.
26 Aug 1926	1:5	Thousands see body; irreverence and disorder cause withdrawal from public view; clash between Fascisti and anti-Fascisti threatened; J Acker, first wife, present; tribute from M Gest.
26 Aug 1926	5:3	Native town, Castellaneta, Italy, indifferent to his death; childhood life; M Guglielmi, sister, grieved at news of death.
27 Aug 1926	3:3, 4	Crowds still try to see body; plans for funeral; 2 memorials proposed; J Dempsey mourns his death.
27 Aug 1926	16:3	Editorial on relative newspaper space given to his death and that of Dr. C W Eliot.
28 Aug 1926	11:3	Decision of burial place rests with brother, A Guglielmi; his horse with open memorial service to him at Break-

		fast Club, Los Angeles; suicide note of P Scott lays death to his.
28 Aug 1926	18:2	Death does not affect stock of United Artist Theatres Circulating Co.
29 Aug 1926	19:1	Plans for funeral.
29 Aug 1926	II 4:5	Tribute by sons of Italy in America.
30 Aug 1926	3:1	P Negri swoons at bier; detailed plans for funeral.
31 Aug 1926	1:3	Funeral services in N.Y.C.; plans to bring body to Hollywood.
01 Sep 1926	8:1	P Seng comments on publicity given him.
01 Sep 1926	23:1	Plans for second funeral service and transportation of body to Hollywood; demand for his pictures.
02 Sep 1926	21:3	Brother, A Guglielmi, consents to burial at Hollywood; plans for second mass abandoned.
03 Sep 1926	17:3	Plans for funeral at Beverly Hills; body starts for Hollywood.
04 Sep 1926	3:6, 7	Catholic Transcript explains his Catholic burial; letter by Dr. H E Meeker on his illness and treatment; crowds wait vainly in Chicago to see funeral car; Warsaw will hold memorial service.
05 Sep 1926	12:5	Troth with P Negri affirmed by her, by S G Ullman and A Guglielmi.
06 Sep 1926	17:6	Dr. S C Wyman, who took active part in making his funeral arrangements, is identified as an impersonator whose real name is S Weinberg.
06 Sep 1926	30:3	Linked with Dr. C W Eliot as artist of life, sermon by the Rev. H E Clute.
07 Sep 1926	21:2	Body reaches Los Angeles.
08 Sep 1926	25:2	Film studios in southern Calif. close for funeral.
09 Sep 1926	1:3	Will; equal bequest to A and M Guglielmi, brother and sister, and Mrs T Werner, aunt of 2nd wife.
09 Sep 1926	23:4	Brother says he will have mausoleum at Hollywood; Catholic News explains burial.
10 Sep 1926	24:2	M Cohen, atty for A and M Guglielmi, brother and sister, says he will contest will if it is unfair.
11 Sep 1926	17:5	Will dispute not settled.
21 Sep 1926	9:2	Line forms 15 hours before performance of *Son of Sheik* in London.
05 Oct 1926	20:1	Relatives demand that brother be co-executor of estate.
06 Oct 1926	27:4	C Rivers denies that he knew P Scott, at inquest on latter's suicide.
12 Oct 1926	30:2	G Ullman made sole executor of estate; A and M Guglielmi contest will.

23 Oct 1926	14:3	T Werner, aunt of 2nd wife, arrives to fight for fortune left to her.
24 Oct 1926	II 6:7	*Valentino as I Knew Him*, by S G Ullman, published.
31 Oct 1926	18:2	Mrs A Celestina says her suicide attempt was for love of him.
07 Nov 1926	IX 17:3	Car designed by him will be exhibited at Automobile Salon in N.Y.C.
08 Nov 1926	19:3	Income tax lien filed in Los Angeles.
26 Nov 1926	21:4	N Rambova, former wife, says he sends spirit messages to her.
29 Nov 1926	21:3	J Acker scouts report from N Rambova of "spirit" messages.
02 Dec 1926	34:2	His "double" brought to US by Mme M Sari.
11 Dec 1926	32:1	Home, autos and horses sold.
12 Dec 1926	18:7	Auction of home called off.
15 Dec 1926	20:5	Personal effects sold.
16 Dec 1926	3:4	Personal effects sold.
23 Dec 1926	10:3	Sale of his art works.
25 Dec 1926	23:2	P Negri sues estate for alleged $15,000 loan.
16 Jan 1927	II 6:8	Valentino excluded from American Theatre Hall of Fame.
10 Feb 1927	14:6	Tax appeals board rejects claims by Jean Acker.
04 May 1927	28:4	Auction nets $96,654.
26 Jul 1927	37:1	Memorial services in London.
27 Jul 1927	1:6	J Mathis dies.
25 Sep 1927	II 7:5	May be in Tussand's Wax Works.
03 Mar 1928	5:4	Balance of estate.
04 Mar 1928	4:4	Accounting of estate.
09 May 1928	2:4	P Joyce sued over car.
10 May 1928	4:3	Joyce settles for car.
25 Jul 1928	8:2	Exhibit of jewelry.
18 Aug 1928	15:5	Suit brought by family against S G Ullman.
17 Feb 1929	IX 5:1	Cult formed in Hungary.
09 Jul 1929	34:7	J Valentino arrives.
30 May 1930	10:6	G Ullman defends against mismanagement.
08 Nov 1930	20:5	S G Ullman — document stolen.
11 Oct 1931	II 6:5	Income tax abatement.
21 Feb 1932	15:8	Estate listed at $130,000.
19 Jul 1936	3:6	Movie companies seek successor.
28 Aug 1938	IV 2:1	Career, portrait.
06 May 1945	VI 24:4	Present popularity discussed.
16 May 1948	II 5:5	30 psychic mediums attempt to communicate.
20 Jul 1951	13:4	A Terry sues Small on Valentino film.
24 Jul 1951	21:8	Hollywood mansion to be torn down.

Date	Ref	Description
06 Jan 1953	22:6	Damage suit against Valentino film settled.
08 Mar 1953	85:4	Falcon Lair bought by Doris Duke.
24 Apr 1960	VI 60	Article on career.
24 Aug 1961	29:1	35th anniversary of death.
01 Oct 1961	43:6	Castellaneta memorial dedicated.
08 Oct 1961	127:3	Valentino statue sparks public criticism.
12 Nov 1961	VI 42	J. Stang art/career.
08 Jan 1966	15:3	"Ciao Rudy" review.
11 Jan 1966	19:6	"Ciao Rudy" correction.
24 Aug 1967	37:2	Anniversary of death.
08 Nov 1967	45:3	Shulman bio review.
19 Nov 1967	VII 44	Review.
20 Nov 1975		Nureyev to portray Valentino in movie.
24 Aug 1976	58:5	1,000 R Valentino fans attend 50th anniversary of his death.
16 Oct 1976	2:3	Home town to preserve name and reputation of R Valentino.
03 Mar 1978		N Rambova reports on graft in the movies.
07 Jun 1978	III 2:4	L. A. City Council approves changing name of Irving Street to Valentino Place.
01 Mar 1984	IV 27:4	D Flamé obituary.
21 Apr 1984		P Ivano obituary.
08 Nov 1991	C 1:1	Review of "The Valentino Cult" film series of R Valentino films at American Museum of Moving Image.
20 Oct 1996	XIII-LI 17:1	*The Shiek* is screened as part of Hampton's Int'l Film Festival.

APPENDIX VIII

Periodical Articles

Acker, Jean. "Does the Ghost of Valentino Live in George Raft?" *Hollywood*, November 1933.
Adams, E. "Horoscope of the Stars: Rudolph Valentino," *Photoplay*, November 1924, p. 107.
"Ah, Valentino!," *New York Times Magazine*, April 24, 1960, p. 60.
Albert, Katherine. "Watch This Hombre!" *Photoplay*, January 1930, p. 31.
"All That Is Mortal of Valentino Lies in a Borrowed Tomb," *Picture Play*, November 1928.
"L'Amant Eternel (Le Fils du Cheik)," *Le Film Complet*, 1939.
"Amour and the Man," *Saturday Review*, October 13, 1956, p. 29.
"As Julio in 'The Four Horsemen of the Apocalypse," *Literary Digest*, March 26, 1921, p. 29.
"At Home After January First 1923," *Photoplay*, September 1922, p. 26.
Balch, David. "The Most Romantic Personality in the World," *Movie Weekly*, August 11, 1923.
Ball, Russel E. "Mr. and Mrs. (with apologies to Briggs)," *Motion Picture Magazine*, August 1923.
Biery, Ruth. "I Slept in Valentino's Haunted House," *Motion Picture Magazine*, November 1928.
_____. "Spirit Messages to Natacha Rambova," *Motion Picture Magazine*, January 1929.
Bodeen, DeWitt. "Rudolph Valentino," *Screen Facts*, Vol. III, No. 5, 1968, pp. 1–27.
Brewster, Eugene V. "Has Valentino Come Back?" *Motion Picture Classic*, March 1926, p. 42.
"Brickbats and Bouquets," *Photoplay*, June 1923, p. 8.

"Brickbats and Bouquets," *Photoplay*, January 1927, p. 12.

Calhoun, Dorothy. "What if They Had Lived?" *Motion Picture Magazine*, December 1930, p. 29.

Cannon, Regina. "Is a Screen Star's Wife Jealous?" *Movie Weekly*, August 11, 1923, p. 13.

Card, James. "Rudolph Valentino," *Image*, May 1958, No. 7, p. 106.

Carr, Harry. "Home Life," *Motion Picture Magazine*, August 1925, p. 32.

_____. "Valentino is Not a Henpecked Husband," *Motion Picture Magazine*, August 1925.

Cebe, G. "L'Homme Fatal et sa Legende," *Ecran* (Paris), November 1976, p. 4.

Cheatham, Maude S. "The Darkest Hours," *Motion Picture Classic*, October 1922, p. 52.

Cocci, John. [Addendum] *Screen Facts*, Vol. III, No. 6, 1968, p. 63.

Crane, E. "Rudolph Valentino, Legend with Feet of Clay?" *Screen Legends*, October 1965, p. 4.

Cross, Joan. "Why the Valentinos Separated," *Movie Magazine*, October 1925.

"Dagmar Wins Part with Valentino," *Photoplay*, October 1924.

Dean, Frances Smith. "Reading Between the Lines in the Valentino–Ramobova Separation," *Moving Picture Stories*, December 29, 1925, p. 19.

De Revere, F. V. "What I Read in His Face," *Motion Picture Magazine*, October 1924, p. 45.

De Saix, Guillot. "Valentino, Son Revolver et le Serpent d'Argent," *Comoedia*, September 25, 1926.

De Sola, Vincente. "Why Valentino Is Attractive to Women," *Movie Weekly*, August 11, 1923.

Dillon, Seamus. "How Valentino Keeps His Figure," *Liberty*, December 27, 1924.

"Dinner with the Valentinos," *Movie Magazine*, September 1925.

Dorgan, Dick. "Giving 'The Sheik' the Once Over from the Ringside," *Photoplay*, April 1922.

_____. "A Song of Hate," *Photoplay*, July 1922, p. 26.

Ellenberger, Allan. "Good Night Valentino," *Classic Images*, May 2003.

"En Este Numero: La Vida Valentino," *Cine-Mundial*, May 1927.

"Eternal Love: Return of the Sheik," *L. A. Weekly*, August 31, 2001.

"Famous Players–Lasky vs. Rudolph Valentino: Affidavit of Rudolph Valentino," *Movie Weekly*, October 21, 1922, through January 6, 1923.

Faulkner, H. H. "A Phrenological Study of Some Famous Stars: Rudolph Valentino," *Photoplay*, March 1922, p. 30.

"Final Acts," *Saturday Evening Post*, July 1978.

Florey, Robert. "Indimenticabile Indimenticato: Rudolfo Valentino," *Rotosei* (Rome), 1957, no. 1–6.

Fontana, Attilio. "La Verita Sulla Giovanezza di Rodolfo Valentino," *Cinema* (Rome), November 10, 1938, vol. III, p. 309.

French, William Fleming. "Valentino, the Man," *Illustrated World*, May 1923, p. 345.

"From Here to Eternity," *Premiere*, November 1994.

Gaddis, Vincent H. "Valentino—Was His Death Foretold?," *Fate Magazine*, July 2, 1949, p. 4.

Gassaway, Gordon. "The Erstwhile Landscape Gardner," *Motion Picture Magazine*, July 1921.

Gatto, Alfonso. "Signora Guglielmi's Son," *Epoca*, July 24, 1952.

Gladwell, Robert. "Valentino ... and His Unseen Guide," *Fate Magazine*, March 1956, p. 6.

Glyn, Elinor. "Rudolph Valentino as I Knew Him," *Modern Screen*, May 1927.

_____. "Rudolph Valentino as I Knew Him," *Modern Screen Magazine*, May 1930, p. 26.

Gnaedinger, L. B. N. "Valentino as a Hall Roomer," *Movie Weekly*, February 14, 1925.

Godowsky, Dagmar. "The Secret Rudolph Valentino Taught Me," *Guideposts*, August 1975.

Goldbeck, Willis. "The Perfect Lover," *Motion Picture Magazine*, May 1922, p. 40.

Golden, Eve. "The Greatest Star: Rudolph Valentino," *Classic Images*, May 1995, p. C10.

"The Good Bad Man Is Back Again," *Photoplay*, October 1924, p. 44.

Good Housekeeping, September 1932. [Portrait].

Grant, Jack. "Has No Permanent Tomb," *Motion Picture Magazine*, July 1931, p. 34.

_____. "Long-Missing Valentino Film Found," *Movie Classic*, September 1934, p. 30.

Gravier, J. M. "Rudolph Valentino," *Lumière du Cinema*, September 1977, p. 20.

"The Great Lover," *Life*, January 2, 1950, p. 36.

"The Greatest Lover," *National Film Theatre* (UK), February 1998.

"The Greatest Stars," *Cosmopolitan*, October 1956, p. 29.

Gruen, John. "Nureyev's Valentino Tango," *Vogue*, August 1977, p. 149.

Hale, Ruth. "What the Boy Still Has," *Judge*, December 2, 1922.

Hall, Alice. "Rudolph the Romantic," *Picturegoer*, January 1922, p. 15.

Hall, Gladys. "He Still Lives for Pola Negri," *Motion Picture Magazine*, January 1935, p. 46.

_____. "In Memorium," *Motion Picture Classic*, September 1927.

_____. "Women I Like to Dance With, by Rudolph Valentino," *Movie Weekly*, January 27, 1923, p. 7.

_____, and Adele Whieley Fletcher. "We Discover Who Discovered Valentino," *Motion Picture Magazine*, June 1923, pp. 20–22.

Hansen, Miriam. "Valentino and Female Spectatorship," *Cinema Journal*, Summer 1986, p. 6.

Henderson, Anabel. "I Was Valentino's Mystery Woman: Part One," *Secret Confessions*, January 1941.

_____. "I Was Valentino's Mystery Woman: Part Two," *Love Revelations*, February 1941.

_____. "I Was Valentino's Mystery Woman: Part Three," *Love Revelations*, March 1941.

_____. "I Was Valentino's Mystery Woman: Part Four," *Love Revelations*, April 1941.
_____. "I Was Valentino's Mystery Woman: Part Five," *Love Revelations*, May 1941.
"Her Years as Valentino's Wife," *New Movie Magazine*, February 1930.
"Her Years as Valentino's Wife," *New Movie Magazine*, August 1930.
Hilborne, Ronald. "King of My Heart For Ever," *Everybody's Magazine*, August 25, 1951.
"His Unknown Love," *Motion Picture Magazine*, January 1930, p. 58.
Hodenfield, Chris. *Rolling Stone*, November 3, 1977, p. 80.
"Hollywood Westerns," *House and Garden*, April 1988.
Holman, Russell. "The Rise of Rudolph," *Pantomine*, February 11, 1922, p. 12.
"House of the Month," *Los Angeles Magazine*, October 1997.
Houston, Jane. "The Sheik Goes Hunting," *Cinema Art*, January 1926, p. 25.
"How Rudolph Valentino Learned About Sex," *Uncensored Magazine*, January 1956.
Howe, Herbert. *Motion Picture Classic*, December 1921, p. 18. [Interview].
_____. "Success—and the Morning After," *Picture Play*, August 1921.
Huff, Theodore. "The Career of Rudolph Valentino," *Films in Review*, April 1952, p. 145.
"I Knew Valentino Best," *Stardom*, May 1942.
"In Memory of Rudolph Valentino," *Girls' Cinema*, August 27, 1927.
Ingram, Rex. "How I Discover Them," *Photoplay*, June 1923, p. 37.
"Is Rodolph Valentino a Bigamist?" *Movie Weekly Magazine*, June 10, 1922, p. 3.
Jacobson, Laurie. "Cult of the Sheik," *Hollywood Studio Magazine*, March 1986.
Jennings, Dean. "The Actor Who Won't Stay Dead," *Colliers*, July 2, 1949, p. 24.
Jordon, Anne. "R Stands for Rudy and Romance," *Movie Magazine*, September 1925.
Kelly, T. Howard. "Red Blood and Plenty of Sand," *Physical Culture*, February, 1923, p. 7.
"Konsten ail vara spanstig," *Filmjournalen, No. 27*, September 2, 1923.
Kutner, Nanette. "Valentino's Own Version of the Tango," *Dance Lovers Magazine*, March 1925, p. 22.
Lambert, Gavin. "Fairbanks & Valentino: The Last Heroes," *Sequence*, No. 8, Spring 1949.
Lampert-Greaux, E. "Projections," *Opera News*, January 8, 1994.
Lane, Wilton. "The Reason Why," *Pictures and Picturegoer*, September 1923, pp. 39–42.
"A Latin Lover," *Photoplay*, September 1921, p. 21. [Portrait].
Lee, Raymond. "The Legend of Valentino, Part One," *Movie Classics*, June 1973, p. 6.
_____. "The Legend of Valentino, Part Two," *Movie Classics*, July 1973.
_____. "The Legend of Valentino, Part Three," *Movie Classics*, August 1973.
Lee, S. "Immortals of the Screen," *Motion Picture Magazine*, October 1933, p. 32.
"Lest We Forget," *Photoplay*, August 1929.
"The Life of Rudolph Valentino," *Vidas Ilustres*, May 1, 1972.
"A Lingering Look at Those Lascivious Latin Lovers," *After Dark*, March 1977.

Literary Digest, January 14, 1922. [Portrait].
Literary Digest, October 2, 1926. [Portrait].
Lo Bello, N. "Home of the Sheik," *Travel*, May 1976.
"Love and Fighting in 'The Son of the Sheik,'" *Mid-Week Pictorial* (*New York Times*), August 5, 1926.
MacGregor, Helen. "A New Portrait of the Well-Known Star," *Shadowland*, August 1923.
Madden, Elsie. "Are They Making Valentino a Saint?" *Motion Picture Magazine*, February 1928, p. 31.
Mademoiselle, July 1957. [Portrait].
"The Man Who Came Back," *Life*, June 20, 1938, p. 54.
Mank, Chaw. "Valentino Still Lives," *Classic Film Collector*, Spring-Summer 1970, p. 35.
Marberry, M. M. "The Overloved One," *American Heritage*, August 1965, p. 84.
McClusky, Thorp. "He Was the World's Greatest Lover," *Man to Man*, August-September, 1950.
McPherson, Mervyn. "Valentino's Career Became a Graveyard Gamble," *Films and Filming*, May 1956, p. 15.
Mencken, H. L. "On Hollywood — and Valentino," *Cinema Journal*, Spring 1970, p. 13.
"A Mental Photograph of Rudolph Valentino," *Pantomime*, April 15, 1922.
Moderwell, Hiriam Kelly. "When Rudy Was a Boy," *Photoplay*, January 1928, p. 29.
Moffitt, C. F. "Censorship for Interviews Hollywood's Latest Wild Idea," *Cinema Digest*, January 9, 1933, p. 9.
"Moran of the Lady Letty," *Photoplay*, April 1922, p. 49.
Motion Picture Magazine, April 1921. [Portrait].
Motion Picture Magazine, January 1922. [Portrait].
Motion Picture Magazine, June 1922. [Portrait].
Motion Picture Magazine, November 1921. [Portrait].
Motion Picture Magazine, September 1923.
Motion Picture Magazine, June 1933, p. 52. [In Memorium].
"Music of the Sound Screen," *New Movie Magazine*, May 1930.
"Mystery at Valentino's Tomb," *Screen Book*, May 1932.
Naldi, Nita. "Great Lovers of the Screen: Rudolph Valentino," *Photoplay*, June 1924, p. 90.
Negri, Pola. "Rudolph Valentino and I! My Great True Love Story," *True Story Magazine*, April 1934.
Nicholai, Boris. "Would Valentino Be a Star Today?" *Motion Picture Magazine*, September 1934, p. 40.
"No Time for Valentino," *Newsweek*, September 5, 1955, p. 66.
"Nureyev Leaps Into Films as Valentino," *Saturday Review*, April 30, 1977.
Peeples, Samuel A. "Out, Brief Candle: the Story of Valentino," *The 8mm Collector*, Spring 1966, p. 6.

Peterson, Roger C. "My Strange Experiences at Valentino's Grave," *The New Movie Magazine*, April 1932, p. 32.
Peterson, Roger E. "Valentino's Memory Gives Them Hope," *Film Pictorial*, September 5, 1936.
_____. "Why Valentino Will Never Be Forgotten," *Film Pictorial*, August 22, 1936.
_____. "Woman Who Solved a Dream at Valentino's Tomb," *Film Pictorial*, September 12, 1936.
Photoplay, January 1922. [Portrait].
Photoplay, June 1922. [Portrait].
Photoplay, April 1924. [Portrait].
Photoplay, September 1938, p. 46. [Revival of *Son of the Sheik*].
Pictorial Review, July 1924. [Portrait].
Pictorial Review, May 1933. [Portrait].
Pitera, Z. "Dookola mitu Valentino," *Kino* (Warsaw), September 1976, p. 60.
Predal, Rene. "Rudolph Valentino," *Anthologie du Cinéma: Series 45*, May 1969.
Price, Matlock. "A Monument to Youth and Romance," *Photoplay*, November 1926, p. 44,
"La Prodigieuse Camérière de Rudolph Valentino," *Cinémagazine*, 1922.
Prophater, Anna. "Rudolph Valentino and Marriage," *Screenland*, October 1923.
"The Psychology of the Sheik," *Movie Weekly*, October 8, 1921.
Queen, Harold. "The Perfect Lover," *Coronet*, January 1951, p. 66.
Quirk, James R. "Close-Ups and Long Shots," *Photoplay*, January 1931, p. 29.
_____. "Close-Ups and Long Shots," *Photoplay*, April 1931, p. 25.
_____. "Presto Chango Valentino!" *Photoplay*, May 1925, p. 36.
_____. "Speaking of Pictures," *Photoplay*, September 1924, p. 27.
_____. "Speaking of Pictures," *Photoplay*, October 1926, p. 27.
_____. "Speaking of Pictures," *Photoplay*, November 1926, p. 27.
Rambova, Natacha. "Valentino's Messages from Beyond the Grave," *The Illustrated Love Magazine*, November 1930, p. 23.
_____. "Why I Married Rudy," *Movie Weekly*, December 16, 1922.
_____. "Why I Married Rudolph," *Movie Weekly*, December 16, 1923.
"Rambova Death Calls Back Interview with Valentino," *Classic Film Collector*, Summer 1966.
Ramsey, Walter. "The Undiscovered Valentino," *Modern Screen*, April 1927.
_____. "The Undiscovered Valentino," *Modern Screen Magazine*, April 1930, p. 29.
"The Real Valentino," *Photoplay*, February 1927, p. 76.
Redfield, Elisabeth. "May a Wife Deny Her Husband Children?" *Liberty*, January 2, 1926.
"Remembering Valentino," *Literary Digest*, August 20, 1927, p. 23.
"Return of the Sheik?" *Time*, August 1, 1949, p. 64.
Review of Reviews, October 1926. [Portrait].
"Rodolfo Valentino: el Inventor del 'Sexy,'" *Nuevo Fotoghama!* (Spain), 1971.

"Rodolph Valentino: Interprète de 'Sangre y Arena' de la Paramount," *Ciné-Mundial*, January 1923.
"Rodolpho Valentino, el Amante Latino de Hace Cuarenta Anos," *Mi Vida*, June 1965.
Roland, Gilbert. "Valentino Smiled, Shook My Hand, and I Trembled," *TV Guide*, November 22, 1975, p. 6.
"Rudolph Valentino," *7 Jours*, November 2001.
"Rudolph Valentino," *Cinefilo*, August 23, 1930.
"Rudolph Valentino," *Classic Movie Magazine*, October 1922.
"Rudolph Valentino," *De Film*, September 2, 1928.
"Rudolph Valentino," *Las Estrellas*, 1981.
"Rudolph Valentino," *Le Film*, August 25, 1929.
"Rudolph Valentino," *Liberty*, Fall 1971.
"Rudolph Valentino," *Line-Up*, April 1974.
"Rudolph Valentino," *Mi Vida*, March 1959.
"Rudolph Valentino," *Movieline*, October 2001.
"Rudolph Valentino," *Photoplay*, August 1927, p. 71. [tribute]
"Rudolph Valentino," *Photoplay*, August 1928, p. 31. [tribute]
"Rudolph Valentino," *This Was Show Business*, 1956.
"Rudolph Valentino Discusses Girls," *True Confessions*, March 1925.
"Rudolph Valentino in 'The Sheik,'" *Look*, August 16, 1938.
"Rudolph Valentino: The Sheik's Lead Man at Falcon Lair," *Architectural Digest*, April 1994.
"Rudolph Valentino: The Sheik's Leading Man at Falcon Lair," *Architectural Digest*, April 1996.
"Rudolph Valentino: The Truth About the Great Lover," *Cosmopolitan*, July 1974.
"Rudolph Valentino: Why?" *Los Angeles Times Sunday Magazine*, August 28, 1938.
"Rudolph Valentino's Persecution," *Screenland*, June 1923.
Ryan, Don. "Has the Great Lover Become Just a Celebrity?" *Motion Picture Classic*, May 1926.
St. Johns, Adela Rogers. "The Haunted Studio," *Photoplay*, December 1927, p. 30.
_____. "Valentino: The Life Story of 'The Sheik,' Part 1," *Liberty*, September 21, 1929.
_____. "Valentino: The Life Story of 'The Sheik,' Part 2," *Liberty*, September 28, 1929.
_____. "Valentino: The Life Story of 'The Sheik,' Part 3" *Liberty*, October 5, 1929.
_____. "Valentino: The Life Story of 'The Sheik,' Part 4," *Liberty*, October 12, 1929.
_____. "The Women in Valentino's Life," *American Weekly*, November 12, 1950.
Sangster, R. M. "In Memorium," *Photoplay*, October 1926, p. 39.
Santley, Joseph. "Now Peace of a Kind Comes at Last (or does it) to Fantastic Falcon Lair," *Sunday Mirror Magazine*, July 31, 1949, p. 2.
Scognomillo, Giovanni. "Rudolph Valentino: Sevgisiv Kalan Bir Ilah," *Hayat* (Turkey), No. 11, 1981.
Sheehan, Kevin. "Falcon's Lair," *American Weekly*, October 16, 1949, p. 23.
"The Sheik," *Photoplay*, November 1921, p. 69.
"The Sheik Rides Again," *World Film News*, 1938, vol. III, p. 156.

"The Sheik: The Story That Made Rudolph Valentino," *The Gentlewoman*, October 1926.

Sheldon, J. [Interview]. *Motion Picture Magazine*, November 1925, p. 24.

Shelton, Josephine. "Signore Valentino Herewith Presents His New Leading Lady, Fraulein Banky," *Motion Picture Magazine*, November 1925.

Shepherd, Thomas. "A Man and His Clothes: An Interview on Dress with Rudolph Valentino," *Movie Digest*, April 1922, p. 30.

Sherwood, C. Blythe. "Enter Julio," *Motion Picture Classic*, November [June?] 1920, p 18.

Sherwood, Robert E. "Review of 'The Sheik,'" *Life*, December 8, 1921.

"Sixteen Years Later the Sheik Rides On," *Cue* (New York), June 18, 1939, p. 9.

Slater, Thomas J. "June Mathis: A Woman Who Spoke Through Silents," *Griffithiana*, Spring 1995.

Slide, Anthony. "Ivan and Valentino: A Unique Partnership," *American Cinematographer*, August 1985, p. 36.

Smith, Agnes. "Not Quite a Hero," *Picture Play*, August 1922.

Smith, B. "Farewell, Great Lover," *Saturday Evening Post*, January 20, 1962, p. 66.

Smith, Frederick James. "Does Rudy Speak from the Beyond," *Photoplay*, February 1927, p. 38.

Stang, J. "Sheik Still Rides!" *New York Times Magazine*, November 12, 1961, p. 42.

"A Stenographer's Chance in Pictures," *Photoplay*, March 1923, p. 42.

"The Story of Valentino's Last Film," *Girls Cinema*, December 11, 1926.

"Studio News & Gossip," *Photoplay*, February 1925, p. 60.

Studlar, Gaylyn. "Discourse of Gender and Ethnicity," *Film Criticism*, Vol. XIII (Winter 1989).

"Supplement Consacré à Rudolph Valentino," *Mon Ciné*, September 1926.

Talley, Alma M. "How Valentino Plays a Love Scene," *Movie Weekly*, August 11, 1923, p. 11.

Tarrington, Thomas. "How Valentino Obtained His Physique," *Movie Weekly*, August 11, 1923.

_____. "Will Fur Fly When the Two Mrs. Valentinos Meet?" *Movie Weekly*, March 3, 1923, p. 18.

Taviner, Reginald. "Why Was Valentino Tried for Bigamy," *Motion Picture Magazine*, July 1931, p. 34.

Theatre, October 1926, p. 39. [Interview].

"This Is Rudolph Valentino," *The Picture Show Annual*, 1926.

"This Was Valentino's Home," *Los Angeles Times Home Magazine*, April 26, 1953.

"To Valentino's Memory," *Photoplay*, July 1930, p. 136.

"The Top 100 Movie Stars of All Time," *Empire*, No. 100, October 1997, p. 200.

Towers, Mary. "Valentino's Power Over Women Explained," *Movie Weekly*, April 7, 1923.

"The Tragedy Of Valentino's Brother's Nose," *Literary Digest*, September 21, 1929, p. 43.

"The Truth About Valentino's Divorce," *Movie Weekly*, October 28, 1922.
"The Truth About Valentino's Divorce," *Movie Weekly*, January 20, 1923, p. 7.
Tully, Jim. "His Popularity," *Motion Picture Classic*, June 1925, p. 16.
_____. "Rudolph Valentino," *Vanity Fair*, October 1926, p. 86.
"Updating," *Screen Facts*, No. 18, 1968.
"Valentino," *Literary Digest*, September 11, 1926, p. 26.
"Valentino and Yellow Journalism," *The Nation*, September 8, 1926, p. 207.
"Valentino, el 'Gran Amante' del Cine Mudo," *Mi Vida*, No. 391, 1966.
"Valentino Loses Out," *Moving Picture World*, October 14, 1922.
"Valentino Mania," *Skrien*, Dec-Jan 1996-97, p. 16–17.
"The Valentino-Negri Romance," *American Weekly*, October 20, 1950.
"Valentino Puts Art Above Good Looks," *Photoplay*, November 1924, p. 37.
"Valentino Returns," *People Weekly*, July 31, 1989.
"Valentino Walks Again," *Screenland*, December 1950.
"Valentino Won't Stay Dead," *Illustrated*, December 30, 1950.
Valentino, Rudolph. "Confidences et Souvenirs," *Ciné-Miroir*, January 1, 1928–March 2, 1928.
_____. "Girls of the Chorus," *Fawcett's Magazine*, September 1925.
_____. "High Lights in the Life of Rudolph Valentino," *Photoplay*, November 1926, p. 63.
_____. "Is the American Girl Playing a Losing Game?" *Metropolitan*, January 1923, p. 40.
_____. "The Motion Picture Novel," *The Bookman*, February 1923, p. 724.
_____. "My Life Story, Part I — Under Italian Skies," *Photoplay*, February 1923.
_____. "My Life Story, Part II — Broadway Nights," *Photoplay*, March 1923, p. 54.
_____. "My Life Story, Part III — Hollywood," *Photoplay*, April 1923, p. 49.
_____. "My Own Story of My Trip Abroad," *Movie Weekly*, March 8, 1924.
_____. "My Own Story of My Trip Abroad," *Movie Weekly*, March 15, 1924.
_____. "My Own Story of My Trip Abroad," *Movie Weekly*, March 22, 1924.
_____. "My Own Story of My Trip Abroad," *Movie Weekly*, March 29, 1924.
_____. "My Own Story of My Trip Abroad," *Movie Weekly*, April 5, 1924.
_____. "My Trip Abroad, Part I," *Pictures and Picturegoer*, June 1925.
_____. "My Trip Abroad, Part II," *Pictures and Picturegoer*, July 1925.
_____. "An Open Letter From Valentino to the American Public," *Photoplay*, January 1923, p. 34.
_____. "Our Jazz Age," *True Confessions*, June 1925, p. 13.
_____. "Valentino's Adventurous Life, by Himself," *Movie Weekly*, February 18, 1922.
_____. "What Is Love? Twelve Men of the Screen Give Their Ideas," *Photoplay*, February 1925.
_____. "What Is the Matter with the Movies?" *Movie Weekly*, June 16, 1923.
_____. "What's the Matter with the Movies?" *Illustrated World*, May 1923.
_____. "When I Come Back," *Motion Picture Classic*, December 1923, p. 22.
_____. "Woman and Love," *Photoplay*, March 1922, p. 41.

_____. "Yes, I am Not an Invalid," *Movie Weekly*, August 11, 1923, p. 3.
"Valentino: Not Just a Gigolo," *In Style*, Sept.-Oct. 1985.
"Valentino: The Undying Legend," *The Hollywood Observer*, Vol. 1, No. 2, Oct. 15, 1968.
"Valentino: Zun Leven Als Mensch en Als Filmkonig," circa 1926.
"The Valentinos' Chateau on the Riviera," *Photoplay*, May 1924, p. 66.
"Valentino's Lawsuit Against Famous Players," *Movie Weekly*, November 1922–January 1923.
"Valentino's Memory," *Photoplay*, August 1930, pp. 75, 115.
"Valentino's Unknown Adventure," *Modern Screen*, November 1933.
"Valentinoville," *Newsweek*, April 10, 1961, p. 52.
Varga, John. "Valentino, First of the Red Hot Lovers," *Hollywood Studio Magazine*, July 1991.
"Veinticinco Años Despues de Su Muerte," *7 Fechas*, July 1952.
"Vilma Banky, Hollywood Star with a Short but Splendid Career," *New York Times*, December 12, 1992.
"The Vogue of Valentino," *Motion Picture Magazine*, February, 1923, p. 27.
Walker, Helen Louise. "His Death a Valuable Publicity Stunt for Those Who Profited from His Last Production," *Motion Picture Magazine*, March 1931, p. 32.
_____. "Valentino's Last Interview," *Motion Picture Magazine*, September 1933.
Waterbury, Ruth. "Screenland's Great Lover Tells His Story," *World Magazine*, November 12, 1922.
_____. "Wedded and Parted," *Photoplay*, December 1922, p. 58.
Waxman, Percy. "The Truth About Rudolph Valentino," *Style*, October 1924, p. 21.
Webb, S. "After Twenty Years, Valentino Still Wows Them," *New York Times Magazine*, May 6, 1945, p. 24.
Weemaes, G. "Rudolph Valentino," *Film en Televisie* (Brussels), May-June 1976, p. 24.
Wehner, George. "The Valentino Death Prophecy," *True Mystic Science*, November 1938.
Wells, Margaret Caroline. "What!!! Valentino???" *Photoplay*, February 1925, p. 70.
Wennersten, Robert. "The Second Mrs. Valentino," *Performing Arts*, February 1978, p. 16.
"What Really Killed Rudolph Valentino," *Physical Culture Magazine*, November 1926.
"When Silence Was Golden," *Screen Greats*, Summer 1971, p. 77.
"When Valentino Went Home," *Parade Magazine*, May 22, 1994.
White, Peter. "What Every Woman Wants," *Picture Play*, May-June 1927.
Wickstead, Richard. "Valentino Writes a Book of Poems," *Movie Weekly*, August 11, 1923.
Wilson, Lois. "The Rudolph Valentino I Know," *Movie Weekly*, June 27, 1925.
Winkler, John K. "I'm Tired of Being a Sheik," *Colliers*, January 16, 1926, p. 28.
Winship, Mary. "When Valentino Taught Me to Dance," *Photoplay*, May 1922, p. 45.
"The Women Valentino Loved," *True Experiences*, March 1939.
"Women Who Enshrine Valentino," *Literary Digest*, February 7, 1931, p. 19.

Woodbridge, A. L. "When Rudy's Belongings Were Sold," *Picture Play*, April, 1927, p. 16.
York, Cal. "Gossip — East & West," *Photoplay*, April 1923, p. 88.
_____. "Gossip — East & West," *Photoplay*, August 1923, p. 68.
_____. "He Who Got Slapped and Why," *Photoplay*, July 1926, p. 78.
_____. "Plays and Players," *Photoplay*, May 1922, p. 86.
_____. "Plays & Players," *Photoplay*, August 1922, p. 67.
_____. "Plays & Players," *Photoplay*, September 1922, p. 64.
_____. "Plays & Players," *Photoplay*, November 1922, p. 70.
_____. "Studio News and Gossip," *Photoplay*, July 1924, p. 52.
_____. "Studio News and Gossip — East and West," *Photoplay*, October 1926, p. 104.

APPENDIX IX

Books

Books Written by Valentino

"Motion-picture stars have written biographies since the beginning. And while Rodolph Valentino is not about to publish his biography, he is about to publish a book of verse, called *Reflections* [renamed *Daydreams*]. It is to be very attractively bound in Chinese red and lettered in gold and black. The contents? Poetry from his own pen; some of it written to various people and some of it written of various people and various things."—*Motion Picture*, August 1923.

Valentino, Rudolph. *Daydreams*. New York: MacFadden Publications, 1923.
Valentino, Rudolph. *How You Can Keep Fit*. New York: MacFadden Publications, 1923.
Valentino, Rudolph. *My Private Diary*. Chicago: Occult Publishing Company, 1929.
Valentino, Rudolph. *The Intimate Journal of Rudolph Valentino*. New York: William Faro, Inc., 1931.

Books Written about Valentino

Argento, Dominick. *The Dream of Valentino*. New York: Boosey & Hawkes, 1998.
Arnold, Alan. *Valentino*. London: Hutchinson, 1952.
Arrese, Jesus Basanez. *Rodolfo Valentino en el 25 Aniversario de Su Muerte*. Madrid: Graficas Bilbao, 1951.
Attolini, Vito. *Rudolph & Rodolfo: La Vita Breve e Felice di Valentino*.
Barnstijn, Loet C. *Myn Levensgeschiedenis door Rudolph Valentino*. Holland: Loet C. Barnstijn's Cinemabibliotheek, 1927.
Botham, Noel. *Valentino, the First Superstar*. London: Metro Publishing, 2002.

_____, and Peter Donnelly. *Valentino: The Love God.* New York: Ace Books, 1976.
Bret, David. *Valentino: A Dream of Desire.* London: Robson Books Ltd., 1998.
Burdon, J. G. *Het Liefde-Leven van Rudolph Valentino.* Amsterdam: Koloniale Boek Centrale, 1927.
Charpentier, Julia Ann. *Valentino: Icon of Love* (eBook). Gemini Books.
Cristalli, Paola. *Valentino — Lo Schermo Della Passione.* Ancona, Italy: Transeuropa Cinegrafie, 1996.
Dalemans Brothers. *Valentino Mania.* Provincie Limburg, 1996.
Dempsey, Amy. *They Died Too Young: Rudolph Valentino.* London: Parragon Books Ltd., 1995.
De Recqueville, Jeanne. *Rudolph Valentino.* Paris: France-Empire, 1978.
Ellenberger, Allan R. *The Valentino Mystique.* Jefferson, N.C.: McFarland & Company, Inc., 2005.
Erhard, Anna Lou. *Rudolph Valentino Is My Spirit Friend: A Biographical Account of an Intimate Experience.* New York: William-Frederick Press, 1959.
Flint, Leslie. *The Voice of Valentino.* London: Regency, 1965.
Fragasso, Humbert R. *Vita Amorosa di Rodolfo Valentino.* New York: Italian Book Company, 1944.
Les Grands Artistes de l'Écran; Rudolph Valentino: His Life — His Pictures — His Adventures. Paris: Les Publications Jean-Pascal.
La Une, A. *La Mort de Rudolph Valentino.* France.
Leider, Emily Wortis. *Dark Lover: The Life and Death of Rudolph Valentino.* Farrar Straus & Giroux, 2003.
Livingston, Beulah. *Remembering Valentino: Reminiscences of the World's Greatest Lover.* New York, 1938.
Mackenzie, Norman. *The Magic of Rudolph Valentino.* London: Research Publishing Co., 1974.
Mank, Charles, Jr. *What the Fans Think of Rudolph Valentino: A Memorial Book.* Staunton, IL: Charles Mank, Jr., 1929.
McKinstry, Carol E. *The Return of Rudolph Valentino.* Los Angeles: Kirby & Gee, 1952.
Morone, Chicca Guglielmi, and Antonio Miredi. *Rodolfo Valentino: Una Mitologia per Immagini.* Turin: Libreria Petrini, 1995.
Newman, Ben-Allah. *Rudolph Valentino: His Romantic Life and Death.* Hollywood: Ben-Allah Company, 1926.
Oberfirst, Robert. *Rudolph Valentino: The Man Behind the Myth.* New York: Citadel Press, 1962.
Pantaleo, Leo. *Il Mistero Rodolfo Valentino.* Milan: Idea Books, 1995.
Peterson, Roger C. *Valentino: The Unforgotten.* Los Angeles: Wetzel Publishing Co., Inc., 1937.
Rambova, Natacha. *Rudolph Valentino Recollections.* New York: Jacobsen-Hodgkinson Corp., 1927.
_____. *Rudy: An Intimate Portrait of Rudolph Valentino by His Wife.* London: Hutchinson & Co. Ltd., 1926.

Ramond, Edouard. *La Vita Amorosa di Rodolfo Valentino* (trans. Enrico Picene). Milano: Mondadori, 1926.

_____. *Valentino und die Frauen* (trans. Hans Blum). Berlin: Johannes Knoblauch, 1927.

_____. *La Vie Amoureuse de Rudolph Valentino*. Paris: Librairie Baundiniere, 1927.

Richards, Scott. *The Reincarnation of Rudolph Valentino*. Scientists of New Atlantis, 1994.

Rodolfo Valentino Divo-Mito del Cinema. Castellaneta, Italy: Museo R Valentino, 1995.

Russell, Lynn. *The Voice of Valentino*. London: Regency Press, 1965.

Scagnetti, Jack. *The Intimate Life of Rudolph Valentino*. New York: Jonathan David Publishers Inc., 1975.

Serradifalco, L. *Aventure Amore di Rodolfo Valentino*. Milano: Ed. Perrinca, 1927.

_____. *Die Liebesabenteuer des Rodolf Valentino*. Berlin: Ross, 1927.

Shulman, Irving. *Valentino. The True Life Story*. New York: Trident Press, 1967.

Spiess, Verlag Volker. *There's a New Star in Heaven ... Valentino*. Berlin: Internationale Filmfestspiele Berlin, 1979.

Steiger, Brad, and Chaw Mank. *Valentino*. London: Corgi Books, 1966.

Tajiri, Vincent. *Valentino: The True Life Story*. New York: Bantam Books, 1977.

Tello, Antonio, and Gonzalo Otero Pizarro. *Valentino: La Seducción Manipulada*. Barcelona : Editorial Bruguera, 1978.

Terhune, Tracy. *Valentino Forever*. Los Angeles: 2004.

Tierney, Tom. *Rudolph Valentino Paper Dolls*. New York: Dover Publications, 1979.

Trinchero, Sergio, and Sergio Russo. *Rodolfo Valentino*. Priuli & Verlucca, 1975.

Ullman, S. George. *The Real Valentino*. London: Pearson, 1927.

_____. *Valentino as I Knew Him*. New York: Macy-Masius, 1926.

Von Sohel, Helmuth. *Rodolfo Valentino— El Amante de Hollywood*. Barcelona: Producciones Editorales, 1977.

Walker, Alexander. *Valentino: An Intimate and Shocking Expose*. New York: Stein and Day, 1976.

Ziazan, Madenasar. *Ashari amenen kehetsik marti (Rudolf Valentino)*. Constantinople: Dbakr. Hovagimyan, 1926.

APPENDIX X

Film Biographies and Stage Productions

Includes film biographies, parodies, film shorts, documentaries, television programs and stage plays

Film Biographies

Valentino (1951). Columbia Pictures Corporation. April 1951.

Produced by Edward Small; directed by Lewis Allen; screenplay by George Bruce, based on the biography *Valentino as I Knew Him* (New York, 1926), by S. George Ullman; cinematography by Harry Stradling, Sr.; art direction by William Flannery; original music by Heinz Roemheld; music supervisor, David Chudnow; set decoration by Howard Bristol; costume design by Travis Banton and Gwen Wakeling (gowns); edited by Daniel Mandell; stunts by Ken Terrell; color consultant, Robert Brower; dance direction by Larry Ceballos; assistant to producer, Jan Grippo.

Cast: Eleanor Parker (Joan Carlisle), Richard Carlson (William King), Patricia Medina (Lila Reyes), Joseph Calleia (Luigi Verducci), Dona Drake (Maria Torres), Lloyd Gough (Eddie Morgan), Anthony Dexter (Rudolph Valentino), Otto Kruger (Mark Towers), Marietta Canty (Tilly), Paul Bryar (Photographer), Eric Wilton (Butler), William Forrest (Dr. Verne), Fred Grahame (Chef), Almira Sessions (Fan Mail Sorter), George Melford, Lester Dorr, Sally Forrest, William Henry.

Review: "This spectacularly awful simulation of a valid biography is about as far from actual history or even intelligence as anything could be. And the quality of writing and acting that has gone into its fustian romance make for some of the corniest histronics that have been loosed on the battered screen in years."—*New York Times*, April 20, 1951.

Sound. Biographical-Drama. Technicolor. 35mm. Running time, 105 minutes. Not rated.

The Legend of Valentino (1975). Spelling-Goldberg Productions. American Broadcasting Company (ABC). November 23, 1975.

Produced by Leonard Goldberg and Aaron Spelling; directed by Melville Shavelson; teleplay by Melville Shavelson; original music by Charles Fox; cinematography by Archie R. Dalzell; editing by John Woodcock; casting by Lynn Stalmaster; art direction by Tracy Bousman; costume design by Nolan Miller; choreography by Anita Mann.

Cast: Franco Nero (Rudolph Valentino), Suzanne Pleshette (June Mathis), Judd Hirsch (Jack Auerbach), Lesley Ann Warren (Laura Lorraine), Milton Berle (Jesse Lasky), Yvette Mimieux (Natacha Rambova), Harold Stone (Sam Baldwin), Alicia Bond (Nazimova), Michael Thoma (Rex Ingram), Constance Forslund (Silent Star), Brenda Venus (Constance Carr), Ruben Moreno (Mexican Mayor), Penny Stanton (Madame Tullio), Jane Alice Brandon (Teenage Girl), Montana Smoyer (Big chested autograph hunter).

Anthony Dexter as the "Great Lover" in the 1951 Columbia film *Valentino*.

Review: "Written and directed by Melville Shavelson with small regard for fact or taste. Just for starters he'd have us believe that screenwriter June Mathis discovered Valentino when he came to burglarize her house while she was writing the script of *The Four Horsemen of the Apocalypse*. In fact, she chose him on the basis of his previous bit parts in movies. The fiction goes on from there with the emphasis on the star's involvement with lesbians and hints of his own homosexuality. As Mathis tells a producer, 'Sex can be the biggest boxoffice of all.' The movie is an insult to its subject and its audience..."—Judith Crist, *TV Guide*, November 19, 1975.

Sound. Biographical-Drama. Color. 35mm. Running time, 120 minutes. Not Rated.

Valentino (1977). Aperature Films. Chartoff-Winkler Productions. Distributed by United Artists [US], Anglo-EMI Films Distributors, Ltd. [UK]. November 1977.

Produced by Irwin Winkler and Robert Chartoff; associate producer, Harry Benn; directed by Ken Russell; screenplay by Ken Russell and Mardik Martin, based on the biography *Valentino, an Intimate Exposé of the Sheik*, by Brad Steiger and Chaw Mank; original music by Stanley Black; cinematography by Peter Suschitsky; editing by Stuart Baird; casting by Maude Spector; production design by Phillip Harrison; costume design by Shirley Russell; hairstyles by Colin Jamison; makeup by Peter Robb-King; production management by Peter Price; assistant director, Jonathan Benson; set design by Steve Cooper; art direction by Tim Hutchinson and Malcom Middleton; property master, Ray Traynor; set dresser, Ian Whittaker; construction manager, Jeff Woodbridge; sound by Ian Fuller, John Mitchell and Bill Rowe.

Cast: Rudolf Nureyev (Rudolph Valentino), Lesie Caron (Alla Nazimova), Michelle Phillips (Natacha Rambova), Carol Kane (Fatty's girl), Felicity Kendal (June Mathis), Seymour Cassel (George Ullman), Peter Vaughn (Rory O'Neil), Huntz Hall (Jesse Lasky), David De Keyser (Josephy Schenck), Alfred Marks (Richard Rowland), Anton Diffring (Baron Long), Jennie Linden (Agnes Ayres), Willian Hootkins (Fatty), Bill McKinney (Jail cop), Don Fellows (George Melford), John Justin (Sidney Olcott), Ken Russell (Rex Ingram), Linda Thorson (Billie Streeter), June Bolton (Bianca De Saulles), Penny Milford (Lorna Sinclair), Dudley Sutton (Willie), Robin Brent Clarke (Jack De Saulles), Anthony Dowell (Vaclav Nijinsky), James Berwick (Fight referee), Marcella Markham (Hooker), Leland Palmer (Majorie Tain), John Alderson (Cop), Hal Galili (Harry Fischbeck), Percy Herbert (Studio guard), Nicolette Marvin (Marsha Lee), Mark Baker (Assistant director), Mildred Shay (Old lady), Lindsay Kemp (Angus McBride), John Ratzenberger, Norman Chancer, Robert O'Neil (Newshounds), Christine Carlson (Tango dancer).

Review: "You have only to peruse one of the published biographies of Rudolph Valentino to affirm that Ken Russell's film about the Italian-born Hollywood idol of the silent era has treated facts with a very elastic dramatic license. Such is Russell's custom, of course. His imagination takes wing, having absorbed the known information, apparently working on the bold assumption that his own sensibilities are attuned to the minds and emotions of the historical figures he chooses to recall."—*Films and Filming*, November 1977.

Sound. Biographical-Drama. Color (DeLuxe). 35mm. Running time, 128 minutes. Rated R.

Parodies

The Shreik of Araby (1923). Mack Sennett Productions. Distributed by Allied Producers and Distributors. March 5, 1923. Produced by Mack Sennett; directed by F. Richard Jones; scenario by Mack Sennett.

Cast: Ben Turpin (A Bill Poster), Kathyrn McGuire (The Girl), George Cooper (Presto, the Magician), Charles Stevenson (Luke Hassen), Ray Grey (The Arab Prince), Louis Fronde (The Chief of Police), Dick Sutherland (The Bandit).

Silent. Comedy/Satire/Short. B & W. 35mm. Running time, 5 reels.

Michelle Phillips as Natacha Rambova and Rudolf Nureyev as Rudolph Valentino in the United Artists film *Valentino* (1977).

Uncensored Movies (1923). Hal Roach Studios Inc. Distributed by Pathé Exchange Inc. December 9, 1923. Produced by Hal Roach; directed by Roy Clements.

Cast: Will Rogers (Lem Skagwillow), Earl Mohan, Marie Mosquini, George Rowe, Noah Young.

Silent. Comedy/Short. B & W. 35mm.

Big Moments from Little Pictures (1924). Hal Roach Studios Inc. Distributed by Pathé Exchange Inc. March 30, 1924. Produced by Hal Roach; directed by Roy Clements; titles by H. M. Walker; cinematography by Robert Doran and Otto Himm; editing by Thomas J. Crizer.

Cast: Will Rogers, Charlie Hall (Chaplin lookalike), Earl Mohan, Marie Mosquini, Guinn 'Big Boy' Williams, Noah Young.

Silent. Comedy/Short. B & W. 35mm.

The World's Greatest Lover (1977). 20th Century–Fox Film Corporation. Produced, directed and written by Gene Wilder; original music by John Morris; cinematography by Gerald Hirschfeld; editing by Anthony A. Pellegrino; production design by

Terence Marsh; art direction by Steven P. Sardanis; set decoration by John Franco, Jr.; costume design by Ruth Myers; makeup by William Tuttle.

Cast: Gene Wilder (Rudy Valentine), Carol Kane (Annie), Dom DeLuise (Zitz), Fritz Feld (Hotel manager).

Sound. Color (DeLuxe). 35mm. Running time, 89 minutes. Rated PG.

Film Shorts

Hollywood: City of Celluloid (1932). Striking aerial photography of empty streets, rolling hills, and orange groves kicks off this fascinating peek into the Hollywood of yesteryear, with particular attention paid to the early studios of the 'Golden Era.' Said to have originated the "Lady in Black" legend.

Taxi Dancer (1996). Favourite Films. U. S. premiere at the Third Annual Hollywood Film Festival, August 4–9, 1999. Produced by Gilbert and Jan Dalemans; directed by Caroline Strubbe; screenplay by Gilbert and Jan Dalemans, and Caroline Strubbe; production design by Eugenie Collet; music composed by de Rode Zee, Eddy Fontaine, Jeff Gielen, Robert Piccart and Luc Vanlessen; edited by Sergio Bigones; cinematography by Paul Vercheval.

Cast: Jeroen Willems (Liftboy).

Summary: Rudolph Valentino, silent film icon, dies in New York at the age of 31. After his early death, a wave of mass hysteria and suicide attempts sweeps America and Europe. Some fans actually follow their idol into death. Later that week, a liftboy at a luxurious hotel is found dead in his room surrounded by photos of the deceased actor. The film tells the story of this liftboy mesmerized by Valentino's magic.

Review: "And unlike Ken Russell's *Valentino* (1976), in which Nureyev attempts unsuccessfully to evoke Rudolph Valentino's mythical appeal, *Taxi Dancer* succeeds in capturing the magical flow of silent film at its best. Far from being ironic the film possesses all the smaller and greater elements typical for the genre."—K. Schippers, *N. R. C. Handelsblad*, Amsterdam, January 1997.

Silent. Short. B & W, 35mm. Running time, 40 minutes.

Good Night, Valentino (2003). Mineralava Productions. Thor Films. January 2003 (Sundance Film Festival). Executive produced by Adam Cohen; produced by Edoardo Ballerini, Jean Philippe Girod, and John Rothman; directed by Edoardo Ballerini; first assistant director, Paul Domick; screenplay by Edoardo Ballerini and John Rothman, adapted from H. L. Mencken's essay "Valentino"; original music by Igor (Khoroshev); production design by Jeffrey MacIntyre; costume design by Carlie Tracey; make-up by Michelle Werner; sound by Samuel Libraty and Frederick Critchlow; editing by Paul Ohnersorgen; color timer, Jim Passon; cinematography by Tim Ives; still photographer, Jeff Vespa.

John Rothman as H. L. Mencken and Edoardo Ballerini as Rudolph Valentino from the short film *Good Night, Valentino* (2003). (Photograph by Jeff Vespa, ©Mineralava Productions 2003.)

Cast: Edoardo Ballerini (Rudolph Valentino), John Rothman (H.L. Mencken), Blaire Chandler (The Maid).

Summary: The true story of a meeting between silent movie idol Rudolph Valentino and famed journalist H. L. Mencken that took place a week before Valentino tragically died at age 31.

Review: "The anger, frustration and pathos felt by Valentino is clearly portrayed in Edoardo Ballerini's compelling and sympathetic performance. His on-screen resemblance to Valentino is uncanny and those familiar with Valentino's films will note he has even mastered the Great Lover's gait. John Rothman, as the usually sardonic Mencken, reveals the uncharacteristic empathy the writer had for Valentino, and, in the process, exposes the profundity of his own sentiments." *Classic Images*, May 2003.

Silent and Sound. Short. B & W and Color. 35mm. Running time, 15 minutes. Not Rated.

Documentaries and Television Programs

The History of the Motion Picture: The Valentino Mystique (1960). ABC Television Network. Produced by Kevin Flood; written and narrated by Paul Killiam; edited by James Syring; opticals by the Film Palace; score by Lee Irwin; research by William K. Everson. This profile of the life, films and phenomenal popularity of Rudolph Valentino traces his early years in Italy, his arrival in New York and his dramatic rise to fame. See how Valentino, in his short life, became one of the most worshipped celebrities of the 20th century. Silent with narration. Documentary. B & W. Running time, 30 minutes. Not Rated.

Swanson and Valentino (1980). Thames Television. Executive producer, Mike Wooler; written, directed and produced by David Gill and Kevin Brownlow; narrated by James Mason. Valentino's brother helps tell the story of the young Italian who became the silver screen's Great Lover—but whose private life failed to match his public image. Silent and Sound. Documentary. Color with B & W footage. Running time, 52 minutes. Not Rated.

The Legend of Valentino (1983). A Wolper-Sterling Production. A Janus Film Release. Produced by Saul J. Turell and Paul Killiam; directed and edited by Saul J. Turell and Graeme Ferguson; written by Saul J. Turell and Paul Killiam; narrated by Frank Gallop; music composed and conducted by Alexander Semmler; music edited by Harry D. Glass; research by William K. Everson and Arthur Knight; treatment by Harvey Bullock; additional scripting by Arthur Knight; format coordinated by Herbert J. Strauss; supervising film editor, Raymond F. Angus; sound engineer, Albert Gramaglia; production staff, Howard Kupperman, Joseph A. Zysman, and Alan Smiler. Grateful acknowledgment is made to Robert Florey, Paul Ivano, George S. Ullman, and Alberto Valentino. Silent with narration and musical score. Documentary. B & W. Running time, 72 minutes. Not Rated.

Against the Odds: Rudolf [sic] ***Valentino*** (1988). Films for the Humanities and Sciences. A series of brief biographies that illuminate the process of personal struggle and, in most cases, achievement. Some were heroes and some villains, but all played a significant role in history. Forty-Seven-part series. Rudolf Valentino: The Italian-born America film actor reached the shores of America without money, skills, or friends; what he had was a dream that brought him to the height of an industry built on changed America's vision of manliness, romance and love. VHS, ISBN Number: 1-56950-983-2. Sound. Documentary. Color. Running Time, 14 minutes. Not Rated.

Biography—Rudolph Valentino: The Great Lover (1995). Produced by Greystone Communications, Inc. for A&E Entertainment. Executive in charge of production, Steven Lewis; executive producers, Craig Haffner and Donna E. Lusitana; produced by Martin Gillam. Explore the compelling saga of Rudolph Valentino, who paved the way for the matinee idols that followed. See clips from his classic movies, and accounts of his death at the age of 31 from blood poisoning. Join *Biography* for the man whose legend could not be cut short like his life, for ten years after his death fan mail poured in, and Hollywood is still looking for the next Valentino. Silent and Sound. Documentary. Color and B & W. Running time, 50 minutes, Not Rated.

Great Romances of the Twentieth Century: Rudolph Valentino and Natasha [sic] ***Rambova*** (1997). Nugus/Martin Productions, Inc. BBC Worldwide Ltd. [UK] Program 2:10. Executive producer, Philip Nugus; produced and directed by Jonathan Martin. He was the Great Lover of the Silent Screen, she was the self-created exotic who fashioned his career. Neither partner in this remarkable marriage was quite what he or she seemed. Sound. Documentary series. B & W and Color. Running time, 26 minutes.

Mysteries and Scandals: Rudolph Valentino. E! Entertainment. Episode 63, aired May 10, 1999. Hosted by A. J. Benza. *Mysteries and Scandals* looks at the life of the "Great Lover," Rudolph Valentino. *Mysteries and Scandals* is your guided tour through the back alleys and backlots that make up the flip side of Hollywood's Walk of Fame. Sound. Documentary series. B & W and Color. Running time, 30 minutes. Not rated.

Alla Nazimova and Rudolph Valentino (2000). Striana Productions. Distributed by Europe Images International. Directed and written by Laurent Preyale. Sound. Documentary / Short. Color. Running time, 26 minutes. Not Rated.

The Young and the Dead (2003). HBO. Produced by Ellin Baumel; co-produced by Julia King; directed by Robert Pulcini and Shari Springer Berman; edited by Robert Pulcini; cinematography by Michael Barrow and Sandra Chandler; original music by Mark Suozzo. For HBO: Executive producer, Sheila Nevins; supervising producer, Julie Anderson; consulting editor, Geoff Bartz. From the 2003 DVD jacket: "An irreverent look at how a fertile imagination and 21st century technology can turn the most unlikely business into an exciting—and profitable—undertaking." A portion of the documentary takes a look at the Rudolph Valentino memorial, held each year at Hollywood Forever Cemetery. Sound. Documentary. Color. Running time, 90 minutes. Not rated.

Stage Productions

Ciao Rudy! (1966). Opened January 7, 1966, in Teatro Sistina, Rome. Music by Armando Trovaioli; lyrics by Pietro Garinei and Sandro Giovanninil; costumes and stage design, Giulio Coltellacci.

Songs: "Ciao Rudy," "Il Porto di New York," "Quattro Palmi di Terra in California," "Piaceva alle Donne," "Bonita e Rosy," "Gente Matta," "Il Mio Nome, "Il Proibizionismo," "Questo si Chiama Amore," "Abbiamo Julio," "Valentino Tango," "Mexico," "Cosí é Lui," "È Lei."

Cast: Marcello Mastroianni (Valentino), Olga Villi (Natacha Rambova), Giuliana Lojodice (June Mathis), Ilaria Occhini (Jean Acker), Raffaella Carrà (Bonnie Glass), Tina Lattanzi (Her mother), Paola Pitagora (President of a fan club), Angela Pagano (Girl-friend), Giusi Raspani Dandolo (A journalist), Paola Borboni (A wealthy heiress), Minnie Minoprio, Loredana Bertè, Violetta Chiarini, Emiliana, Lorenza Guerrieri, Mita Medici, Carmen Scarpitta, Marzia Ubaldi, Raffaella Carrà, Nina Da Padova, Eleonora Nura, Minni Minoprio, Simona Sarlisi.

Review: "The lobby consensus— the official reviewers will not get at it until tonight — was that this attempt to evoke the life and era of the first great 'Latin lover' of the silent films suffers primarily from lack of an attitude. It cannot make up its mind, the preview audience seemed to think, whether to treat Valentino as a comic or as a tragic character."—*New York Times*, January 8, 1966.

Note: A new version, with Alberto Lionello as Valentino, was produced in 1973.

Rudolph Valentino (1988). Scuola Teatro Colli, Bologna. Directed by Emanuele Montagna; written by Giuseppe Liotta; original music by Fabrizio Festa; costumes by Barbara Ragazzi and Gianni Di Lorenzo.

Cast: Emanuele Montagna (Rudolph Valentino), Grazia Minarelli (Natacha Rambova), Patrizia Bracaglia (June Mathis), Andrea Drangoni (George Ullman), Elisa Cheli (Jean Acker).

Review: "Slow rhythm, disconnected development, acting somewhat over the top, nice music, acceptable scenery and costumes. Valentino became a myth thanks also to a collective mania, fed by his funeral, a piece of theatre, in acts and scenes. The version presented here, on a text by Giuseppe Liotta (flat, superficial and overly 'literary'), directed by Emanuele Montagna, who also plays Valentino, attempts to take a distance from the myth in order to approach the man himself, restoring him his curiously adolescent humanity, the sum of faults and virtues, of which the gutter-press of the period and the films themselves had deprived him. However, Rudy comes out even worse off. Whatever peace he might have found in his eternal sleep has definitely been lost, for this work does little more than to disturb his hard-won oblivion, lending no new lustre and leaving his splendour largely unrenewed. It would have been better, perhaps, to remain forgotten…"— Elena D'Armento, the Italian daily *Corriere del Giorno*, March 2, 1988.

Rudolph Valentino My Love (1992). Theatrical Company "Gli Esauriti" in collaboration with the Crest Theatre Company. A play in two acts by Leo Pantaleo; costumes and direction, Leo Pantaleo; stage-design, Pasquale Strippoli.

Cast: Rosalba Gravina (Natacha Rambova), Laura Federzoni (Pola Negri), Lina Antonante (Governess), Marina Lupo (Louella O. Parsons), Luisa Coppola (Vilma

Banky), Angela Leandro (Evelin Hugues), Tiziana Risolo (Germain Dor), Dea Cinzy (Bonnie Glass), Carmela Antonante (Maidservant), Mariangela Lincesso, Francesco Cavallo, Franco Nacca, Angelo Cardellicchio (Members of the Club: "Life Is Short, Art Eternal"), Viviana Caressa (Maidservant), Aurelia Nacca, Giusy Stravalaci, Amalia Massafra, Antonella Veglia, Daniela da Prato, Maria Vittoria Colapietro, Chiara Favale, M. Rosaria Villani and Roberta Leserri (Valentino's widows), Adriano Calzolaro (Valentino's voice off stage).

Review: "A festival of self-love, phasing into paradox at the beginning of the second act, when the spirit of Valentino is called up on stage. Only his voice is heard, denouncing the construction of a personality condemned to perform continually and, inevitably, his private solitude…"— Giuseppe Mele, *Corriere del Giorno*, August 5, 1992.

The Dream of Valentino (1994). World Premiere, January 15, 1994, Eisenhower Theatre, Kennedy Center, Washington, D.C. Washington Opera Company. Opera in two acts. Libretto by Charles Nolte; music by Dominick Argento; stage design, John Conklin; costumes, Valentino Garavani; conductor: Christopher Keene.

Songs: "The Dream Of Valentino: Valentino Dances."

Cast: Robert Brubaker — Tenor (Valentino), Suzanne Murphy — Soprano (June Mathis), Edrie Means (Jean Acker), Julia Anne Wolf (Natacha Rambova), Julian Patrick (George Ullman).

Review: "This piece, intended to bring back to life the first great lover of the cinema, instead [had] a rather deadening effect on the audience. The lion's share, however, went to the ladies, so many, and so good, radiant and majestic in period costumes designed by Valentino. The question is why Charles Nolte, author of the accessible and almost elementary English libretto, and Argento have chosen to completely ignore Valentino's presumed homosexuality, while recognizing that of his women, for example the lesbianism of his first and second wives. The stylist Valentino justly defends the overall 'look' of the opera, which is indeed fantastic and highly sophisticated. As theatregoers, we Italians are undoubtedly the utter bottom. Nothing is ever good enough."— Alessandra Farkas, *Corriere della Sera*, January 17, 1994.

Running time, 135 minutes.

Valentino, the Musical (1998). Opened May 6, 1998, at the Judith Anderson Theatre, New York, and ran for 16 performances.

Music by Charles Mandracchia; lyrics by Francesca DeJosia and Charles Mandracchia; book by Francesca DeJosia and Charles Mandracchia.

Songs: "Castellaneta," "New York Is All Around," "Santa's Nite," "Mamma, I Miss You," "The Lover's Waltz," "Hollywoodland," "The Difference in You," "A Hollywood Marriage Sham," "Million Dollar Baby," "Great Valentino," "Art Deco Women," "Tender Sweet Romance," "Somewhere Far Beyond," "Battle Song," "Valentino Soliloquy," "Locked Forever Away."

Original Cast: Charles Mandracchia (Rudolph Valentino), Kathy Robinson,

Jason Cammorata, Melodee Shea Curry, Dan O'Brien, Michele Patzakis, Kristin Reitter, Victoria J. Rowe, Jonathan Stewart, Megan Thomas.

Review: "Bravissimo! Valentino sings his way into your heart."— Gail Sheehy, *Vanity Fair*.

APPENDIX XI

Quotations about Valentino

"I think Rudolph Valentino and I could be good friends because we have a lot in common. We're both interested in poetry, art and collecting antiques. I would like to talk with Rudy, but that doesn't mean I'd like him as my lover."[1] — KENNETH ANGER, writer.

"The first time I knew Valentino was on his way was when we were going on location and stopped to pick him up. There he was, all dressed up and said very grandly, 'I'm sorry folks, I can't have you in for coffee and breakfast rolls because it's my butler's day off.' Our driver said to me, 'Why the dumb S.O.B., I loaned him that clean shirt he's wearing!' But Valentino had guts and nerve to think big, which was right. He was different; he wasn't like the others. Yes, he did have magnetism. He could throw it around and he did when he realized it."[2] — GERTRUDE ASTOR, actress.

"I always tried to save Valentino from the suffering, the heart-aches, the awakening which were mine. You know he lived up here, next door to me. I used to warn him, tell him that the American public is more fickle than even the most fickle of women. Tried to save him again and again, but Rudy only laughed. He couldn't believe me. What happened to poor old Francis X. could never happen to Rudolph Valentino!"[3] — FRANCIS X. BUSHMAN, actor.

"Valentino had an air of sadness. He wore his success gracefully, appearing almost subdued by it. He was intelligent, quiet and without vanity, and had great allure for women, but had little success with them, and those whom he married treated him rather shabbily.... No man had greater attraction for women than Valentino; no man was more deceived by them."[4] — CHARLIE CHAPLIN, actor.

"As a human being, Valentino was no more unique than any of the other superstars we've come to know. He was simply the first exemplar of what a new medium, the cinema, can do to magnify a famous face to the point of hypnotizing the audience and frightening the victim."[5] —ALISTAIR COOKE, author.

"What a face, what a star. His movies still play today. Now that's a fine tribute to him [Valentino]."[6] —FRANCES DEE, actress.

"I was honored and thrilled to receive the [Rudolph] Valentino Award. I really don't know too much about his films, I'm sorry to say. But, even today he has a name to be reckoned with."[7] —FAYE DUNAWAY, actress.

"The 'Great Lover of the Screen,' a title earned, indeed, by Valentino's acting ability. One of the biggest film stars, when stars truly were stars. I met him as a young lad. He was mild-mannered, kind and quite dapper. He became a big name with United Artists along with my father, Mary Pickford and later Gloria Swanson."[8] —DOUGLAS FAIRBANKS, JR., actor.

"Of all the hundreds of players I have directed, from the era of silents to the present day, I have never met anyone who had a more sensitive and impressionable nature."[9] —GEORGE FITZMAURICE, director.

"Valentino was one of the biggest stars of the silent era. Female fans panted after him. You could say my father [John Gilbert] inherited the mantle that had been carried by Valentino."[10] —LEATRICE GILBERT FOUNTAIN, author.

"Rudolph Valentino was a really charming young man when I knew him, and kept up all the attractive mannerisms in his ordinary life which delighted his followers on the screen. Although an Italian by birth his life seemed to me to resemble in more ways than one that of a popular Spanish toreador, even to the sudden tragic death at the height of his career."[11] —ELINOR GLYN, author.

"Certainly, it was a magnetic personality that caused Rudolph Valentino to stand out above all other screen lovers and to become the idol of millions, in every corner of the globe."[12] —D. W. GRIFFITH, director.

"Ah, Valentino. The name had magic. Back in his heyday, as well as today, that rather says it all doesn't it?"[13] —SYNDEY GUILAROFF, hair stylist.

"One of the big ones. His early death created a sensation. Just say the name Valentino and his image comes to mind."[14] —BOB HOPE, comedian.

"Of course I remember Valentino. Valentino smoldered didn't he? That was fine with me. I got his message loud and clear, even at a young age."[15] —MARSHA HUNT, actress.

"I must say, as I get older, a guilty pleasure of mine [watching Valentino's films] and hardly no one knows this."[16] —ELEANOR KEATON, wife of Bustor Keaton.

"His name conjures up mystery, romance and all those wonderful things that had to do with glamour in early Hollywood."[17]—SALLY KIRKLAND, actress.

"An early favorite film star of mine in my youth. Millions of fans in Europe. On reflection, a very compelling actor. His premature death caused riots and many bitter tears."[18]—FRANCIS LEDERER, actor.

"One of the forever stars—a true heartthrob and a genuine movie legend!"[19]—JANET LEIGH, actress.

"He [Valentino] was marvelous looking, more like some sleek jungle creature, a panther, than a man. I was just out of my mind. Imagine! I was a kid, and he was the big star, yet he wasn't on the make ever, which pleased me, because I was very young. I found him a very gentle person, a sweet man, charming and seemingly well bred, far less flamboyant than his wife. There was never any of that 'sheik' stuff with him, any more than there was 'exotica' with me later on. Valentino was a nice Italian man who liked fixing cars. That's how the 'Great Lover' spent his time, puttering around with the custom-made cars he collected."[20]—MYRNA LOY, actress.

"An amazing legend, a legend and mystery that endures to this very day. If the word superstar was in vogue in the 1920s, it surely would have been applied to Valentino and deservedly so."[21]—RODDY MCDOWALL, actor.

"Rudy was one of our neighbors [in Whitley Heights], and we saw him often on our daily walk. He was a great dog lover and would walk his dogs. We would usually meet him about dusk, and he and my husband would stop and chat. I wasn't very interested in what they were talking about, so I would usually walk on ahead."[22]—MARION MACK, actress.

"Being neighbors, we came to know Rudy a great deal better than many who claimed to know him well. While he may have stirred his feminine followers with lawless impulses, he stirred us only with compassion."[23]—FRANCES MARION, screenwriter.

"He was and is a tremendous star. What a gorgeous man with a beautiful talent."[24]—MARION MARSH, actress.

"He was one who was catnip to women."[25]—H. L. MENCKEN, writer.

"I just saw him as a sweet young Italian who happened to be a pretty good actor and who happened to be very handsome. Other women found him to be very seductive and sexy. I found him to be just a lot of fun, much like an older brother."[26]—PATSY RUTH MILLER, actress.

"To most young actresses in Hollywood, including me, Rudolph Valentino had about as much sex appeal off the screen as a lemon. But that wasn't the half of it. The matinee idol of millions of adoring women, the personification of male mastery in love, Rudolph Valentino was in his own married life so far from being masterful as to be that most pitiful of all males, the henpecked husband."[27] — COLLEEN MOORE, actress.

"Of course I don't see all that stuff in Rudie that the fair young things rave about. He isn't a wild animal. He's a sweet, adorable, charming boy — not the least spoiled or conceited..."[28] — NITA NALDI, actress.

"A great star, a wonderful actor and a true gentleman. I loved his movies, how I would love to have played opposite him. They have a memorial for him every year that is still well attended."[29] — MARY PHILBIN, actress.

"A true immortal of the screen. That old saying comes to mind — 'they don't make 'em like that anymore.'"[30] — CHARLES "BUDDY" ROGERS, actor.

"When he wore sideburns, we wore sideburns. We combed our hair á la Valentino. If he wore a beret, we wore a beret."[31] — GILBERT ROLAND, actor.

"Valentino was three Gables and four Taylors rolled into one."[32] — DAMON RUNYON, author.

"Valentino was a great friend and favorite of my mother Adela Rogers St. Johns. He visited us at our Malibu home when I was a young girl. He was ever so handsome, polite, and a quiet reflective man. I wish I could remember more about him. He died soon after another famous Hollywood romantic icon, Barbara La Marr, another close friend of mother's. It was a tough year for her."[33] — ELAINE ST. JOHNS, writer.

"Rudy was an exceptionally all-around person. He read avidly, preferring history, poetry and biography to fiction; he spoke four languages; he loved prize fights and was himself the best amateur boxer in the entire screen colony; he wrote a book of poems and studied painting with no less a tutor than Beltran-Masses, court painter of Spain; he collected rare jades, ivories, firearms, armor and costume plates; he was equally at home in the saddle of the wildest horse as on a ballroom floor; he often went into our kitchen and cooked some favorite Italian, Spanish or French dish with the same serious interest and enjoyment that he would display in a fencing bout or tennis match. His charm, his character and his career were unique. There will never be another like him."[34] — NORMA TALMADGE, actress.

"Like most Latins, Valentino could be gay one minute and down in the lowest depths, the next. He took his career very seriously and, more than once, I have seen him sink into absolute despondency as a result of some unkind or flippant story in the daily press that 'belittled his dignity.' He, himself, would never say an unkind word about anyone."[35] — ESTELLE TAYLOR, actress.

"A real star, a true star. Valentino was a fine actor as well. He is one of the few early silent stars still remembered today."[36] — FAY WRAY, actress.

The Complete Filmography of Rudolph Valentino

During his career, Rudolph Valentino was credited under many names, including: Rudolph DeValentino, M. De Valentina, M. Rodolfo De Valentina, M. Rodolpho De Valentina, R. De Valentina, Rodolfo di Valentina, Rudolpho De Valentina, Rudolpho di Valentina, Rudolpho Valentina, Rodolph Valentine, Rudolpho De Valentine, Rudolph Valentine, Rodolfo di Valentini, Rodolph Valentino, Rudi Valentino, Rudolfo Valentino, Rudolf Valentino, Rudolph Volantino.

Unconfirmed Roles as an Extra

Several film historians claim that Rudolph Valentino appeared as an extra in the following films. They are listed here as a source of reference.

The Battle of the Sexes (1914). Majestic Motion Picture Company. Distributed by Mutual Film Corporation. April 12, 1914. Directed by D. W. Griffith; screenplay by Daniel Carson Goodman, based on his novel *The Single Standard*; cinematography by G. W. Bitzer; camera operator, Karl Brown; edited by James Smith and Rose Smith.

Cast: Donald Crisp (Frank Andrews), Lillian Gish (Jane Andrews, the daughter), Robert Harron (John Andrews, the son), Mary Alden (Mrs. Frank Andrews), Owen Moore (Cleo's lover), Fay Tincher (Cleo), W. E. Lawrence (uncredited), Rodolpho Guglielmi (uncredited dance extra).

Note: According to James Card, former curator of the George Eastman House/ International Museum of Photography, Valentino can be seen as a dance extra in the excerpts from this film that survive in the J. Stuart Blackton compilation film *The March of the Movies* (1933). [Source: Spiess. *There's a New Star in Heaven ... Valentino*, p. 32.] This is a lost film.

My Official Wife (1914). Vitagraph Company of America / Broadway Star Features. Distributed by General Film Co. August 1914. Directed by James Young; scenario adaptation by Marguerite Bertsch, based on the play *My Official Wife* by Richard Henry Savage.

Cast: Clara Kimball Young (Helene Marie), Harry T. Morey (Arthur Bainbridge Lennox), Earle Williams (Sacha).

Note: Rudolph Valentino has a bit part as a Russian Cossack. The autobiography of Albert E. Smith, head of the Vitagraph Company (*Two Reels and a Crank*, Garden City: Doubleday, 1952, pp. 192–194) claims that Valentino approached Smith for a job and was cast as an extra in this film. It should be noted that many of Smith's claims have been disallowed by later researchers. [Source: Spiess. *There's a New Star in Heaven... Valentino*, p. 32.] This is a lost film.

The Quest of Life (1916). Famous Players–Lasky. Distributed by Paramount Pictures. September 25, 1916. Direction and scenario by Ashley Miller, based on the play *Ellen Young* by Gabrielle Enthoven and Edmund Goulding; cinematography by Walter Stradling.

Cast: Florence Walton (Ellen Young), Julian L'Estrange (Alec Mapleton), Royal Byron (Percy), Daniel Burke (Baronti), Russell Bassett (Ellen's father), Mrs. William Bechtel (Ellen's mother), Maurice Walton (Maurice Bretton), Kathleen Townsend (uncredited), Robert Brower (uncredited).

Note: Rudolph Valentino is an extra in a dance hall sequence. This is a lost film.

Seventeen (1916). Famous Players–Lasky. Distributed by Paramount Pictures. November 2, 1916. Presenter, Daniel Frohman; directed by Robert G. Vignola; scenario by Harvey Thew, based on the novel *Seventeen* (New York: Harper & Brothers, 1916) by Booth Tarkington.

Cast: Louise Huff (Lola Pratt), Jack Pickford (William Sylvanus Baxter), Winifred Allen (May Parcher), Madge Evans (Jane Baxter), Walter Hiers (George Cooper), Dick Lee (Genesis), Richard Rosson (Johnny Watson), Julian Dillon (Joe Bullit), Helen Lindroth (Mrs. Baxter), Anthony Merlo (Mr. Baxter).

Note: Rudolph Valentino can be seen in the crowd during a wedding sequence.

The Foolish Virgin (1916). Clara Kimball Young Production Company. Distributed by Lewis J. Selznick Enterprises. December 26, 1916. Direction and scenario by Albert Capellani, based on the novel *The Foolish Virgin* (New York: D. Appleton, 1915) by Thomas Dixon; cinematography by Jacques Monteran, Hal Young and George Peters.

Cast: Clara Kimball Young (Mary Adams), Conway Tearle (Jim Anthony), Paul

Capellani (Dr. Mulford), Agnes Mapes (Ella Swanson), Catherine Proctor (Nance Anthony), Sheridan Tansey (Jim), William Welsh (Jim's father), Marie Lines (Jane), Edward Elkas (Harden), Jacqueline Morhange (Dora).

Note: Film historian John Cocci identified Valentino as appearing as an extra in this film. [Source: *Screen Facts*, Vol. III, No. 6 (1968).]

Extra and Supporting Roles

Patria (1917). Pathé [International Film Service]. January 14, 1917; part 3 of a 15-episode serial.

Produced by Leopold Wharton and Theodore Wharton; directed by George Fitzmaurice, Jacques Jaccard, Leopold Wharton and Theodore Wharton; assistant director, James Gordon; screenplay by J. B. Clymer and Charles W. Goddard, based on the novel *The Last of the Fighting Channings* by Louis Joseph Vance; art direction by E. Douglas Bingham and Archer Chadwick; cinematography by Levi Bacon, John K. Holbrook, Ray June and Lew Tree.

Cast: Irene Castle (Patria/Elaine), Warner Oland (Baron Huroki), Milton Sills (Captain Donald Parr), Marie Walcamp (Bess Morgan), George Majeroni (Senor de Lima), Allan Murnane (Rodney Wrenn), Dorothy Green (Fanny Adair).

Additional Cast: Wallace Beery, Nigel Barrie, Charles Brinley, Jack Holt, George Lessey, M. W. Rale, Leroy Baker, **Rudolph Valentino**, F. W. Stewart, Elsie Baker, Howard Cody, Frank Honda, Sojin, Robin H. Townley.

Review: "From the standpoint of the box office — and, indeed from many others — International's 'Patria' serial by Louis Joseph Vance, starring Mrs. Vernon Castle, is probably the best feature of that kind ever produced." — *Variety*, November 24, 1916.

Note: Film historian DeWitt Bodeen claimed that Valentino appeared as an extra in the third episode during the midnight frolic scene. [Source: *Screen Facts*, Vol. III, No. 5 (1968).] Chapters 1, 2, 3, 4, and 10 survive at the Museum of Modern Art in New York.

Silent. Action. B & W. 35mm. Running time, 15 episodes. © International Film Service, Inc., 21 December 1916.

Alimony (1917). Paralta Plays, Inc., A C. L. Yearsly Picture. Distributed by First National Exhibitors' Circuit, Inc. December 3, 1917.

Supervised by Robert Brunton; directed by Emmett J. Flynn; story by Hayden Talbot; art direction by R. Holmes Paul; cinematography by L. Guy Wilky.

Cast: Lois Wilson (Marjorie Lansing), George Fisher (Howard Turner), Josephine Whittell (Bernice Bristol Flint), Wallace Worsley (John Flint), Arthur Allardt (Elijah Stone), Joseph J. Dowling (William Jackson), Ida Lewis (Mrs. Lansing), Margaret Livingston (Florence), Alice Taafe (Extra, uncredited), **Rudolph Valentino** (Dancer, uncredited).

Review: No data found.
Note: This is a lost film. No negatives or prints are known to exist.
Silent. Drama. B & W. 35mm. Running time, 6 reels.

A Society Sensation (1918). Bluebird Photoplays, Inc. (also distributed). September 23, 1918.

Directed by Paul Powell; screenplay by Hope Loring and Paul Powell, based on the short story, "The Borrowed Duchess" (publication unknown) by Perley Poore Sheehan; cinematography by E. G. Ullman.

Cast: Carmel Myers (Sydney Parmelee), **M. Rodolpho De Valentina** (Dick Bradley), Lydia Yeamans Titus (Mrs. Jones), Alfred Allen (Captain Parmelee), Fred Kelsey (Jim), ZaSu Pitts (Mary), Harold Goodwin (Tommy).

Summary: Captain Parmelee, a fisherman, believes that he is a nobleman. Mrs. Jones, a social climber in San Francisco, hears of the old man's allegation and decides to play a trick on Mrs. Bradley, the social leader. Mrs. Jones borrows Parmelee's daughter, Sydney, and introduces her as a duchess. Dick Bradley (Valentino) falls in love with the girl, and when her claim to nobility is found out to be false he follows her back to the fishing village. There he has a fight with a fisherman who is also in love with Sydney and tries to kidnap her so she cannot marry Bradley. The fisherman finally decides on Mary, another village girl, and Sydney and Bradley set off on their honeymoon.

Review(s): " Rodolpho De Valentino makes a very American Dick Bradley despite the fact he is a fairly recent arrival from Italy."—*Variety*, October 4, 1918.

"… [T]he audience gave it and Rodolph Valentino the 'razz' good and proper; playing it up with a lot of new paper which had Valentino starred top of Carmel Myers and which also had some of his recent pictures slapped all over it, they could appreciate the crudity of the picture itself. That was what they razzed more than the star."—*Variety*, April 2, 1924 [reissue].

Note: Working title, *The Borrowed Duchess*. This film is available on video.

Silent. Comedy-drama. B & W. 35mm. Running time, 5 reels. © Bluebird Photoplays, Inc., 11 September 1918.

All Night (1918). Bluebird Photoplays, Inc. (also distributed). November 30, 1918.

Directed by Paul Powell; scenario by Fred Myton, based on the story "One Bright Idea" (*All-Story Weekly*, 29 June–20 July, 1918) by Edgar Franklin.

Cast: Carmel Myers (Elizabeth Lane), **M. Rudolpho De Valentina** (Richard Thayer), Charles Dorian (William Harcourt), Mary Warren (Maude Harcourt), William Dyer (Bradford), Wadsworth Harris (Colonel Lane), Jack Hull (Butler).

Summary: William Harcourt is on the verge of bankruptcy, but has been promised a million dollars by Bradford, an eccentric who never closes a deal without seeing a man in his home. Harcourt, who has fired his servants, is trying to entertain Elizabeth Lane and Richard Thayer (Valentino) when the telegram announcing Bradford arrives. The Harcourts beg Elizabeth and Richard to pose in their places while they pretend to be servants. Bradford arrives and decides to stay all night. Colonel Lane arrives to take his daughter Elizabeth, but is mistaken by Bradford for a crazy uncle, and is locked in the storeroom over night. In the morning Harcourt comes clean to Bradford, but still gets his million. Elizabeth and Richard have fallen in love with each other over night.

Review: "There are no vulgar situations shown at any time in the picture. It has been directed very cleverly and in a refined manner. It is a good offering and should have universal appeal."—*Motion Picture News*, November 2, 1918.

Note: This film is available on video.

Silent. Comedy-drama. B & W. 35mm. Running time, 5 reels. © Bluebird Photoplays, Inc., 9 November 1918.

The Married Virgin (1918). Maxwell Productions. Distributed by State Rights; General Films Co.; Fidelity Pictures Co. December 1918.

Supervised and directed by Joseph Maxwell; story and scenario by Hayden Talbot.

Cast: Vera Sisson (Mary McMillan), **Rodolfo di Valentini** (Count Roberto di San Fraccini), Frank Newberg (Douglas McKee), Kathleen Kirkham (Mrs. McMillan), Edward Jobson (John McMillan).

Summary: Mary McMillan, the daughter of a rich contractor, loves Douglas McKee, an up-and-coming young lawyer. Her stepmother has an affair with a young opportunist, Count Roberta [Valentino], and they agree to elope whenever they can obtain the finances. The Count seeks to blackmail the contractor, but the plan fails and he forces Mary to marry him, even though he still plans to elope with her stepmother on the earnings of the marriage settlement. She is fearful he will not keep his promise and plans to disfigure him with acid. In the struggle, their automobile is dashed over the cliff and she is killed. The Count escapes, but McKee finds a loophole in a long-forgotten law for the girl he loves.

Review: "A poor picture. It is an unhappy subject, with hardly any sympathetic situations to relieve it. More than four out of five reels are consumed in presenting the despicable doings of the villain. He is an Italian nobleman, a married woman being in love with him."—*Harrison's Report*, July 17, 1920 (from reissue as *Frivolous Wives*).

Review from re-release at Silent Movie Theatre: "Reportedly, Valentino preferred the film to remain in oblivion, but he needn't have worried: It's no worse than countless other society melodramas of the period. Its continuity is murky but it has elaborate sets and handsome actual locales, notably a substantial sequence filmed at the Hotel Del Coronado. Seen today it seems lurid and contrived, but there's no denying the impact of Valentino's smoldering presence, and his ability to shade a stereotypical villain with both an insolent irony and a touch of melancholy regret."—Kevin Thomas, *Los Angeles Times*, March 1, 2000.

Note: This film is available on video and DVD. Reissued in 1920 as *Frivolous Wives*.

Silent. Drama. B & W. 35mm. Running time, 6 reels.

The Homebreaker (1919). Thomas H. Ince Corporation. Distributed by Famous Players–Lasky Corp. / Paramount Pictures. April 20, 1919.

Presented and supervised by Thomas H. Ince; directed by Victor L. Schertzinger; story by John Lynch; scenario by R. Cecil Smith; titles by Irvin J. Martin; art direction by C. Tracy Hoag; edited by Duncan Mansfield; cinematography by John S. Stumar.

Cast: Dorothy Dalton (Mary Marbury), Douglas MacLean (Raymond Abbott), Edwin Stevens (Jonas Abbott), Frank Leigh (Fernando Poyntier), Beverly Travis (Marcia Poyntier), Nora Johnson (Lois Abbott), Mollie McConnell (Mrs. White), **Rodolfo di Valentini** (extra).

Summary: Mary Marbury, a saleswoman for Abbott and Son, plans to be married to the junior member of the firm. When she returns from a trip, she finds him rather indifferent. He has also become friendly with a so-called Russian baron and the latter's sister, who spends money extravagantly and leads a wild life. When his father, Jonas, asks for Mary's advice, she convinces him to strike out on his own, indulging in dancing and matching his son in general merriment. Mary recognizes the baron as a crook, who, with his assumed sister, she had seen put off a train for misconduct. She traps him and his accomplices shortly after they rob Jonas' private safe and they are arrested. Abbott comes to his senses and Mary forgives him.

Review: "It is a delightful offering, this one that presents the star as a traveling saleswoman, and as you may guess, the characterization is embroidered in the plot for all that it stands for in the world of realities. The story is human and bright and truly representative of its personages, and if it is developed along extravagant lines, this is because the comedy values demand it."—*Motion Picture News*, May 17, 1919.

Note: Working title, *Miss Marbury and Others*. This is a lost film; no negatives or prints are known to exist. Valentino's role was cut to one scene. [Source: "The Career of Rudolph Valentino," *Films in Review*, April 1952.]

Silent. Comedy-Society. B & W. 35mm. Running time, 5 reels. © Thos. H. Ince Corp., 4 April 1919.

The Delicious Little Devil (1919). Universal Film Mfg. Co. (also distributed). May 20, 1919.

Presented by Carl Laemmle; directed by Robert Z. Leonard; scenario by John B. Clymer and Harvey F. Thew, based on their story "Kitty, Mind Your Feet" (publication unknown); cinematography by Allen G. Siegler.

Cast: Mae Murray (Mary McGuire), Harry Rattenbury (Patrick McGuire), Richard Cummings (Uncle Barnley), **Rudolpho De Valentine** (Jimmie Calhoun), Ivor McFadden (Percy), Bertram Grasby (Duke de Sauterne), Edward Jobson (Michael Calhoun), William V. Mong (Larry).

Song: "Oh, You Delicious Little Devil," words by Alfred Bryan, music by Buddy DelSylva. Remick Publishers.

Summary: The story concerns a young Irish tenement girl who supports a family of three. Out of a job, she applies for a place as a dancer in a disreputable roadhouse, and in order to get that position adopts a "past" as the former flame of the Duke de Sauterne. She falls in love with Jimmy Calhoun (Valentino), the son of a millionaire contractor, who is afraid to propose because of her lurid past. Complications develop when the Duke de Sauterne arrives, but all ends well as Jimmy's Irish father congratulates the girl's Irish father.

Review: "... [D]elightfully fresh and pleasing and the character work good." —*Motion Picture World*, April 26, 1919.

Note: A print of this film exists in the Nederlands Filmmuseum archives.

Silent. Comedy. B & W. 35mm. Running time, 6 reels, 5,650 ft. © Universal Film Mfg. Co., Inc., 18 April 1919.

The Big Little Person (1919). Universal Film Mfg. Co., Inc. (also distributed). May 1919.

Directed by Robert Z. Leonard; scenario by Bess Meredyth, based on the novel *The Big Little Person* (New York, 1917) by Rebecca Lane Hooper Eastman.

Cast: Mae Murray (Arathea Manning), Clarissa Selwynne (Mrs. Manning), **M. Rodolpho De Valentina** (Arthur Endicott), Allan Sears (Gerald Staples), Mrs. Bertram Grassby (Marion Beemis).

Summary: A top ear specialist has diagnosed Arathea Manning's loss of hearing as incurable. Added to her burden is the fact that her lover, Arthur Endicott (Valentino), is ashamed of her affliction and is afraid that the suicide of her father would discolor his good name. Arathea meets an inventor, Gerald Spriggs, who has perfected a machine that enables her to hear until a spoiled child robs her of her newfound happiness during a visit to her former school. Soon she becomes a secretary at the inventor's company where Endicott visits and is told that he is responsible for her deafness. His feelings soon change from shame to cold-heartedness, and an unsuspected brutality becomes the means by which Arathea regains her hearing.

Review: No data found.

Note: This is a lost film; no negatives or prints are known to exist.

Silent. Drama. B & W. 35mm. Running time, 6 reels. © Universal Film Mfg. Co., Inc., 20 May 1919.

Virtuous Sinners (1919). Pioneer Film Corp. Distributed by State Rights / Pioneer Film Corp. May 25, 1919.

Directed by Emmett J. Flynn.

Cast: Norman Kerry (Hamilton Jones), Wanda Hawley (Dawn Emerson), Harry Holden (Eli Barker), David Kirby (Stool Pigeon), Bert Woodruff ('Twenty Years' McGregor), Eunice Woodruff (Child), **Rodolfo di Valentini** (bit part as a down-and-outer in the slums).

Summary: McGregor, assistant to Eli Barker at the mission, finds Dawn Emerson huddled in a corner during a pouring rain and carries her inside. Later Dawn becomes an organist at the mission. One evening, Hamilton Jones, society cracksman, wanders into the slums to dispose of stolen goods. Passing the mission he hears Dawn's voice lifted in song and enters. The girl captivates him and Jones becomes a regular visitor at the mission. The two fall in love. A stool pigeon, who is also in love with Dawn, is jealous of Jones and plans to ruin him. While rescuing a child McGregor is run over by an automobile and is taken to a hospital. To pay for the operation, Jones robs a house, and the police, informed by the decoy, arrest him. At Jones' trial the evidence goes against him until Barker testifies that the theft was to pay for McGregor's operation. Jones is paroled and returns to Dawn who has never lost faith in him.

Review: "At the press exhibition, at the Pioneer Film Corporation's projection rooms, the reviewers periodically emitted snorts at the namby-pamby trash set forth during the course of five reels."—*Variety*, May 16, 1919.

Note: A print of this film exists in the Library of Congress.

Silent. Drama-Crime. B & W. 35mm. Running time, 5 reels. © Pioneer Film Corp., 10 April 1919.

A Rogue's Romance (1919). Vitagraph Company of America (also distributed). June 9, 1919.

Presented by Albert E. Smith; directed by James Young; story by H. H. Van Loan; scenario by James Young; cinematography by Max Dupont.

Cast: Earle Williams (Jules Marin/M Picard), Brinsley Shaw (Henri Duval), Harry von Meter (Leon Voliere), Herbert Standing (Anton Deprenay), Sidney Franklin (Burgomaster), Karl Formes (Brulon).

Additional Cast: Marian Skinner, Harry Dunkinson, Mathilde Comont (billed as Mme. Comounte), Peaches Jackson, Jeanette Trebaol, Pat Moore, Mrs. Griffith, William H. Orlamond, **Rudolph Volantino**, Gladys McMurray, Kathyrn Adams, Maude George.

Summary: Picard, society crook, returns from the front with the Croix de Guerre, adopts the name of Jules Marier, and settles down at Montoir, with three little orphans he assumes charge of. When one of the children is ill, he is forced to borrow the automobile of Mlle. Deprenay, but leaves his cross as security. He returns the car but the police are hot on his trail. Under the guise of Du Bois, alleged Scotland Yard Secret Service agent, he meets Mlle. Deprenay again at a social gathering. A necklace is stolen and Picard forces its return from Voliere, whom he recognizes as a former associate. Picard tells Mlle. Deprenay that love for her has caused his reformation. He foils a plot by Voliere to swindle some innocent stockholders, hands all the stolen money over to the head detective, who is pursuing him, assures him that Picard no longer exists, and escapes with Mlle. Deprenay to begin a new life.

Review: No data found.

Note: This is a lost film; no negatives or prints are known to exist.

Silent. Drama-Crime. B & W. 35mm. Running time, 5 reels. © The Vitagraph Co. of America, 17 May 1919.

Out of Luck / Nobody Home (1919). The New Art Film Co. Distributed by Famous Players–Lasky Corp. / Paramount Pictures. August 24, 1919.

Directed by Elmer Clifton; assistant director, Leigh R. Smith; scenario by Lois Zellner; cinematography by Lee Garmes and John Leezer.

Cast: Dorothy Gish (Frances Wadsworth), Ralph Graves (Malcolm Dale), Raymond Cannon (Crandall Park), Vera McGinnis (Mollie Rourke), George Fawcett (Rockaway Smith), Emily Chichester (Sally Smith), **Rodolph Valentine** (Maurice Rennard), Norman McNeil (Rosebud Miller), Kate V. Toncray (the Strong-Minded Aunt), Porter Strong (Eddie, the Pup), Vivian Montrose (Florence Wellington).

Summary: A superstitious Frances Wadsworth advises her friend, Florence Wellington, to elope because the stars decree it. Florence does so, and Frances falls in love with Malcolm Dale, best man at the ceremony. Unfortunately, Malcolm proposes on Friday the thirteenth, and the cards tell Frances, who is a brunette, that a blonde woman will enter Malcolm's life. Frances is further dismayed when the cards prophesy that a dark man is to cross her fate. A dark fortune hunter soon appears and makes love to Frances, and persuades her to wed him. The ceremony is postponed when a black cat jinxes it. Frances goes to the deserted apartment of her newlywed friends, who are away, and there she meets Malcolm. Burglars raid the place and tie the two up, but the thieves are caught, the fortune hunter exposed, and the lovers united.

Review: "The star and cast measure up high caliber as clever light comedians and comediennes and the direction could not have been improved upon. A slight story and a small plot tangible enough for farce-comedy is developed easily by the continuity writer."—*Motion Picture News*, September 6, 1919.

Note: This is a lost film; no negatives or prints are known to exist. After the film was released with the title *Nobody Home*, the title was changed to *Out of Luck* to accommodate Guy Bolton, who wrote to the producers that his play entitled *Nobody Home* had been produced not long before.

Silent. Comedy. B & W. 35mm. Running time, 5 reels, 4,794 ft. © D. W. Griffith, 18 August 1919.

The Eyes of Youth (1919). Garson Productions. Distributed by Equity Pictures Corp. October 26, 1919.

Produced by Harry Garson; directed by Albert Parker; adaptation by Charles E. Whittaker; scenario by Albert Parker, based on the stage play *Eyes of Youth* (New York opening, August 22, 1917) by Max Marcin and Charles Guernon; technician, John M. Voshell; cinematography by Robert Edeson.

Cast: Clara Kimball Young (Gina Ashling), Gareth Hughes (Kenneth Ashling), Pauline Starke (Rita Ashling), Sam Southern (Asa Ashling), Edmund Lowe (Peter Judson), Ralph Lewis (Robert Goring), Milton Sills (Louis Anthony), Vincent Serrano (the Yogi), William Courtleigh (Paolo Salvo), Norman Selby (Dick Brownell), **Rudolfo Valentino** (Clarence Morgan), Edward Kimball.

Song: "Eyes of Youth," words and music by Irving Berlin. Berlin Publishers.

Summary: When Gina Ashling expresses a desire to look into the future and see what the final outcome of each of three decisions would be, a yogi permits her to gaze into a crystal ball and the action leading up to each final situation is shown. The happy ending is reached when the disillusioned girl makes the fourth decision.

Review: "Here is a picture that you can go the limit on intensely exploiting and you should satisfy all classes of patrons. It has a novel theme tying up a series of three separate and distinct plots and is lavishly mounted, cleverly directed, and portrayed by a capable cast of well know screen artists."—*Motion Picture News*, December 15, 1919.

Note: This film is available on video.

Silent. Fantasy-Drama. B & W. 35mm. Running time, 7 reels; 78 minutes.

An Adventuress (1920). Fred J. Balshofer. Distributed by Republic Distributing Corp. April 10, 1920.

Presented and directed by Fred J. Balshofer; story and screenplay by Charles Taylor and/or Tom J. Geraghty; cinematography by Tony Gaudio.

Cast: Julian Eltinge (Jack Perry, also known as Mam'selle Fedora), Fred Covert (Lyn Brook, also known as Thelma), William Clifford (Dick Sayre), Leo White (Prince Halbere), Virginia Rappe (Zana), **R. De Valentina** (Jacques Rudanyi), Stanton Beck (Grand Duke Nebo), Charles Millsfield (Pom Pom), Alma Francis (Eunice), Lydia Knott (Clifford Townsend's Mother). Additional cast: Frank Bond, Fontain La Rue, Frank Gastrock, William Pearson, Frederick Heck.

Summary: A revolutionist in favor of a monarchy makes an effort to destroy the republican form of government in Alpania, a European country by the sea. Perry, Brook and Sayre, three Americans, arrive. Perry offends the monarchists, is caught and sentenced to execution, but Brook rescues him. Perry, disguised as a woman, flirts with the royal leaders under the name of Fedora, while Brook, in a similar disguise, masquerades as Thelma. Both are highly successful as women, and Perry wins the love of Zana, an Alpanian girl. Perry is again captured and becomes the pilot of an enemy airplane. He succeeds in making a landing and drives off in an automobile, chased by his foes, but eludes them and reaches America with Zana.

Review: No data found.

Note: "Balshofer shot this film in 1918, under the title *Over the Rhine*, as an anti–German war drama. Although contemporary trade articles speculated that Metro had contracted with Balshofer to release *Over the Rhine*, the film was never released under that title due to diminished interest in war films after the armistice. The film was released in 1920 as *The Adventuress* with some plot alterations. In 1922 Balshofer copyrighted the film under the title *The Isle of Love*, and released it on a state rights basis. Balshofer's autobiography gives the additional information that he planned two endings as the war drew to a close, planning to use a more moral ending if the German peace initiative bore no results. Further information in the autobiography states that a version of the film with newly shot material was released later with a plot less anti–German and more comic. This version, according to Balshofer, was also augmented with outtakes of Rudolph Valentino, originally billed as R. De Valentina, to take advantage of his recent popularity, and he received second billing to Eltinge. It is unclear if the changes involving Valentino's performance were made in 1920 or 1922."—*American Film Institute Catalog.*

This film exists at the George Eastman House, Rochester, New York.

Silent. Adventure-Comedy-Drama. B & W. 35mm. Running time, 5 reels. © Republic Distributing Corp. 10 April 1920.

Passion's Playground (1920). Katherine MacDonald Pictures Corp. Distributed by First National Exhibitors' Circuit, Inc. April 1920.

Presented by Sam E. Rork; directed by J. A. Barry; scenario by C. N. Williamson and A. M. Williamson, based on the novel *The Guests of Hercules* (New York, 1912) by Charles Norris Williamson and Alice Muriel Williamson; cinematography by Joseph Brotherton.

Cast: Katherine MacDonald (Mary Grant), Norman Kerry (Prince Vanno Della Robbia), Nell Craig (Marie Grant), Edwin Stevens (Lord Dauntry), Virginia Ainsworth (Lady Dauntry), **Rudolph Valentine** (Prince Angelo Della Robbia), Alice Wilson (Dodo Wardropp), Howard Gaye (James Hanaford), Fanny Ferrari (Idina Bland), Sylvia Jocelyn (Molly Maxwell), Walt Whitman (Cure of Roquebrune).

Summary: Mary Grant, a convent girl, goes to Monte Carlo, and because of her winnings becomes the center of attraction. Prince Vanno Della Robbia (Valentino) falls in love with Mary, and introduces her to his brother, Prince Angelo, whose bride turns out to be Mary's friend Marie Grant, who had run away from the convent with a married man. The brothers know nothing of Marie's past and Mary promises to keep the secret. Idina Bland, outraged at Prince Angelo's marriage, tells the secret but Marie falsely asserts the story is not true of her but of Mary. Mary, by her silence, admits guilt. She leaves Monte Carlo but an old friend, Molly Maxwell, arrives and tells the truth. Prince Vanno goes in search of the innocent Mary and wins her.

Review: "The film is weak through the story, and everything else in connection appears to be in line with that."—*Variety*, June 11, 1920.

Note: Working title, *The Guests of Hercules*. This is a lost film; no negatives or prints are known to exist.

Silent. Drama. B & W. 35mm. Running time, 5 reels. © Attractions Distributing Corp., 10 May 1920.

The Cheater (1920). Screen Classics, Inc. Distributed by Metro Pictures Corporation. June 7, 1920.

Presented by Maxwell Kargar; directed by Henry Otto; scenario by Lois Zellner, based on the play *Judah* (London, 1890) by Henry Arthur Jones; cinematography by William M. Edmond.

Cast: May Allison (Lilly Meany, aka Vashti Dethic), King Baggott (Lord Asgarby), Frank Currier (Peg Meany), Harry von Meter (Bill Tozer), May Geraci (Eve Asgarby), Percy Challenger (Mr. Prall), Lucille Ward (Mrs. Prall), P. Dempsey Tabler (Doctor), Alberta Lee (Nurse), **Rudolph Valentino** (Extra).

Summary: Lily Meany, fortune teller and member of an underworld gang of sharpers in London, conceives the plan of posing as a mystic who can work miracles. Lord Asgarby seeks her aid for his crippled daughter and Lily, escorted by her confederates, becomes a member of the household. The child learns to love Lily so when the mending of a broken doll inspires the girl with faith in Lily's healing powers, the experiment brings success regardless of its undeserving motive. When the father, a widower, also falls in love with Lily, the shame of her deceit comes upon her. Confession leads to the woman's restoration and a happy marriage to Asgarby follows.

Review: "Theme, treatment and interest are of the highest order, as would be inevitable in a picture made from a play by Henry Arthur Jones, one of England's most brilliant dramatists. But it has its defects in screen form."—*Variety*, July 30, 1920.

Note: This is a lost film; no negatives or prints are known to exist.

Silent. Drama-Society. B & W. 35mm. Running time, 6 reels. © Metro Pictures Corp., 21 Jun 1920.

Once to Every Woman (1920). Universal Film Mfg. Co. Distributed by a Universal-Jewel Production de Luxe. September 6, 1920.

Presented by Carl Laemmle; directed by Allen Holubar; story by Allen Holubar; scenario by Allen Holubar and Olga Linek Scholl; edited by Viola Mallory (uncredited); cinematography by Fred LeRoy Granville.

Cast: Dorothy Phillips (Aurora Meredith), William Ellingford (Matthew Meredith), Mrs. Margaret Mann (Mother Meredith), Emily Chichester (Patience Meredith), Elinor Field (Virginia Meredith), Robert Anderson (Phineas Scudder), Mary Wise (Mrs. Thorndyke) **Rudolph Valentino** (Juliantimo), Rosa Gore (Mrs. Chichester Jones), Frank Elliott (Duke of Devonshire), Dan Crimmins (Mr. Chichester Jones).

Song: "Once to Every Woman," words and music by Ben Bolt and Thomas English.

Summary: Aurora Meredith is a privileged daughter, and her family puts everything aside so that she might have everything she longs for. She has a good voice that comes to the attention of a wealthy woman, who agrees to cultivate Aurora's talent and sends her abroad. In the three years away from home she becomes a great singer and forgets all about the sacrifices her family has made. She returns to America to escape the attentions of an ardent admirer, Juliantimo (Valentino), and is soon the idol of the public. The admirer follows, and after being rejected once again plots his revenge. One evening at the opera he shoots her from a box in the crowded theater and then commits suicide. She recovers but her voice is gone. Her former friends and associates now desert her, and she returns to her home where she is overcome by sorrow. On the death of her mother her singing voice comes back, and she marries her country love who has waited all this time for her.

Review: "Amid all his [Holubar] massed effects he has worked in sympathy. The ending is ridiculously out of keeping with fact, but serves for ordinary purposes. The acting was uniformly good."—*Variety*, December 17, 1920.

Note: Working titles, *Ambition* and *The Gorgeous Canary*. This is a lost film; no negatives or prints are known to exist.

Silent. Drama. B & W. 35mm. Running time, 7 reels.

The Wonderful Chance (1920). Selznick Pictures Corp. (also distributed). September 27, 1920.

Directed by George Archainbaud; story by H. H. Van Loan; scenario by Mary Murillo and Melville Hammett.

Cast: Eugene O'Brien (Lord Birmingham / "Swagger" Barlow), Tom Blake ("Red" Dugan), **Rudolph de Valentino** (Joe Klingsby), Joseph Flanagan (Haggerty), Warren Cook (Parker Winton), Martha Mansfield (Peggy Winton).

Summary: "Swagger" Barlow, just released from Sing Sing, is determined to go straight, and confides this to his pal, "Red" Dugan. Red decides that they should have money first and goes out to make his last haul but is shot while making his escape. The only doctor in whom they can confide needs plenty of "hush money," so Barlow goes out on one last haul to pay for Red's treatment. Soon after, while dodging Haggerty, a detective who suspects him of the recent robbery, Barlow is mistaken in the lobby of the Ritz-Carlton for Lord Birmingham. The real Lord Birmingham has been ambushed by some crooks led by Joe Klingsby (Valentino) and is being held for ransom. Barlow assumes the identity of Lord Birmingham and is wined and dined and finally attends a party where he falls in love with Peggy Winton, a member of a prominent family. Through Red, Barlow learns the fate of the real Birmingham and rescues him and becomes Barlow again. After a robbery in which Barlow is implicated, Peggy learns that Birmingham is not Barlow and that she is in love with the wrong man. However, a promise to go straight in the future helps to make the outlook rosy.

Review: "At that the picture is a fairly good one and has some real splendid double exposure photography, showing O'Brien in a dual role. It's hokum, as far as the story is concerned, and full of improbable situations, but will do in the smaller places."—*Variety*, July 21, 1922 [for the 1922 reissue].

Note: aka *The Thug*. Prints of this film exist at NYC's Museum of Modern Art and at the George Eastman House, Rochester, NY. At one time this film was available on video.

Silent. Drama-Crime. B & W. 35mm. Running time, 5 reels, 5,137 ft. © Selznick Pictures Corp., 5 October 1920.

Stolen Moments (1920). American Cinema Corp. Distributed by State Rights / Pioneer Film Corp. October 14, 1920.

Directed by James Vincent; story by H. Thompson Rich; scenario by Richard Hall.

Cast: Marguerite Namara (Vera Blaine), **Rudolph Valentine** (Jose Dalmarez), Albert L. Barrett (Hugh Conway), Henrietta Simpson (Hugh's Mother), Arthur Earle (Carlos, the Butler), Walter Chapin (Richard Huntley), Aileen Pringle [billed as Aileen Savage] (Inez Salles), Alex K. Shannon (Campos Salles, Her Father), Gene Gauthier (Alvarez, His Son).

Summary: Vera Blaine, an orphan and the ward of rising young attorney Hugh Conway, is attracted to Jose Dalmarez (Valentino), a Brazilian novelist visiting New York. He asks her to marry him and go back with him to Brazil but she refuses when she realizes he has no honest intentions. Regrettably, she has given him a book with an inscription suggesting she is very much in love with him. Dalmarez returns to New York with Campos, his former lover's brother, swearing revenge. Hugh, who has married Vera, and his friend Richard invite Dalmarez to dinner. Neither is aware of the past association of Vera and Dalmarez. When he is alone with Vera, Dalmarez threatens to disclose her past unless she visits him. She does, and begs for the return of the book she had given him, but he refuses. They struggle, and she finds a heavy instrument and strikes him, leaving him for dead. She returns the next night for the book, and upon entering the house is discovered by Richard, who is investigating the murder case. Later that evening Campos returns through a window to obtain letters sent by his sister to Dalmarez, and is shot in a scuffle with Richard. Before dying he confesses to the murder of Dalmarez. Vera and her husband find happiness in the future with the past safely behind them.

Review: "The picture will hold the interest of the average screen patron. It is melodramatic in tone but the suspense is cleverly maintained and it is sufficiently well acted to make the illusion complete. Marguerite Namara is a trifle stagey for present day demands, but plays a strong emotional role with sincerity and power." —*Moving Picture World*, June 11, 1921.

Note: An incomplete print of this film exists in the UCLA Archives. Some scenes were filmed in Savannah, Georgia, and St. Augustine, Florida.

Silent. Drama. B & W. 35mm. Running time, 6 reels. © American Cinema Corp., 14 Oct 1920.

Starring Roles

The Four Horsemen of the Apocalypse (1921). Metro Pictures Corp. March 24, 1921 [New York City premiere, March 6, 1921].

Produced and directed by Rex Ingram; assistant directors, Joseph Calder and Amos Myers; scenario by June Mathis, based on the novel *The Four Horsemen of the Apocalypse* (translated by Charlotte Brewster Jordan of *Los Cuatros Jinetes del Apocalipsis*; New York, 1918) by Vincente Blasco-Ibáñez; titles by Jack W. Robson; art direction by Joseph Calder and Amos Myers; music by Louis F. Gottschalk; edited by Grant Whytock; cinematography by John F. Seitz, Starrett Ford (assistant) and Walter Mayo (assistant).

Cast: Pomeroy Cannon (Madariaga, the Centaur), Josef Swickard (Marcelo Desnoyers), Bridgetta Clark (Doña Luisa), **Rodolph Valentino** (Julio Desnoyers), Virginia Warwick (Chichi), Alan Hale (Karl von Hartrott), Mabel Van Buren (Elena), Stuart Holmes (Captain von Hartrott), Jean Hersholt (Professor von Hartrott), John Sainpolis [St. Polis] (Etienne Laurier), Alice Terry (Marguerite Lurier), Mark Fenton (Senator Lacour), Derek Ghent (René Lacour), Nigel De Brulier (Tchernoff), Bowditch M. Turner (Argensola), Edward Connelly (Lodgekeeper), Wallace Beery (Lieutenant-Colonel von Richthosen), Harry Northrup (the Count), Arthur Hoyt (Lieutenant Schnitz), Jacques D'Auray (Captain d'Aubrey), Noble Johnson (Conquest), Claire De Lorez (Mlle. Lucette, a model), Isabelle Keith (German woman), Fred Kelsey (uncredited), Henry Klaus (Heinrich von Hartrott), Jacques Lanoe (German woman's husband), Bull Montana (French butcher), Curt Rehfeld (Major Blumhardt), Brinsley Shaw (Celendonio), Georgia Woodthorpe (Lodgekeeper's wife), Minnehaha (the Old nurse), Kathleen Key (Georgette), Beatrice Dominguez (Dancer), Ramon Samaniego [Novarro] (Dancer, uncredited), Carmen Samaniego (Dancer, uncredited).

Songs: "Chi Chi," words and music by Walter Havenschild (Photoplay Publishing); "I Have a Rendezvous with You," words by Tillie Jay and Nancy Jay, music by Ernst Luz (Photoplay Publishing); "In the Ruins," music by Leo Kempinski (Photoplay Publishing); "Julio," words by Ernst Luz, music by Harry Olsen (Photoplay Publishing).

Summary: Julio Desnoyers (Valentino), the pampered son of Madariaga, a wealthy cattleman, falls in love with Marguerite Laurier, the wife of the French jurist. Marguerite's husband goes to war, and is blinded after a heroic career as a captain in the army. Marguerite, in order to make restitution for her flirtations with Julio, becomes a Red Cross nurse, finds her blind husband and resolves to devote the remainder of her life to his care. Julio discovers her in a convalescent camp and rekindles his efforts to win her. Here, and again at home with her husband, Marguerite struggles with her desire to go with Julio and the call of duty to her husband, but right triumphs in the end. Julio dons the French uniform, and after distinguishing himself for his brave fighting qualities is killed in a hand-to-hand skirmish with one of his cousins, who is an officer in the German army.

Review: "The performance of Rudolph Valentino, who plays Julio Desnoyers, was one of the marvels of the evening. Mr. Valentino's acting has sincerity and depth; he gives a colorful, fascinating and sympathetic portrayal of a complex character." —*New York Morning Telegraph*, March 9, 1921.

Note: This film is available on video.

Silent. Epic drama. B & W. 35mm. Running time, 11 reels. © Metro Pictures Corp., 24 Mar 1921.

Uncharted Seas (1921). Metro Pictures Corp. April 25, 1921.

Directed by Wesley Ruggles; scenario by George Edward Jenks, based on the story, "The Uncharted Seas" (*Munsey's Magazine*, September 1920) by John Fleming Wilson; art direction by John Holden; cinematography by John F. Seitz.

Cast: Alice Lake (Lucretia Eastman), Carl Gerard (Senator Tom Eastman), **Rudolph Valentino** (Frank Underwood), Robert Alden (Fred Turner), Charles Hill Mailes (Old Jim Eastman), Rhea Haines (Ruby Lawton).

Summary: Though her husband Tom Eastman is a drunk, Lucretia is convinced by her father-in-law to give his son one more chance before leaving him. On an expedition to the Arctic Circle, Eastman becomes disillusioned and orders the ship to return. At this point, another ship, commanded by Frank Underwood (Valentino), who loves Lucretia, arrives and Lucretia joins his ship. When Eastman arrives at home, he accuses his wife of infidelity and gets a divorce. Meanwhile, Lucretia and Frank are detained for months until finally the icebergs crush and demolish their ship. After a treacherous journey across the frozen ice in a dog sled, they are rescued by a government patrol craft and all ends well.

Review: "... [A]nd Rudolph Valentino, with very little chance for acting, makes the most of what there is, with his discriminating sense of dramatic value."—*Los Angeles Examiner*, May 2, 1921.

Note: This is a lost film; no negatives or prints are known to exist.

Silent. Romantic melodrama. B & W. 35mm. Running time, 6 reels. © Metro Pictures Corp., 26 Apr 1921.

The Conquering Power (1921). Metro Pictures Corp. New York City premiere, July 8, 1921.

Produced and directed by Rex Ingram; adaptation by June Mathis, based on the novel *Eugene Grandet* (1883) by Honore de Balzac; technical directors, Ralph Barton and Amos Myers; cinematography by John F. Seitz.

Cast: Alice Terry (Eugénie Grandet), **Rudolph Valentino** (Charles Grandet), Eric Mayne (Victor Grandet), Ralph Lewis (Père Grandet), Edna Demaurey (Pere Grandet's wife), Bridgetta Clark (Lucienne des Grassins), Mark Fenton (Monsieur des Grassins), Ward Wing (Adolph des Grassins), Edward Connelly (Notary Cruchot), George Atkinson (Bonfons Cruchot), Willard Lee Hall (the Abbé), Mary Hearn (Nanon), Eugène Pouyet (Cornoiller), Andrée Tourneur (Annette), Rolfe Sedan (Annette's suitor, uncredited).

Summary: Charles Grandet goes to live with his uncle, Pere Grandet, a miserly and frugal old man. During the visit, Charles' father, who is deeply in debt, commits suicide. Charles, who must adjust to his diminished circumstances, falls in love with his cousin, Eugenie, and leaves to seek his fortune. When his uncle learns of their plan, he intercepts their letters and lies to Charles that Eugenie has married. Pere Grandet's greed catches up with him in a terrifying sequence: he is locked into his counting room with the ghosts of those whose lives he has destroyed. In his efforts to escape, he overturns a heavy piece of furniture, which crushes him to death with its burden of gold.

One day while sitting in a garden, Eugenie recognizes a bearded stranger that wanders in as Charles. He explains that he thought her married, the misunderstanding is cleared up, and the two are left to enjoy future happiness together.

Review: "The photoplay falls short of its ideal chiefly because it is an adaptation of a novel and retains much of the nature of a novel. The acting of *The Conquering Power* is exceptionally good. Rudolph Valentino, the Julio of *The Four Horsemen*, gives a finished performance as Charles Grandet."—*New York Times*, July 10, 1921.

Note: This film is available on video.

Silent. Drama. B & W. 35mm. Running time, 7 reels. © Metro Pictures Corp., 28 Nov 1921.

Camille (1921). Nazimova Productions. Distributed by Metro Pictures Corp. September 26, 1921.

Directed by Ray C. Smallwood; adaptation and scenario by June Mathis, based on the novel *La Dame aux Camelias* (1848) by Alexandre Dumas; art direction and costume design by Natacha Rambova; cinematography by Rudolph Bergquist.

Cast: Alla Nazimova (Camille, Marguerite Gautier), **Rudolph Valentino** (Armand Duval), Arthur Hoyt (Count de Varville), Zeffie Tilbury (Prudence), Rex Cherryman (Gatson), Edward Connelly (Duke), Patsy Ruth Miller (Nichette), Consuelo Flowerton (Olimpe), Mrs. Oliver (Manine), William Orlamond (Monsieur Duval).

Summary: Armand Duval [Valentino], a young and unrefined law student, falls in love with Marguerite Gautier, known as Camille, one of the most infamous women in Paris. The couple forsakes their friends and family and goes to the country where the days pass blissfully. They need money, so Armand arranges with his lawyer to give Marguerite his small inheritance. Armand's father visits Marguerite and after much persuasion, she consents to give up Armand and never see him again. She returns to her old life, drowning her sorrow in debauchery. One evening at a gambling house, she sees Armand, who, unaware of Marguerite's promise to his father, denounces her before the crowd. Forsaken and ill, Marguerite dies in her home, while clasping the copy of *Manon Lescaut*, was Armand's only gift to her.

Review: "But second to the star is the Armand of Rudolph Valentino. There are many opportunities for obtrusiveness in the role, but he keeps it correct to the minutest detail. And he looks Armand as no one else has in the past. It will do much to enhance his reputation."—*Variety*, September 16, 1921.

Note: This film is available on video.

Silent. Romantic drama. B & W. 35mm. Running time, 6 reels, 5,600 ft. © Nazimova Productions, 21 Sep 1921.

The Sheik (1921). Famous Players–Lasky. Distributed by Paramount Pictures Corp. November 20, 1921 [Los Angeles premiere: October 30, 1921].

Presented by Jesse Lasky; directed by George Melford; scenario by Monte M. Katterjohn, based on the novel *The Shiek* (London, 1919) by Edith Maude Hull; music by Roger Bellon (re-release); cinematography by William Marshall.

Cast: **Rudolph Valentino** (Sheik Ahmed Ben Hassan), Agnes Ayres (Lady Diana Mayo), Patsy Ruth Miller (Zilah, a marriage market prospect), George Waggner (Youssef, a tribal chieftain), Frank Butler (Sir Aubrey Mayo), Charles Brinley (Mustapha Ali, Diana's guide), Lucien Littlefield (Gatson, the French valet), Adolphe Mejou (Raoul de St. Hubert), Walter Long (Omar, the bandit), Sally Blane (Arab child, uncredited), Loretta Young (Arab child, uncredited), Polly Ann Young (Arab child, uncredited).

Summary: Diana Mayo, British, haughty and proud, goes to the Sahara desert where she disguises herself as a slave girl and meets Sheik Ahmed [Valentino] in a gambling casino. Later, he captures her but she refuses his advances. As she tries to escape, she is almost caught by the bandit Omair. The Sheik finds her and returns her to his camp. While out riding with a guest, she is captured by Omair. As she is about to kill herself, the Sheik arrives and slays Omair. The Sheik is wounded in the fight, and Diana nurses him back to health. Even so, he treats her coldly and she decides to return home. No longer hiding her love, she pleads with him, and several days later they return to society on their honeymoon.

Review: "The acting could not be worse than the story, but it is bad enough. Mr. Valentino is revealed as a player without resource. He depicts the fundamental emotions of the Arabian sheik chiefly by showing his teeth and rolling his eyes, while Agnes Ayres looks too matronly to lend much kick to the situation in which she finds herself."—*Variety*, November 11, 1921.

Note: This film is available on video and DVD.

Silent. Melodrama. B & W. 35mm. Running time, 7 reels, 6,579 ft. © Famous Players–Lasky Corp., 25 Oct 1921.

Character Studies (1921— some sources say 1923); aka *Carter DeHaven in Character Studies*). Production and crew information unknown.

Cast: Carter De Haven (Himself), Roscoe "Fatty" Arbuckle (Himself), Buster Keaton (Himself), Harold Lloyd (Himself), Douglas Fairbanks (Himself), **Rudolph Valentino** (Himself), Jackie Coogan (Himself).

Summary: Carter De Haven "impersonates" Roscoe Arbuckle, Buster Keaton, Harold Lloyd, Jackie Coogan, Douglas Fairbanks, and Rudolph Valentino by applying make-up. Each actor is portrayed by himself.

Review: No data found.

Silent. Short / Comedy. B & W. 35mm. Running time, six minutes.

Moran of the Lady Letty (1922). Famous Players–Lasky. Distributed by Paramount Pictures Corp. February 12, 1922.

Presented by Jesse L. Lasky; directed by George Melford; screenplay by Monte

M. Katterjohn, based on the novel *Moran of the Lady Letty; a Story of Adventure off the California Coast* (New York, 1898) by Frank Norris; cinematography by Bert Glennon and William Marshall.

Cast: Dorothy Dalton (Moran [Letty Sternersen]), **Rodolph Valentino** (Ramon Laredo), Charles Brinley (Captain Sternersen), Walter Long (Captain Kitchell), Emil Jorgenson (Nels), Maude Wayne (Josephine Herrick), Cecil Holland (Bill Trim), George Kuwa ("Chopstick" Charlie), Charles K. French (Tavern owner), William Boyd (Bit, uncredited), George O'Brien (Deck hand, uncredited).

Summary: In San Francisco, Ramon Laredo [Valentino], young and wealthy, meets Moran, an unconventional girl who sneers at the immaculately dressed young man. Ramon is shanghaied and taken aboard a smuggling schooner bound for Mexico. He is treated brutally by Captain Kitchell. Moran's ship catches fire and she is the lone survivor. When Kitchell's crew boards the burning vessel, Ramon finds Moran unconscious and dressed as a man. Ramon attempts to keep her sex a secret from Kitchell and falls in love with her. Once they arrive in Mexico, Ramon and Moran discover some treasure on the beach, and when Kitchell tries to steal it, a fight takes place between them. Later, in San Francisco, Kitchell breaks loose and attacks Moran, but Ramon saves her. Kitchell topples overboard and is drowned. Ramon holds Moran and announces that he intends to marry her.

Review: "Rodolf Valentino, as the hero, of course, is not so well-suited to the sea. He fits better into the romantic and melodramatic excesses of the story. Of course, he's supposed to be a wealthy young blood who has been shanghaied and falls in love with the sure-footed Moran of the Lady Letty, so you do not expect him to be salty, but even if you make this allowance for him, he is too slick. He doesn't impress one as the kind of youth who would be attracted by Moran, except momentarily, or attractive to her. In some of his scenes he is persuasive, but in others it seems a pity that he ever left the ballroom. And it is through his character, too that the story becomes just movie stuff, so he naturally is not as acceptable as the others."—*New York Times*, February 6, 1922.

Note: This film is available on video.

Silent. Adventure melodrama. B & W. 35mm. Running time, 7 reels, 6,360 ft. © Famous Players–Lasky Corp., 15 Feb 1922.

Beyond the Rocks (1922). Famous Players–Lasky. Distributed by Paramount Pictures. May 7, 1922.

Presented by Jesse L. Lasky; directed by Sam Wood; screenplay by Jack Cunningham, based on the novel *Beyond the Rocks* (New York, 1906) by Elinor Glyn; cinematography by Alfred Gilks.

Cast: Gloria Swanson (Theodora Fitzgerald), **Rodolph Valentino** (Lord Bracondale), Edythe Chapman (Lady Bracondale), Alec B. Francis (Captain Fitzgerald), Robert Bolder (Josiah Brown), Gertrude Astor (Morella Winmarleigh), Mabel Van Buren (Mrs. McBride), Helen Dunbar (Lady Ada Fitzgerald), Raymond Blathwayt

(Sir Patrick Fitzgerald), F[rank] L. Butler (Lord Wensleydon), June Elvidge (Lady Anningford).

Summary: Lord Bracondale [Valentino] rescues Theodora Fitzgerald from drowning when her rowboat capsizes. To please her father, she marries a wealthy, elderly man named Josiah Brown. Later, while climbing the Alps, Theodora is again saved by Lord Bracondale when she slips over the side of a precipice. They meet again in Paris, fall in love, but agree that they must part forever. In London fate brings them together once more at the residence of Lady Anningford. Bracondale again declares his love but Theodora resists his pleadings to elope with him. She writes her husband that she is coming home and at the same time writes a note to Bracondale, confessing her love for him, but bidding him farewell. Morella Winmarleigh, who is in love with Bracondale, obtains the letters and switches them. Brown confronts Bracondale, and resolves to sacrifice himself for his wife's happiness. During an exploring party to Arabia, Bracondale and Theodora follow Brown. Bandits attack Brown's party, and he is fatally wounded just as Bracondale and Theodora arrives. Before he dies, Brown joins the lovers' hands and wishes them happiness.

Review: "Gloria Swanson can wear clothes. So can Rodolph Valentino. And the talents of each are given full play... if this situation is reached through a series of incredible incidents, and if the leading characters do little else but wear clothes, and if, also, much of the action takes place on apparently artificial mountains and before what seem to be painted back drops, can the result be called an interesting photoplay?"—*New York Times*, May 8, 1922.

Note: In April 2004 a copy of this film was discovered in a private collection. A restored print will be screened by the Nederlands Filmmuseum in 2005.

Silent. Society melodrama. B & W. 35mm. Running time, 7 reels, 6,740 ft. © Famous Players–Lasky Corp., 7 May 1922.

Blood and Sand (1922). Famous Players–Lasky. Distributed by Paramount Pictures. September 10, 1922 [Los Angeles premiere, August 5, 1922].

Presented by Jesse L. Lasky; directed by Fred Niblo; scenario by June Mathis, based on the novel *Sangre y Arena* (Buenos Aires, 1908) by Vicente Blasco-Ibáñez, and the play *Blood and Sand* (New York opening, September 20, 1921) by Tom Cushing; edited by Dorothy Arzner; cinematography by Alvin Wyckoff.

Cast: **Rodolph Valentino** (Juan Gallardo), Lila Lee (Carmen), Nita Naldi (Doña Sol), George Field (El Nacional), Walter Long (Plumitas), Rosa Rosanova (Señora Augustias), Leo White (Antonio), Marie Marstini (El Camaciones), Charles Belcher (Don Joselito), Fred Becker (Don José), Jack Winn (Potaje), Harry Lamont (El Ponteliro), Gilbert Clayton (Garabato), George Periolat (Marquise de Guevera), Sidney De Gray (Dr. Ruiz), Dorcas Matthews (Señora Nacional), William Lawrence (Fuentes).

Song: "You Gave Me Your Heart," words by Frances Wheeler and Harry B. Smith, music by Ted Snyder (Berlin Publishing).

Summary: Juan Gallardo [Valentino] becomes one of Spain's most noted bullfighters and weds his childhood sweetheart, Carmen. He is a great friend of Plumitas, a bandit, for he robs the rich in order to give to the poor. Gallardo is happy with his wife, but she worries when he performs in the arena. Gallardo falls under the charm of Dona Sol, the widow of a diplomat. Gallardo is badly wounded in the arena and nursed back to health by Carmen, but does not forget Dona Sol. Gallardo loses popularity and Carmen begs him to quit bullfighting, but he refuses. At a bullfight Dona Sol is sitting with a handsome stranger and betrays Plumitas to the authorities. Plumitas makes a dash for freedom and is shot down. Gallardo, bereft of his old passion, goes down before the first charge of the bull he faces. He dies in his wife's arms, realizing at last that his love for her is strong.

Review: "Rodolph Valentino acts his part of the bull-fighter. Mr. Valentino has not been doing much acting of late. He's been slicking his hair and posing for the most part. But here he becomes an actor again. He makes one know Juan Gallardo as a real person with thoughts and feelings, as well as mannerisms and a fine physique."—*New York Times*, August 7, 1922.

Note: This film is available on video and DVD.

Silent. Drama. B & W. 35mm. Running time, 9 reels, 8,110 ft. © Famous Players–Lasky Corp., 15 August 1922.

The Young Rajah (1922). Famous Players–Lasky. Distributed by Paramount Pictures. November 12, 1922.

Presented by Jesse L. Lasky; directed by Philip Rosen; assistant director, Mervyn LeRoy; screenplay adapted by June Mathis, based on the novel *Amos Judd* (New York, 1895) by John Ames Mitchell, and the play *Amos Judd, a Play in a Prologue and Four Acts* (July 26, 1919) by Alethea Luce; costume design by Natacha Rambova; cinematography by James C. Van Trees.

Cast: **Rudolph Valentino** (Amos Judd), Wanda Hawley (Molly Cabot), Pat Moore (Amos Judd as a boy); Charles Ogle (Joshua Judd), Fanny Midgley (Sarah Judd), Robert Ober (Horace Bennett), Jack Giddings (Austin Slade), Edward Jobson (John Cabot), Josef Swickard (Narada), Bertram Grassby (Maharajah), J. Farrell MacDonald (Tehjunder Roy), George Periolat (General Gadi), George Field (Prince Musnud), Maude Wayne (Miss Van Kovert), William Boyd (Stephen Van Kovert), Joseph Harrinton (Dr. Fettiplace), Spottiswoode Aitken (Caleb).

Song: "The Young Rajah," music by Aubrey Stauffer (M. Schwartz Publishers).

Summary: An Indian prince is brought to America to escape the revolution and is placed in the care of Joshua Judd. The prince, who has a strange ability to see into the future, is raised as Amos Judd [Valentino], and becomes a star athlete at Harvard. There he falls in love Mary Cabot. On the day before their wedding, he foresees a plot hatched by the revolutionists to kill him. Amos goes into hiding but is attacked and then rescued. He is told he is needed by his people so he returns to India without Mary but is hopeful because he dreams of his marriage to her in the future.

Review: "Can you imagine Mr. Valentino an Indian Prince and the hero of a college crew? Think of the clothes he can wear and the manners he can assume. Is anything lacking—except in the real acting of which Mr. Valentino is capable when he is not used merely to decorate an incredible tale that does not save itself by being openly and freely fanciful, but proceeds solemnly as if you were expected to believe it." — *New York Times*, November 6, 1922.

Note: This is a lost film; no negatives or prints are known to exist. A short segment once owned by Leslie Flint of England's Valentino Memorial Guild is the only known surviving remnant.

Silent. Romantic drama. B & W. 35mm. Running time, 8 reels, 7,705 ft. © Famous Players–Lasky Corp., 25 Oct 1922.

The Sheik's Physique (circa 1922; exact year of release unknown).

Cast: **Rudolph Valentino** (Himself).

Summary: "Rudolph Valentino drives his automobile to the beach and changes into a swimming suit to spend a leisurely afternoon relaxing. Having fallen asleep, he awakens to discover that he is late for an undefined appointment, realizes that his car is gone, and that he must hitch a ride back into town."— *Progressive Silent Film List*.

Review: No data available.

Note: The film was likely part of a compilation split reel, or perhaps even a home movie reportedly shot by Paul Ivano. Available as an extra on select videos and DVDs.

Silent. Short. B & W. 35mm. Running time, three minutes.

Rudolph Valentino and His 88 American Beauties (1923). Selznick International. Directed by David O. Selznick.

Cast: **Rudolph Valentino** (Himself), Norma Niblock (Miss Toronto), Eugenia Gilbert (Miss Los Angeles), Reba Owen (Miss New York City), Mildred Adams (Miss Baltimore), Gloria Hellar (Miss Wichita).

Summary: Rudolph Valentino judges a beauty contest at New York's Madison Square Garden for the Minerva Beauty Clay Company.

Review: No data available.

Note: Aka *Valentino Beauty Contest in the USA*. The film features beauty contest contestants from Toronto, Ontario; Los Angeles, California; New York, New York; Baltimore, Maryland; Wichita, Kansas; Boston, Massachusetts; Rochester, New York; Pittsburgh, Pennsylvania; Seattle, Washington; Philadelphia, Pennsylvania; Dayton, Ohio; Buffalo, New York; Salt Lake City, Utah; Vancouver, British Columbia; Atlantic City, New Jersey; Fort Worth, Texas; Providence, Rhode Island; Columbus, Ohio; Chicago, Illinois; Portland, Oregon; and Birmingham, Alabama. This was Selznick's second film production. A print exists in the Film Preservation Associates film collection [35mm positive]. Also available as an extra on select videos and DVDs.

Silent. Documentary / Short. B & W. 35mm. Running time, 13 minutes.

Monsieur Beaucaire (1924). Famous Players–Lasky. Distributed by Paramount Pictures. August 18, 1924.

Presented by Adolph Zukor; produced and directed by Sidney Olcott; screenplay by Forrest Halsey, based on the novel *Monsieur Beaucaire* (New York, 1900) by Booth Tarkington, and the play *Monsieur Beaucaire, a Play, in Dramas by Present-Day Writers* (New York opening, December 2, 1901) by Evelyn Greenleaf Sutherland; art direction by Natacha Rambova; costume design by George Barbier; edited by Patricia Rooney; cinematography by Harry Fischbeck.

Cast: **Rudolph Valentino** (Duke of Chartres/Beaucaire), Bebe Daniels (Princess Henriette), Lowell Shermann (King Louis XV), Lois Wilson (Queen of France), Doris Kenyon (Lady Mary), Paulette Duval (Madame Pompadour), John Davidson (Richelieu), Oswald Yorke (Miropoix), Flora Finch (Duchesse de Montmorency), Louis Waller (François), Ian MacLaren (Duke of Winterset), Frank Shannon (Badger), Templar Powell (Molyneux), H. Cooper Cliffe (Beau Nash), Downing Clarke (Lord Chesterfield), Yvonne Hughes (Duchesse de Flauhault), Harry Lee (Voltaire), Florence O'Denishawn (Colombine), George Barbier, Blanche Craig (Ball guests at Bath, uncredited), Tony D'Algy (Bit, uncredited), Andre Daven (Duc de Nemours, uncredited), Brian Donlevy (Ball guest at Bath, uncredited), Nat Pendleton (Barber, uncredited).

Songs: "Red Red Rose," words by Fred Roth, music by Mel Shaver (Robbins Engel Publishers); "Rudolph Valentino's Love Song," words by Beth Young, music by Ignay Waghalte (Marks Publishers).

Summary: At the court of Louis XV the Duke of Chartres [Valentino] romances Princess Henriette, but is offended by the King's order to marry her and flees to England. Posing as Monsieur Beaucaire, the French ambassador's barber, he visits Bath, becomes infatuated with lady Mary Carlisle, entices her disguised as a noble, is denounced by Lord Winterset, defeats the latter's hired bullies, returns later and is introduced by the ambassador in his true colors. He is pardoned by the King but rebuffed by the now eager Lady Mary. He returns to France and is reconciled to Henriette.

Review: "If any costume play has ever drawn, *Monsieur Beaucaire* certainly ought to draw, for the reason that the picture, aside from starring Rudolph Valentino, one of the most popular male stars of our day, has been directed by Sidney Olcott, a director whose name, because of recent performances, means much to the box-office. In addition, the story bears the name of one of the most popular novelists of our day— Booth Tarkington."—*Harrison's Reports*, October 11, 1924.

Note: This film exists but is not available on video.

Silent. Romantic drama. B & W. 35mm. Running time, 10 reels, 9,932 ft. © Famous Players–Lasky Corp., 29 Jul 1924.

A Sainted Devil (1924). Famous Players–Lasky. Distributed by Paramount Pictures. November 17, 1924.

Presented by Jesse L. Lasky and Adolph Zukor; directed by Joseph Henabery; scenario by Forrest Halsey, based on the short story "Rope's End" (*Cosmopolitan*, May

1913) by Rex Beach; art direction by Lawrence Hitt; cinematography by Harry Fischbeck.

Cast: **Rudolph Valentino** (Don Alonzo De Castro), Nita Naldi (Carlotta), Helen D'Algy (Julieta Valdez), Dagmar Godowsky (Doña Florencia), Jean Del Val (Casimiro), Antonio D'Algy (Don Luis), George Siegmann (El Tigre), L. Rogers Lytton (Don Baltasar), Isabel West (Doña Encarnación), Louise Lagrange (Carmelita), Rafael Bongini (Congo), Frank Montgomery (Indian Spy), William Betts (Priest), Edward Elkas (Notary), A. De Rosa (Jefe Politico), Ann Brody (Duennnna), Evelyn Axzell (Guadalupe), Marie Diller (Irala), Genevieve Belasco.

Summary: Don Alonzo Castro [Valentino], a wealthy South American, is engaged to Julietta. His jealous former lover, Carlotta, conspires with an outlaw, El Tigre, to raid the hacienda and kidnap Julietta on their wedding night. Castro pursues them and sees a woman, whom he believes to be Julietta, surrender to El Tigre's advances. Castro goes to the city and finds El Tigre's favorite café. There they fight and El Tigre is killed by his enemy Don Luis. Afterward, Castro finds that Julietta is safe in a convent and they are reunited.

Review: "Mr. Valentino is interesting as the young man eager to set eyes upon the girl he is to marry, and his youthful admiration for Julietta, after she steps from her carriage, is quite natural. Later he is too deliberate in his actions, especially when he goes to find Julietta, who has returned to a convent. He walks so slowly that his ankles almost appear to touch in the timed strides. Those who admire Mr. Valentino will enjoy this film, and they will be quite thrilled by the latter sequences."—*New York Times*, November 24, 1924.

Note: This is a lost film; no negatives or prints are known to exist.

Silent. Melodrama. B & W. 35mm. Running time, 9 reels, 8,633 ft. © Famous Players–Lasky Corp., 5 Nov 1924.

The Eagle (1925). Art Finance Corp. Distributed by United Artists. November 8, 1925.

Produced by John W. Considine, Jr. (uncredited); directed by Clarence Brown; assistant director, Charles Dorian (uncredited); screenplay by Hans Kraly, based on "Dubrovsky" in *Prose Tales of Alexander Poushkin* (translated from the Russian by T. Keane; London, 1894) by Alexander Sergeevich Pushkin; titles by George Marion, Jr.; art direction by William Cameron Menzies; costume design by Adrian; technical advisor, Michael Pleschkoff (uncredited); edited by Hal C. Kern; cinematography by George Barnes and Devereaux Jennings (uncredited).

Cast: **Rudolph Valentino** (Lt. Vladimir Dubrovsky, aka the Black Eagle and Marcel Le Blanc), Vilma Banky (Masha Troekouroff), Louis Dresser (the Tsarina, Catherine II), Albert Conti (Captain Kuschka), James A. Marcus (Kyrilla Troekouroff), George Nichols (Judge), Carrie Clark Ward (Aunt Aurelia), Spottiswoode Aitken (Dubrovsky's Father), Mario Carillo (Marcel Le Bland, French tutor, uncredited), Gary Cooper (Masked Cossack, uncredited), Jean De Briac (uncredited), Otto Hoffman (Man whose purse is stolen, uncredited), Eric Mayne (Official asking for signature, uncredited), Michael Pleschkoff (Captain Kushcka of the Cossack Guard, scenes deleted), Russell Simpson (the Eagle's lieutenant and coach driver, uncredited), Gustav von Seyffertitz (Court servant at dinner, uncredited).

Songs: "Eagle Overture," music by Lee Erwin (General Publishers); "You're My Love," words by Dailev Paskman, music by Bert Reisfeld (Marks Publishing).

Summary: Lieutenant Vladimir Dubrovsky [Valentino] is sentenced to death for rejecting the Czarina's love, but he escapes and becomes the leader of a lawless gang. His intent is to kill a landowner who has cheated his father. Disguised as a French tutor for his daughter, he gains the man's trust. Dubrovsky soon falls in love with her and gives up his original objective. Just as things are going well, he is arrested by the Czarina's troops and must face the firing squad. At the last moment he receives the Czarina's pardon is allowed to leave the country with his beloved.

Review: "In this production, which might suit several male screen celebrities, including the agile Douglas Fairbanks, Mr. Valentino acquits himself with distinction. He appears to have benefited by Clarence Brown's direction and to have appreciated that Miss Banky was a valuable asset to his picture."—*New York Times*, November 9, 1925.

Note: This film is available on video and DVD.

Silent. Romantic comedy. B & W. 35mm. Running time, 7 reels, 6,755 ft. © Art Finance Corp., 16 Nov 1925.

Cobra (1925). Ritz-Carlton Pictures. Distributed by Paramount Pictures. November 30, 1925.

Directed by Joseph Henabery; assistant directors, Barton Adams and Richard Johnston; screenplay by Anthony Coldeway, based on the play *Cobra* (New York opening, April 22, 1924) by Martin Brown; art direction by William Cameron Menzies; costume design by Adrian; costumes executed by Lillian M. Turner; technical advisor, Eugene Hornboestel; edited by John H. Bonn; cinematography by J. D. Jennings and Harry Fischbeck.

Song: "Playing at Love" (British edition issued in England), words and music by William Helmore (Day Publishers).

Cast: **Rudolph Valentino** (Count Rodrigo Torriani), Hector V. Sarno (Vittorio Minardi), Claire de Lorez (Rosa Minardi), Nita Naldi (Elise Van Zile), Casson Ferguson (Jack Dorning), Gertrude Olmstead (Mary Drake), Henry A. Barrows (Henry Madison), Lillian Langdon (Mrs. Porter Palmer), Eileen Percy (Sophie Binner), Rosa Rosanova (Marie).

Summary: Count Rodrigo Torriani [Valentino], a true ladies' man, meets Jack Dorning, who sees some good in him and brings him into his antique business. There Torriani meets Mary Drake and finds that he has a genuine affection for her. Later, Dorning's wife Elise offers herself to the Count. He refuses her advances and that same night she perishes in a hotel fire. The Count goes abroad for several months and when he returns once again tries to court Mary, but finds that Dorning is in love with her. Out of respect for his friend, the Count treats his affair with Mary lightly. The Count is out of their lives forever.

Review: "Mr. Valentino takes advantage of the opportunity to wear a variety of clothes. [Valentino's] acting is acceptable, but he is not indifferent to his much exploited looks."—*New York Times*, December 7, 1925.

Note: This film is available on video and DVD.

Silent. Society-Drama. B & W. 35mm. Running time, 7 reels, 6,895 ft. © Rudolph Valentino, 3 Dec 1925.

The Son of the Sheik (1926). Feature Productions. Distributed by United Artists. September 5, 1926 [Los Angeles premiere, July 9, 1926, Grauman's Million Dollar Theater; New York premiere, July 25, 1926, Mark Strand Theater].

Produced by John W. Considine, Jr.; directed by George Fitzmaurice; scenario adapted by Frances Marion, Fred De Gresac and Paul Girard Smith (uncredited), based on the novel *Sons of the Sheik* (Boston, 1925) by Edith Maude Hull; titles by George Marion, Jr.; art direction by William Cameron Menzies; props by Irving W. Sindler; costumes by Adrian; original music by Gerard Carbonara; edited by Hal C. Kern; cinematography by George Barnes.

Songs: "My One Arabian Night," words and music by James Bradford, Art Gutman and Art Jones (Mills Publishers); "Son of the Sheik," words by Edwin Powell, music by Miro Mosay (Chilton Publishers); "That Night in Araby," words by Billy Rose, music by Ted Snyder (Waterson Publishers).

Cast: **Rudolph Valentino** (Ahmed/Sheik), Vilma Banky (Yasmin), George Fawcett (André), Montagu Love (the Moor Ghabah), Karl Dane (Ramadan), Bull Montana (Ali), B. Hyman (Pincher), Agnes Ayres (Diana, the Sheik's wife), Charles Requa (Pierre), William Donovan (S'rir), Erwin Connelly (the Zouve), George Fiske (Rudolph Valentino's stunt double).

Summary: The passionate and jealous Ahmed [Valentino] is quick to anger, much like his father. He meets Yasmin, a bejeweled dancing girl, and he falls in love with her. Captured, held for ransom, and tortured by Ghabah, Ahmed escapes, seething with revenge. Yasmin has suddenly vanished, convincing Ahmed that she has deserted and betrayed him. In reality, she has been kidnapped. Ahmed, hurt and bitter, vows retribution, and when next he sees Yasmin, he snatches her up and carries her off to the desert. Though she pleads with him to release her, and tries to explain what happened, he rapes her. Rebuked by his father [Valentino in a dual role], Ahmed regrets his treatment of Yasmin, even more so when he learns that she is guiltless. In retaliation, he overpowers the bad guys, saving the foul Ghabah for last.

Review: "In its setting of desert sands, those picturesque mounds and valley formed by the wind, this latest offering of Valentino makes a very good romantic picture. It is a Western thriller in an Arabian atmosphere, except for the exotic Eastern love affair, which no noble hero of the wide, open spaces of the West would ever be let in for in moving pictures, no matter how much he really felt like it."—*New York Times*, July 26, 1926.

Note: This film is available on video and DVD.

Silent. Melodrama. B & W. 35mm. Running time, 7 reels, 6,685 ft. © Feature Productions, 24 Aug 1926.

What Price Beauty? (1928). S. George Ullman. Distributed by Pathé Exchange. January 28, 1928.

Executive producer, **Rudolph Valentino**; produced by Natacha Rambova; directed by Thomas Buckingham; story and scenario by Natacha Rambova; titles by Malcom Stuart Boylan; costume design by Adrian; cinematography by J. D[evereaux] Jennings.

Cast: Nita Naldi (Rita Rinaldi), Natacha Rambova, Pierre Gendron (John Clay), Virginia Pearson (Mary), Dolores Johnson, Sally Winters, La Supervia, Marilyn Newkirk, Victor Potel, Caroline Rankin, Templar Saxe, Leo White, Myrna Loy (Vamp).

Review: No data found.

Note: Produced in 1925. This is a lost film; no negatives or prints are known to exist.

Silent. B & W. Melodrama. 35mm. Running time, 5 reels, 4,000 ft. © S. George Ullman, 18 Jan 1928.

Archival Appearances in Films, on Television and on Video

March of Time: The Movies Move On (1939). RKO Radio Pictures, Inc. Produced by Louis De Rochemont. Celebrity footage includes: Renée Adorée, Douglas Fairbanks, Mack Sennett, **Rudolph Valentino**, Jack L. Warner. A "March of Time" presentation of the evolution of movies compiled primarily from film clips of silent movies through the early sound pictures to the present (1939) date. Sound. Short-Documentary. 35mm. B & W. Running time, 19 minutes.

Unholy Partners (1941). Metro-Goldwyn-Mayer. Produced by Mervyn LeRoy and Samuel Marx; directed by Mervyn LeRoy; screenplay by Earl Baldwin, Bartlett Cormack and Lesser Samuels. Cast: Edward G. Robinson, Laraine Day, Marsha Hunt. **Rudolph Valentino** appears, uncredited, in archival footage. Sound. B & W. 35mm. Running time, 94 minutes.

Herrliche Zeiten (1950). [West Germany] Comedia-Film GmbH. Distributed by Academy. April 23, 1951. Produced by Rühmann Heinz; directed by Günter Neumann and Erik Ode. Celebrity footage includes: Enrico Caruso, Charles Chaplin, Emil Jannings, Mia May, Max Schmeling, **Rudolph Valentino**. Sound. Documentary. B & W. 35mm.

Fifty Years Before Your Eyes (1950). Warner Bros. Produced by Alfred Butterfield; directed by Robert Youngson; original music by Howard Jackson and William Lava. Celebrity footage includes: Calvin Coolidge, Lou Gehrig, Al Jolson, Prince Charles, Babe Ruth, **Rudolph Valentino**. Sound. Documentary. B & W. 35mm. Running time, 72 minutes.

Screen Snapshots: Memorial to Al Jolson (1952). Columbia Pictures Corporation. Produced and directed by Ralph Staub. Jack Benny narrates utilizing archive footage that traces the career of Al Jolson, and rare off-stage shots of Jolson with stars such as Bob Hope, Eddie Cantor and Pat O'Brien. Includes archival footage of **Rudolph Valentino**. Sound. Documentary-Short. B & W. 35mm. Running time, 9 minutes.

The Love Goddesses (1965). Janus Film. Distributed by Continental Distributing, Inc. Produced and written by Graeme Ferguson and Saul J. Turell; directed by Saul J. Turell; original music by Percy Faith. Celebrity footage includes: Agnes Ayres, Clara Bow, Maurice Chevalier, Bette Davis, Greta Garbo, Rita Hayworth, Myrna Loy, Pola Negri, Gloria Swanson, **Rudolph Valentino**, Mae West. Sound. Documentary. B & W / Technicolor. Running time, 87 minutes.

Dora et la Lanterne Magique (1978). [France] Cinéma 9. Directed by Pascal Kané; screenplay by Pascal Kané and Raoul Ruiz. Cast: Gérard Boucaron (L'ogre), Mathalie Manet (Dora), Rita Maiden (Magdelène, la Bonne Fée). **Rudolph Valentino** appears, uncredited, in archival footage. Sound. Eastmancolor. Running time, 100 minutes.

Hollywood Sex Symbols (1988). Celebrity footage includes: Theda Bara, Charles Chaplin, Clark Gable, Elvis Presley, **Rudolph Valentino**. Video. Documentary-Short. B & W / Color. Running time, 40 minutes.

Death Scenes 2 (1992). Executive producer, Ray Atherton; produced by Nick Bougas; directed and written by Nick Bougas. Celebrity footage includes: Jeffrey Dahmer, Bela Lugosi, Charles Manson, Sal Mineo, **Rudolph Valentino**. Video. Documentary. B & W / Color.

Fame in the Twentieth Century (1993) [UK]. Celebrity footage includes: Lucille Ball, Marlon Brando, James Dean, Judy Garland, Cary Grant, Adolf Hitler, Grace Kelly, Bruce Lee, Marilyn Monroe, Princess Diana, Ronald Reagan, Wallace Simpson, Barbra Streisand, Elizabeth Taylor, **Rudolph Valentino**. An examination of the nature of fame in the Twentieth Century. Television series (eight episodes). Sound. Documentary. B & W / Color. Running time, 50 minutes.

The Roaring Twenties (1996). Celebrity footage includes: Charles Chaplin, Jack Dempsey, Charles A. Lindbergh, Will Rogers, **Rudolph Valentino** (sporting a beard), Johnny Weissmuller. Video. Sound. Documentary-Short. B & W / Color. Running time, 35 minutes.

Notes

Introduction

1. "Valentino, Type of Film Appeal," *New York American*, August 24, 1926.

One. "Pink Powder Puffs"

1. S. George Ullman, *Valentino as I Knew Him* (New York: Macy-Masius, 1926), p. 184.
2. *Blackstone Hotel*, 636 South Michigan Avenue, between East Harrison Street and East Balbo Drive, Chicago. Valentino stayed at the Blackstone Hotel on many of his visits to the Windy City. Most notably this was where he read for the first time, over breakfast, the now infamous "Pink Powder Puffs" editorial in the *Chicago Tribune*. Built in 1910, the Blackstone was known as the "Hotel of the Presidents," hosting more than a dozen American leaders, including Woodrow Wilson, Franklin D. Roosevelt and John F. Kennedy. Except for the usual modernization and updating of services, the Blackstone remains very much as it was when Valentino stayed there.
3. Ullman, *Valentino as I Knew Him*, p. 59.
4. Harry T. Brundidge, *Twinkle, Twinkle Movie Star!* (New York: E. P. Dutton & Co., Inc., 1930), p. 73.
5. Ullman, *Valentino as I Knew* Him, p. 71.
6. Ibid., p. 185.
7. *Aragon Ballroom*, 1106 West Lawrence Avenue, at North Winthrop. While Valentino never actually visited the Aragon Ballroom, it would indirectly play an important and very frustrating part of the last month of his life. The massive and lavishly decorated Aragon Ballroom first opened its doors on July 15, 1926, in the heart of Chicago's Uptown district. Little did the owners realize how much public attention — and grief for Valentino — the installation of a seemingly innocent powder machine in the men's washroom would generate. The ballroom continued drawing huge crowds for nearly forty years until the regular dances ended in February 1964. The Aragon still functions today, hosting such events as wrestling matches, roller-skating and rock concerts (and, on rare occasions, dances). As for the infamous powder machine, they removed it long ago from the Aragon's washroom, but perhaps on a sultry summer evening the faint sound of a coin inserted and lever pulled can still be heard.

8. "Pink Powder Puffs" [editorial], *Chicago Tribune*, July 18, 1926.
9. "Personal Puff," *Time*, August 2, 1926.
10. Dick Dorgan, "A Song of Hate," *Photoplay*, July 1922.
11. Ibid.
12. Dick Dorgan, "Giving 'The Sheik' the Once Over from the Ringside," *Photoplay*, April 1922.
13. Irving Shulman, *Valentino: The True Life Story* (New York: Trident Press, 1967), pp. 164–65.
14. Ullman, *Valentino as I Knew Him*, p. 121.
15. "The Sheik of Film-Araby," *Theatre*, October 1926.
16. *Photoplay*, July 1923.
17. James Gavin, *Intimate Nights: The Golden Age of New York Caberet* (New York: Grove Weidenfeld, 1991), p. 54.
18. Emily W. Leider, *Dark Lover: The Life and Death of Rudolph Valentino* (Farrar Straus & Giroux, 2003), p. 126.
19. *Los Angeles Mirror*, February 28, 1961.
20. John K. Winkler, "I'm Tired of Being a Sheik," *Colliers*, January 16, 1926, p. 28.
21. Unsourced clipping, NYPL, June 18, 1938.
22. "In This Corner Valentino, Battler," *Los Angeles Evening Herald*, July 30, 1926.
23. "Rudy's Jeweled Fist Would Avenge Slur," *Los Angeles Examiner*, July 20, 1926.

Two. The Boxer, the Sage and the Accidental Fiancée

1. "Valentino Seeking Fight with Editor," *New York Times*, July 21, 1926.
2. Jack Dempsey, with Barbara Piatelli, *Dempsey* (New York: Harper & Row, 1977), p. 195.
3. Ibid., p. 196.
4. Frank "Buck" O'Neil was 6'1" and weighed 195 pounds, compared to Valentino's reported 5'11" and 167 pounds.
5. "Oh, Rudy, What if 'He's' a Lady," *Los Angeles Examiner*, July 22, 1926.
6. Dempsey, *Dempsey*, p. 196.
7. Ullman, *Valentino as I Knew Him*, p. 193; "'Valentino Packs Punch,' Claim of N.Y. Mitt Experts," *Los Angeles Evening Herald*, July 22, 1926.
8. Fred Hobson, *Mencken: A Life* (New York: Random House, 1995), p. 270.
9. Edoardo Ballerini to author, February 2003, Hollywood, California.
10. H. L. Mencken, "Valentino," *Baltimore Evening Sun*, August 30, 1926.
11. "The Sheik of Film — Araby," *Theatre*, October 1926.
12. Mencken, "Valentino," *Baltimore Evening Sun*, August 30, 1926.
13. John Rothman in telephone interview with author, February 2003.
14. "The Sheik of Film-Araby," *Theater*, October 1926.
15. Adela Rogers St. Johns, "Valentino: The Life Story of the Sheik," *Liberty*, October 12, 1929, p. 73.
16. General Umberto Nobile (1885, Lauro, Italy–1978, Rome). Nobile was an Italian aeronautical engineer and pioneer in Arctic aviation who, in 1926, with the Norwegian explorer Roald Amundson and Lincoln Ellsworth of the United States, flew over the North Pole in the dirigible *Norge*, from Spitsbergen (now Svalbard), north of Norway, to Alaska — in short, completing the flight from Europe to North America.
17. Ullman, *Valentino as I Knew Him*, p. 195. Major Wallace McCutcheon (1880–1928), a World War I veteran and a pioneer filmmaker, married actress Pearl White in 1918, even performing with her in the film *The Black Secret* (1919). Unfortunately, McCutcheon, undone by nerve gas and the strain of war, divorced White in 1921. He was later placed in a Washington, D.C. sanitarium, eventually committing suicide in Los Angeles in January of 1928.
18. Ullman, *Valentino as I Knew Him*, p. 194.
19. Ibid.
20. Ibid., p. 195.

21. Leider, *Dark Lover*, p. 358.
22. Louella O. Parsons, *The Gay Illiterate* (Garden City, New York: Doubleday, Doran and Co., Inc., 1944), p. 91.
23. Pola Negri, *Memoirs of a Star* (New York: Doubleday & Company, 1970), p. 258.
24. Ibid., pp. 258–259.
25. Parsons, *The Gay Illiterate*, p. 92.
26. Negri, *Memoirs of a Star*, p. 260.
27. St. Johns, "Valentino: The Life Story of the Sheik," *Liberty*, October 12, 1929, p. 71.
28. Harry Carr, "Untold Tales of Hollywood," *Smart Set*, March/May 1930.
29. St. Johns, "Valentino: The Life Story of the Sheik," *Liberty*, October 12, 1929, p. 72.
30. Mary Irene Curzon Ravensdale, 2nd Baroness, *In Many Rythms* (London: Weidenfeld, 1953), p. 69.
31. Ibid.
32. Negri, *Memoirs of a Star*, pp. 273–274.
33. St. Johns, "Valentino: The Life Story of the Sheik," *Liberty*, October 12, 1929, p. 72.
34. "Valentino Denies Negri Engagement," *Nashville Banner*, March 16, 1926.
35. "Calls Negri Bridal Likely," *New York Times*, July 8, 1926.
36. "Marry Again? Absurd! Says Movie Sheik," *Glendale Evening Press*, November 14, 1925.
37. St. Johns, "Valentino: The Life Story of the Sheik," *Liberty*, October 12, 1929, p. 74.

Three. Mending Fences

1. "Rudy's Red Suspenders," *Variety*, July 28, 1926.
2. Ibid.
3. The Globe Theater was located at 205 W. 46th Street. In 1958 it was renamed the Lunt-Fontaine Theatre.
4. "Follies Girl Prostrated with Grief," *New York American*, August 24, 1926.
5. Ibid.
6. Ullman, *Valentino as I Knew Him*, p. 203.
7. "In This Corner Valentino, Battler," *Los Angeles Evening Herald*, July 30, 1926.
8. Ullman, *Valentino as I Knew Him*, p. 201.
9. Ibid., p. 202.
10. Ibid., p. 182.
11. John Origen Herrick, born August 3, 1898, Chicago, Illinois. With *Chicago Tribune* as reporter, editorial writer and correspondent, Washington staff, 1921–35. Herrick died of lung cancer on December 24, 1955, in Albuquerque, New Mexico.
12. "Valentino's Challenge Is Ignored by Editor," *Los Angeles Evening Herald*, July 21, 1926.
13. Gene Siskel, "The Valentino Legend Stirs a Revival," *Chicago Tribune*, June 28, 1977.
14. Bruce Dold, the editorial department of the *Chicago Tribune*, in communication to author, January 16, 2002.
15. Clifford Samuel Raymond was born on November 11, 1875. He joined the *Chicago Tribune* on September 1, 1898, as a correspondent, later reporting on the activities of the Illinois state legislature before writing editorials in 1907. He was the author of several books, including *Our Very Best People* (1930) and *The Honorable John Hale* (1946). Raymond died after a long illness on October 21, 1950, in Highland Park, Illinois.
16. Lloyd Wendt, *Chicago Tribune: The Rise of a Great American Newspaper* (New York: Rand McNally & Company, 1979), p. 494.
17. "Valentino Seeking Fight with Editor, *New York Times*, July 21, 1926.
18. Schuyler Parsons, *Untold Friendships* (Boston, Houghton Mifflin, 1955), p. 125.
19. Norma Talmadge, "Valentino as I Knew Him," *New York Daily News*, August 25, 1926.
20. "How Valentino Keeps His Figure," *Liberty*, December 27, 1924.
21. "Estelle Balks at Watching Jack Fight," *Los Angeles Examiner*, August 31, 1926.

22. Brundidge, *Twinkle, Twinkle, Movie Star!*, p. 77.
23. Ullman, *Valentino as I Knew Him*, pp. 203–204.
24. "'Rudy' Told Friend of Early Death," *Hollywood Daily Citizen*, August 23, 1926.
25. Talmadge, "Valentino as I Knew Him," *New York Daily News*, August 26, 1926.
26. Natacha Rambova, *Rudy: An Intimate Portrait of Rudolph Valentino by His Wife* (London: Hutchinson & Co. Ltd., 1926), p. 115.
27. Ullman, *Valentino as I Knew Him*, pp. 176–177.
28. Adolph Zukor, with Dale Kramer, *The Public Is Never Wrong: The Autobiography of Adolph Zukor* (New York: Putnam, 1953), pp. 217–218.
29. Talmadge, "Valentino as I Knew Him," *New York Daily News*, August 25, 1926.

Four. "Doctor, Am I a Pink Puff?"

1. Ullman, *Valentino as I Knew Him*, p. 210.
2. "Rudy Better After Relapse," *New York Daily News*, August 17, 1926.
3. St. Johns, "Valentino: The Life Story of the Sheik," *Liberty*, September 21, 1926.
4. John Kobal, *People Will Talk* (New York: Alfred K. Knopf, 1985), p. 64.
5. *George White's Scandals of 1926* was the eighth incarnation of the popular revue. It opened at the Apollo Theatre on June 24, 1926, and continued for 424 performances.
6. "Rudy's Host Quits Hospital Secretly," *New York Daily News*, August 28, 1926.
7. "Say Valentino Out of Danger," *Los Angeles Record*, August 19, 1926.
8. "Rudolph Valentino Goes Under Knife," *New York American*, August 16, 1926.
9. Alberto Valentino to Kevin Brownlow, *Hollywood: Swanson & Valentino* (Thames Television, 1980).
10. Leider, *Dark Lover*, p. 381.
11. Brundidge, *Twinkle, Twinkle Movie Star!*, p. 74.
12. Harold D. Meeker (1876–1945), who was born in Bound Brook, New Jersey, received his Bachelor of Arts degree in 1898 from Wesleyan University, which later awarded him an honorary degree of Master of Science. He graduated from the College of Physicians and Surgeons of Columbia University in 1902 and then served as an intern at the City Hospital. Meeker was a consulting surgeon to the Polyclinic Hospital and a former Professor of Surgery for a long period on the faculty of the Polyclinic Medical School. Until his death on May 26, 1945, he was best known to the public as the surgeon who operated on Rudolph Valentino. Obituary, *New York Times*, May 28, 1945.
13. "Surgeon Explains Valentino Death," *New York Times*, September 4, 1926.
14. "Valentino Collapses," *Los Angeles Times*, August 16, 1926.
15. "Valentino Has Operation After Collapse Here," *New York Herald Tribune*, August 16, 1926.
16. "Film Star's Condition Critical," *Los Angeles Evening Herald*, August 16, 1926.
17. Ullman, *Valentino as I Knew Him*, p. 212.
18. Michael Morris, *Madam Valentino* (New York: Abbeville Press, 1991), p. 185.
19. "Film Star's Condition Critical," *Los Angeles Evening Herald*, August 15, 1926.
20. Pola Negri, "Rudy Valentino and I! My Great True Love Story," *True Story*, April 1934.
21. "Cruel Director Keeps Pola from Rudy's Bedside," *Illustrated Daily News*, August 17, 1926.
22. "Rudy Better After Relapse," *New York Daily News*, August 17, 1926.
23. "Rudy Fights for Life After Operation," *New York American*, August 17, 1926.
24. "Dancer Lauds Stricken Star," *New York American*, August 19, 1926.
25. Ibid.
26. "Rudy Cheers Up as Pola Plans to Fly to Him," *New York Daily News*, August 19, 1926.
27. "Follies Girl Says Rudy Asked Her to Marry Him," *New York Daily News*, August 24, 1926.
28. Leider, *Dark Lover*, p. 380.
29. "Huge Crowds Await News of Film Star," *Los Angeles Examiner*, August 18, 1926.
30. Ullman, *Valentino as I Knew Him*, p. 213.

31. "Fate of Valentino Hangs in Balance," *New York American*, August 18, 1926.
32. Ibid.
33. "Watch Over Life Thread of Valentino," *Chicago Tribune*, August 18, 1926.

Five. Final Days

1. "Rudy Cheers up as Pola Plans to Fly to Him," *New York Daily News*, August 19, 1926.
2. "Rudy Given First Food Since Knife," *Los Angeles Record*, August 18, 1962.
3. "Valentino Still Wages His Grim Fight for Life," *New York Herald Tribune*, August 19, 1926.
4. Ibid.
5. "Hope Rules as Valentino's Life Battle Nears Climax," *New York American*, August 19, 1926.
6. "Rudy Dead," *New York Evening Graphic*, August 18, 1926.
7. "Say Valentino Out of Danger," *Los Angeles Record*, August 19, 1926.
8. "Doctor Refutes Graphic's Story of Valentino False," *New York Telegraph*, August 21, 1926.
9. "Valentino on Mend; Crisis Not Reached," *Chicago Tribune*, August 19, 1926.
10. "Valentino Winning," *Los Angeles Times*, August 20, 1926.
11. "Valentino's Death Shadow Fades Away," *New York American*, August 20, 1926.
12. "Rudy Getting Better as Marquise Calls," *New York Daily News*, August 20, 1926.
13. "Valentino's Death Shadow Fades Away," *New York American*, August 20, 1926.
14. "Rudy Getting Better as Marquise Calls," *New York Daily News*, August 20, 1926.
15. "Here's First Interview with Sheik," *Los Angeles Record*, August 21, 1926.
16. "Valentino Wins Fight for Life; Crisis Passes," *New York Herald Tribune*, August 20, 1926.
17. "Rudy's Friend Stricken Now," *New York American*, August 21, 1926.
18. "Restless Night for Valentino," *Los Angeles Record*, August 20, 1926.
19. Dagmar Godowsky, *First Person Plural: The Lives of Dagmar Godowsky* (New York: Viking Press, 1958), p. 161.
20. "Valentino Host at Party Has Operation," *New York Daily News*, August 21, 1926.
21. Ullman, *Valentino as I Knew Him*, p. 214.
22. "Valentino's Condition Reported Very Serious," *Los Angeles Times*, August 22, 1926.
23. "Valentino Life Flickers in Relapse," *New York American*, August 22, 1926.
24. "Valentino Has Relapse; Pleurisy Set In," *Chicago Tribune*, August 22, 1926.
25. "Valentino's Strength Ebbing," *New York Daily News*, August 23, 1926.
26. Negri, "Rudy Valentino and I! My Great True Love Story," *True Story*, April 1934.
27. "Valentino Low; Crisis Near," *Chicago Tribune*, August 23, 1926.
28. "Valentino Sinking Fast," *New York American*, August 23, 1926.
29. Mgr. Edward F. Leonard (1870, New York, NY–November 27, 1940, New York, NY), continued as pastor of St. Malachy's Catholic Church, known as the "Actor's Church," until his death in 1940. In a 1937 testimonial, song and dance man George M. Cohan expressed the esteem in which Father Leonard was held when he said: "I never met any priest who was so loved, so revered and so admired as Mgr. Leonard" ("Mgr. Leonard Dies; 'Actors' Priest,' 70," *New York Times*, November 28, 1940). Actors Douglas Fairbanks, Jr. and Joan Crawford were married by Mgr. Leonard at St. Malachy's in 1929. And in 1936, because of the late hours kept by actors in the theater section that he ministered to, Leonard received permission from Cardinal Hayes to institute a weekly mass at 4 o'clock Sunday mornings. Father Leonard died of heart disease after a year's illness.
30. "Valentino Sinking Fast," *New York American*, August 23, 1926.
31. Ullman, *Valentino as I Knew Him*, p. 216.
32. "Valentino's Strength Ebbing," *New York Daily News*, August 23, 1926.
33. "Valentino Low as 4 Doctors Fight Pleurisy," *New York Herald Tribune*, August 23, 1926.
34. Ibid.
35. Ullman, *Valentino as I Knew Him*, p. 217.
36. "Valentino Lies Hovering on Borderline of Death," *Los Angeles Times*, August 23, 1926.
37. "Valentino Low as 4 Doctors Fight Pleurisy," *New York Herald Tribune*, August 23, 1926.

Six. Monday, August 23, 1926

1. "Nation Mourns Valentino," *New York American*, August 24, 1926.
2. "Pola Breaks Reading Final Words—to Her," *New York Daily News*, August 31, 1926.
3. "Mourns Death of Valentino," *Chicago Tribune*, August 24, 1926.
4. Ullman, *Valentino as I Knew Him*, pp. 217–218.
5. "Valentino Is Dead!" *Wisconsin News*, August 23, 1926.
6. Parsons, *The Gay Illiterate*, p. 93.
7. Father Joseph F. Congedo (1883, Galatina, Italy–November 1, 1954, Morristown, NJ), the founder and pastor of Sacred Hearts Church (307 East Thirty-third Street), continued as pastor of the church he founded in 1915 until his death in 1954, and also founded St. Joseph's Villa Camp for Boys in Hackettstown, New Jersey.
8. "Priest, Born Near Actor, Administers Last Rites," *New York American*, August 24, 1926.
9. "Valentino Is Dead!" *Wisconsin News*, August 23, 1926.
10. "Valentino Dies with a Smile as Lips Touch Priest's Crucifix," *New York Daily News*, August 24, 1926.
11. "Nation Mourns Valentino," *New York American*, August 24, 1926.
12. "Valentino Is Dead!," *Wisconsin News*, August 23, 1926.
13. "Valentino," *Time*, August 30, 1926.
14. "Throngs See Rudy's Coffin," *New York American*, August 24, 1926.
15. "Ill Luck in Love Thorn in Valentino Path to Success," *Chicago Tribune*, August 26, 1926.
16. "Pola Negri Prostrated," *Los Angeles Times*, August 24, 1926.
17. "Grief-Stricken Pola Negri Sobs for Rudy in His Deserted Home," *New York American*, August 24, 1926.
18. Ibid.
19. Parsons, *The Gay Illiterate*, p. 93.
20. Negri, *Memoirs of a Star*, p. 283.
21. "Valentino and Pola Were to Wed Next Year," *Chicago Tribune*, August 24, 1926.
22. "Pola Negri Leaves for N.Y. Today," *Illustrated Daily News*, August 25, 1926.
23. "Legend of Valentino, Part 1," *Movie Classics*, June 1973, p. 13.
24. *Atlanta Georgian*, September 11, 1929.
25. Letter from Ditra Flamé to S. George Ullman, February 13, 1961. Courtesy of Tracy Terhune from his private collection.
26. Thanks to Jim Craig of the Valentino discussion group.
27. "Death Comes to Valentino; Film World Mourns Loss," *New York Herald Tribune*, August 24, 1926.
28. "Valentino Passes with No Kin at Side; Throngs in Street," *New York Times*, August 24, 1926.
29. "Brother to Bury Rudolph in Beloved Adopted Land," *New York American*, August 25, 1926.
30. "Pola to Claim Body; Rambova Just Silent," *New York American*, August 25, 1926.
31. "Only Doctors Present as Death Came to Valentino," *Illustrated Daily News*, August 24, 1926.
32. Campbell's advertising, circa 1926.
33. "Foundling Named After Valentino Left with Police," *New York American*, August 24, 1926.

Seven. Ballyhoo

1. "Rudy Spent Huge Income," *New York American*, August 24, 1926.
2. "Valentino Income Nearly $1,000,000 Year, Is Estimate," *Illustrated Daily News*, August 24, 1926.
3. M. M. Marberry, "The Overloved One," *American Heritage*, August 1965.
4. "Film World Mourns for Rudy," *Los Angeles Times*, August 24, 1926.
5. "Jack Dempsey Still Upset," *New York Times*, August 27, 1926.
6. "Film World Mourns for Rudy," *Los Angeles Times*, August 24, 1926.

7. Even though the *Graphic* boasted a readership of more than 100,000, they had difficulty operating in the black since no respectable business would advertise in the tabloid. By 1932, the *Evening Graphic* was no more.
8. "Native City Wants Film Sheik's Body," *Los Angeles Record*, August 25, 1926.
9. "News and Other Values" [editorial], *New York Times*, August 27, 1926.
10. "Embalmer's Art Preserves Film Lover in Death," *New York American*, August 24, 1926.
11. "150 Police Fight Valentino Rioters," *New York American*, August 25, 1926.
12. Adela Rogers St. Johns to Kevin Brownlow in *Hollywood: Swanson and Valentino* (New York: HBO Video, 1980).
13. "100 Hurt as 30,000 Fight to View Body of Valentino," *New York Herald Tribune*, August 25, 1926.
14. Ibid.
15. "Thousands in Riot at Valentino Bier," *New York Times*, August 25, 1926.
16. "Foul Play Hint in Death of Rudy," *New York Evening Graphic*, August 25, 1926.
17. "Valentino and Yellow Journalism," *The Nation*, September 8, 1926.
18. "Spirit Declares Sheik Poisoned," *New York Evening Graphic*, August 24, 1926.
19. "Doctor Denies Arsenic Story; Pecora Ready to Act," *New York Daily News*, August 24, 1926.
20. "Doctor Suspects Poisoning, Urges Autopsy on Rudy," *New York Daily News*, August 25, 1926.
21. Untitled article, *New York Daily News*, August 26, 1926.
22. "Thousands in Riot at Valentino Bier," *New York Times*, August 25, 1926.

Eight. The Fight for Rudy's Body

1. "Crowds Struggle to See Dead Sheik," *Los Angeles Record*, August 24, 1926.
2. Google Groups/ alt.elvis.king, April 5, 1998.
3. Adolph Zukor, *The Public Is Never Wrong*, p. 219.
4. "Valentino's Sister Wants Home Burial," *New York American*, August 26, 1926.
5. "Actors Funeral Plans Are Laid," *Hollywood Daily Citizen*, August 24, 1926.
6. "Pola Negri Will Leave for East Today," *Los Angeles Times*, August 25, 1926.
7. "Valentino View Barred," *New York American*, August 26, 1926.
8. "Valentino Funeral Closed to Public," *New York American*, August 27, 1926.
9. Ibid.
10. "Valentino View Barred," *New York American*, August 26, 1926.
11. "Sheik's Brother Delays Decision on Burial Site," *New York American*, August 26, 1926.
12. "Valentino View Barred," *New York American*, August 26, 1926.
13. Ibid.
14. "Vatican Organ Raps Mob Demonstration," *Hollywood Daily Citizen*, August 26, 1926.
15. "Public Now Barred at Valentino's Bier," *New York Times*, August 26, 1926.
16. "Police Charge Drives 5,000 from Door to Valentino Bier," *New York Herald Tribune*, August 26, 1926.
17. Ibid.
18. "Valentino Rests in Peace," *Los Angeles Times*, August 27, 1926.
19. "Valentino Burial Postponed Until Brother Arrives," *New York Herald Tribune*, August 28, 1926.
20. "'Circus Crowd' at Valentino Bier Assailed," *Los Angeles Examiner*, August 27, 1926.
21. Schulman, *Valentino*, p. 27.
22. "'Circus Crowd' at Valentino Bier Assailed," *Los Angeles Examiner*, August 27, 1926.
23. "Valentino Funeral Closed to Public," *New York American*, August 27, 1926.
24. "Lays Death to Valentino's," *New York Times*, August 28, 1926.
25. "Crowds Still Try to View Valentino," *New York Times*, August 27, 1926.
26. "'Circus Crowd' at Valentino Bier Assailed," *Los Angeles Examiner*, August 27, 1926.

27. "Film World's Center Suggested for Tomb by Doug and Mary," *New York American*, August 27, 1926.
28. "Hollywood Seeks Tomb of Valentino," *New York American*, August 28, 1926.
29. *Illustrated Daily News*, August 28, 1926.
30. "Pola Stays in Seclusion Here on Way to N.Y." *Chicago Tribune*, August 29, 1926.
31. "Pola Negri Speeds East for Valentino Funeral," *New York Herald Tribune*, August 29, 1926.
32. Ben Lyon to Kevin Brownlow, *Hollywood: Swanson and Valentino* (New York: HBO Video, 1980).

Nine. Requiem in New York

1. "Pola Prays at Casket," *Los Angeles Times*, August 30, 1926.
2. "Pola Negri Here for Valentino Funeral To-Day," *New York Herald Tribune*, August 30, 1926.
3. "Pola, Faints, Faints, FAINTS," *New York Daily Mirror*, August 30, 1926.
4. "Pola Prays at Casket," *Los Angeles Times*, August 30, 1926.
5. Ibid.
6. "Pola Faints Seeing Rudy," *New York American*, August 30, 1926.
7. Ibid.
8. "Pola Prays at Casket," *Los Angeles Times*, August 30, 1926.
9. "Star Mourned by Chicagoans," *New York American*, August 31, 1926.
10. "Last Journey for Valentino Waits Brother," *New York Daily News*, August 31, 1926.
11. Ibid.
12. "Silent Crowds See Valentino Cortege," *New York Times*, August 31, 1926.
13. "Film Stars Sob as Mass Is Sung for Valentino," *New York Herald Tribune*, August 31, 1926.
14. "Valentino's Last Words for Pola," *Los Angeles Examiner*, August 31, 1926. "Silent Crowds See Valentino Cortege; Screen Stars Weep," *New York Times*, August 31, 1926.
15. "Valentino Dying Message for Pola," *New York American*, August 31, 1926.
16. "Silent Crowds See Valentino cortege," *New York Times*, August 31, 1931.
17. "Pola in Love! Mary Insists," *New York American*, September 1, 1926.
18. "Friends Plan Last Journey of Valentino," *New York American*, September 1, 1926.
19. Ibid.
20. "Valentino Body to Lie in Hollywood," *New York American*, September 2, 1926.
21. "Ballyhoo for Valentino Funeral Told in Court," unidentified source, November 6, 1930.
22. "Valentino Body to Lie in Hollywood," *New York American*, September 2, 1926.
23. Ibid.
24. "Valentino Body Starts for Coast," *New York Times*, September 3, 1926.
25. Ibid.
26. "Memorial Service for 'Rudy' Held at Emerald Bay," *Illustrated Daily News*, September 3, 1926.

Ten. The Journey West

1. Alberto Valentino to Kevin Brownlow, *Hollywood: Swanson and Valentino* (New York: HBO Video, 1980).
2. "Middle West Pays Tribute to Valentino," *New York American*, September 4, 1926.
3. "Valentino's Catholic Burial," *The Catholic News of New York*, September 10, 1926.
4. "Pola Negri Affirms Troth with Valentino," *New York Times*, September 5, 1926.
5. "Why Marriage Was a Failure in My Case," *New York American*, September 5, 1926.
6. "'Dr.' Wyman Exposed as Former Convict," *New York Times*, September 6, 1926.
7. "Repudiated by Ullman: Wyman Not His Representative Says Valentino's Manager," *New York Times*, September 6, 1926.

8. "She Sobs Her Grief," unidentified source, September 6, 1926.
9. "Los Angeles Reverently Greets Star," *Los Angeles Examiner*, September 7, 1926.
10. Patrick O. Kerrigan (1927–1992) to author, June 1990.
11. Hedda Hopper, *From Under My Hat* (Garden City: Doubleday & Company, Inc., 1952), pp. 170–171.
12. Ravensdale, *In Many Rhythms*, p. 69.
13. Studios throughout Los Angeles ceased filming that morning so that a selected group of film folk could attend the funeral.
14. "Valentino Rites Solemn; Pola Swoons at Services," *Los Angeles Examiner*, September 8, 1926.
15. Ravensdale, *In Many Rhythms*, p. 70.
16. Robert Parrish, *Growing Up in Hollywood* (New York: Harcourt Brace Jovanovich, 1976), p. 36.
17. Ibid., pp. 36–37.
18. Jack Scagnetti, *The Intimate Life of Rudolph Valentino* (New York: Jonathan David Publishers Inc., 1975), p. 128.
19. Ravensdale, *In Many Rhythms*, p. 70.
20. "Unknown Friend's Tiny Bouquet on Grave," *Los Angeles Examiner*, September 8, 1926.
21. "Last Honors Paid to Valentino," *Illustrated Daily News*, September 8, 1926.
22. Ravensdale, *In Many Rhythms*, p. 70.
23. "Star at Rest in Hollywood," *Los Angeles Examiner*, September 8, 1926.
24. Allan R. Ellenberger, "Hollywood Cemetery: Where All the Stars ARE in Heaven! (Part 1 of 2)," *Classic Images*, March 1998.
25. "Pola Negri Returns to Film Work Today," *Los Angeles Examiner*, September 8, 1926.
26. "Film Pioneers' Memorial Plan Is Proposed," *Hollywood Daily Citizen*, August 24, 1926.
27. "Valentino Park Proposed Here," *Hollywood Daily Citizen*, August 25, 1926.
28. Blanche Yurka, *Bohemian Girl* (Athens, Ohio: University Press, 1970), pp. 123–124.

Tour 1— New York

1. "The Planless City," *New York Times*, November 22, 1965.
2. *New York Herald-Tribune*, August 22, 1926.
3. "Valentino's Records Here," *Los Angeles Times*, November 4, 1930.
4. "My Life Story: Chapter II — Broadway Nights," *Photoplay*, March 1923, p. 112.
5. Ibid.
6. "Tries to Join Valentino," *New York Times*, October 31, 1926.
7. "My Life Story: Chapter II — Broadway Nights," *Photoplay*, March 1923, p. 111.
8. "Dancer Lauds Stricken Star," *New York American*, August 19, 1926.
9. "My Life Story: Chapter II — Broadway Nights," *Photoplay*, March 1923, p. 58.
10. Leider, *Dark Lover*, p. 71.
11. "My Life Story: Chapter II — Broadway Nights," *Photoplay*, March 1923, p. 58.
12. Ibid., p. 54.
13. Ibid., p. 111.
14. Henderson, "I Was Valentino's Mystery Woman," *Secret Confessions*, January 1941.
15. Herbert Howe, "Stepping Out with The Movie Crowd in Hollywood & New York," *Photoplay*, June 1923, pp. 41–42.
16. "June Mathis Falls Dead in Theatre," *Los Angeles Examiner*, July 27, 1927.
17. "My Life Story: Chapter II — Broadway Nights," *Photoplay*, March 1923, p. 54.
18. Leider, *Dark Lover*, pp. 70–71.
19. "Rudy Better After Relapse," *New York Daily News*, August 17, 1926.
20. "Frank E. Campbell, Undertaker, Dies," *New York Times*, January 20, 1934.
21. Leider, *Dark Lover*, p. 226.

22. "My Life Story: Chapter II — Broadway Nights," *Photoplay*, March 1923, p. 111.
23. Ibid., p. 56.

Tour 2 — Hollywood

1. "My Life Story: Chapter III — Hollywood," *Photoplay*, April 1923, p. 96.
2. "Valentino Brother Hits Wedding Tale," *Reno Evening Gazette*, November 12, 1945.
3. Viola Dana to Kevin Brownlow, *Hollywood: Swanson & Valentino* (Thames Television, 1980).
4. *Los Angeles Times*, November 23, 1921, Section 2, p. 7.
5. "Ghost of Valentino Lurks in Death Try Over Love," *Los Angeles Herald-Express*, May 20, 1953.
6. Paul Zolle, *Hollywood Remembered: An Oral History of Its Golden Age* (New York: Cooper Square Press, 2002), p. 321.
7. Ezra Goodman, *The Fifty Year Decline and Fall of Hollywood* (New York: Simon and Schuster, 1961), p. 442.
8. In 2001, the All Star Cafe lost its lease at the Knickerbocker and moved up the street to the Vogue Theater, 6675 Hollywood Boulevard.
9. Leider, *Dark Lover*, p. 174.
10. "Kerrigan's Niece Near Death After Clothing Burns," *Los Angeles Examiner*, December 27, 1924.
11. "My Life Story: Chapter III — Hollywood," *Photoplay*, April 1923, p. 52.
12. Rambova, "Why I Married Rudy," *Movie Weekly*, December 16, 1922, p. 7.
13. Valentino, "The Darkest Hours," *Motion Picture Classic*, October 1922, p. 52.
14. Leider, *Dark Lover*, p. 86.

Tour 3 — West Hollywood

1. "Valentino: Was His Death Foretold?" *Fate*, July 1949, p. 6.
2. Leider, *Dark Lover*, pp. 132–133.

Tour 4 — Beverly Hills

1. "Pola Negri Will Soon Own Rudolph Valentino Home," *Los Angeles Examiner*, October 1, 1934.
2. Marion, *Off with Their Heads*, p. 118.
3. "My Life Story: Chapter III — Hollywood," *Photoplay*, April 1923, p. 96.
4. Negri, *Memoirs of a Star*, p. 272.
5. Pickford, *Sunshine and Shadow*, p. 308.

Tour 5 — Downtown Los Angeles

1. "My Life Story: Chapter II — Broadway Nights," *Photoplay*, March 1923, p. 112.
2. "My Life Story: Chapter III — Hollywood," *Photoplay*, April 1923, p. 96.
3. Ibid., p. 50.
4. "Studio News and Gossip — East and West," *Photoplay*, October 1926, p. 104.
5. Chaplin, *My Autobiography*, p. 186.
6. "Valentino: Lover and Legend," *Los Angeles Mirror*, August 26, 1949.

Tour 6 — Suburban Los Angeles and Environs

1. "My Life Story: Chapter III — Hollywood," *Photoplay*, April 1923, pp. 50–51.
2. Ibid., p. 51.
3. "Few See Arrival of Valentino in Coffin," *Los Angeles Record*, September 7, 1926.

Appendix II. The Medical Diagnosis, Operation and Treatment

1. *New York Times*, September 4, 1926.

Appendix III. Tributes and Eulogies

1. These tributes were culled from the following newspapers: *Chicago Tribune, Cleveland Plain Dealer, Glendale Daily Press, Hollywood Daily Citizen, London Daily Express, London Daily News, London Times, Los Angeles Evening Herald, Los Angeles Examiner, Los Angeles Illustrated Daily News, Los Angeles Record, Los Angeles Times, New York American, New York Daily News, New York Herald-Tribune, New York Times, New York World*.

Appendix V. The Last Will and Testament

1. "Lawyer Backs Valentino Will," *Los Angeles Times*, February 5, 1931; "Torn Evidence in Valentino Court Case," unsourced, February 5, 1931; "Rudy's Good-by Scene Disputed," *Los Angeles Times*, February 6, 1931.

Appendix VI. The Estate

1. *The Estate of Rudolph Valentino*, p. 4.

Appendix XI. Quotations about Valentino

1. Kenneth Anger's Icons. http://www.grandstreet.com/gs/gs57/anger.html.
2. "A Golden Hour for Silent Star," *Los Angeles Times*, October 2, 1975.
3. "What Killed Francis X. Bushman," *Photoplay*, January 1928.
4. Chaplin, *My Autobiography*, p. 186.
5. "Movie Idols, Media and Autumn Mists," *BBC News*, October 26, 1997.
6. Dee to Jimmy Bangley, Academy Salute to Preston Sturges, Los Angeles.
7. Dunaway to Jimmy Bangley, West Hollywood, California, January 2001.
8. Fairbanks in telephone interview to Jimmy Bangley, West Hollywood, California, Summer 1996.
9. Unsourced and undated clipping, NYPL.
10. Fountain in telephone interview with Jimmy Bangley, West Hollywood, California, Summer 1996.
11. Elinor Glyn, *Romantic Adventures* (London: Nicholson, 1936), p. 300.
12. From a press book edited on the occasion of the 1938 re-release of *The Son of the Sheik*.
13. Guilaroff to Jimmy Bangley, West Hollywood, California, December 1996.

14. Hope to Jimmy Bangley, Roundtable West's 25th Anniversary, Beverly Hills.
15. Jimmy Bangley, "Marsha Hunt," *Classic Images*, April 1997, No. 262.
16. Keaton to Jimmy Bangley.
17. Kirkland to Jimmy Bangley, West Hollywood, California, January 2003.
18. Roundtable West, La Quinta, California.
19. Leigh to Jimmy Bangley, Roundtable West, Beverly Hills.
20. Myrna Loy and James Kotsilibas-Davis, *Being and Becoming* (New York: Knopf, 1987), p. 38.
21. MacDowall to Jimmy Bangley.
22. Michael G. Ankerich, *Broken Silence: Conversations with Twenty-Three Silent Film Stars* (Jefferson, N. C.: McFarland, 1993), p. 196.
23. Frances Marion, *Off with Their Heads*, p. 118.
24. Marsh in telephone interview with Jimmy Bangley, December 1998.
25. Mencken, "Valentino," *Baltimore Evening Sun*, August 30, 1926.
26. Ankerich, *Broken Silence*, p. 200.
27. Colleen Moore, *Silent Star* (Garden City, New York: Doubleday, 1968), p. 98.
28. "Great Lovers of the Screen," *Photoplay*, June 1924.
29. Philbin to Jimmy Bangley, West Hollywood, California, Summer 1988.
30. Rogers in telephone interview with Jimmy Bangley, West Hollywood, California, August 1998.
31. *Variety*, September 1, 1976.
32. Unsourced and undated clipping, NYPL.
33. St. Johns in telephone interview with Jimmy Bangley, Los Angeles, 1995.
34. From a press book edited on the occasion of the 1938 re-release of *The Son of the Sheik*.
35. Ibid.
36. Wray in telephone interview with Jimmy Bangley, Los Angeles, 1999.

Bibliography

General

Anderson, Gillian B., comp. *Music for Silent Films: 1894–1929.* Washington, D.C.: Library of Congress, 1988.
Anger, Kenneth. *Hollywood Babylon.* New York: Dell, 1975.
_____. *Hollywood Babylon II.* New York: E. P. Dutton, 1984.
Ankerich, Michael G. *Broken Silence: Conversations with Twenty-Three Silent Film Stars.* Jefferson, N. C.: McFarland, 1993.
Ardmore, Jane. *The Self-Enchanted. Mae Murray: Image of an Era.* New York: McGraw-Hill Book Co., 1959.
Basinger, Jeanine. *Silent Stars.* Hanover, N.H.: Wesleyan University Press; University Press of New England, 2000.
Basquette, Lina. *Lina: DeMille's Godless Girl.* Fairfax, VA: Denlinger's Publishers, 1990.
Baxter, John. *The Hollywood Exiles.* New York: Taplinger, 1976.
Benda, Wladyslaw T. *Masks.* New York: Watson-Guptill, 1944.
Bent, Silas. *Ballyhoo: The Voice of the Press.* New York: Boni and Liveright, 1927.
Bland, Alexander. *The Nureyev Valentino: Portrait of a Film.* Studio Vista, 1977.
Boller, Paul F., Jr., and Ronald L. Davis. *Hollywood Anecdotes.* New York: William Morrow, 1987.
Bondanella, Peter. *Italian Cinema.* New York: Continuum, 1995.
Brody, Iles. *The Colony: Portrait of a Restaurant — And Its Famous Recipes.* New York: Greenberg, 1945.
Brownlow, Kevin. *Behind the Mask of Innocence.* New York: Alfred A. Knopf, 1990.
_____. *Hollywood: The Pioneers.* New York: Alfred A. Knopf, 1979.
_____. *The Parade's Gone By...* New York: Dutton, 1981.
_____. *The War, the West and the Wilderness.* New York: Alfred A. Knopf, 1979.
Brundidge, Harry T. *Twinkle, Twinkle Movie Star!* New York: E. P. Dutton, 1930.
Chaplin, Charles. *My Autobiography.* New York: Simon and Schuster, 1964.
Chaplin, J. P. *Rumor, Fear, & the Madness of Crowds.* New York: Ballantine Books, 1959.
Cohen-Stratyner, Barbara Naomi. *Biographical Dictionary of Dance.* New York: Macmillan, 1982.

Cook, David A. *A History of Narrative Film*, 2nd Edition. New York: W. W. Norton, 1990.
Crystal, David. *The Cambridge Biographical Encyclopedia*. Cambridge: Cambridge University Press, 1988.
Dempsey, Jack, with Barbara Piatelli. *Dempsey*. New York: Harper & Row, 1977.
DeShazo, Edith. *Everett Shim, 1876–1953: A Figure in His Time*. New York: Clarkson N. Potter, 1974.
Drew, William M. *Speaking of Silents: First Ladies of the Screen*. Vestal, N.Y: Vestal Press, 1989.
Drexel, John. *The Facts on File Encyclopedia of the Twentieth Century*. New York: Facts on File, 1991.
Ellenberger, Allan. *Ramon Novarro: A Biography of the Silent Film Star*. Jefferson, N.C.: McFarland, 1999.
Florey, Robert. *Hollywood d'Hier et Aujourd'hui*. Paris: Editions Prisma, 1979.
_____. *La Lanterne Magique*. Lausanne: La Cinémathèque Suisse, 1966.
Garraty, John A., and Mark C. Carnes. *American National Biography*. New York: Oxford University Press, 1999.
Gavin, James. *Intimate Nights: The Golden Age of New York Cabaret*. New York: Grove Weidenfeld, 1991.
Glyn, Anthony. *Elinor Glyn: A Biography*. Garden City, N.Y.: Doubleday, 1955.
Glyn, Elinor. *Romantic Adventure*. London: Nicholson, 1936.
Godowsky, Dagmar. *First Person Plural: The Lives of Dagmar Godowsky*. New York: Viking, 1958.
Golden, Eve. *Golden Images*. Jefferson, N.C.: McFarland, 2001.
Goldwyn, Samuel. *Behind the Screen*. New York: George H. Doran, 1923.
Goodman, Ezra. *The Fifty Year Decline and Fall of Hollywood*. New York: Simon and Schuster, 1961.
Griffith, Richard, and Arthur Mayer. *The Movies*. New York: Simon and Schuster, 1957.
Harmon, Justin. *American Cultural Leaders: From Colonial Times to the Present*. Santa Barbara, CA, 1993.
Hart, James D. *A Companion to California*. New York: Oxford University Press, 1978.
Hobson, Fred. *Mencken: A Life*. New York: Random House, 1995.
Janis, Elsie. *So Far, So Good! An Autobiography*. New York: E. P. Dutton, 1932.
Jenkins, Alan. *The Twenties*. New York: Universe Books, 1974.
Katz, Ephraim. *The Film Encyclopedia*. New York: Harper Collins, 1994.
Knight, Marion A., and Mertice M. James (eds.). *The Book Review Digest: Books of 1926*. New York: H. W. Wilson, 1927.
Kobal, John. *People Will Talk*. New York: Alfred K. Knopf, 1985.
Lambert, Gavin. *Nazimova: A Biography*. New York: Alfred K. Knopf, 1997.
Lamparski, Richard. *Lamparski's Hidden Hollywood: Where the Stars Lived, Loved and Died*. New York: A Fireside Book, 1981.
Lasky, Jesse L., with Don Weldon. *I Blow My Own Horn*. Garden City, N.Y.: Doubleday, 1957.
Liebman, Roy. *From Silents to Sound*. Jefferson, N.C.: McFarland, 1998.
Lloyd, Ann (ed.). *Movies of the Silent Years*. London: Orbis Publishing, 1984.
Loos, Anita. *Kiss Hollywood Good-Bye*. New York: Ballantine, 1975.
Loy, Myrna, and James Kotsilibas-Davis. *Being and Becoming*. New York: Knopf, 1987.
Macklin, Jack. *World's Strangest True Ghost Stories*. New York: Sterling Pub. Co., 1991.
Marion, Frances. *Off with Their Heads: A Serio-Comic Tale of Hollywood*. New York: Macmillan, 1972.
Menjou, Adolphe, and M. M. Musselman. *It Took Nine Tailors*. New York: McGraw-Hill, 1948.
Moore, Colleen. *Silent Star*. Garden City, New York: Doubleday, 1968.
Morris, Michael. *Madam Valentino*. New York: Abbeville Press, 1991.
Negri, Pola. *Memoirs of a Star*. New York: Doubleday, 1970.
O'Leary, Liam. *Rex Ingram, Master of the Silent Cinema*. Dublin: Academy Press, 1980.

Parish, James Robert. *The Hollywood Celebrity Death Book*. Las Vegas, NV: Pioneer Books, 1993.
Parkinson, Mary Jane. *The Kellogg Arabian Ranch: The First Fifty Years*. Arabian Horse Association of Southern California, 1977.
Parrish, Robert. *Growing Up in Hollywood*. New York: Harcourt Brace Jovanovich, 1976.
Parry, Melanie. *Chambers Biographical Dictionary*. New York: Larousse Kingfisher Chambers, 1997.
Parsons, Louella O. *The Gay Illiterate*. Garden City, N.Y.: Doubleday, Doran, 1944.
Parsons, Schuyler Livingston. *Untold Friendships*. Boston: Houghton Mifflin, 1955.
Pickard, Roy. *A Companion to the Movies: From 1904 to the Present Day*. New York: Hippocrene Books, 1972.
Pickford, Mary. *Sunshine and Shadow*. Garden City, N.Y.: Doubleday, 1955.
Pratt, George C. *Image: On the Art and Evolution of the Film* (ed. Marshall Deutelbaum). New York: Dover, 1979.
Preston, Wheeler. *American Biographies*. New York: Harper, 1940.
Ravensdale, Mary Irene Curzon, 2nd Baroness. *In Many Rythms*. London: Weidenfeld, 1953.
Richman, Harry. *A Hell of a Life*. New York: Duell, Sloan and Pearce, 1966.
Room, Adrian. *Dictionary of Pseudonyms*. Jefferson, N.C.: McFarland, 1998.
St. Johns, Adela Rogers. *Love, Laughter and Tears: My Hollywood Story*. New York: Doubleday, 1978.
Shirley, Glenn. *The Story of Texas Guinan*. Austin, TX: Eakin Press, 1989.
Silvester, Christopher. *The Grove Book of Hollywood*. New York: Grove Press, 1998.
Sinclair, Marianne. *Those Who Died Young*. New York: Penguin Books, 1979.
Skolsky, Sidney. *Don't Get Me Wrong—I Love Hollywood*. New York: Putnam, 1975.
Soares, André. *Beyond Paradise: The Life of Ramon Novarro*. New York: St. Martin's Press, 2002.
Stewart, John. *Filmarama, Volume I: The Formidable Years, 1893–1919*. Metuchen, N.J.: Scarecrow Press, 1975.
_____. *Filmarama, Volume II: The Flaming Years, 1920–1929*. Metuchen, N.J.: Scarecrow Press, 1977.
Thompson, David. *A Biographical Dictionary of Film*. New York: Alfred A. Knopf, 1994.
Torrence, Bruce. *Hollywood: The First Hundred Years*. New York: Zoetrope, 1982.
Urdosikova, Blazena. "Rudolph Valentino" in *Kino Ponrepo*. Prague: Filmovy Ustav, 1970.
Valerio, Anthony. *Valentino and the Great Italians*. New York: Freundlich Books, 1986.
Walker, Stanley. *Mrs. Astor's Horse*. New York: Frederick A. Stokes, 1935.
Wallace, David. *Hollywoodland*. New York: St. Martin's Press, 2002.
_____. *Lost Hollywood*. New York: St. Martin's Press, 2001.
Wallace, W. Stewart. *A Dictionary of North American Authors Deceased Before 1950*. Toronto: Ryerson Press, 1951.
Weaver, John T. *Twenty Years of Silents, 1908–1928*. Metuchen, N.J.: Scarecrow Press, 1971.
Wendt, Lloyd. *Chicago Tribune: The Rise of a Great American Newspaper*. New York: Rand McNally, 1979.
Yurka, Blanche. *Bohemian Girl*. Athens: Ohio University Press, 1970.
Zollo, Paul. *Hollywood Remembered: An Oral History of Its Golden Age*. New York: Cooper Square Press, 2002.
Zukor, Adolph, with Dale Kramer. *The Public Is Never Wrong: The Autobiography of Adolph Zukor*. New York: Putnam, 1953.

Reference Books

Combined Retrospective Index to Book Reviews in Scholarly Journals, 1866–1974, Vol. IX. Arlington and Iverness: Carrollton Press, 1981.
Contemporary Theatre, Film and Television: Volume 22. Detroit: Gale Group, 1999.

Cumulated Dramatic Index, 1909–1949. Boston: G. K. Hall & Co., 1965.
Dictionary of the Arts. New York: Facts on File, 1994.
The New York Public Library, Catalogue of the Theatre and Drama Collections, Part III — Non-Book Collection. Boston: G. K. Hall, 1976.
The New York Times Theater Reviews, 1920–1970. New York: New York Times and Arno Press, 1971.
Variety Obituaries. New York: Garland Publications, 1905–1994.
Variety Television Reviews, Vol. 7, 1960–1962. New York: Garden Publishing, 1989.
Who's Was Who in the Theatre, 1912–1976. Detroit: Gale, 1978.

Index

Aaliyah 117
Abrams, Hiram 35, 40, 45, 158, 173
Abrazze, Nicolo 84, 174
Academy of Motion Picture Arts and Sciences 143
Acker, Edith 174
Acker, Jean 13, 15, 28, 30, 34, 39, 47, 53, 57, 71, 73–74, 79, 82, 83–84, 91, 109, 114, 116, 117, 121, 122, 123, 126, 127, 128, 131, 139, 144, 146, 147, 158, 174
Acker, Margaret 73–74, 83, 109, 174
Adams, Marcus 158
Adrian 127
An Adventuress (film) 127, 244–245
Against the Odds: Rudolf Valentino (documentary) 225
Aitken, Spottiswood 127
Alexandra, Queen Mother 26
Alexandria Hotel (Los Angeles) 15, 16, 142, 143
Algonquin Hotel (New York) 22
Alimony (film) 79, 237–238
All Night (film) 238–239
All Star Cafe (Hollywood) 129
Alla Nazimova and Rudolph Valentino (documentary) 226
Allegra, Pietro 76

Allison, May 36, 175
Ambassador Hotel (Los Angeles) 54, 56, 95, 142, 145, 146
Ambassador Hotel (New York) 19, 20, 21, 24, 33, 35, 36, 40, 46, 54, 79, 81, 84, 87, 88, 92, 106–108, 156
American Museum of Natural History (New York) 119
Anger, Kenneth 230
Apollo Theater (Hollywood) 125–126
Apollo Theatre (New York) 36, 112
Aragon Ballroom (Chicago) 10–11
Arbuckle, Roscoe "Fatty" 41, 117
Archainbaud, George 158
Arts Association of Hollywood 98
Asher, E. M. 175
Aspiration 123–124
Astor, Gertrude 127, 175, 230
Astor, Mary 158
Astor Hotel (New York) 112
The Auditorium (Los Angeles) 142
Ayres, Agnes 32, 120, 127, 159, 175

Baby Peggy 135
Baggot, King 175
Balboni, Silvano 98, 100, 101, 135–136, 159, 175

Ballerini, Edoardo 1–2, 21, 23, 224
Baltimore Evening Sun 23
Balzar, Robert L. 139
Bank of America 132
Banks, Monty 175
Banky, Vilma 138, 159
Bara, Theda 135
Barberetti, Calise 174
Barham, Frank E. 175
Barker, Reginald 159, 175
Barnes, George 128
Baron Long's Watts Tavern 145
Barrymore, John 43, 48, 114, 145, 159, 175
Barrymore, Lionel 159
Battey, Dr. Golden R 38
Battle of the Sexes (film) 235–236
Bedtime Stories for Grownups (book) 43
Beekman Street Hospital 112
Beery, Noah 159
Beery, Wallace 160
Beetson, Fred W. 160, 175
Belasco, David 160
Bell, Monta 185
Bellamy, Madge 84, 160, 174
Bellevue Hospital (New York) 60
Beltran-Masses 55–56, 139
Ben-Allah 94
Benda, Marion 30, 37, 40–41, 112–113, 116, 122, 134, 160

Index

Bent (play) 112
Beranger, Clare 175
Bern, Paul 175
Bernie, Ben 174
Bey, Rahman 29–30, 115
Beyond the Rocks (film) 124, 127, 253–254
The Big Little Person (film) 149, 241
Big Moments from Little Pictures (film) 222
Biltmore Hotel (Los Angeles) 142, 143, 144
Biography—Rudolph Valentino: The Great Lover (documentary) 225–226
The Birth of a Nation (film) 129, 142
Black Feather (Spirit guide) 10
Blackstone Hotel (Chicago) 9, 17
Bliss, Cornelius 113
The Blonde Saint (film) 89
Blood and Sand (film) 12, 45, 53, 124, 127, 129–130, 143, 144, 254–255
Blue, Monte 160
Blythe, Betty 160
Boardman, Eleanor 98, 175
Bogart, Dr. Arthur 37
Bogart, Humphrey 134, 147
Bonelli, Richard 96
Borden, Olive 175
Borrelli, Judge Francis 82
Borzage, Frank 160
Boulevard Cafe (New York) 110
Boulevard Park Station (Los Angeles) 93
Bourbon, Ray 15
Bowes, Major Edward 49–50, 160, 174
Boyertown Casket Company 58
Brabin, Charles 160
Brand, Harry 175
Breakfast Club 79
Brennon, Herbert 161
Brent, Evelyn 175
Briggs, H. B. R. 175
The Bronx Zoo 120
Brooke, Tyler 175
Brooklyn Information and Culture Center (BRIC) 120
Brooks, Louise 174
Broun, Heywood 161
Brown, Clarence 57, 161, 175
Brown, Melville W. 175
Brown Derby (Hollywood) 105

Browning, Tod 175
Brown's "Drive It Yourself" Automobile Company (New York) 66
Brulatour, Jules 174
Brunswick Records (New York) 108–109
Brunton, Robert 131
Buck, Gene 174
Bunky Valentino 147
Burham, Roger Noble 123
Burkan, Nathan 174
Burke, John B. 175
Burns, William J. 174
Bushman, Francis X. 182, 230, 275
Buys, Gypsy 139

Cabrillo, Juan 148
Cagney, James 117
Calder, Senator William M. 92
Calvary Cemetery (Los Angeles) 89, 91
Camille (film) 127, 251
Campbell, Frank 58, 66, 69, 73, 76, 89, 117
Campbell, Mrs. Thomas 175
Cantwell, Bishop 91
Capitol Theater (New York) 49–50
Carey, Harry 138
Carmen, Jewell 175
Carminati, Tullio 175
Carnegie Hall (New York) 116
Carr, Harry 26
Carr, Mary 175
Carrillo, Marion 175
Carroll, Frank 174
Caruso, Enrico 59, 63, 64, 114, 117
Cassidy, Hopalong 147
Castellaneta (Italy) 63, 71, 72, 78, 84
Castle, Vernon 117
Celestina, Angeline 110–112
Central Park (New York) 16, 30, 113
Central Station (Los Angeles) 94
Cerverra, Carmen 8
Chalupec, Elinor 28
Chandler, Harry 175
Chaney, Lon 161, 174
Chaplin, Charlie 1, 27, 43, 72, 79, 95, 97, 130, 134, 136, 144, 145, 147, 161, 175, 230
Chaplin, Frank 37, 175
Character Studies (film) 252
Chase, Charles 175

The Cheater (film) 127, 245–246
Chez-Fysher (New York) 109
Chicago Grand Opera 96
Chicago Herald-Examiner 17, 153, 155
Chicago Opera Company 84
Chicago Tribune 9, 10, 11, 15, 17, 18, 19, 30, 31, 116, 153, 154, 155
Christie, Al 134, 161
Christie, Charles 161, 175
Church of Sacred Heart of Jesus and Mary (New York) 52, 88
Church of the Good Shepherd (Beverly Hills) 89, 91, 95, 96, 138, 174
Ciao Rudy! (play) 226–227
Ciccolini, Guido 84
Cinema Film Corporation 61
Clayton, Ethel 175
S. S. *Cleveland* (ship) 120
Clifford, Ruth 175
Clift, Montgomery 117
Cline, Eddie 175
Club Lido (New York) 40–41, 108
Clune's Auditorium 142
Cobra (film) 19, 57, 131, 259–260
Coconut Grove 145
Coffin, Ray 175
Cohan, George M. 161
Collier, William, Jr. 174
Collins, E. R. 175
Colonial Theatre (New York) 110
The Colony (New York) 34, 36, 40, 116
Colorado River Bridge 93
Columbia University 38
Combs, Perry 122
Concannon, Father Patrick 174
Congedo, Father Joseph 52, 88, 173
Connelly, Edward J. 127
Connelly, Erwin 127
The Conquering Power (film) 127, 171, 250–251
Considine, John, Jr. 33–34, 93, 161, 175
Considine, John, Sr. 175
Conte Blancamane (ship) 24
Coogan, Jack 175
Coogan, Jackie 175
Coogan, Lillian 175
Cooke, Alistair 231
Cooper, Gary 138

Cortez, Ricardo 161
The Cosby Show (television) 120
Crawford, Joan 110, 117, 130
Crosby, Bing 130
Crosland, Alan 162
Cruz, Celia 117
Cruze, James 162, 175
Cryer, Mayor George E. 175
Cryer, Isabel 175
Cunningham & O'Connor Mortuary (Los Angeles) 94, 143, 148
Curzon, Lady Mary *see* Ravensdale, Baroness
Curzon, Lord 26

Dale, Frances 175
Dana, Viola 123
Dane, Karl 127
Daniels, Bebe 27, 43, 127, 162, 185, 175
Dannemora State Hospital 92
Dark Lover: The Life and Death of Rudolph Valentino (book) 4
Darmond, Grace 121, 123
Davies, Ethel 175
Davies, Marion 25, 27, 54, 56, 71, 72, 93, 94, 97, 98, 130, 162, 175
Davies, Rose 175
Davis, Bette 134
Davis, Mildred 175
Daydreams (book) 63
Death Scenes 2 (documentary) 262
Dee, Frances 231
de la Falaise de Coudray, Marquis 84, 173
de la Motte, Marguerite 175
The Delicious Little Devil (film) 95, 149, 240–241
Delmonico's (New York) 110
De Longpre, Paul 123
De Longpre Park 101, 123–124
Del Rio, Dolores 123, 175
Del Vecchio, Dr. M 67–68
DeMille, Cecil B. 129, 162, 175
de Mille, William C. 175
De Mond, Maurice 175, 183
Dempsey, Jack 19–21, 30, 33, 62, 117, 154, 162
Denny, Reginald 162, 175
de Saulles, Bianca 116
de Saulles, John 113, 116
Dexter, Anthony 220
Di Calzi, Mike 40
Dillon, John S. 175
Dix, Richard 83, 162, 173

Dixon, Edward A. 175
Dixon, Jane 174
Doane, Warren 175
Dolly Sisters 26
Donlin, Mike 175
Donnelly, Ruth 174
Donohue, Father William 173
Donovan, Catherine 89
Doob, Oscar 17, 62
Dora et la Lanterne Magique (film) 262
Dorgan, Dick 11–12, 15, 17, 31
Dorgan, Thomas "Tad" 11
Dove, Billie 175
The Dream of Valentino (opera) 228
Duke, Doris 139
Dunaway, Faye 231
Dunkinson, Harry 127
Dunn, Winfred 175
Dunne, Rev. Father Patrick 174
Du Pont, E. A. 175
Durante, Jimmy 138
Durham, Dr. Paul 37, 38, 41, 46, 47, 54, 116
Dwan, Allan 162

Eagels, Jeanne 117
The Eagle (film) 33, 57, 61, 62, 115, 127, 258–259
Eddy, Don 175
Ederle, Gertrude "Trudy" 79
Edwards, Gus 32
Egan, Betty 175
Eldridge, Fred W. 175
Eliot, Dr. Charles 63–64
Ellis, Richard 124
Ellis Island (New York) 120
Empire State Building (New York) 105, 112
Engel, Joseph 121
Exhibitor's Herald 174
The Eyes of Youth 243–244
Eyton, Charles 54–56, 71, 93, 175

Fager, Raymond A. 179
Fairbanks, Douglas 78, 86–87, 95, 97, 125, 128, 136, 140, 141, 173, 175
Fairbanks, Douglas, Jr. 110, 117, 231
Fairbanks, Robert 175
Faire, Virginia Browne 175
Falcon Lair 24, 27, 54–56, 79, 126, 137, 138–139, 180
Falcon Lair's Stables 139
Fame in the Twentieth Century (documentary) 262

Famous Players-Lasky 9, 12, 34, 44, 54, 56, 95, 113, 120, 124–125, 129, 131; *see also* Paramount Studios
Fascisti League of North America 69, 74, 75–76
Felger, Dr. Louis 54, 94, 175
Fenton, Mark 127
Ferdinand III, Saint 148
Ferguson, Helen 175
Ferris, Dick 175
Fielding, Margaret 175
Fields, W. C. 148
The Fifth of July (play) 112
Fifty Years Before Your Eyes (documentary) 262
Film Daily 174
Finch, Flora 127
Finch, Peter 138
Fineman, Bernard P. 175
Fitzmaurice, George 95, 162, 175, 231
Flame, Ditra 57, 144, 146, 147
Fleming, Victor 163
Flint, Motley H. 175
Florentino, Rudolph 125–126
Flower Hospital (New York) 73
Flynn, Emmett 79, 175
The Foolish Virgin (film) 236–237
Forbes, Genevieve 31
Forbidden Paradise (film) 25
Ford, John 175
Ford Center for the Performing Arts (New York) 112
Forest Lawn–Hollywood Hills Cemetery (Hollywood) 130
Formosa Apartments (Hollywood) 126, 144
Forty-eighth Street Theatre (New York) 98, 115
Fountain, Leatrice Gilbert 231
The Four Horsemen of the Apocalypse (film) 14, 126, 127, 130, 136, 148, 171, 248–249
Fox, William 163
Foy, Brian 143
S. S. *France* (ship) 24
Frank, A. 175
Frank, Pearl 40, 46, 67
Frank E. Campbell's Funeral Church (New York) 3, 54, 56, 57, 58, 64, 68–69, 73, 75, 76, 77, 82, 83, 84, 88, 89, 100, 117, 119; Gold Room 58–59; riots at Valentino funeral and 64–67
Franklin, Sidney 127

Frann, Mary 138
Frawley, William 138
Frederick, Pauline 139, 144
French Hospital (New York) 110
Freud, Sigmund 19
Friganza, Trixie 175

Gable, Clark 134
Gabor, Eva 138
Gad, Sven 89
Gallagher, Richard 173
Gallery, Tom 175
Gallo, Fortuno 174
Galloway, Frank 175
Garden of Allah (West Hollywood) 135
Garland, Judy 117
Gaudio, Tony 127
George Ullman Agency, Inc. 135
George White's Scandals (revue) 36–37, 40, 112
Gerard, Carl 127
Gerrard, Douglas 139, 144, 146, 175
Gest, Morris 163
Ghost Stories Magazine 67
Giannini, A. P. 175
Gibson, Hoot 163, 175
Gilbert, John 43, 163, 174
Giolito's (New York) 113
Giordano, Dominick *see* Florentino, Rudolph
Gish, Lillian 175
Glass, Bonnie 29, 84, 109–110, 115, 174
Globe Theatre (New York) 30
Glynn, Elinor 26–27, 95, 96, 154, 163, 175, 231
Godowsky, Dagmar 36, 149
Golden State Limited 90
Goldwyn, Francis Howard 98
Goldwyn, Samuel 95, 98, 163, 175
Goldwyn, Samuel, Jr. 98
Goldwyn Pictures 130
Good Night Valentino (film) 21, 23, 223–224
Good Samaritan Hospital (Los Angeles) 98
Goulding, Edmund 175
Gradenigo, Count 175
Grand Central Terminal 19, 35, 81, 87, 88–89, 106, 108
Grange, Harold "Red" 163
Grauman, Mrs. D. J. 175
Grauman, Sid 144, 164
Grauman's Chinese Theater (Hollywood) 105

Grauman's Million Dollar Theater (Los Angeles) 32, 144
Gray, Gilda 164
Great Romances of the Twentieth Century: Rudolph Valentino and Natasha [sic] (documentary) 226
The Greatest Thing in Life (film) 142
Green, Alfred E. 175
Grey, Lita 175
Gribbon, Eddie 176
Griffin, Frank 176
Griffith, Corinne 176
Griffith, D. W. 129, 136, 142, 231
Griffith, Raymond 164
Gross, Frank 40
Guasti, Segundo, Jr. 175
Guglielmi, Ada (sister-in-law) *see* Valentino, Ada
Guglielmi, Alberto (brother) *see* Valentino, Alberto
Guglielmi, Gabriella Barbin (mother) 112, 132
Guglielmi, Jean (nephew) *see* Valentino, Jean
Guglielmi, Maria (sister) 39, 45, 71, 89, 164, 178, 179; *see also* Strada, Maria
Guilaroff, Sydney 231
Guinan, Texas 29, 40–41, 84, 114, 115, 116, 117, 174
Guinan, Tommy 29, 115

H & H Automat (New York) 113–114
Haggerty, James 176
Haggin, Ben Ali 29, 30, 110, 174
Haines, Rhea 127
Haisman, Irene 176
Hale, Alan 176
Hall of Arts Studios (Hollywood) 126, 180
Hallam Cooley Agency 135
Hamburger, M. A. 175
Hamilton, Neil 164
Hammerstein, Oscar 59, 117
Hammill, Captain 65–66, 69
Hampton, Hope 164, 174
Hampton Studios 136
Hanson, Einar 176
Harbor Sanatorium (New York) 46, 116–117
Hardart, Frank 114
Harding, Ann 139
Harding, Warren G. 92
Harris, Dr. Louis L 77–78

Harron, John 176
Hart, William S. 175, 176
Hartman, Gretchen 176
Harvard University 31, 63, 128
Hastings Hotel 134; *see also* Regent Hotel (Hollywood)
Hawkes, Emily 98, 100, 115
Hawley, Wanda 127
Hays, Will H. 164
Hayworth, Rita 117, 138
Hearst, William Randolph 78, 95, 96, 97, 175
Hein, Florence 54, 79
Held, Anna 59, 117
Hellman, Irving 176
Hellman, Marco 175
Henderson, Anabel 114
Hendricks, Ben, Jr. 176
Henley, Hobart 176
Henson, Jim 117
Hergesheimer, Joe 95
Herrick, John Origen 31
Herrliche Zeiten (film) 261
Hersholt, Jean 164, 176
Hill, A. J. 175
Hilton, Nicky 138
Hines, Johnny 173
History of the American Language (book) 21
The History of the Motion Picture: The Valentino Mystique (documentary) 225
Hitchcock, Alfred 138
Hoffman, Milton 176
Hollis, Hylda 176
Hollywood and Highland (Hollywood) 126, 128
Hollywood Athletic Club 126
Hollywood Babylon (book) 15
Hollywood Cemetery (Hollywood Forever Cemetery) 8, 89, 91, 94–95, 96–98, 100–101, 126–128, 129, 131
Hollywood: City of Celluloid (film) 223
Hollywood Freeway 129, 133
Hollywood Heritage Museum 129
Hollywood High School 128
Hollywood Hospital 95, 124
Hollywood Hotel 105, 121, 128
Hollywood Paladium 125
Hollywood Renaissance Hotel 126
Hollywood Sex Symbols (short) 262
Holmes, Stuart 16
Holt, Jack 165
Holubar, Allen 127

Holy Cross Cemetery 146
The Homebreaker (film) 127, 240
Homeric (ship) 58, 71, 78, 87, 88
The Hooden Falcon (film) 34
Hope, Bob 231
Horn, Joseph 114
Horowitz, Vladimir 117
Hotel des Artistes (New York) 117
The Hotel Imperial (film) 39, 48, 54, 56, 98
Houdini, Harry 84, 174
Howard, Jules 138, 184
Howe, Herbert 14, 176
Hughes, Betty 42
Hughes, Lloyd 165
Hull, William H. 89
Hunt, Marsha 231
Hunter, Rachel 138
Hurlock, Madeline 176

Ingram, Rex 165
International Beauty Contest 8
Intimate Nights (book) 15
Ivano, Paul 16, 126, 129, 131

J. P. Morgan Chase & Co. (New York) 108
Jazzland 145
Jeffries, Jeff 165
Jenny (Spirit guide) 10, 38, 43; *see also* Mathis, Virginia
Jessel, George 174
Johnson, Alice 123
Johnson, William A. 174
Johnston, Ann 124
Johnston, Julianne 176
Joller, Dr. A. A. 44, 46
Jones, F. Richard 176
Joy, Leatrice 165
Joyce, Peggy Hopkins 26, 114
Julliard School 3

Kabar (Valentino's dog) 146–147
Kann, "Red" 174
Kaplan, Izzy 84
Karamano, George 176
Karger, Maxwell 121, 127
Kashmiri Love Song 108–109
Kaufman Astoria Studios (Long Island) 120
Keaton, Buster 165, 176
Keaton, Eleanor 231
Keeler, Ruby 174
Keene, D. 177
Kelley, Edward 174

Kemp, John W. 175
Kennedy, Jacqueline 108
Kent, Sidney R. 165, 173
Kenyon, Doris 89
Kerrigan, J. Warren 95, 129, 176
Kerrigan, Patrick O. 95
Kerrigan, Virginia Richdale 94–95, 129
Kerrigan, William W. 95, 129, 176
Kerry, Norman 16–17, 62, 72, 79, 95, 142, 146, 165, 175, 176
Kid Dugan (comic strip) 11
King Cole Room (New York) 114
Kirkham, Kathleen 127
Kirkland, Sally 232
Kirkwood, James 126, 176
Kleine, George 174
Klemfuss, Harry C. 64, 76, 89
Knickerbocker Hosptial 66
Knickerbocker Hotel (Hollywood) 129
Knickerbocker Hotel (New York) 114
Kodak Theater (Hollywood) 128
Kosloff, Theodore 131, 136
Kosloff's Imperial Russian Ballet School 131
Kraly, Hans 176
Kyne, Peter B. 176

La Badie, Florence 117
Lackaye, Wilton 174
Lady in Black 122, 125, 144, 146, 147
Laemmle, Carl 149
Laemmle, Edward 176
La Marr, Barbara 7–8, 62
Lamb, Thomas W. 115
Lampton, L. E. 177
Langdon, Harry 175
La Plante, Laura 165, 176
La Rocque, Rod 138, 165, 176
La Salle Street Station (Chicago) 90
Las Encinas Hospital (Pasadena) 148
Lasky, Jesse L. 12, 127, 165, 175, 176
Lasky-DeMille Barn (Hollywood) 129
Lasky Ranch (Hollywood) 129–130
Lederer, Francis 232
Lee, Dixie 130
Lee, Lila 176

Lee, Peggy 110
The Legend of Valentino (documentary) 225
The Legend of Valentino (film) 220
Leigh, Janet 232
Leighton, Louis 176
Leni, Paul 176
Lennon, John 117
Leonard, Father Edward 49, 52–53, 83–84, 91, 173
Leonard, Robert Z. 176
Lesser, Irving 174
Levee, M. C. 175
Lewis, George 176
Lewis, Ralph 127
The Life of Cellini (film) 30, 33, 35
Lincoln Center for the Performing Arts 3
Lincoln Heights Jail (Los Angeles) 122
Livent Producing Organization 112
Lloyd, Hal E. 175
Lloyd, Harold 97, 140, 176
Loew, Marcus 166, 173
Loew's State Theater (New York) 29
London Daily Herald 63
The Lone Ranger (television) 147
Long, Baron 145
Long, Walter 127
Los Angeles Athletic Club 144
Los Angeles Central Library 144
Los Angeles Pet Memorial Park 146–147
Los Angeles Philharmonic 142
Los Angeles Record 148
Los Angeles Times 4, 81, 187–199
The Lot 136
Louden, Dorothy 117
Loughborough, Lady Sheila 26–27
Love, Montague 174
The Love Goddess (documentary) 262
Loy, Myrna 232
Lubistch, Ernst 25, 176
Lucas, Mary 174
Lyle, A. 177
Lyon, Ben 49, 79–80, 83, 166, 173
Lyric Theatre (New York) 112

MacArthur, A. 176
Macdonald, Katherine 176

Index

MacGowan, Robert 176
MacIntosh, Captain Alastaire 173
MacKenna, Kenneth 173
Mack, Marion 232
Mackaill, Dorothy 174
Macpherson, Jeanie 166, 176
Madison Square Garden 109
Mahoney, Charles W. 176
Mahoney, Luther 97, 176, 179
Mancini, Zunilda 123
Manhattan Detention Complex 106
Manning, Dr. G. Randolph 38, 47
Mansfield, Duncan 127
March of Time: The Movies Move On (film) 261
Marchetti, Guilda 176
Marchetti, Joseph 175
Marion, Frances 139, 232
Mark Strand Theater (New York) 24, 115
Markiewz, Marie 42
Marmont, Percy 166
The Married Virgin (film) 127, 239
Marsh, Marion 232
Martin, Billy 117
Maryland Hotel (Pasadena) 147–148
Mason, Shirley 176
Mathis, June 34, 62, 91, 94, 95, 97, 98–101, 115, 117, 127, 135–136, 166, 176
Mathis, Virginia 94, 112, 135–136; *see also* Jenny
Mathis, William 135
Maxim's (New York) 16
Maxim's Restaurant-Caberet (New York) 109
May, Thomas 175, 176
Mayer, Louis B. 72, 130, 175
Mazziotta, Ralph 109McAvoy, May 176
McCarey, Leo 176
McCarthy, Five-yard 17–18
McCormick, John 166, 175, 176
McCrae, Henry 176
McCullough, Robert 173
McCutcheon, Major Wallace 24, 174
McDonald, Francis 176
McDonald, G. W. 177
McDonald, Violet 176
McDowall, Roddy 232
McFadden, Bernarr 63
McGeechie, Cora 176
McGowan, Roxana 176

McGraw-Hill Companies 113
McGregor, Malcom 174
McHugh, Charles 176
McKenna, Father Joseph 173
McManus, George 176
McNeil, Allen 176
McRae, Henry 175
Mdivani, Prince 138, 145, 146
Meeker, Dr. Harold 38, 43, 46–47, 48, 51, 53, 85, 87, 156–157
Meighan, Thomas 79, 166, 174
Melford, George 166
Mencken, H. L. 1, 21–23, 167, 174, 232
Menillo, Frank 49, 51, 87–88, 117, 173
Menjou, Adolphe 127, 183
Merman, Ethel 117
Meselope (Spirit guide) 10
Methodist Hospital (Arcadia) 148
Metro-Goldwyn Pictures 50
Metro Studios 105, 121, 130
Metropolitan Opera House 109
Miley, Jack 44
Miller, Marilyn 84, 174
Miller, Patsy Ruth 176, 232
Mills, Marilyn 176
Mills Hotel (New York) 119
Mineralava Beauty Clay Company 9
Mineralava Tour 119
Mines, W. W. 175
Minnelli, Vincente 138
Minskoff Theatre (New York) 112
Miranda, Carmen 138
Mr. Gilfeather (comic strip) 11
Mix, Tom 140
Monnette, Oro E. 175
Monroe, Marilyn 8, 110, 134
Monsieur Beaucaire (film) 14, 34, 120, 127, 256–257
Montmartre Cafe 130
Monument to the Stars (Beverly Hills) 140
Moore, Colleen 167, 176, 232–233
Moran of the Lady Letty (film) 252–253
Moreno, Antonio 72, 167, 174
Moreno, Daisy Canfield 176
Morgan Stanley 115
Morosco, Walter 176
Morris, H. Landon 176
Mother of Sorrows Church 174

Motion Picture News 174
Movieland Wax Museum 148
Moving Picture World 174
MTV Studios 112
Mullen's Gymnasium (Chicago) 30
Mullins, Father Michael 96, 97, 174
Murphy, John L. 176
Murray, Charlie 167
Murray, Mae 28, 95, 114, 138, 145, 146, 149, 167, 176
Mussolini, Benito 69, 75–76
My Life Story (article) 63
My Official Wife (film) 236
Mysteries and Scandals: Rudolph Valentino (documentary) 226

Nagel, Conrad 140
Naldi, Nita 167, 233
Nash, Jean 26
The Nation (magazine) 67
Nazimova, Allah 128, 135, 149
NBC Studios (Hollywood) 125
Negri, Pola 4, 25–28, 30, 39, 44, 45, 47–48, 51, 54–56, 58, 71, 78, 79–80, 81–82, 83–86, 87–88, 89, 90, 91, 92–93, 94, 95–96, 97, 98, 108, 130, 139, 140, 143, 167, 174, 176
Neilan, Marshall 167, 175, 176
Nelson, Ricky 8
New York American 40, 63, 64
New York Daily Mirror 62, 81, 84
New York Daily News 41, 62, 63
New York Evening Graphic 3, 40, 44, 63, 67
New York Evening Journal 19
New York Evening Telegram 174
New York Life Insurance Company 109
New York Public Library 113
New York Times 3, 4, 63–64, 75, 92, 108, 199–204
New York World 56
New York's Century Theatre 119
Newsweek (magazine) 114
Niblo, Fred 140
Nissen, Greta 174
No Foolin' (revue) 30, 37
Nobile, General Umberto 24
Nobody Home (film) 243
Nolan, Warren 174
Norge (airship) 24

Normand, Mabel 176
Northridge Earthquake 134
Notorius B.I.G. 117
Novarro, Ramon 15, 72, 142, 167
Novello, Ivor 114
Novic, Ely 96–97
N'Sync 8
Nureyev, Rudolf 222

O'Brien, George 167, 174
O'Connell, Rev. Father Daniel 174
O'Connor, Joseph 94
O'Connor, Mary 176
Odell, Maude 174
Olcott, Sidney 176
Old King Cole (painting) 114
Olmstead, Gertrude 176
O'Malley, Agnes 176
O'Malley, Pat 176
On Golden Pond (play) 112
Onassis, Jackie Kennedy 117
Once to Every Woman (film) 127, 246–247
O'Neal, Ella 176
O'Neil, Frank "Buck" 19–21, 106
Onotri, Demetri 84
O'Reilly, Father James 173
Orlamond, William 127
Orpheum Theatre (Brooklyn) 110
Osborne, Jack 148
Osborne, Ozzy 148
Out of Luck (film) 243

Pacheaco, Mildred 147
Palace Theatre (New York) 110
Palmer, Clara 174
Pantages Theater (Hollywood) 105, 134
Paramount Studios 97, 131, 132; *see also* Famous Players-Lasky
Parker, Dorothy 117
Parker, Edward 174
Parker, Robert 176
Parrish, Robert 96–97
Parsons, Harriet 52
Parsons, Louella O. 25, 52, 54–56, 136, 168, 176
Parsons, Schuyler 32–33
Pasa-Hambra Railroad Crossing (Los Angeles) 93, 148
Passion (film) 25
Passion's Playground (film) 89, 245
Patria (film) 237

Patten, Thomas 176
Pecoria, Ferdinand 68
Pennsylvania Station (New York) 108
Pershing Square Center 142
Persian Garden (New York) 115
Peters, House 174
Phelps, Katherine 148
Philbin, Mary 84, 174, 176, 233
Phillips, Dorothy 127, 176
Phillips, Michelle 222
Photoplay (magazine) 11, 12, 14, 31, 63, 101, 110
Piana, Enrico 175
Pickfair 140–141
Pickford, Charlotte 176
Pickford, Jack 174, 176
Pickford, Mary 38, 43, 77, 78, 83, 86–87, 95, 97, 110, 125, 136, 140, 141, 168, 174, 176
Pickford-Fairbanks Studio 136
Pierce, Lola 68, 174
Pink Powder Puffs (editorial) 9, 10–11, 13, 14, 17, 18, 21, 22, 30–32, 35, 62, 98, 116, 153–155
Pitts, ZaSu 176
Plantation Club 145
The Playground (nightclub) 29, 115
Plaza Hotel (New York) 114
Pollard, Harry 176
Polyclinic Hospital (New York) 37, 38, 42, 43, 44, 46, 47, 48, 50, 53, 54, 56, 57, 67, 110, 156
Poole, Dr. Eugene 48, 49
Pope John Paul II 1, 75
Powers, P. A. 175
Presley, Elvis 8
Price, Guy 176
Price, Matlock 101
Prince (Valentino's dog) 146–147
Princess Diana 8
Princess Fatima 92
Pringle, Aileen 21, 22, 24, 117, 176
The Prisoner of Chance (book) 45
Providencia Ranch (Hollywood) 129

The Quest of Life (film) 236
Quigley, Martin J. 174
Quirk, James R. 12, 14, 24, 36, 52, 68, 70, 72, 89, 174, 176
Quirk, Lawrence 70

Radio City Music Hall (New York) 105
Ralph's (Hollywood) 131
Ralston, Jobyna 176
Rambova, Natacha 4, 9–10, 13, 15, 16, 23, 26, 28, 34, 39, 43–44, 46, 54, 71–72, 82, 83, 91, 108, 109, 114, 117, 119, 122, 129, 130, 131, 132, 135, 136, 138, 144, 145, 148, 168, 178, 179
Rand, Ayn 117
Rapf, Harry 168, 176
Rappe, Virginia 127
Ravensdale, Baroness 26–27, 95, 96, 97, 176
Rawles, Dr. William Bryant 47, 58, 67
Raymond, Clifford Samuel 31–32
Reachi, Manuel 175
Reachi, Maria 32
Read, George 138
Rector's (New York) 110, 115
Reddy, Joseph 176
Regent Hotel 122, 134; *see also* Hastings Hotel (Hollywood)
Reid, Wallace 7, 62, 130
Reilly, William 174
Reinhardt, Max 25
Reiss, F. G. 168
El Relicario 108
Rialto Theater (Los Angeles) 144
Rich, Irene 168
Richman, Harry 37, 41, 174
Rihga Royal Hotel (New York) 116
Riley, Corinne 174
The Ritz (Hollywood) 131
Ritz-Carlton Hotel (Atlantic City) 32
RKO Warner Twin (New York) 115
Roach, Hal 175
The Roaring Twenties (documentary) 262
Roberts, Theodore 168
Rockefeller Center (New York) 105, 114
Rockett, Al 168
Rogers, Charles "Buddy" 141, 233
Rogers, Will 8, 140
A Rogue's Romance (film) 127, 242–243
Roland, Gilbert 233
Roland, Ruth 95, 176

Rolph, Mayor James J. 95, 168, 176
Romano, Frank 174
Romano, Michael A. 174
Romero, Juan 139
Roosevelt Hotel (Hollywood) 105
Roosevelt Theater (Chicago) 30
Rork, Sam 89
Rosanova, Rosa 53
Rosie O'Grady's Bar (New York) 115
Rosson, Richard 169
Rothman, John 23, 224
Rothstein, Arnold 110
Rowland, Richard 121, 169, 174
Rubens, Alma 169
Rudami, Rosa 97, 176
Rudolph Valentino (book) 4
Rudolph Valentino (play) 227
Rudolph Valentino and His 88 American Beauties (film) 109, 256
Rudolph Valentino: His Romantic Life and Death (book) 94
Rudolph Valentino Memorial Association (Chicago) 82, 90
Rudolph Valentino My Love (play) 227–228
Rudolph Valentino National Memorial Committee 89
Rudolph Valentino Productions 131–132, 136
Rudy's Music Shop (New York) 115
Ruffu, Anthony 76
Ruggles, Wesley 176
Runyon, Damon 233
Russell, Rosiland 138
Russell, William 176
Ryan, James 176

St. Clair, Malcom 169, 174
St. Ensullins Church 174
St. Johns, Adela Rogers 23, 25–26, 27, 28, 36, 65, 70–71, 145, 176
St. Johns, Elaine 233
St. Johns, Ivan 176
St. Joseph's Church (Rio de Janeiro) 82
St. Malachy's Church 49, 71, 82, 83, 85, 86, 110, 173
St. Phillip Church of Pasadena 174
St. Polis, John 127

St. Regis Hotel (New York) 114
The Sainted Devil (film) 34, 120, 257–258
Salm, Count Alex 120
Samuel Goldwyn Studios 136
San Carlo company 84
San Fernando Mission (Mission Hills) 148
San Jacinto Cemetery 146
Santa Monica Boulevard School 96
Santschi, Mrs. Thomas 185
Savage, Nellie 174
Sawyer, Joan 29, 113, 115
Scaramouche (film) 15
Schallert, Edwin 176
Schenck, Joseph M. 27, 33, 35, 39–40, 42, 43, 49, 51–53, 54, 61, 63, 72, 85, 89, 108, 169, 174
Schenck, Nicholas M. 169, 174
Schulberg, B. P. 169, 176
Scott, Peggy 77
Screen Snapshots:Memorial to Al Jolson (short) 262
Sedan, Rolfe 127
Seiter, William A. 176
Selig, Col. William N. 175
Selznick, David O. 109
Senelle, Valeria 174
Sennett, Mack 175
Seventeen (film) 236
Shaeder, Fred 174
Shapiro, Victor 174
Shearer, Norma 139, 169
Sheehan, Winfield S. 175
The Sheik (film) 12, 32, 92, 124, 125, 127, 128, 145, 251–252
The Sheik's Physique (film) 256
Shelden, E. Lloyd 176
Sheraton-East Hotel (New York) 108
Sherman, Lowell 49
Ship Cafe (Venice) 148–149
The Shreik of Araby (film) 221
Shubert, Lee 169–170
Siegman, George 176
Sills, Milton 170
Simpson, William 175
Sinatra, Frank 138
Siskel, Gene 31
Sisson, Vera 127
Sixty Club 143
Sloman, Edward 176
Smith, Carmen 175
Smith, Guy 58
A Society Sensation (film) 238

The Son of the Sheik (film) 9, 17, 18, 24, 30, 32, 33, 34, 61, 62, 79, 89, 96, 115, 120, 126, 136, 144, 260–261
A Song of Hate 11–12, 31
Southern Pacific Golden State Limited 93
Southland Geriatric Center 149
Spargo, John 174
Spearman, Frank 176
Spitzell, Herman 176
The Squall (play) 98
The Squaw Man (film) 129
Stahl, John M. 176
A Star Is Born (film) 138
Stevensen, Hayden 176
Stewart, Raymond W. 179
Stewart, Rod 138
Stolen Moments (film) 247–248
Stone, Lewis 89, 170
Strada, Gabriella 73
Strada, Maria (sister) 73; *see also* Guglielmi, Maria
Strand Theater (Brooklyn) 32, 120
Stravinsky, Igor 117
Stromberg, Hunt 170, 176
Sunset Strip (West Hollywood) 135
Swanson, Gloria 84, 139, 170, 174
Swanson and Valentino (documentary) 225
Sweet, Blanche 170, 176
Swickard, Josef 127

Tain, Marjorie 145
Talmadge, Constance 83–84, 86, 174
Talmadge, Margaret 170, 176
Talmadge, Natalie 170, 176
Talmadge, Norma 27, 33, 34, 35, 40, 42, 49, 63, 83–84, 86, 108, 170, 174, 233
Tate, Sharon 139
Taxi Dancer (film) 223
Taylor, Elizabeth 138
Taylor, Estelle 30, 33, 170, 176, 233
Taylor, Sam 176
Terry, Alice 171
Thalberg, Irving 139, 171, 176
Thomajan, P. K. 176
Thomas, Danny 138
Thomas, Olive 7, 59, 62, 117
Thomson, Fred 139
The 300 Club (New York) 116
Thym, Georgia 106, 116

Time (magazine) 11
Times Square 112–116
Tinee, Mae 155
The Tombs 106
Tonello, Mgr. Joseph 174
Tonto 147
Trianon Ballroom (Chicago) 82
Trueblood, Ralph 176
Tunney, Gene 19
Turnbull, Hector 176
Turpin, Ben 176
Tynan, Brandon 174

Ullman, Beatrice 37, 52, 81, 83, 87, 88, 174, 176
Ullman, S(amuel) George 2, 9–10, 21, 24, 25, 28, 30, 31, 32, 33, 34, 36, 37, 38, 39, 40, 41, 42, 43, 44, 45, 46, 47, 48, 49, 50, 51–53, 54, 57, 58, 61, 66, 68, 69, 71–72, 75, 76, 77, 81–82, 83, 84, 86, 87–88, 89, 90, 91, 92, 93, 95, 112, 122, 124, 131–132, 135, 141, 156, 174, 175, 177, 178, 179, 180
Ulric, Lenore 37, 171
Unbiased Commission for the Investigation of Psychic Phenomena 67
Uncensored Movies (film) 222
Uncharted Seas (film) 127, 250
Unholy Partners (film) 261
United Artists Corporation 19, 34, 35, 44, 61, 62, 64, 116, 132, 136
United Studios 19, 131
Universal Studios 95, 129, 149

Valencia, Adlelaide 87
Valentino (book) 4
Valentino (1951, film) 219–220
Valentino (1977, film) 220–221
Valentino, Ada 24, 128, 136
Valentino, Alberto 24, 37, 39, 45, 48, 54, 57, 58, 71, 72, 77–78, 87–88, 89, 90, 91, 92, 94, 96, 97–98, 122, 128, 136–137, 149, 171, 176, 178, 179, 182, 185
Valentino, Jean 24, 57, 137, 146, 179
Valentino, Jean Acker *see* Acker, Jean
Valentino, Robert 60
Valentino, Rudolph: Alberto buys crypt for 101; annual memorial service for 101; attraction of 1–2; boxing and 19–21; burial place discussed 58, 71–72, 78, 87–88; contract with Famous Players-Lasky 9; corpse described 68; crowds at New York funeral of 73, 74–75; death of, 3, 53; death premonition of 33–34; death rumors of 67–68; diagnosis of 38; estate of 61, 180–186; Fascisti at funeral of 69, 75–76; funeral party leaves New York 88–89; ghost of 129, 131, 132, 136; happiness of 23; Hollywood funeral of 95–96; interment at Hollywood Cemetery 96–98; last will and testament 177–179; marriage and 25, 28; medical diagnosis of 156–157; memorial (planned) at Hollywood Cemetery 99–101; memorials of 72–73, 78, 98; monument dedicated in Castellaneta 72; New York funeral of 8, 76–77, 82–84; operation of 3; physical fitness of 33; "Pink Powder Puffs" editorial and 153–155; Pola Negri and 25–28; Pola Negri's reported engagement to 28, 30, 56, 91; riots at New York funeral of 64–67; Roman Catholic burial and 91; sexuality of 1, 11–18; sickness of 32–33, 37–53; slave bracelet of 13, 30; *Son of the Sheik* premiere and 24; suicides of fans 77, 124; supernatural beliefs of 10; tributes to 158–172; wax dummy at funeral of 70–71
Valentino As I Knew Him (article) 63
Valentino As I Knew Him (book) 4, 13, 36
Valentino Building (Hollywood) 132
Valentino Memorial Shrine 126
Valentino, the Musical (musical play) 228–229
Valli, Virginia 176
Van Cleave, George 176
Van Horn, Nora 83, 174
Variety 30, 174
Vernon County Club (Los Angeles) 15, 145

Vidor, Florence 171
Vidor, King 98, 176
Vignola, Robert 98
Villa Valentino (Hollywood) 105, 129, 132, 137, 180–182
Virginia Theater (Atlantic City) 32
Virginia Hotel (Long Beach) 52
Virtuous Sinners (film) 127, 241–242
Von Ettisch, R. T. 176
Von Stroheim, Erich 171, 175

Waldorf Astoria Hotel (New York) 112
Waldron, John 176
Walk of Fame (Hollywood) 133–134
Walker, H. M. 176
Walker, Johnnie 176
Walsh, Raoul 25
Wannamaker, John 36
Warburton, Barclay, Jr. 36–37, 40–41, 46, 112, 116–117, 118
Ward, Carrie Clark 127
Warner, Jack L. 171
Warner Bros. Studios 130
Warner-Hollywood Studios 136
Warsaw Imperial Academy of Dramatic Arts 25
Washington Square 119
Waters, Margaret Neff 179
WEAF 50
Webb, Clifton 83, 173
Webb, Millard 176
Weber, Lois 176
Wehner, George 43
Weinberg, Stephen Jacob *see* Wyman, Dr. Sterling
Werner, Teresa 39, 43–44, 108, 117, 119, 178, 179, 186
Wertzel, Sol 175
West, Mae 117
West, Roland 171, 176
What Price Beauty? (film) 261
Whelan, Tim 176
White, Frances 36
White, George 171–172
Whitley Heights (Hollywood) 129, 132
Williams, Frances 41
Williams, Kathlyn 54–56, 71, 93, 176
Williams, Mervin 98
Wilson, Cary 176
Wilson, Lois 84, 172, 174
Winchel, Walter 57

Winter Garden Theatre (New York) 110, 115
Wittenburg College 31
Wollen, Ann 148
The Wonderful Chance (film) 247
Wood, James 175
Woodlawn Cemetery (The Bronx) 77
Woodlawn Cemetery (Santa Monica) 122
Woodmansten Inn (The Bronx) 115
Woodruff, Eunice 127

Woods, A. H. 172
Woolworth, F. W. 117
Workman, Boyle 175, 176
The World's Greatest Lover (film) 222–223
Wray, Fay 233
Wyman, Cynthia 88
Wyman, Dr. Sterling 73, 87, 88, 89, 92, 174
Wynne, Hugh 176

"You Are the Star" mural 134
You Know Me (comic strip) 11
Young, George G. 175

Young, Mrs. George G. 176
The Young and the Dead (documentary) 226
The Young Rajah (film) 11, 14, 127, 255–256
Yurka, Blanche 98–100

Zadora, Pia 141
Zela (lion cub) 131
Ziegfeld, Florenz 172
Ziegfeld Follies 29
Zukor, Adolph 12, 34–35, 49, 71, 87, 116, 172, 174

www.ingramcontent.com/pod-product-compliance
Lightning Source LLC
Chambersburg PA
CBHW081542300426
44116CB00015B/2722